THE CLASSICS
OF WESTERN
SPIRITUALITY

THE CLASSICS OF WESTERN SPIRITUALITY
A Library of the Great Spiritual Masters

President and Publisher
Kevin A. Lynch, C.S.P.

EDITORIAL BOARD

PSEUDO-MACARIUS
THE FIFTY SPIRITUAL HOMILIES AND THE *GREAT LETTER*

TRANSLATED, EDITED AND WITH AN INTRODUCTION BY
GEORGE A. MALONEY, S.J.

PREFACE BY
KALLISTOS WARE

PAULIST PRESS
NEW YORK • MAHWAH

Copyright © 1992 by George A. Maloney, S.J.

Library of Congress Cataloging-in-Publication Data

Pseudo-Macarius.
    [Spiritual homilies. English]
    The fifty spiritual homilies; and, The great letter/Pseudo-Macarius; edited and translated with an introduction by George A. Maloney; preface by Bishop Kallistos of Diokleia.
      p. cm.—(Classics of Western spirituality)
    Includes bibliographical references and index.
    ISBN 0-8091-0455-5 (cloth)—ISBN 0-8091-3312-1 (pbk.)
    1. Mysticism—Orthodox Eastern Church—Early works to 1800. 2. Sermons, Early Christian. I. Maloney, George A., 1924– . II. Pseudo-Macarius. Great letter. English. 1992. III. Title: Fifty spiritual homilies. IV. Title: 50 spiritual homilies. V. Title: Great letter. VI. Series.
BR65.P823S6513 1992
248—dc20   92-4736
                                              CIP

Published by Paulist Press
997 Macarthur Boulevard
Mahwah, New Jersey 07430

Printed and bound in the
United States of America

CONTENTS

PREFACE   xi

INTRODUCTION   1

NOTES TO INTRODUCTION   27

GENERAL ABBREVIATIONS   33

HOMILIES ONE–FIFTY   35

INTRODUCTION TO THE *GREAT LETTER*   249

THE *GREAT LETTER*   253

NOTES TO THE FIFTY HOMILIES   272

NOTES TO THE *GREAT LETTER*   286

BIBLIOGRAPHY   289

INDEX   294

Editor of this Volume

GEORGE A. MALONEY, S.J. was ordained in Rome as a priest of the Russian Byzantine Rite, April 18, 1957. He earned a doctorate in Oriental Theology June 21, 1962, summa cum laude from the Pontifical Oriental Institute.

In 1965 he launched an ecumenical journal, *Diakonia,* to promote dialogue between Orthodox Christians and Roman Catholics. He served as editor of all the Eastern Rite articles for the *New Catholic Encyclopedia.*

He is fluent in several languages, including Russian and Greek. He has travelled extensively in Russia, Greece, Egypt, Lebanon, Jordan, Israel, and Turkey in an attempt to meet the Eastern Christian groups and to understand their religious background. Especially fruitful were two summers spent on Mt. Athos.

Fr. Maloney is the founder and director of the John XXIII Institute for Eastern Christian Studies at Fordham University. He teaches Oriental theology and spirituality on the master and doctoral levels.

Fr. Maloney has established himself as an outstanding author of works on prayer and Eastern Christian Spirituality as applied to the daily life of Western Christians. Some of his books include *The Cosmic Christ; Inward Stillness; Bright Darkness; Listen, Prophets; Nesting in the Rock; Jesus, Set Me Free!; Theology of Uncreated Energies;* and *Inscape—God at the Heart of Matter.*

Author of the Preface

BISHOP KALLISTOS WARE was born in Bath in 1934 and studied Classics, Philosophy and Theology at the University of Oxford. Received into the Orthodox Church in 1958, he was ordained a priest in 1966. In the same year he was appointed Spalding Lecturer in Eastern Orthodox Studies at Oxford, and in 1970 he became a Fellow of Pembroke College. In 1982 he was consecrated titular Bishop of Diokleia and made an Assistant Bishop in the Orthodox Archdiocese of Thyateira and Great Britain. He is a monk of the Monastery of St. John the Theologian in Patmos. He is the author of many books, including *The Orthodox Church* and *The Orthodox Way,* and he is a co-editor of the new English translation of *The Philokalia.*

Dedicated to Colleen and Bill Green

Acknowledgments
Deepest thanks to Dorothy Reeme and Suzy Caruther for their patience in deciphering my writing and typing up the manuscript and many footnotes. Thanks to Reverend Anthony Paul Clarkson, O.C.S.O., who allowed me to read excerpts from his doctoral thesis, *Christ in the Writings of Pseudo-Macarius;* to Bernard McGinn, editor of this Paulist Series, for his encouragement to help in obtaining some needed Greek texts; and to Georgia Christo for her editorial hints and helps.

PREFACE

"I read Macarius and sang," wrote John Wesley in his diary for July 30, 1736. There are countless others, alike in Eastern and in Western Christendom, who have experienced a similar joy through reading Macarius. The Homilies are written with a warmth of feeling, an affectivity and enthusiasm, that are instantly attractive. Their message is one of hope, light and glory:

> The soul that is counted worthy to participate in the light of the Holy Spirit by becoming his throne and habitation, and is covered with the ineffable glory of the Spirit, becomes all light, all face, all eye. There is no part of the soul that is not full of the spiritual eyes of light. That is to say, there is no part of the soul that is covered with darkness (H. [= *Homilies,* Collection II] 1:2).

Yet at the same time the Homilies are devoid of facile optimism. The Christian journey, Macarius warns us, is a struggle, a spiritual combat that continues right up to the end of our life: "I have not yet seen any perfect Christian or one perfectly free" (H. 8:5). If Macarius is to be termed an enthusiast, yet his is an enthusiasm rooted in the realism and austerity of the desert.

Who is the author of the Spiritual Homilies? His precise identity is a mystery and is likely to remain such, unless fresh evidence comes unexpectedly to light. The complex debate concerning "Pseudo-Macarius" during the past seventy years is carefully summarized by Father George Maloney in his Introduction. There is general agreement that the author of the Macarian writings has no connection with the Coptic Desert Father, St. Macarius of Egypt (c. 300–c. 390). The milieu presupposed in the Homilies is definitely Syria rather than Egypt. Although the language used by the author is Greek, his highly distinctive vocabulary and imagery are Syrian. This is indicated with full and convincing detail in the latest study of the Macarian problem, written by Columba Stewart, OSB: *"Working the Earth of the Heart." The Messalian Controversy in History, Texts, and Language to AD 431* (Oxford, 1991). Dom Columba concludes that the Homilies date basically from the 380s, and were probably written in Mesopotamia or Asia Minor.

Macarius has links of some kind with the ascetic and "charismatic" movement known as Messalianism. Originating in Syria during the second half of the fourth century, Messalianism spread rapidly throughout the Mediterranean and was condemned as heretical at a series of synods, including the Council of Ephesus in 431. The Messalians were accused of undervaluing the sacraments and overemphasizing dreams, visions and the practice of continual prayer. It is difficult, however, to establish exactly what they believed and did. Like the twentieth-century "charismatic" movement, they were not a clearly defined group, and their standpoint was very probably misunderstood by those who condemned them.

Several of the phrases and images associated with the Messalians occur prominently in the text of the Homilies, although other Messalian tenets are more or less absent. Those who classify the Homilies as Messalian are bound to concede that they represent a moderate and qualified type of Messalianism. Hermann Dörries, in his fundamental study *Die Theologie des Makarios/Symeon* (Göttingen, 1978), even suggests that Macarius is, if anything, *anti*-Messalian, although the Messalians may have made use of him. A growing number of specialists are agreed, at any rate, on one point: when Messalian language appears in the Homilies, there is nothing specifically heretical about the way in which it is employed. In common, therefore, with Christians in the East and West during the past fifteen centuries, we today can continue to honor the Homilies as a classic of the spiritual life.

Macarius is existential and intuitive in his approach, and his Homilies lack an organized structure. Parts of them were evidently written in response to actual inquirers and take the form of questions and answers, as with the so-called "Shorter Rules" of St. Basil the Great. Macarius was not writing an abstract treatise, but was offering inspiration and practical advice to particular groups of ascetics; and so the teaching is tailored to their circumstances. This gives to the Homilies something of the spontaneity and immediacy that mark the *Apophthegmata* or Sayings of the Desert Fathers.

PREFACE

Yet, however unsystematic in form, the Homilies presuppose a single underlying pattern of the Christian life. Beneath an ever-varying imagery, evocative and colorful, the basic message of Macarius is very simple. Our spiritual journey falls into three main stages:

1. Initially the heart is under the dominion of evil. This is a consequence of Adam's disobedience: the Homilies take a somber view of the fall, and place heavy emphasis on the reality of inherited human sinfulness. "From the time that Adam transgressed the command, the serpent entered and became master of the house, and became like a second soul with the real soul" (H. 15:35). Although humans do not altogether forfeit freedom of the will, evil is pervasive and stubborn, and cannot be overcome without the assistance of divine grace.

2. Next comes the stage of spiritual struggle, when the heart is indwelt simultaneously by both sin and grace, the one fighting against the other. "There are some persons in whom grace is operative and working in peace. Within, however, evil is also present hiddenly, and the two ways of existing, namely, according to the principles of light and darkness, vie for dominance within the same heart" (H. 17:4).

3. Finally there comes the stage when sin is cast out from the heart by the Holy Spirit, working in cooperation with our human will. Cleansed from evil, the soul is now united to Christ the heavenly Bridegroom and is "mixed" or "mingled" with the divine Spirit, in this way attaining a state higher than that enjoyed by Adam before the fall. "When your soul has fellowship with the Spirit and the heavenly soul enters into your soul, then you are a perfect man in God and an heir and son" (H. 32:6). Macarius describes this third stage as "dispassion" or "freedom from passions" (*apatheia*), as "renewal above nature" or "new creation," and also as "divinization." Yet even so a person still continues subject to temptation and liable to fall: "Satan is never quieted.... As long as a person dwells in this world and is living in the flesh, he is subject to warring" (H. 26:14). There is no inalienable perfection in this present life.

Such is the basic progression envisaged by Macarius: from a heart possessed by evil, to a heart indwelt by sin and grace, and then ultimately to a heart that belongs to God alone.

What value do the Macarian Homilies possess for us today? There are perhaps two ways in which they speak especially to our condition. In the first place, ours is an age that values concrete experience more than theoretical systems. Here the affective spirit of Macarius and his concern with inner subjectivity possess an immediate appeal. He exploits to the full the language of feeling and conscious awareness, employing as his key words *plerophoria* ("confidence" or "assurance": cf. 1 Thess. 1:5), *aisthesis* ("sensation" or "feeling"), *peira* ("experience"), *energeia* ("energy") and *dynamis* ("power"). Christianity, as Macarius understands it, involves much more than assent to reasoned arguments or outer obedience to a moral code. It consists above all in the awakening of our spiritual senses, so that we attain a direct, palpable awareness of God's Holy Spirit dwelling in our hearts.

Secondly, alike in physics, philosophy and psychology, we are today finding it less and less helpful to distinguish sharply between mind and matter, between soul and body. We are inclined to concur with that great Christian prophet of the eighteenth century, William Blake: "Man has no Body distinct from his Soul, for that call'd Body is a portion of Soul discern'd by the five Senses." In the words of C.G. Jung, "Spirit is the living body seen from within, and the body the outer manifestation of the living spirit—the two being really one." With this vision of the human person as an undivided unity Macarius is in broad agreement, as Fr. Maloney makes clear. In the Homilies the body is described as the "likeness" of the soul, its outward expression and reflection; it is the two together that constitute "the house of God" (H. 30:3,7). Our Christian vocation is not to "save our soul" but to become "spirit enfleshed" (H. 47:15). There is no salvation for the soul apart from the body; divinization signifies the transformation of the total person, soul and body together.

Particularly striking is the manner in which Macarius spells out this unified anthropology in eschatological terms. His understanding of the Christian hope is firmly holistic, not dualist. Since our human nature is a single, unified whole, we are committed to believing in the resurrection of the body rather than the immortality of the soul. We look beyond the severance of soul and body at physical death—which is something deeply *un*natural—to their reintegration at the last day. Again and again Macarius refers to the future glory of the resurrection body in the age to come: this forms one of the dominant *leitmotifs* in the Homilies.

This glory of the body, however, does not belong only to the End but is foreshadowed at various moments throughout salvation history. Before the fall the bodies of Adam and Eve shone with light in Paradise, and they were "covered with God's glory in place of clothing" (H. 12:8). Once they had fallen into sin, this robe of glory was taken away from them and they were left naked (cf. Gen 3:7). Then at Moses'

PREFACE

descent from Mount Sinai, after the giving of the Law, the final restoration of our bodily glory was briefly anticipated when his face shone so brightly that he had to cover it with a veil (cf. Exod 34:29–35): "He went up as a mere man; he descended, carrying God with him. . . . The Word of God was his food and he had a glory shining on his countenance" (H. 12:14). A far more significant foretaste of the eschatological glory came at Christ's own transfiguration: "As the body of the Lord was glorified when he climbed the mount and was transfigured into the divine glory and into infinite light, so also the bodies of the saints are glorified and shine like lightning" (H. 15:38). What happened then to the Savior will happen to all true Christians in the age to come:

> In so far as anyone, through faith and zeal, has been deemed worthy to receive the Holy Spirit, to that degree his body also will be glorified in that day. What the soul now stores up within shall then be revealed as a treasure and displayed externally in the body. . . . The glory of the Holy Spirit rises up from within, covering and warming the bodies of the saints. This is the glory they interiorly had before, hidden in their souls. For what they now have, that same then pours out externally into the body (H. 5:8–9).

To express this holistic anthropology, Macarius employs more particularly the biblical notion of the heart. The Macarian spirituality is indeed a "spirituality of the heart," to use Fr. Maloney's phrase. In the Homilies, as in scripture, the term "heart" denotes much more than merely our emotions and affections (which in the Old Testament are located, not primarily in the heart, but in the belly, entrails or guts). The heart is the moral and spiritual center of the entire human person. It is the seat not just of our feelings but of our intelligence and wisdom, and corresponds to what we today mean by the conscience.

In this way, the heart designates the human person as a whole, regarded as a spiritual subject. It is the ground or core of our being, the "inner self" (cf. Eph 3:16–17)—what in Zen Buddhism is termed "the center of the lotus." It is at the same time the place where we come face to face with God, where the grace of the Spirit is active (Rom 8:27; Gal 4:6). Once the heart is understood in this comprehensive way, it is surprising how many scriptural texts acquire sharper significance. When, for instance, it is said, "The heart is deep" (Ps 64:6)—a key text in Orthodox spirituality—the meaning is that the human person as a whole is a profound mystery. The divine appeal, "My child, give me your heart" (Prov 23:26), affirms that we are to entrust to God our entire being. By the same token, when the Hesychasts of the Christian East speak about "prayer of the heart," they have in mind prayer of the total person—spirit, soul, body.

Macarius for his part clearly understands the heart in this all-embracing biblical sense:

> The heart itself is but a small vessel, yet dragons are there, and there are also lions; there are poisonous beasts and all the treasures of evil. There also are rough and uneven roads; there are precipices. But there too is God, the angels, the life and the Kingdom, the light and the apostles, the heavenly cities and the treasures of grace—all things are there (H. 43:7).

"There are infinite depths to the human heart," Macarius states elsewhere (H. 15:32). While denoting the physical organ located in our chest, it is clearly a symbol of much more than this, existing as it does at a whole series of interconnected levels:

1. The heart is first of all the central and controlling element in our physical structure: "The heart directs and governs all the other organs of the body" (H. 15:20). When the heart ceases to function, bodily death ensues.

2. The heart is likewise the place in which the intellect is situated: "For there, in the heart, the mind (*nous*) abides as well as all the thoughts of the soul and all its hopes" (H. 15:20). In Macarius' symbolic scheme, there is no dichotomy between head and heart: we think with our heart.

3. The heart includes what we today designate as "the unconscious," whether personal or collective.

4. As moral center, the heart is the point where grace and sin are experienced: "There is found the office of justice and of injustice. There is death and there is life" (H. 15:32).

5. The heart is in this way also the point of self-transcendence, where we encounter God. It is "the palace of Christ," where he "sets up his Kingdom" (H. 15:33).

Through the heart, then, divine grace permeates our entire personhood, not only transforming the soul but penetrating also "throughout all parts of the body" (H. 15:20). The heart is the symbol of our personal unity, the center where the physical and non-material, the created and the uncreated converge. It is the point of meeting:

xvi

between body and soul;
between the unconscious and the conscious;
between human freedom and divine grace.

In a writer as unsystematic (outwardly) as Macarius no one could reasonably demand completeness; and there are indeed obvious omissions, which some interpret as defects. Relatively little is said in the Homilies about the sacraments of baptism and the eucharist, about the priesthood and the ecclesiastical hierarchy. Are we to see in this a deliberate and typically "Messalian" devaluation of the visible, institutional church? Yet such arguments from silence are often insecure. Nowhere does Macarius actually deny efficacy to the sacraments; and, particularly in Collection I of the Homilies, there are passages where sacramental baptism is clearly affirmed as the foundation of our life in Christ (see, for example, *Logos* 43).

Another attitude in the Homilies which might be thought one-sided is their apparent neglect of the apophatic approach or *via negativa*. God is repeatedly described through the symbolism of fire and light—and here Macarius exercised a decisive influence over later Byzantine Hesychasm—but no use at all is made of the complementary symbol of the divine darkness, to which St. Gregory of Nyssa attached such crucial importance. Throughout the Homilies we find an affirmation of images, whereas nothing is said about prayer as "a laying-aside of thoughts," to use the phrase of Evagrius of Pontus (d. 399); nowhere is it stated that in mystical contemplation our mind is to transcend all discursive thinking, all words and visual forms.

Yet it would be wrong to conclude from this that Macarius is in no sense an apophatic theologian, for he has in fact a strong awareness of God as mystery. He uses the same argument *a fortiori* as is found in Philo and St. Basil. We do not even understand our own selves, he insists: "Who can see or lay hold of the soul? Or what is its nature? It has no visible appearance. A person does not know himself, until the time that the Lord reveals this to him." Ignorant as we are of our own true nature, how much less can we claim to understand the nature of God! "What shall we say? Where is the invisible God to be found? Is he beneath the sea? Or under the earth? Who can seize hold of him or catch sight of him? Not a single created thing." By love alone can the soul grasp God (*Homilies*, Collection III, 18:1: ed. V. Desprez, *Sources chrétiennes* 275, pp. 218–20). Macarius' standpoint here is exactly that of *The Cloud of Unknowing*: "He may well be loved, but not thought. By love may he be gotten and holden; but not by thought."

For all their warm enthusiasm, the Macarian Homilies are not an unbalanced work. While Pentecostal, they are also Christ-centered. While primarily concerned with the inner awareness of God's presence in the heart, they are also outward-looking: "This is purity of heart, that, when you see the sinners and the weak, you have compassion and show mercy toward them. . . . There is no other way to be saved except through your neighbor" (H. 15:8; 37:3). Macarius strongly emphasizes the need for us to "work the earth of the heart" through our own human efforts—"When the will of man is lacking, God himself does nothing" (H. 37:10—but he is in no sense Pelagian: "Everything is to be ascribed to divine grace" (H. 5:5). He has a keen perception of the tragedy of human sin, yet he never loses sight of the primal beauty of our created personhood: "Great is the dignity of humanity!" (H. 15:22)—we are actually higher, not lower, than the angels. With their message of hope, their repudiation of all destructive self-hatred, their insistence that there is indeed a *good* form of self-love, the Homilies offer profound encouragement to each one of us. It is not difficult to appreciate why, in the monasteries of Mount Athos, they are given as spiritual reading to novices. Like Wesley, let us also read Macarius and sing.

INTRODUCTION

All religions struggle with presenting a vision of God and the means whereby God and human beings can be in communication and eventually come to a final goal of intimate communion. Judaism and Islam basically present a God, most transcendent to his creation, who communicates through word revelations about his nature, the purpose of creation, and the nature of human beings and their final goal. God speaks through his appointed prophets. Such communications are gathered up in the Hebrew Bible for the Jews and in the Koran for the Muslims.

The Far Eastern religions, especially Hinduism and Buddhism, stress primarily the immanence of God in all creation, especially the fulfillment of human striving to be found in the *advaita* experience of nonduality. The human person finds completion in total immersion in the Absolute Being.

Christianity's strength consists in maintaining the antinomy of "both/and." God is both transcendent to his creatures and also immanently indwelling in his human children in intimate personal relationships. The Good News is that God is love and love unites, but also differentiates. A triune community of love, the Trinity, unites with human beings in a unity of love through the Word of God made flesh, Jesus Christ, and his Holy Spirit. Yet divine love also preserves the difference within God as Father, Son, and Spirit, at the same time as it maintains the union of the divine persons with each unique human being, made freely by God according to his own image and likeness.

Two Emphases In Christianity

As Christianity developed out of Judaism, influenced greatly by the Hellenic *paideia*, we see in the spiritual writings of the early Fathers of the Church, especially in the more ancient writings of Christians in the

East (today this would roughly correspond to the Near and Middle East), two main accents or tendencies that would continue as two distinct schools of Christian spirituality. Rooted in the latter books of the Old Testament and the New, we see the parallelism between *life* and *light*.

The Semitic emphasis in the Old Testament (as Christians term the Hebrew Bible) and in much of the New is said to stress the dynamic, the voluntaristic, the existential and psychological, the process of continued growth in interpersonal relations between God and human beings. The emphasis is on *life*.

The Hellenic influence, especially from Platonism and Stoicism, is characterized in general by the emphasis placed on *light*, which represents reality as a world of static ideas, abstract and logical. The Christian Platonists, such as Clement of Alexandria, Origen, and Evagrius, developed the spiritual life as a form of Christian Gnosticism. The Christian is the Gnostic who is called to know God, to possess him and to see him. This is not mere intellectualism. It is a spiritual gift, a mystical vision that transcends all materiality. The human soul, once purified from all the worldly stains that prevent it from contemplating God as the Eternal One, becomes a mirror that reflects God. This is the nature of humanity: to reflect God as in the mirror of our human souls.

Semitic Christianity grew up around Antioch and spread out into two directions: (1) that of St. Irenaeus and the theologians who would follow his holistic and incarnational approach; and (2) that of Pseudo-Macarius. It will become clearer why most commentators on Macarius's writings prefer to call him by this title. But this unknown author would be the key writer in the tradition of spirituality that stresses the existential transformation of the total human person, body, soul, and spirit, into the experienced indwelling of the Trinity. Such a spirituality goes beyond human reason. In its apophatic but experiential knowledge of the "heart" one does not see God in visions, but, like Moses, hears God in the burning bush. Encountering God as speech through his Word, human beings are to listen and respond by loving obedience. God is life, and he shares this with the humble and pure of heart. This emphasis draws heavily from the Johannine Gospel.

The Antiochene school of spirituality in the East accepted this Semitic concept as an essential part of Christ's message. Christ is the Life, the true and full Life for all human beings, called by God's gratuitous choice to be children of God. Salvation is a process of entering more fully into the new life in Christ.

Under the influence both of heresies and of Platonism and other non-Christian philosophies that became the main vehicle for the so-called Alexandrian school of spirituality, the spiritual life gradually moved away from the existential, holistic life-approach to a more intellectual emphasis. Werner Jaeger, who has focused on early Christianity and Greek *paideia,* shows that Greek humanism and Hellenic culture provided categories of thought for many early Christian thinkers.[1]

Gradually, the message of St. John's Gospel, with its strong accent on experiencing the risen Lord Jesus as the life of Christians' souls, was seen merely as the primitive message. It was preserved somewhat longer in regions where Christianity had penetrated before Hellenic philosophy had a chance to intervene, as in East Syria where through political, doctrinal, and linguistic differences, an Aphraates and an Ephrem developed a Christian spirituality outside of any distinct philosophical system.

It is in this form of early Christianity that we must place Pseudo-Macarius. He will continue this Semitic, holistic approach to the Christian life. Yet because of his contacts with the writings of Clement of Alexandria, Origen, and, above all, St. Basil and St. Gregory of Nyssa, he and his later disciples were able to correct some of the weaknesses of a "feeling" religion, as we will point out in dealing with the Messalian heresy and Pseudo-Macarius's writings.

The Macarian Question: Spirituality of the Heart

Pseudo-Macarius, a Syrian monk, wrote fifty spiritual homilies and some letters and responses to questions (known collectively as the "Macarian corpus"). He continues the Semitic tradition with its accent on the total, existential encounter with God in the "heart."

In this Macarian optic, God is found in a holistic manner within the heart and not in the mind as the ground of one's being. Macarius insists on the total encountering in ever-increasing awareness and even "feeling" of the presence of the indwelling Trinity through the power of the Holy Spirit. He describes in his fifteenth homily the mythic use of the word *heart* as the focus where God meets humanity in its concrete existence. The divinizing effect of the Holy Spirit works through grace to lead human beings into ever mounting levels of transcendent possibility and realized human development according to our image and likeness, that is Jesus Christ:

> His very grace writes in their hearts the laws of the Spirit. They should not put all their trusting hope solely in the scriptures written in ink. For divine grace writes on the "tables of the heart" (2 Cor 3:3) the laws of the spirit and the heavenly mysteries. For the heart directs and governs all the other organs of the body. And when grace pastures the heart, it rules over all the members and the thoughts. For there, in the heart, the mind abides as well as all the thoughts of the soul and all its hopes. This is how grace penetrates throughout all parts of the body.

Such an affective spirituality sought to integrate body, soul, and spirit in prayer to experience God's indwelling presence in the purified Christian as a transforming light. We will see that this Macarian theme is the beginning of the Taboric light, the light Christ appeared in on Mount Tabor. It is the goal of the hesychastic mysticism of St. Symeon the New Theologian (d. 1022) and the followers of St. Gregory Palamas (d. 1359).

Other accents in this "heart" spirituality placed great emphasis on the transcendence of God, the need for *penthos* or a continued weeping for one's sinfulness, the striving to attain incessant prayer, the theme of the cohabitation of sin and grace, the value of profound humility to attract the mercy and healing of God's love, and the stress on the conscious awareness of the indwelling Trinity through grace as uncreated energies of love.

History of the Macarian Manuscripts

Before we can deal with the authorship of the fifty spiritual homilies of Pseudo-Macarius, we need to study the history of the manuscripts in order to place the time in which the author lived and uncover some historical evidence about his identity and possible background.

Recent patristic scholarship, especially of the past three decades, has given us a greater understanding of Pseudo-Macarius and the literary corpus attributed to him. Studying the manuscript history of these writ-

4

ings, embracing the well-known selection of the fifty spiritual homilies along with other homilies, but also sayings and various letters attributed to Pseudo-Macarius, commentators and editors have given us an orderly presentation of the various collections of Macarian materials.

The Macarian manuscripts are classified according to four main types, or, to use the better term coined by H. Berthold, *collections*,[2] plus the Arab-Coptic manuscript (TV), a very ancient one. It is important to summarize briefly the contents of these collections.

Collection I.[3]   This is the longest of the five collections and contains all of Collection IV and more. Here we find sixty-four homilies and letters called not homilies, but *logoi* in the manuscripts.[4] A special feature of this collection is the presence of *Logos* I, what is known as the *Great Letter*. Much scholarly writing has gone into investigating whether this is a spurious work (a copy of St. Gregory of Nyssa's *De Instituto Christiano*), or whether Pseudo-Macarius or perhaps his disciples wrote it and asked St. Gregory to retouch it, giving it a more philosophical underpinning and removing any evident Messalian teachings.[5]

Collection II.[6]   This is the best known source of Macarius's homilies, coming from an intelligent selection of manuscripts known in the West since 1559, giving the traditional fifty spiritual homilies. It is this edition, first printed with a Latin translation by Jean Picot in 1559, and improved in later editions by H. J. Floss from a Berlin Codex,[7] that formed the basic version for the text reprinted in J.-P. Migne's *Patrologia Graeca* (*PG*).

This translation of the spiritual homilies will use the Greek text found in J.-P. Migne. I will also consult the latest critical edition of H. Dörries, E. Klostermann, M. Kroeger to correct difficult readings.[8] I have chosen to translate the fifty spiritual homilies as found in Collection II since this has been the most popular text in both the East and the West. It is this collection that offers the most representative version of the Macarian corpus, no doubt purified of any seeming "heretical" statements or ambiguous readings. From the sixteenth century down to the present day, it has been the version favored by those who, in both the Western and Eastern forms of Christianity, have been most influenced by this mysterious person that tradition has simply called St. Macarius. Because of its importance, I also have included an original English translation of the famous and much disputed *Great Letter*.

Collection III.[9]   This collection contains forty-three *Logoi* in three manuscripts.[10] It includes other seemingly authentic Macarian homilies not found in Collection II of the fifty homilies. Two-thirds of this collection gives new homilies edited for the first time in 1961 by E. Klostermann and H. Berthold.[11]

Collection IV.[12] This collection contains twenty-six homilies, which have not yet been edited individually since all of them are found in Collection I. It, like Collection I, begins with the *Great Letter.*

Who Is Macarius?

Having outlined the four main collections of manuscripts and critical editions, we are now in a position to investigate the problem of who the author of the fifty spiritual homilies and other Macarian writings really is. Much scholarly investigation has been done on this problem and yet there has not been a convincing conclusion that has been accepted by all patristic scholars.

One reason for this difficulty in determining the author is that parts of the corpus have been attributed to various persons bearing the name of Macarius. In the second half of the fourth century, in which these writings were most likely written, there were several noted figures bearing the name of Macarius. Macarius Magnes (c. 400) appears as the bishop of Magnesia and author of a five-volume work called the *Apocriticus,* of which we possess only a part.[13] Palladius (c. 363–431) in his *Lausiac History,* one of the earliest eye-witness accounts of the Egyptian teachers and leaders of the fourth century, writes of the heroic ascetic Macarius the Alexandrian (c. 295–394), who was in charge of a monastic colony of hermits in the Nitrian desert.[14]

The most important personage of the Egyptian desert to whom the fifty spiritual homilies were attributed almost universally until such authorship was challenged in the nineteenth century by a monk of Mount Athos, Neophytos Kavsokalivites, was St. Macarius the Egyptian. He is mentioned in the writings of Palladius and Rufinus (c. 345–410). This Macarius entered the desert of Scetis when he was thirty years old. He lived as a hermit for sixty years and was renowned for his great gifts of spiritual direction of hermits, discernment, healing, and prophecy. Later manuscripts attribute a number of writings to him, including sayings, letters, prayers, homilies, and treatises.[15] However, scholars find no basis for such prolific literary work on the part of Macarius of Egypt. His only authentic work is his *Letter to his Children* (i.e., disciples), as Gennadius of Marseilles informs us.[16]

From internal evidence of the Macarian texts, we see that the author is a person of high culture. He speaks and writes Greek correctly and with ease. He is a citizen of the Roman Empire. He belongs to the Greek world as well as the Syrian. His language also betrays Latinisms that could be explained by a period he may have passed in the army or in imperial administration before he became a monk. His numerous comparisons are taken from the political, military, and economic world of Late Antique Rome. Thus, the King who is Christ resembles the Byzantine emperor. His palace resembles that of Constantinople or Antioch.

Macarius/Symeon of Mesopotamia

H. Dörries discovered that some of the ancient manuscripts attributed the authorship to one Symeon of Mesopotamia, who was known as a Messalian.[17] The location of Symeon is at least correct, because on the basis of recent scholarship on the contents of the homilies, the author is usually considered to have been a monk who lived in northeast Syria in the middle of the fourth century.

The author mentions wars between the Romans and the Persians and the Romans and the Goths. There is also mention made of Indian and Saracen invasions. The Syrian method of naming the months of the year is used, and there is note of recent persecutions for the faith. The author shows a familiarity with Mediterranean cities and with the institutions existing in the late Empire. He uses phrases and images that occur in earlier Syriac literature. The type of ascetical practices he praises was common in the Syrian world. The author mentions the Euphrates river, known by him for its torrential floodings. He surely did not live in Egypt, for he mentions that the greatest rivers in his northern regions freeze over in winter. He alludes to systems of irrigation found in Lower Mesopotamia. Cities are described as fortified, as castles of the Persian frontier. His language is full of Aramaenisms, or at least it manifests a Semitic way of thinking.

Furthermore, his religious universe is similar to that found in Syriac Christian literature. For example, his scriptural texts are akin to the Syriac version of the Gospels, known as the *Diatessaron*. He uses certain apocrypha of Syrian origin and teaches points of doctrine that are typically Syrian, for example, the Holy Spirit is referred to as Mother (Spirit-*Ruho*, is feminine in both Syriac and Hebrew). His use of symbols is similar to that of Syrian writers, such as Aphraates, St. Ephrem, and the like. The most convincing arguments in favor of placing the author in northeast Syria, that is, the Mesopotamia region, rather than in

Egypt, come from the similarity of certain ideas found in the homilies with those of the Messalians, a heretical group of Syrian Christians condemned at synods and councils in the fourth and fifth centuries.

Was Macarius a Messalian?

The problem of whether Macarius was really the Symeon of Mesopotamia listed as one of the key leaders in the Messalian movement of the fourth century arose among scholars only in recent times. What occasioned it was an article by Dom L. Villecourt in 1920.[18] Villecourt discovered in certain writings attributed to Pseudo-Macarius Messalian texts that had been condemned by several councils and synods between 390 and 431.[19]

Messalianism must be looked at as a general movement rather than a distinct sect. It comes from the Syriac word *messalleyane*, which means "those who pray" (*Euchites* in Greek). It refers to those ascetics whose whole discipline consisted in seeking to pray always, even to the exclusion of fasting or any other practices. They also sought to avoid manual labor in order to receive the outpouring of the Holy Spirit. They minimized the efficacy given to the sacraments, especially to Baptism and the Eucharist, and they opposed the clerical hierarchy. Intense prayer for them would alone uproot the passions within each person so that one could eventually reach *apatheia,* or a state of passionlessness. In this state, any asceticism, such as controlling one's thoughts, and any moral failings would become innocent since there would be no longer any passions.[20]

This movement spread rapidly under the leadership of Dadoes, Sabbas, Adelphios, Hermas, and Symeon.[21] It is this latter Symeon that is listed in one of the most ancient manuscripts, the Arab-Coptic TV manuscript, as the author of the homilies and letters included in that collection.[22] Churches and monasteries were won over by the tenets of this movement, starting mainly in Mesopotamia, then moving to Armenia, Pamphylia, and Lycaonium through Antioch. Soon Cappadocia came under its influence, as the movement spread to Egypt and Carthage.

The hierarchy reacted swiftly and the first stage of Messalianism was condemned in 390 in the Synod of Side in Lycaonium in which twenty-five bishops met, presided over by Amphilochius of Iconium, friend and disciple of St. Basil. In 426 a synod was presided over by Sisinnios, who wrote letters to the bishops of Pamphylia. The most important condemnation of Messalianism came in the ecumenical Council of Ephesus (431), when the bishops approved the letter of Sisinnios and anathematized some propositions taken from the ascetical book of the Messalians, the *Ascetikon*. We know, therefore, that the *Ascetikon* was written between 390 and 431. It could have been written by Symeon of Mesopotamia, as several authors maintain.

After the condemnation of certain propositions found in the *Ascetikon*, the texts of the homilies and other works attributed to Pseudo-Macarius were apparently purged of any glaring Messalian errors. Perhaps this best explains why these "orthodox" teachings of Pseudo-Macarius were attributed to the venerable St. Macarius of Egypt and thus gained respectability as reliable teachings reflecting antiquity and the best in the ascetical practices of the Church.

We can make some provisional conclusions on the question of how Messalian Pseudo-Macarius actually was. It is clear on the basis of comparisons between the Macarian corpus and the *Ascetikon* that some parts of the Macarian corpus were censured in the Council of Ephesus (431). However, the texts of the fifty spiritual homilies and the *Great Letter* were never formally condemned. Symeon of Mesopotamia was doubtless a Messalian, though probably a moderate one. We can tie this problem of Messalian influences in the Macarian corpus to Pseudo-Macarius's relationships with the Cappadocians, especially Basil and Gregory of Nyssa.

Relationships with the Cappadocians

From internal evidence it is clear that Pseudo-Macarius had contact with the monasticism and spirituality of the Cappadocian Fathers, of whom Basil and Gregory of Nyssa were the most important. His fifty homilies and other works show a balance of asceticism, mysticism, and theology that must have been helped by such contacts. He shows similarities to Syrian asceticism, but from Basil he received the emphasis on the importance of the Holy Spirit, which enabled him to bring forth a supple but firm ascetical structure, a respect for sacraments and traditions through the teachings of the hierarchy, and an openness to the inner divine voice.[23]

Like St. Basil in his *Rules* for his monks, Pseudo-Macarius addressed his audience not as "monks," but as "Christians." Both he and Basil believed that all Christians are called to live the Gospel radically and follow Christ completely. Macarius takes an intermediate position between primitive asceticism, centered on the ideal of virginity, and the eremitical life. Both writers aim to teach those Christians who take seriously the "commands" of the Lord and live together in a sharing fraternity. The monasticism of Macarius is little tied to clergy and faithful. His principal aim, as that of Basil, is to present a radical asceticism and mysticism based on the Old and New Testaments. More than Basil, Macarius highlights individual subjectivity—he can be called one of the first teachers of spiritual, interior experiences.

St. Gregory of Nyssa

Macarius, or Pseudo-Macarius/Symeon of Mesopotamia, was clearly more in contact with St. Gregory of Nyssa than with the other Cappodocians. Gregory was knowledgeable about the Messalianism that had influenced the Cappadocian monks of the first stage of the movement.[24] In Gregory's *Treatise on Virginity* (371–378), he sought to correct or guard the young monks tempted by the Messalian style of life by proposing the balanced example of his brother, St. Basil.[25] Gregory expressed an admiration for Mesopotamian monks, who seemed to him a bit uncultured yet deeply spiritual. These could have been the ascetics and disciples of Macarius-Symeon.[26] The absence of Gregory at the Council of Side suggests that the assembled bishops took advantage of this fact to condemn the Messalians toward whom he had shown proof of sympathy.

R. Staats, in his work on the disputed relation of Macarius's *Great Letter* and the *De Instituto Christiano*,[27] supposedly written by Gregory, rejects W. Jaeger's position, as pointed out earlier.[28] Staats maintains that either Gregory, shortly before his death, or one of his disciples edited the *De Instituto Christiano* to encourage the Messalian moderates, like Symeon of Mesopotamia. Since this work attributed to Gregory parallels two-thirds of the first part of Macarius's *Great Letter*, one of the two writings necessarily depends on the other. Jaeger holds that the *Great Letter* is a developed paraphrase of Gregory's *De Instituto*, or at least that there is a common source both authors were using, but this seems improbable.[29] Staats concludes that the *Great Letter* of Macarius/Symeon is the original. Gregory's *De Instituto Christiano* is an attempt to translate the ideas of Macarius-Symeon on spiritual asceticism for a wider audience by lessening the Messalian expressions and infusing into the *Letter* some philosophical notions.

M. Canévet also rejected the authenticity of Gregory as the primary source for Macarius's *Great Letter*.[30] She argues that there are differences in vocabulary, exegesis of scriptural texts, and theology between the *De Instituto* and other works of Gregory. These differences can be explained by the Macarian model that inspired Gregory, who took it and refashioned it in order the better to propagate the true ascetical and mystical teachings found in Macarius's *Great Letter*.[31]

Conclusion

The question is very complex, and only a full study of the works of Gregory and of the Macarian corpus will be able to produce a final answer. It is clear from internal evidence that there are many points of similarity between the two writings. In both we find a theological vision centered on the creation of man according to the image and likeness of God. There is also a spiritual exegesis, more allegorical with Macarius, more philosophical with Gregory, by which both authors extend the interpretations of Origen. There is a similar teaching on the spiritual senses. Another recurring similarity is that both authors highlight the idea of growth in the life to come and an infinite progress, tied to the incomprehensibility of God, perceived in a manner more experiential in Macarius, more philosophical by Gregory. Both keep together the tension between the doctrine of the spiritual senses and that of the incomprehensibility of God, between the awesome Otherness of God and our impossibility to touch him on the one hand, and, on the other, our access through God's grace and our supernatural elevation to an intimate, immanent union with Jesus Christ.

Macarius ignores the mystical darkness (*gnophos*) that Gregory develops so originally in his mystical treatises, especially in his *Life of Moses* and *Commentary on the Song of Songs*. Macarius knows little about the dark night of the spirit, but develops much on the transforming light of the risen Lord Jesus through his Holy Spirit, which makes Christians into sharers in Christ's Taboric light.

We can conclude that Macarius depends on Gregory on many points, while Gregory was certainly inspired by the lived experience of the Holy Spirit found in the monks of Syria around Mesopotamia, of whom Macarius is one of the most articulate and balanced of witnesses.

MACARIAN DOCTRINE

In reading the Macarian writings, we must avoid looking for a neatly arranged system of spiritual teachings geared to Christians of all generations and of all styles of life. As we will see in the fifty homilies, much of the material either is presented in the direct form of questions from disciples and answers from the master, Macarius, or develops a given theme applicable to his audience of fellow monks. Therefore, we are dealing with a practical monastic pedagogy and only in such a setting do we discover the typical traits of Eastern Christian asceticism. The preponderant accent is on the spiritual combat and the interiorization of one's spiritual life, with special stress placed on the personal and intimate experience of fire and baptism in the Holy Spirit that effects a mystical oneness with the indwelling Jesus Christ.

Evidently, from the details of the life of the monks given in the homilies, we see a coenobitic form that does not present a regimented life of fixed hours for communal prayer. Macarius/Symeon favors much individual freedom of gifts, but above all charity. The eminent role is given to the action of the Holy Spirit and the importance of interior prayer as the way to perfection. He calls his audience simply "Christians," for he is presenting them a way of life that follows Christ as perfectly as possible, as outlined in the Gospel precepts. He advises his Christians to give up marriage and to be separated from the "world." Macarius cites St. Paul's advice in 1 Corinthians 7:34: "The unmarried woman or the virgin is concerned with the Lord's interest, is intent on being holy both in body and in mind."

Renounce Oneself

One chief emphasis throughout the writings of Macarius is the call not only to serve God absolutely by renouncing through spiritual and actual poverty all attachments to persons and things, but also to enter into the depths of one's soul and do the inner spiritual battle—to renounce even one's false self. He explains in his *Great Letter* what true renouncement of oneself means:

> What does it mean to renounce one's own self except to give oneself completely to the fraternity and never to accomplish, absolutely, one's own desires, but to be totally available to the Word of God.[32]

Christian charity, found in serving those closest to oneself, is the true criterion of how much a monk has entered into the inner battle to forsake self-centeredness by the healing love of Jesus Christ living within and bringing the Christian the help of his Holy Spirit to live in love for others.

INTRODUCTION

Dignity of the Human Person

Macarius presents throughout his writings a very positive view of human nature, both before and after the fall of Adam and Eve. The first editor of *Collection II*, most probably John Picot (1559),[33] begins the fifty homilies with the homily on the vision of the prophet Ezekiel (Ez 1:4–2:3). Here we see Macarius's typical use of allegory in his scriptural exegesis, much along the lines of Origen. The covering of the human soul with the beauty and ineffable glory of God's Spirit is Macarius's description of the intrinsic beauty and dignity of the human person, both before sin had diminished God's glory from within the soul, and after, by means of the restoration of this inner light. The recovering of this light is the goal to which Macarius wants to lead Christians.

We also see here the beginnings of the doctrine developed by Origen and St. Gregory of Nyssa on the spiritual senses, which have been lost through sin but restored by the Spirit of the Risen Jesus. The idea of the Taboric light, as a luminous vision of God made perceptible even to the eyes of the body, was to develop in the fourteenth century with the hesychasts of Mount Athos. We can safely say that Macarius did not conceive of the light in this way, but rather as a symbol of God's indwelling presence in the more advanced Christian.

Macarius always returns to the basic goodness of human nature. To deny this is to deny God's power and immanence in his human creatures, made by him according to his own image and likeness (Gn 1:26). Homily 15 brings out the intrinsic goodness of man and woman through God's gratuitous willing to share his beauty and nature with them:

> See how great are the heavens and the earth, the sun and the moon. But the Lord was not pleased to find his rest in them, but in humanity alone. Man, therefore, is of greater value than all other creatures, and perhaps I will not hesitate to say, not only visible creatures, but also those invisible, namely, "the ministering spirits" (Heb 1:14). For it was not of Michael or Gabriel, the archangels, that God said: "let us make men to our image and likeness" (Gn 1:26), but he said it concerning the spiritual makeup of the human, I mean, the immortal soul.[34]

Sin

As Macarius is rooted in Scripture, so his teaching on sin is less legalistic and more centered on what sin has done to God's image in

INTRODUCTION

human beings. Sin is something that goes against human nature. It has come from outside, since God created man and woman as very good.

> We have received into ourselves something that is foreign to our nature, namely, the corruption of our passions through the disobedience of the first man which has strongly taken over in us, as though it were a certain part of our nature by custom and long habit. This must be expelled again by that which is also foreign to our nature, namely, the heavenly gift of the Spirit, and so the original purity must be restored.[35]

The author is rich in concrete examples showing how evil penetrates into the depths of the human soul. It becomes like a second "soul" joined to the first.[36] Two forces now inhabit the human soul: God and his angels and Satan and his powers of evil. The human person has lost the glory of God that inhabited the first man and woman. Now he or she is covered with a garment, a veil, a heavy fog, smoke—all Macarian examples to convey how the image of God is not destroyed by sin, but covered over and no longer reflecting the glory of God's light.[37]

Human Free Will

Jesus Christ, by his risen presence living within the Christian, permeates from within the human soul by the divine light of his Spirit. From God's side of this relationship to his human children springs the grace brought about by Jesus, the Savior. He comes with the Father and Holy Spirit to inhabit the Christian in a new and redeeming way. Now grace has preceded and is operative in the Christian soul to move the free will to make choices that help him or her surrender to the alluring love of God rather than to the enticements of the devil.

Here again we see Macarius's optimism about God's creating human nature as good, a goodness that sin can never fully corrupt or destroy. The freedom of the human will is one of his main teachings. No power, not even God, can take it away. God will do nothing to force the human will. God waits upon the movement of our will. God and the devil both desire to win over the human soul.

God's grace is always present, even as the presence of evil exerts its power over the human person. Man stands in the midst of these two adversaries and needs only to exercise faith, hope, and love in God's revelation that the Trinity dwells within the human soul. "I tell you that the human mind is a good match for the enemy, and evenly balanced against him; and a soul of that kind when it seeks, finds help and succor, and redemption is granted it. The contest and struggle is not an unequal one."[38] Whether to do good or evil, the Christian is in a position to assent to whatever course of action he or she decides upon. As long as God allows us this freedom of choice, there can be no complete and total Christian perfection in this earthly dimension of life.

The Spiritual Combat

Thus the true Christian must engage constantly in the inner spiritual combat to fight against sin and the evil powers. God is there testing the sincerity and steadfastness of the human will.

> ... who hears the word comes to repentance and, after this through God's providence grace withdraws for the development of the man. He enters into training and the tactics of war. He enters into the struggle and conflict against Satan. And after a long race and struggle, he carries off the victory and becomes a Christian.[39]

Macarius gives a solidly orthodox teaching on the interrelationships between God's unmerited grace and man's free will to cooperate with grace and thus actively work for his salvation. Macarius always insists that the Christian could not even begin to make a move toward the Good, toward God, without God's graceful help. Even the desire for God himself comes from him, never from human creatures alone. "Never think that you have preceded the Lord in virtue according to him who says: 'It is he, who works in you, both to will and to do for his good pleasure'" (Phil 2:13).[40]

Need for Humility

Macarius, along with all the great spiritual teachers of true Christianity, extolled the need for humility. By praying incessantly and being inwardly attentive to the living presence of the triune God, we come to live in God's real world, a world that gives us the conviction that we are utterly dependent on God. This produces a profound humility. The "more perfect" a person becomes, the nearer one approaches God's perfection, the more she or he is deeply aware of how little one has truly responded to God's influence and grace in this earthly journey.

INTRODUCTION

Such true humility combines with an ardent longing for more and more of God:

> For the sign of Christianity is this, that one be pleasing to God so as to seek to hide oneself from the eyes of men. And even if a person should possess the complete treasures of the King, he should hide them and say continually: "The treasure is not mine, but another has given it to me as a charge. For I am a beggar and when it pleases him, he can claim it from me. . . . And the more they apply themselves to the art of growing in perfection, the more they reckon themselves as poor, as those in great need and possessing nothing. . . . This is the sign of Christianity, namely, this very humility." [41]

Vices and Virtues

In Macarius's writings we find a consistent presentation of the spiritual combat of fourth-century Eastern Christian monasticism and asceticism. This is called *praxis,* or what the human being must do to cooperate with grace to eradicate the deep roots of the eight capital sins.[42] When sins are overcome we can begin to develop the virtues that come from conversion and putting on the mind of Jesus Christ by an inner revolution (Eph 4:7).

We find such traditional words as inner attention (*prosochi*), guarding of the heart, vigilance, sobriety (*nepsis*), and purifying the heart used to express the inner state of alertness necessary to check every thought (*logismos*) at the entry way to our consciousness. Weeping for one's alienation and exile and shame at turning away from God's tender love and the fear of losing that love for eternity is stressed by Macarius in his development of *penthos.*[43]

Discernment

As a spiritual director of monks seeking inner union with Christ, Macarius stresses the need of the Holy Spirit's gift of discernment (*diakrisis*). Pride in making spiritual progress must be checked through a constant vigilance of the thoughts that lead to vainglory and pride. Discernment of spirits is absolutely necessary to eradicate any forces that would take the monk away from an ever-increasing conscious self-surrendering at each moment.

Macarius insists on the need of much prayer and asceticism in order

16

to receive the discernment of spirits from the Holy Spirit and thus be able to recognize each of the evil demons disguised behind various phantasms. The author of the homilies always returns to the test Christ gives in the Gospel. It is the fruit produced that measures the movement of one's surrender to the guidance of the Holy Spirit. This is St. Paul's test also (Gal 5:22).

To be guided by a mature and advanced spiritual soul-friend is absolutely necessary for the Christian, especially in the early stages of the spiritual combat. Beginners should search for a person who is guided by the Spirit and who knows from personal experience of the "heart" the path to perfection.[44]

Cohabitation of Grace and Sin

St. Gregory of Nyssa was the major proponent of the theory of the spiritual life as a process of continued growth, using the word *epectasis* from St. Paul's "stretching forth for the finish" in Philippians 3:13. This is also essential to Macarius's vision.[45] Macarius shows a constant progression that can never be finished, since the co-habitation in the same person of sin and grace will always exist in our earthly life. For him, grace always finds sin present, so there is always at least the possibility of turning away from God on our part. Grace always gives us the power to fight against this, however, if we truly desire a conversion. We are always being healed, saved, redeemed, being divinized by the loving grace of God's Spirit, who, both in this life and in the next, never tires of drawing us into his own image and likeness through his Son, Jesus Christ. Grace never suppresses nature's weaknesses, sufferings, or death. We accept such brokenness as a part of education and grow in faith and humility and eventually into pure love.

> But who, indeed, has ever arrived at perfection and tasted and directly experienced that world? I have not yet seen any perfect Christian or one perfectly free. But, although a person may be at rest in grace and arrive at experiencing mysteries, revelations and the immense consolation of grace, nevertheless, sin still abides in him.[46]

Pray Unceasingly

Macarius, like all of the desert Christian mystics, stresses greatly the centrality of unceasing prayer as the air in which a true Christian should live daily. He considers all virtues as interrelated, forming, as it were a spiritual chain, with the first link as foundational to all others in the spiritual life, namely, incessant prayer.

> The summit of all zeal toward the good and peak of all virtuous practices is in one's striving in prayer, thanks to which we can obtain each day the rest of the virtues and demand them of God.[47]

We cannot, according to Macarius's teaching, do anything except to cry out to the Lord and demand the aid of his grace, in which consists the foundation of prayer. The Spirit then comes in response to accomplish in us the virtues.

> Prayer produces among those who are worthy of it a certain mystical communion (*koinonia*) of holiness with God, thanks to the action of the Spirit. It brings about a certain union with the Lord that fills the human spirit with an inexpressible love. And each day he who is moved to continue in prayer is drawn by the love of the Spirit to a love and a desire that is full of fire for God. Each one receives the grace from the Spirit of the perfection of a free will. It is God who gives this gift.[48]

The state of pure prayer or incessant prayer of the heart is tied to the guarding of the heart. Macarius, along with the leading Eastern Fathers, views the heart as the center of the human spirit, where one can communicate and surrender oneself totally in love to God. Ultimately, he maintains that pure prayer or true prayer, which we would call today "contemplative prayer," becomes equivalent to the fire of God's Spirit transforming the Christian into love, in every thought, word, and deed.

> To fly into the divine air and enjoy the liberty of the Holy Spirit (2 Cor 3:18) may be one's desire, but, if he does not have wings given him, he cannot. Let us pray to God that he gives us "the wings of a dove" (Ps 55:7) of the Holy Spirit so we may fly to him and find rest (*anapausis*) and that he may separate and take away from our soul and body such an evil wind namely, sin itself, inhabiting the members of our soul and body.[49]

INTRODUCTION

Baptism of the Holy Spirit

A Christian cannot reach what Macarius calls "true prayer," different from "natural prayer," without the power of the Holy Spirit. The Spirit alone can teach the Christian that prayer in which the mysteries of God are taught directly to the soul. The soul then knows the sweetness, the spiritual experience, the joy, and the various forms of ecstasy.

Macarius is one of the first witnesses of what modern Christians would call the baptism in the Holy Spirit. He conceives this to be an ongoing process of surrendering to the indwelling guidance of the Holy Spirit to the degree that the individual cries out for the Spirit to heal the roots of sinfulness that lie deeply within the soul. When one begins consistently to give himself or herself over entirely to seeking the love of Christ in all things, then, according to Macarius, that person is receiving the baptism in the Holy Spirit of Jesus Christ. The sign of the true progress in the baptism of the Spirit is the continued desire to surrender to the Spirit's gifts, especially faith, hope, and love. This is directly dependent on the individual's maintaining humility and a state of constant compunction or *penthos*.

Receiving from the Holy Spirit inner knowledge of God's omnipotence and one's own human sinfulness, the individual will be granted the gift of spiritually weeping for his or her sins. The desert fathers, along with Macarius, were convinced that this weeping kept them from sinning and that this was the only way to true salvation, to the true life, whereby God would come and dwell within them.

It is interesting that Macarius, possibly influenced by the writings of the Syrians Aphraates and Ephrem, refers to the Holy Spirit as Mother. Spirit (*Ruho*) is feminine in Syriac and also in Hebrew.[50] The Holy Spirit is described by Macarius as "Rachel, the true mother, the heavenly Grace."[51] "And from that time until the time of the last Adam, the Lord, man did not see the true Heavenly Father and the Good and Kind Mother, the grace of the Spirit."[52] It is the Holy Spirit who gives birth to Christians in the divinizing process that makes them truly children of God (1 Jn 3:1) and brothers and sisters to Jesus Christ.[53]

Centrality of Jesus Christ

For Macarius, the Incarnation is the high point of human history through which the Godhead has come down into our world of matter and has redeemed us in the person of Jesus Christ. Macarius stresses not so much what Jesus has done in his lifetime (other than the key of

19

INTRODUCTION

manifesting through death on the cross the infinite love of the Father for us), but what he is now doing for us and with us by his gloriously risen life within us.

In typical Syrian style of allegory, Macarius describes Jesus as "paradise, tree of life, pearl, crown, builder, cultivator, sufferer, one incapable of suffering, man, God, wine, living water, lamb, bridegroom, warrior, armor, Christ, all in all."[54] Other images he uses to bring out the centrality of Jesus for the Christian are spread throughout the corpus: Christ the Master, the Father who brings us new divine life, the King, the Physician, Savior and Redeemer, Pilot, Rider and Charioteer, Farmer and skilled Craftsman, Foundation, Rock, and Pearl. All such attributes convey to the reader his deep love for Jesus Christ. Although he does not yet synchronize the name of Jesus with his breath, nevertheless, he prepares the way for the hesychastic fathers who centered their praying incessantly around the breathing continually, day and night, of the name and hence the presence of Jesus.

This mystical union with Jesus Christ brings about the peak of all Christian perfection, which consists in the love of God with one's whole heart and soul. This takes over the consciousness of the individual so that one may live continually in the love of God pouring out in his heart (Rom 5:5) by the Spirit. Macarius, in a rare sharing with the reader, gives us an account of the intimate love of Christ he had attained:

> After I received the experience of the sign of the cross, grace now acts in this manner. It quiets all my parts and my heart so that the soul with the greatest joy seems to be a guileless child. No longer am I a man that condemns Greek or Jew or sinner or worldling. Truly, the interior man looks on all human beings with pure eyes and finds joy in the whole world. He really wishes to reverence and love all Greeks and Jews.[55]

INFLUENCE OF THE MACARIAN CORPUS

The Macarian writings spread very quickly and had great influence, both in Syriac Christianity and in the wider Christian world. Thus, we see a strong influence of Macarius/Symeon on Diadochus, bishop of Photice in Epirus, one of the great ascetics of the fifth century. Like Macarius, he stressed the need of a consciousness of the Spirit's operating grace.[56] St. Mark the Hermit also shows a decided dependence on

20

the basic themes treated by Macarius, along with a similar vocabulary and terminology to express religious experience of expanded consciousness of affectivity toward the indwelling Jesus Christ.[57]

One of the popular lives of the saints that had great influence on early Christian writing was the *Life* of the monk Hypatius (c. 366–446). It was written by his disciple, the Syrian Callinicus.[58] We find in this work certain Macarian phrases that deal with the nature of "true Christianity," as well as the practice of unceasing prayer of the heart and the virtues. This demonstrates that its author knew the Macarian corpus, especially the homilies.

Macarius's writings had strong influence on later Syrians, especially the Nestorian mystics of the seventh and eighth centuries. Such writers as Dadiso Qatraya (c. second half of the seventh century), Isaac of Ninevah (c. 660–680), and Joseph Hazzaya (eighth century) were influenced by ideas from the Macarian corpus.

Byzantine Influence

Among the Byzantine writers we find the influence of Macarius on Symeon Metaphrastes (c. 900–984), who in his famous *Menologion,* a collection of the lives of the saints, presented many extracts from the works of Macarius. The greatest Macarian influence is seen on the eleventh-century Byzantine mystic St. Symeon the New Theologian (949–1022), especially in his *Hymns of Divine Love*[59] and his *Catecheses.*[60] Symeon's descriptions of the awareness of the presence of the indwelling Trinity, the experience of grace, of man's sinful condition without salvation, of the mysticism of the indwelling Spirit and the need for the baptism in the Spirit, along with the mysticism of Jesus Christ as light, all show a strong Macarian influence. Nevertheless, he does not appeal too often by name to this fundamental source.[61]

Macarius's writings had a special impact on the Byzantine hesychastic writers who developed the techniques on Mount Athos for the prayer of the heart, using one's breathing and the Jesus Prayer.[62] Such writers include Nicephorus the Hesychast (c. 1230),[63] St. Gregory of Sinai (1255–1346), and St. Gregory Palamas (1296–1359) who cites Macarius often in his Triads. St. Gregory of Sinai brought a renaissance to fourteenth-century Mount Athos with his use of the Jesus Prayer, combined with his writings on the hesychastic style of spirituality.[64] Gregory of Sinai's stress on holistic integration of body, soul, and spirit, the feeling of God's interior presence and an abiding consciousness of grace, all show a definite influence from Macarius. This Macarian influence on Gregory passed on to Patriarch Callistus and Ignatius of Xanthopoulos in the *Directions to Hesychasts*.[65] Nicholas Cabasilas (1320–1391), famous for his *Life in Christ* and his *Commentary on the Divine Liturgy*, took over the theme of the prayer of the heart and the spiritual senses from Macarius's writings and inserted such perspectives into his sacramental spirituality with its accent on a dynamic encounter with the risen Jesus Christ.[66] Finally, parts of Macarius in the eleventh-century paraphrase of Symeon Metaphrastes were included in the Greek *Philokalia* edited by St. Macarius of Corinth and St. Nicodemus of the Holy Mountain (Venice, 1782).

Slavic Influence

Slavic spirituality as found among the Bulgarians, Serbians, Slovaks, Ukrainians, and Russians, and also Romanians, has always highlighted many aspects of the Macarian spirituality of the heart. The Slavs received Christianity from the Greek Church and along with it a rich patristic theology and spirituality. We find Macarius's works translated into Slavonic before the sixteenth century in the form of selected excerpts found in anthologies and florilegia.

St. Nil Sorsky (1433–1508), who spent several years on Mount Athos and near Constantinople, brought back to Russia the spirituality of hesychasm and the use of the Jesus Prayer. In his works and letters we find an original synthesis of basic Macarian themes of prayer of the heart, *penthos* (weeping for sins), interior poverty, and humility.[67] The greatest Macarian influence came through the translation into Slavonic by Paissy Velichkovsky (1722–1794) of the Greek *Philokalia*, the collection of the hesychastic writings of the "neptik" Fathers, or those who practice inner attentiveness, who depended greatly on Macarius. One of the most popular of all Russian saints, St. Seraphim of Sarov (1759–1833), meditated on the *Homilies* of Macarius frequently. His teaching, as well as his experience of the indwelling Trinity as transforming even the body with its Taboric light, find their source in Macarius.[68]

One final Slavic work that recently has had great popularity in the West is the anonymous *The Way of the Pilgrim*.[69] This describes a simple peasant who walks as a pilgrim through parts of Siberia, reciting the Jesus Prayer as he learned it from the *Philokalia*. This simple Christian mantra offers Westerners eager for a more interior, simplified, contemplative prayer a synthesis of the elements that Macarius stressed in his homilies: *nepsis* or constant interior vigilance over one's thoughts; unceasing prayer; fiery prayer that takes flame within the heart and transforms one into the experience of being risen in Christ through the power of the indwelling Holy Spirit.

Influence on the West

Until the invention of the printing press in the West in the fifteenth century, Macarius's influence was mostly indirect. John Cassian (c. 360–435), called by St. Benedict the "Master," brought the monasticism he had seen lived among the hermits and members of the communities of the Egyptian and Syrian deserts to the West through the monasteries he founded in southern France. It is in his two classics, the *Institutes* and the *Conferences*, that he borrows from Macarius's teachings on perfection and on the gifts of the Holy Spirit.[70] St. Benedict (d. 547), by relying on Cassian's writings, gives a similar teaching in his *Rule*.

In the later Middle Ages, we find a distinct Macarian influence in the West in the writings of the Spiritual Franciscans. The rise of the spirituality of St. Francis throughout Europe was in part a reaction against the abstract and impersonal theology of Scholastic theologians and a longing for a more intimate union with Jesus Christ. Angelo of Clareno (c. 1260–1337) and his companions, persecuted by Roman officials, fled to Thessalonika and there made translations of certain Macarian writings. With the arrival of the printing press and the first Latin translation of the fifty spiritual homilies by John Picot in 1559, however, Macarius began to have much greater influence in the West, especially among the Protestant Reformers. The Protestant Pietist authors of the seventeenth and eighteenth centuries found in his writings an authority of the early Church to mount a reaction against Protestant Scholasticism.

Influence among Protestant Spiritual Writers

Protestant spiritual authors found in the writings of Macarius a personalistic, intimate, and charismatic approach in great contrast to the heavy Scholasticism that had taken over both the classical Roman and Protestant theological circles. The Pietists and their predecessors and followers looked for and found in Macarius a basis for much of their teaching. John Arndt (1555–1621), a German Lutheran pastor and spiritual writer, is said to have known the homilies of Macarius by heart. In his writings, such as *De Vero Christiano* and his *Paradiesgartlein*, he injects whole passages rephrased from Macarius.[71] His disciple, John Gerhard (1582–1637), the outstanding Lutheran theologian of the seventeenth century, brought a revival of patristic interpretation of Holy Scripture to Germany through the reading of Macarius.[72] A direct impetus for Macarian influence among Protestant Pietists was given by Gottfried Arnold (1666–1714), who made a German translation of the Macarian *Homilies*. This prepared the way for lay communal, almost monastic, communities that developed in Europe and America.[73] Arnold held that the true doctrine of justification by faith alone was taught by Macarius and hence he belonged to the pristine apostolic tradition. Against the static State Lutheran Church he preached perfection as he saw it taught by Macarius—a process leading to divinization through constant vigilance over one's heart. In France the Huguenot Pastor Pierre Poiret (1646–1719) had immense influence on pietist groups in France, Holland, and England. He too envisioned the Christian life as a mystical journey of progressive transformation, a theme he found in Macarius.[74] His admiration for Macarius is seen in his statement: "There is no need to recall to the man who has eyes for reading that the whole of mystical theology is found in Macarius."[75]

The writings of such men as Arndt, Arnold Kopken, and Christian Hoburg (the latter two of the seventeenth century) were often reprinted for popular reading and meditation. Through them Macarius's influence entered deeply into the segment of Western Christianity that was eager for a more immediate, direct contact with God in a conversion experience. We can see this influence of Macarius, although indirectly, through the writings of Arndt's *De Vero Christiano*, and even in Soren Kierkegaard (1813–1855). The latter's approach, stressing a radical faith conversion and total following of Christ, is typically Macarian.[76] The Macarian corpus is also said to have influenced Madame Guyon.[77]

In Great Britain, Macarius's writings enjoyed a following in eighteenth-century revivalism. In 1721 an Anglican clergyman, Thomas Haywood, made the first English translation of the homilies under the title *Primitive Morality, or The Spiritual Homilies of St. Macarius the Egyptian*. This translation influenced Samuel Wesley (1662–1735) and his son John (1703–1791). It was John, the inspiration for Methodism, who made a new translation of selected homilies of Macarius that were published in the first volume of his *Christian Library* (1749).[78] The influence of Macarius was not as great among Catholics, although we find here and there individual Catholic spiritual writers recommending his writings for spiritual reading. He was recommended to Jesuit novice-masters immediately after the writings of Cassian. Msgr. L. de Segur (1820–1881) often cites Macarius in his devotional work *La Pieté et la Vie Interieure*.[79]

We can see, therefore, that Macarius's influence through the centuries, both among Eastern and Western Christian writers, came about mainly through his fifty spiritual homilies. The writers influenced by Macarius were usually of a more pietistic or mystical attraction. Readers of such works made contact with one of the classics of early Christian writing on the spiritual life, a work that emphasized a process of continued growth through a daily baptism in the Holy Spirit. Johannes Quasten summarizes the influence of Macarius on succeeding generations of Christians: "These Homilies entitle their author to a preeminent position in the history of early Christian mysticism and have proved a source of inspiration to modern mystics."[80]

Contemporary Importance of Macarius

Today we find many Christians throughout the world seeking a more intimate relationship with God. The far-off God of Scholastic theology of the Middle Ages is just too remote to have an impact on most modern citizens. Contemporary Christians who are serious about following Christ desire to experience God more directly and immediately.

We also see a great movement afoot in all Christian Churches that can be called the charismatic renewal. Innumerable Christians of the Orthodox, Roman Catholic, and Protestant groups, and even those coming out of Judaism or no formal church membership, are beginning to meet Jesus Christ in a most personal, living experience as their Lord and Savior. They are being fed by meditation on Holy Scripture, especially the Gospels, and are crying out for deeper healings of the psyche and for the gifts of the Holy Spirit in order to grow in the interior life, and then to exercise such gifts of service to the world around them.

It was for this reason that I have undertaken this translation of the fifty homilies of Pseudo-Macarius, as well as the *Great Letter*.[81] I believe Macarius is a source of solid orthodox teaching for all who seek more seriously to journey inwardly and to surrender to the indwelling Trinity's infinite love and transforming power. His accent on the charismatic gifts of healing, knowledge, and wisdom, his interpretation of Scripture in an allegorical sense through the guidance of the Spirit, his stress on the gifts of pure or true prayer (which for Macarius means incessant prayer), are much needed today.

INTRODUCTION

The reader should be cautioned not to approach the writings of Macarius expecting a type of spiritual teaching common to modern writers. His spirituality is almost impossible to understand if one wishes to systemize it. Because he was a mystic, solidly rooted in Holy Scripture and the early patristic tradition of the ascetics of the desert, his writings reveal a wide spectrum of emphasis and very often apparent contradictions. One can point out faulty, fuzzy language, at least if one were to push his words to their logical conclusion. Macarius wants to lead the reader into an inner Christian experience that lies beyond our translation of such words as knowledge, experience, feeling, or awareness. For this reason he resorts to an abundance of parables and analogies, allegories used to convey the hidden mystery of God's love for his human creatures, much as Jesus himself taught in the Gospels.

One great source of aid to modern readers is his accent on interior discipline and the control of the thoughts and passionate desires of the individual. With his stress on humility and love, Macarius can call charismatic Christians away from objectivizing the gifts of the Spirit as a source of personal power, tools that could so easily lead them on a vanity trip. Others who fear emotionalism within the charismatic renewal will find in Macarius an excellent balance in teaching about the gifts of the Holy Spirit and the need to surrender to the Spirit's indwelling presence in communicating the mind of the Father through his Son.

The greatest value in reading this volume of the fifty homilies and the *Great Letter* is to be brought back in very simple language, nontheological in the sense of scholastic abstractions, to the basic message found in the Gospels. These writings, if one keeps in mind the particular time and place and audience they were intended for, can be applicable to all, regardless of whether we live a Christian life in marriage, in the single state, or in the religious life of vows.

Macarius challenges us to become true Christians by living the Gospel message of humility and love in service at all times. He shows powerfully and simply the meaning of life in his various question-and-answer sections that touch on the psychology of creaturely attachments, on worldliness, on the importance of prayer and ascetical disciplines, but especially on the meaning of the resurrection in the life of each individual. His teaching on interiority is a message that challenges a modern Christian to seek the Kingdom of God over everything else, so that in a purified heart all things will be added unto him or her.

There is also an ecumenical thrust to Macarius's writings. Catholics and Orthodox should feel at home with him, since both churches have maintained, through their mystical and ascetical writings, contact with the teachings of the inner life as presented by Macarius. Evangelical and Pentecostal Protestants also will feel at home with Macarius's scriptural teachings and the stress on the openness to the Holy Spirit and the personal experience of God's grace working in their lives.

Because Macarius, as represented chiefly by the homilies, brings us back to a more simplified, pristine form of Christianity that reduces to the most basic elements of what it means to be a Christian, I have sought to introduce these classic texts to modern Christians. Previously there was only one complete translation of the fifty homilies in English (done by A. J. Mason in 1921), but it was in rather archaic language and was not readily available.[82] There was no existing English translation of the *Great Letter*. I thought it was time to do a more modern translation, and especially to bring together a summary of the scholarship done on the Macarian corpus in the present century.

Conclusion

The proof of the orthodoxy and sublime teaching of Macarius on spiritual perfection and the interior, mystical life, in harmony with Holy Scripture and the patristic traditions, lies only in the reading. If a Christian has begun to experience the dying to self through the rigorous asceticism propounded by Jesus Christ and Macarius, he or she will also begin to experience to some degree the transfiguring presence of the risen Lord within as the center of all human activity.

The heart, as Blaise Pascal insisted, has its own reasons. I pray that the reader will not look for logical proofs or mere techniques in this work, but will find in it sparks that, as Macarius had hoped, would ignite the divine Fire, the Holy Spirit, within each person's heart and bring him or her into that inner resting of the Great Sabbath that only God can reveal. Such resting or integration, paradoxically, will also become a restless striving, a stretching out toward Infinity, toward the Unpossessable that makes all other possessions vain.

NOTES

1. Werner Jaeger, *Early Christianity and Greek Paideia* (Cambridge, England, 1961).

2. H. Berthold, *Makarios/Symeon: Reden und Briefe. Die Sammlung*

I des Vaticanus Graecus 694 (B), 2 vols., in *GCS (Die Griechischen Christlichen Schriftsteller)* (Berlin, 1973).

3. Berthold has edited these texts in the two volumes of *Makarios/Symeon*.

4. *Collection I* is found almost completely in two manuscripts of the thirteenth century. According to Berthold's introduction, these are *Vaticanus Graecus 694 (B)* and *Atheniensis B.N. 423 (b)*.

5. W. Jaeger edited this text and insisted that it really was first written by St. Gregory of Nyssa with the name of *De Instituto Christiano*. Cf. Jaeger's *Two Rediscovered Works of Ancient Christian Literature: Gregory of Nyssa and Macarius* (Leiden, 1954). But recent authors have doubted this, especially J. Gribomont and Vincent Desprez in his *Pseudo-Macaire: Oeuvres Spirituelles Homélies propres a la Collection II* (Paris, 1980). See also M. Canévet, "Le 'De Instituto Christiano' est-il de Grégoire de Nysse?" *Revue des Études Grecques* 82 (1969): 404–23; and R. Staats, *Gregor von Nyssa und die Messalianer*, Patristische Texte und Studien 8 (Berlin, 1968). Staats summarizes the opinions of the other authors who consider the *Great Letter* of Pseudo-Macarius as the original work and explain the *De Instituto Christiano*, normally attributed to St. Gregory of Nyssa, as an attempt to translate the ideas of Pseudo-Macarius/Symeon of Mesopotamia on the ascetical life in a more literary language. They argue that this was done in order to lessen the Messalian expressions and to infuse into the *Letter* some philosophical notions more acceptable to the Greek intelligentsia. The basis for rejecting St. Gregory of Nyssa as the author comes from comparing the vocabulary, biblical exegesis, and theology of the *De Instituto* and those of other works of St. Gregory. J. Gribomont explains these difficulties precisely by the Macarian model, which inspired Gregory himself or his disciples to refashion it in order better to propagate the ideas of Symeon of Mesopotamia. The question is very complex and necessitates a more "global" confrontation of the works of Gregory and Macarius.

6. The critical edition is that of H. Dörries, E. Klostermann, and M. Kroeger, *Die 50 Geistlichen Homilien Des Makarios*, Patristische Texte und Studien 6 (Berlin, 1964). This edition gives an introduction with the history of the text of the *Homilies* and the different editions in various languages.

7. Cod.Berol.gr.16. It is this improved text of H. J. Floss that is used in the Migne collection (J.-P. Migne, *PG* 34:449–822), along with the still more improved text of the 1770 edition printed in Venice. The text

INTRODUCTION

for the *Great Letter* is also found in *PG* 34:409–41 (the edition of H. J. Floss).

8. See above, note 6. The French patristic series *Sources Chrétiennes* has undertaken an ambitious editing of all four collections, under the direction of Vincent Desprez. *Collection III* was published in 1980; *Collection I* and *IV* will soon appear as the second volume, with *Collection II* to follow.

9. The latest edition is by Vincent Desprez as *SC. 275*, using the critical text of Klostermann and H. Berthold (see below, note 11).

10. These manuscripts, forming the basis for the critical editions of Klostermann and Berthold, are: *Atheniensis B.N. 272 (C)*; Athos, *Panteleimon 129 (R)*; and *Mosquensis, Bibliothèque synodale, gr. 177 (M)*.

11. E. Klostermann and H. Berthold, *Neue Homilien des Makarios/Symeon aus Typus III*, Texte und Untersuchungen (Berlin, 1961).

12. This collection is found in an ancient manuscript of the eleventh century in Greek, *Parisinus Gr. 973 (X)*, copied in the monastery of Xerochoraphion near Milet. Parts of *Collection IV* are found in two other manuscripts of *Collection III*. See H. Berthold's introduction to *Collection I* above, in footnote 2.

13. An English edition was made by T. W. Crafer, *The Apocriticus of Macarius Magnes* (London: SPCK, 1919). Cf. J. Quasten, *Patrology* (Utrecht, 1960), vol. 3, pp. 486–88.

14. See Palladius, *Lausiac History*, and the treatment in J Quasten, *Patrology*, vol. 3, pp. 168–69.

15. Ibid., pp. 161–62. Cf. also J. Meyendorff, "Messalianism or Anti-Messalianism? A Fresh Look at the Macarian Problem," *Kyriakon. Festschrift in honor of J. Quasten*, vol. 2 (Münster, 1971), pp. 285–290, esp. p. 590, n. 2.

16. Gennadius of Marseilles, *De viris illustribus X* (*PL* 58:1065 sq.).

17. Cf. H. Dörries, *Symeon von Mesopotamien. Die Überlieferung der Messalianischen Makarios Schriften*, Texte und Untersuchungen 55 (Leipzig-Berlin, 1941).

18. Dom L. Villecourt, "La date et l'origine des Homélies Spirituelles' attribuées à Macaire," *Comptes rendus des sessions de l'Académie des Inscriptions et Belles-Lettres* (Paris, 1920), pp. 250–58.

19. On the history and the errors attributed to Messalianism, see G. Bareille, "Euchites," *Dictionnaire de théologie catholique*, vol. 5, c. 1454–465. The sources are assembled by P. Kmosko in his introduction to his *Livre des Degrés* in *Patrologia Syriaca*, ed. R. Graffin, 3 vols. (Paris,

29

1894–1926), vol. 3, cc. CLXX–CCXCIII. See also A. Guillaumont, "Messaliens," *DS* 10:1074–83.

20. One can discover by reading the sources that dealt with Messalianism in the fourth and fifth centuries three different stages of this movement. The first is known through the writings of Epiphanius (*Panarion* 80, in *PG* 42:756–64), and the second text cited by Kmosko, which describes groups of unstable "enthusiasts" about the year 377. The second group is described in the writings of Theodoret and Timothy. The third is known through the writings of St. John Damascene, who groups various extracts from the book of the Messalians, *The Ascetikon*. It is in the lists of Timothy and of John Damascene that we find resemblances, even word for word, with pseudo-Macarian texts.

21. Kmosko, *Livre des Degrés*, c. CXCII.

22. H. Dörries, *Symeon von Mesopotamien. Die Überlieferung der messalianischen Makarios-Schriften*, Texte und Untersuchungen 55, 1 (Leipzig, 1941). Dörries is the chief exponent of Symeon of Mesopotamia as being the author of the *Homilies* and other works attributed to Macarius of Egypt. He traces out quite convincingly the Messalian elements in Macarius/Symeon's writings.

23. Vincent Desprez, "Macaire (Pseudo)," *DS* 11:25–26.

24. A. Wilmart, "Origine veritable des homélies pneumatiques," *Revue d'Ascetique et de Mystique* 1 (1920): 361–77.

25. *Treatise on Virginity* 23. 3–6 (see *SC* 119:530–53).

26. R. Staats, "Die Asketen aus Mesopotamien in der Rede des Gregor von Nyssa 'In suam ordinationem,'" *Vigiliae Christianae* 21 (1967): 167–79.

27. R. Staats, *Gregor von Nyssa und die Messalianer*, Patristische Texte und Studien 8 (Berlin, 1968).

28. Cf. above, footnote 5.

29. Jaeger, *Two Rediscovered Works*, pp. 174–207.

30. Canévet, "Le 'De Instituto Christiano.' "

31. See J. Gribomont as cited by V. Desprez in *Pseudo-Macaire* (*SC* 275), p. 53.

32. *Great Letter*, p. 260.

33. Cf. notes 6 and 7 above.

34. Homily (hereafter H.) 15:22. Cf. H. 24. This latter homily forms a whole with III, 24 (*Collection III* in *SC* 275:263ff.).

35. H. 4:8.

36. St. John Damascene writes that the literal understanding of two persons within the human soul through sin was condemned in the

Council of Ephesus (431) as a teaching of Messalianism. See *De Haeresibus* 80, 2–3 (*PG* 94:729a).

37. For such images, see H. 2:1, 2 and 9:11, 122. See also H. 8:3, 42; 26:25; and 43:7.

38. H. 3:6.

39. H. 27:20.

40. H. 37:49.

41. H. 15:37.

42. Western spirituality under the influence of the writings of Gregory the Great gives a different lineup of the capital sins, with only seven. The eight sources of all passions, sins, and thoughts are catalogued in Eastern Christian tradition as gluttony, fornication, covetousness, anger, sadness, *acedia* (spiritual ennui), vainglory, and pride. See I. Hausherr, "L'Origine de la théorie orientale des huit pechès capitaux," *Orientalia Christiana*, vol. 30 (Rome, 1933), pp. 164–75.

43. A classic work on this patristic theme of *penthos* is that of Iréneé Hausherr, *Penthos la doctrine de la componction dans l'Orient chrétien*, Orientalia Christiana Analecta, no. 132 (Rome, 1944) (see bibliography for English translation). See also G. Maloney, "Brokenness unto Life," in *The Prayer of the Heart* (Notre Dame, Ind., 1981), pp. 80–102.

44. *Collection III*, 7:2. See "Direction spirituelle en Orient," *DS* 3:1008sq; and *Spiritual Direction in the Early Christian East* (Kalamazoo, 1990).

45. P. Deseille, "Epectase," *DS* 4:785–88. T. Spidlik: "L'eternitá e il tempo, la *zoe* e il *bios*, problema dei Padri Cappadoci," *Augustinianum* 16 (1976): 107–16. For Macarius, this stretching out to possess God as infinite Beauty and Love is a restlessness that knows no end or satiety, and yet it brings a true resting in the possession of the already-achieved level of oneness with Infinity.

46. H. 8:5.

47. *Great Letter;* see Jaeger, *Works*, pp. 268,19–269,3.

48. *Collection I*, H. 4:1 and 4.

49. H. 2:3.

50. See V. Desprez, *Collection III* (*SC* 275), pp. 35–36, note 9.

51. *Collection I*, H. 61:2.

52. H. 28:4. Cf. *Collection III*, H. 16:2, 3.

53. H. 30:2.

54. H. 31:4.

55. Hom. 8:6.

56. E. Des Places in his introduction to his edition of the works of

Diadochus, *Diadoque de Photice, Oeuvres Spirituelles, SC* 5 (Paris, 1955), pp. 9–81. Cf. Quasten, *Patrology,* vol. 3, pp. 509–13.

57. His writings can be found in *PG* 65:893–1140. Cf. Quasten, *Patrology,* pp. 504–09.

58. See G. J. M. Bartelink in his Introduction to *Vie d'Hypatios, SC* 177 (Paris, 1971), pp. 9–44.

59. See my translation and introduction to Symeon's *Hymns of Divine Love* (Denville, N.J., 1975).

60. The critical edition of B. Krivocheine is in *SC* 96 (Paris, 1963). An English translation is D. J. deCatanzaro, *Symeon the New Theologian: The Discourses,* The Classics of Western Spirituality (Mahwah, N.J.: Paulist, 1980).

61. For a presentation of his mysticism, see G. Maloney, S.J., *The Mystic of Fire and Light* (Denville, N.J., 1975).

62. For an explanation of the hesychastic spirituality and the historical origins of the Jesus Prayer, see Maloney, *The Prayer of the Heart.*

63. Jean Meyendorff, *St. Grégoire Palamas et la Mystique Orthodoxe* (Paris, 1959), pp. 60–64 (trans., *St. Gregory Palamas and Orthodox Spirituality,* New York, 1974).

64. See the writings of St. Gregory of Sinai in *Writings from the Philokalia on Prayer of the Heart,* tr. M. Kadloubovsky and G. E. H. Palmer (London, 1951), pp. 35–94.

65. Ibid., pp. 162–273.

66. B. Bobrinskoy, "Nicholas Cabasilas and Hesychast Spirituality," *Sobornost* 5 (1969): 483–505.

67. G. Maloney, *Russian Hesychasm—the Spirituality of Nil Sorskij* (The Hague, 1973).

68. V. Lossky, *The Mystical Theology of the Eastern Church* (London, 1957), pp. 227–35.

69. *The Way of a Pilgrim,* tr. E. French (London, 1930).

70. A. Kemmer, *Charisma Maximum, Unterschuung zu Cassians Vollkommenheitslehre und seiner Stellung zum Messalianismus* (Louvain, 1938), pp. 92–109.

71. See Quasten, *Patrology,* vol. 3, pp. 162–63.

72. See L. Bouyer, *Orthodox Spirituality and Protestant and Anglican Spirituality,* vol. 3 of *A History of Christian Spirituality* (London, 1969), pp. 100–02.

73. Ibid., pp. 174–75.

74. E. Benz, *Die Protestantische Thebais zur Nachwirkung des Maka-*

INTRODUCTION

rios des Egypters im Protestantismus des 17 und 18 Jahrhunderts in Europa und Amerika (Wiesbaden, 1963), pp. 26–28.

75. Ibid., p. 26.

76. M. M. Thulstrup, "Soren Kierkegaard," *DS* 8:1723–29.

77. See Louis Guerrier, *Madame Guyon: Sa vie, sa doctrine, et son influence* (Orleans, 1881).

78. A. C. Outler, *John Wesley* (New York, 1964), pp. 9, n. 26; p. 31; 368–82; 432–35.

79. See J. Revet, "Louis-Gaston de Segur," *DS* 14:1781–83.

80. Quasten, *Patrology*, vol. 3, p. 162.

81. An earlier version, containing only the fifty homilies, was published as G. Maloney, S. J., *Intoxicated with God* (Denville, N.J., 1978).

82. A. J. Mason, *Fifty Spiritual Homilies of St. Macarius* (London: SPCK, 1921). A recent reprint of this work was published by *Eastern Orthodox Books* (Willits, 1974), with an introduction by Ivan M. Knotzevich, but it contains very little of the more recent scholarship on the Macarian corpus.

General Abbreviations

DS *Dictionnaire de spiritualité ascetique et mystique doctrine et histoire.* Edited by Marcel Viller, assisted by F. Cavallera, J. de Guibert, et al. Paris: Beuchesne, 1937– . Fifteen volumes to date (to Thiers; March 1990).

GCS *Die griechischen christlichen Schriftsteller der ersten drei Jahrhunderte.* Berlin: Akademie Verlag, 1897– .

PG *Patrologiae cursus completus. Series Graeca.* Edited by J.-P. Migne. Paris, 1857–1866. 161 volumes.

PL *Patrologiae cursus completus. Series Latina.* Edited by J.-P. Migne. Paris, 1844–1864. 221 volumes.

SC *Sources chrétiennes.* Edited by Jean Daniélou et al. Paris: Editions du Cerf, 1940– .

TU *Texte und untersuchungen zur Geschichte der altchristlichen Literatur.* Edited by Oskar Leopold von Gebhardt and C. G. Adolf von Harnack. Berlin: Akademie Verlag, 1883– .

H Homilies Collection II   p-XI

THE FIFTY
SPIRITUAL HOMILIES

HOMILY 1

An allegorical interpretation of the vision written down by the Prophet (Ez 1:4–2:1)

1. When Ezekiel the prophet beheld the divinely, glorious vision,[1] he described it in human terms but in a way full of mysteries that completely surpass the powers of the human mind. He saw in a plain a chariot of Cherubim, four spiritual animals. Each one had four faces. On one side each had the face of a lion, on another side that of an eagle, while on the third side each had the face of a bull. On the fourth side each had the face of a human being. To each of the faces were attached wings so that one could not discern any front or posterior parts. Their backs were full of eyes and likewise their breasts were covered with eyes so that there was no place that was not completely covered with eyes.

And there were three wheels for each face, a wheel within a wheel. And in the wheels there was inserted a spirit. And Ezekiel saw what appeared to be the likeness of a man and under his feet there was an artistic setting in sapphire. And the Cherubim and the animals pulled the chariot on which sat the Lord. In whichever direction he wished to go, he merely pointed his face in that direction. He was under the cherubim as it were the hand of a man carrying and balancing it.

2. And all of this which the prophet saw in ecstasy or in a trance was indeed true and certain, but it was only signifying and foreshadowing something no less hidden, something divine and mysterious, "a mystery hidden for generations" (Col 1:26) but that "has been revealed only in our time, the end of the ages," (1 Pt 1:20) when Christ appeared. For the prophet was viewing the mystery of the human soul that would receive its Lord and would become his throne of glory. For the soul that is deemed to be judged worthy to participate in the light of the Holy Spirit by becoming his throne and habitation, and is covered with the beauty of ineffable glory of the Spirit, becomes all light, all face, all eye. There is no part of the soul that is not full of the spiritual eyes of light. That is to say, there is no part of the soul that is covered with darkness but is totally covered with spiritual eyes of light. For the soul has no imperfect part but is in every part on all sides facing forward and covered with the beauty of the ineffable glory of the light of Christ, who mounts and rides upon the soul. It is similar to the sun that is the same all

37

over, without any imperfect part, but is completely all light, brilliantly shining. It is totally light in all of its parts. Or it is similar to fire, which like light is the same all over, having in itself no part that is before or behind, either greater or less.

Thus the soul is completely illumined with the unspeakable beauty of the glory of the light of the face of Christ and is perfectly made a participator of the Holy Spirit. It is privileged to be the dwelling-place and the throne of God, all eye, all light, all face, all glory and all spirit, made so by Christ who drives, guides, carries, and supports the soul about and adorns and decorates the soul with his spiritual beauty. For Scripture says, "There was the hand of a man under the Cherubim" and this is why Christ is the one who is carried by the soul and still directs it in the way.

3. The four animals that bore the chariot were a type of the leading characteristics of the soul. For as the eagle rules over all the other birds and the lion is king of the wild beasts and the bull over the tamed animals and man rules over all creatures, so the soul has certain dominant powers that are superior to others. I am speaking of the faculties of the will: conscience, the mind and the power of loving. For it is through such that the chariot of the soul is directed and it is in these that God resides. In some other fashion also such a symbolism can be applied to the Heavenly Church of the saints.

In this text of Ezekiel's vision it is said that the animals were exceedingly tall, full of eyes (Ez 10:4). It was impossible for anyone to comprehend the number of eyes or grasp their height since the knowledge of such was not given. And in a like manner the stars in the sky are given for man to gaze upon and be filled with awe, but to know their number is given to no man. So in regard to the saints in the Heavenly Church it is permitted to all who only enter into it and enjoy it as they strive to live in it. But to know and comprehend the number of the saints is given only to God.

The Rider, then, is carried by the chariot and the animals with all eyes, or, in a way, he is carried by every soul that has become his throne and exists now as eye and light. He is mounted on the soul and guides it with the reins of the Spirit, directing it according to his knowledge of the way.

Just as the spiritual animals went, not wherever they themselves wished, but only in the direction that he knew and wished to direct them, so also he holds the reins and guides the human souls by his Spirit and they follow, not by their own habit as they wish, but as he leads them

38

to Heaven. At times he leaves the body and leads and directs the soul toward Heaven by wisdom. And again when he wishes, he comes in the body and through thoughts directs the soul. At other times, he is so minded that he leads the soul to the ends of the earth and shows it the revelations of hidden mysteries.

Oh, what a good and useful and the only authentic Charioteer! In a similar way our bodies will be judged worthy of this honor in the resurrection which even now the human soul is given an anticipated grasp of such a glory by being mingled with the Spirit.

4. That the souls of the just become heavenly light, the Lord himself has told his Apostles: "You are the light of the world" (Mt 5:14). For he himself, who first transformed them into light, has ordered and commanded them to be light to the world. He said: "No one lights a lamp to put it under a tub; they put it on the lampstand where it shines for everyone in the house. In the same way your light must shine in the sight of men" (Mt 5:15–16). That is to say, do not hide the gift that you have received from me, but give it to all who desire it. And again he said: "The lamp of the body is the eye. It follows that if your eye is sound, your whole body will be filled with light. But if your eye is diseased, your whole body will be all darkness. If then, the light inside you is darkness, what darkness that will be!" (Mt 6:22–23).

Just as the eyes are the light of the body and when the eyes are healthy and sound, then the whole body is enlightened, so also on the contrary, if anything should happen to render the eyes darkened, then the whole body is in darkness. Thus the Apostles were called and ordained to be the eyes and the light of the whole world. For this reason the Lord told them: "If you, who are the light of the world, will persevere and not turn away, behold, then the whole body of the world will be enlightened. But if you, who are light, should be led into darkness, how great is that darkness, which is nothing less than the world." Thus the Apostles, who were made light, brought light to those who believed and enlightened their hearts by the heavenly light of the Spirit by whom they themselves had been enlightened.

5. And since they themselves were salt, they seasoned and salted every believing soul by the salt of the Holy Spirit. For the Lord told them: "You are the salt of the earth" (Mt 5:13). He meant by earth the souls of upright men. For they ministered to the souls of men the heavenly salt of the Spirit, seasoning them and keeping them free from decay and from anything harmful, away from the fetid condition they were in. Indeed, it is just as flesh—if it is not salted, it will decay and give off a

stench, so that all bypassers will turn aside from the fetid odor. Worms crawl all over the putrid meat; there they feed, eat, and burrow. But when salt is poured over it, the worms feeding on that meat perish and the fetid odor ceases. It is indeed the nature of salt to kill worms and dispel fetid odors.

In like manner every soul not seasoned with the Holy Spirit and made a participator of the heavenly salt which is the power of God grows corrupt and is filled with the stench and fetidness of bad thoughts so that the countenance of God turns away from the awful stench of vain and dark thoughts and from the disorderly affections that dwell in such a soul. The harmful and wicked worms which are the spirits of wickedness and the powers of darkness crawl up and down in such a soul. There they feed, burrowing deeply inside. They crawl all over and devour it and thoroughly corrupt it. "My wounds stink and are festering" (Ps 38:5).

If indeed the soul takes refuge in God, believes and seeks the salt of life, which is the good and human-loving Spirit, then the heavenly salt comes and kills those ugly worms. The Spirit takes away the awful stench and cleanses the soul by the strength of his salt. Thus the soul is brought back to health and freed from its wounds by the true salt in order again to be useful and ordered to serve the Heavenly Lord. That is why even in the Law, God uses this example when he ordered that all sacrifices be salted with salt (Lv 2:2, 13).

6. It was, therefore, necessary that the sacrifice first be killed by a priest. After it died, it was cut in pieces and seasoned with salt, then placed on the fire. Unless the priest first kills the lamb, it is not salted nor is it brought to the Lord as a burnt offering. Similarly also our soul must approach the High Priest Christ to be slain by him and die to its own thoughts and the wicked life which it was living, that is, to die to sin. Thus the life of wicked passions must go out of it.

Just as the body, after the soul has left it, is dead and has no longer life in it as it had before (neither does it hear nor walk), so after Christ, the Heavenly High Priest, by the grace of his power, puts to death our life to the world, it dies to the life of corruption that it formerly lived. It no longer hears nor speaks nor moves about in the darkness of sin because the evil passions which possessed the soul have by grace left it. Thus the Apostle exclaims, saying: "The world is crucified to me and I to the world" (Gal 6:14). For the soul, which still lives in the world and in the darkness of sin, has not yet been put to death by him, but still has the soul of wickedness in it, that is, it still harbors the power of the dark *ordering of passions, etc.*

THE FIFTY SPIRITUAL HOMILIES

passions of sin. It is nurtured by such a sinful soul and is not of the Body of Christ nor is it of the body of light, but it is a body of darkness and is still a part of that darkness. But those, on the contrary, who possess a soul of light, that is, they possess the power of the Holy Spirit, they are a part of the light.

7. But someone may say: How is it that you say the soul is a body of darkness since it is born of darkness? Listen well to this example. Just as the coat or garment that you wear was made by someone else, still you wear it.[2] Likewise, another builds a house and nevertheless you live in it. In the same way Adam violated the command of God and obeyed the deceitful serpent. He sold himself to the devil and that evil one put on Adam's soul as his garment—that most beautiful creature that God had fashioned according to his own image, as also the Apostle says: "He has done away with it by nailing it to the cross; and so he got rid of the Sovereignties and the Powers" (Col 2:15).

This was the very reason why the Lord came in order to cast them out and reclaim man as his very own house and temple. For this reason the soul is said to be the body of the darkness of wickedness as long as the darkness of sin lives in it because there it lives in the perverse world of darkness and there it is held captive. Thus Paul calls it the body of sin, the body of death, saying ". . . with him to destroy this sinful body" (Rom 6:6). And again he says: "Who will deliver me from the body of this death?" (Rom 7:24).

Contrariwise the soul that believes in God and has been freed of the sordidness of sin is lifted through death out of the life of darkness once the soul has accepted the light of the Holy Spirit as its life. By that means it has come to life and spends its life in the Spirit forever after, because it is now held captive by the divine light. The soul is neither by nature divine nor by nature part of the darkness of wickedness, but is a creature, intellectual, beautiful, unique, and admirable. It is a beautiful likeness and image of God. Into that likeness the wickedness of the passions of the dark world entered through the fall.[3]

8. A conclusion, therefore, is that the soul is united in will with whatever it is joined and bound to as its master. Either it has, therefore, the light of God in it and lives in that light with all of his powers, abounding with a restful light, or it is permeated by the darkness of sin, becoming a sharer in condemnation.

The soul, therefore, that wishes to live with God in rest and eternal light must approach, as we said above, to the true High Priest, Christ, and be slain and die to the world and to its former life of darkness and

41

wickedness and be transported into another life to enter into a divine communication. When someone dies in a city, he is unable to hear the voices of others around him. He does not hear their conversation nor the sounds they make, but he is completely dead and is transported to another place where there are no voices, none of the noises of the city. In a like manner the soul, after it has been slain and dead to that city of evil passions where it once earlier lived, hears no longer in itself the voice of the darkened thoughts. It no longer hears the conversation and the noise of frivolous arguments or of the noisy crowd of the spirits of darkness. For it is transported to the city full of goodness and peace, to the city of divine light. There it lives and listens, there it converses, speaks, and reasons. There it performs spiritual works very worthy of God.

9. Let us, therefore, pray that we may be put to death by his power and die to the world of the wickedness of darkness and that the spirit of sin may be extinguished in us. Let us put on and receive the soul of the heavenly Spirit and be transported from the wickedness of darkness into the light of Christ. Let us rest in life forever. For just as on the racetrack the chariot that takes the lead becomes an obstacle, pressing and checking and preventing the others from stretching out and reaching the goal first, so do the thoughts of the soul and of sin run the race in man. If the thought of sin gets the upper hand from the start, it becomes an obstacle, checking and hindering the soul from approaching God to carry off the victory against sin.

But where God himself truly mounts and guides the soul, he always obtains the victory, skillfully directing and leading with expertise the chariot of the soul to a heavenly mind forever. God does not wage war against wickedness, but since he possesses all power and authority of himself, he brings about the victory by himself. Therefore the Cherubim go, not where they wish, but where the Rider in control directs them. Wherever he inclines them, there they go and he supports them. For Scripture says, "The hand of a man was under them" (Ez 10:21).

Holy souls are led and guided by the Spirit of Christ, who directs them wherever he wishes them to go. Sometimes he leads them by his will through heavenly thoughts, sometimes through the body. Wherever he wishes, there they minister to him. Just as the feet of the birds are the wings, so the heavenly light of the Spirit takes up the wings of thoughts worthy of the soul and leads and directs the soul as he knows best.

10. Therefore, when you hear such things, look to yourself and see whether you really possess these things in your own soul. These are not mere and empty words, but we are dealing with a work that truly goes on

in the soul. And if you do not possess these very important spiritual goods but you are lacking in them, be moved to sorrow, grieve and be continually in mourning as one who is still dead in regard to the Kingdom. And as one lies wounded, continually cry out to the Lord and ask with confidence that he may deign to give you this true life.

And so God, who made your body, did not give it life from its very own nature nor from the body itself, nor from the food, drink, clothing, and footwear that he gave the body, but he arranged it that your body, created naked, should be able to live by means of such extrinsic things as food, drink, and clothing. (If the body were to attempt to exist only by its own constituted nature without accepting these exterior helps, it would deteriorate and perish.) In a similar way, it is so with the human soul. It does not have by nature the divine light, even though it has been created according to the image of God. For, indeed, God ordered the soul in his economy of salvation according to his good pleasure that it would enjoy eternal life. It would not be because of the soul's very own nature but because of his Divinity, of his very Spirit, of his light, that the soul would receive its spiritual meat and drink and heavenly clothing which are truly the life of the soul.

11. As, therefore, the body, as was said above, does not have life in itself, but receives it from outside, that is, from the earth, and without such material things of the earth it cannot live, so also the soul, unless it be regenerated into that "land of the living" (Ps 27:13) and there be fed spiritually and progress by growing spiritually unto the Lord and be adorned by the ineffable garments of heavenly beauty flowing out of the Godhead, without that food in joy and tranquility, the soul cannot clearly live.

For the divine nature has the bread of life who said: "I am the bread of life" (Jn 6:35), and "the living water" (Jn 4:10), and the "wine that gladdens the heart of man" (Ps 104:15), and "the oil of gladness" (Ps 45:8), and the whole array of food of the heavenly Spirit and the heavenly raiment of light coming from God. In these does the eternal life of the soul consist. Woe to the body if it were to rely solely on its own nature, because it would by nature disintegrate and die. Woe also to the soul if it finds its whole being in its own nature and trusts solely in its own operations, refusing the participation of the Divine Spirit because it does not have the eternal and divine life as a vital part of itself.

For just as it happens to sick men that, when the body can no longer take food, all the genuine friends, relatives, and loved ones lose all their hope for life and grieve, so God and all the holy angels are saddened by

43

those who do not eat the heavenly food of the Spirit and do not live in a state of incorruption.[4] These things, I repeat, are not simply words spoken, but are the work of the spiritual life, the work of truth, which is brought forth in the worthy and faithful soul.

12. If, therefore, you have become a throne of God and the Heavenly Charioteer has mounted you and your whole soul is a spiritual eye[5] and has become totally light, and if you have been nourished with that heavenly food of the Spirit and you have drunk from the water of life and you have put on the raiment of ineffable light, if finally your interior man has experienced all these and has been rooted in the abundance of faith, then, behold, you already live the eternal life, indeed, with your soul resting with the Lord.[6]

Look, you have received these things truly from the Lord so that you may live the true life. If, however, you are not conscious of having experienced any of these things, weep, mourn and groan because you have not yet been made a participator of the eternal and spiritual riches and you have not yet received true life.[7] Therefore, be worried at your poverty, beseeching the Lord night and day because you have settled for the serious poverty of sin.

Would that one be anxious about his penury! And would that we not live as though we are complacent in our smugness, because whoever is so burdened in this way should seek and cry out incessantly to the Lord and he will soon obtain redemption and heavenly riches, just as the Lord said in his story of the unjust judge and the widow. "How much more shall God avenge them who cry out to him night and day? Yes, I say unto you, he shall quickly vindicate them" (Lk 23:7). To whom be glory and power for ever. Amen.

HOMILY 2

On the reign of darkness, that is, of sin and that God alone is capable of taking sin away from us and freeing us from the slavery to the evil prince.

1. The reign of darkness, the evil prince, after humanity at the beginning was taken captive, surrounded and clothed the soul as if it were a human form with the vestiture of the power of darkness.[8] "And they made him king and they clothed him with regal garments and from head to foot he would walk in royal robes." So likewise he clothed the soul and all its substance with sin. That evil prince corrupted it com-

pletely, not sparing any of its members from its slavery, not its thoughts, neither the mind nor the body, but he clothed it with the purple of darkness. Just as the whole body suffers and not merely one part alone, so also the entire soul was subjected to the passions of evil and sin. The prince of evil thus clothed the whole soul, which is the chief member and part of humanity, with his own wickedness, that is, with sin. And so the entire body fell a victim to passion and corruption.

2. When, indeed, the Apostle says "Put off the old man" (Eph 4:22), he refers to the entire man, having new eyes in place of the old, ears replacing ears, hands for hands, feet for feet. For the wicked one has defiled the entire person, soul and body, and dragged him down and subjected him to the old man, polluted, impure, and an enemy of God, "not subject to God's law" (Rom 8:7). That is, man is under sin so that he no longer can see freely but sees evilly, hears evilly, and has swift feet to perpetrate evil acts (Ps 58:3). His hands work evil and his heart meditates evil deeds.

Let us, therefore, beg God to put off from us the old man because he alone is able to take away from us sin and because they are stronger who have taken us captive and hold us in their kingdom. He, indeed, has promised that he would free us from this slavery. For just as the sun shines and the wind blows together, each having its own body and nature, yet no one can separate the wind from the sun unless God alone who can calm the wind so it blows no more, similarly sin is also mixed with the soul even though each has its own nature.

3. It is, therefore, impossible to separate the soul from sin unless God should calm and turn back this evil wind, inhabiting both the soul and body. As anyone who watches a bird flying may wish that he himself could fly, yet still he cannot fly, being without wings, so also a man may have the will to be pure, to be without blame and spotless, to be always without evil and in communion with God, yet he does not truly have the power.

To fly into the divine air and enjoy the liberty of the Holy Spirit (2 Cor 3:18) may be one's desire, but, if he does not have wings given him, he cannot. Let us pray to God that he give us "the wings of a dove" (Ps 55:7) of the Holy Spirit so we may fly to him and find rest and that he may separate and take away from our soul and body such an evil wind, namely, sin itself, inhabiting the members of our soul and body.[9] For this he alone is able to do. For it says: "Behold, the Lamb of God who takes away the sins of the world" (Jn 1:29). He alone has shown this mercy to those who believe in him by redeeming them from sin, and he always confers this ineffable salvation on those who are always waiting and who assiduously seek him and who put all their hope in him.

4. As a certain strong wind blows in a dark and gloomy night and strikes all the plants and seeds, moving them this way and that in shaking agitation, so also man, who has fallen under the power of the night of the devil of darkness, also lies in night and darkness, and is moved, buffeted, and shaken by the stiff blowing wind of sin, and through all his nature (namely, in his soul, thoughts, and mind) is thoroughly affected. All the members of the body are shaken; not one part of the soul or the body is immune from the passions of sin dwelling in us. In a similar way there is a day of light and the divine wind of the Holy Spirit, breathing through and refreshing souls who live in the day of the divine light. It passes through the whole nature of the soul, the thoughts and the entire substance of the soul and all the members of the body, as it recreates and refreshes them with a divine and ineffable tranquillity.

This is what the Apostle said: "We are not sons of the night nor of the darkness, for you all are sons of light and sons of the day" (1 Thes 5:5). And just as in that other state of error the old man put on the whole, complete man and wears the garment of the kingdom of darkness, the cloak of blasphemy, unbelief, audacity, vainglory, pride, avarice, concupiscence, and all the other similar adornments of the kingdom of darkness, ragged, impure, and contaminated, so here, on the contrary, all who have put off the old and earthly man and from whom Jesus has removed the clothing of the kingdom of darkness have put on the new and heavenly man, Jesus Christ, so that once again the eyes are joined to new eyes, ears to ears, head to head, to be completely pure and bearing the heavenly image.[10]

5. And the Lord has clothed them with the garments of the kingdom of unspeakable light, the garment of faith, hope, love, joy, peace, goodness, human warmth, and all the other divine and living garments of light, life, and ineffable tranquillity. The result is that, as God is love and joy and peace and kindness and goodness, so too the new man may become by grace.

And just as the kingdom of darkness and sin are hidden in the soul until the day of resurrection when the very body of sinners will be covered over with the darkness that is now hidden in the soul, so also the kingdom of light and the heavenly Image, Jesus Christ, now mystically illumines the soul and holds dominion in the souls of the saints. Indeed, Christ is hidden from the eyes of men. Only with the eyes of the soul is he truly seen, until the day of resurrection, when even the body itself will reign with the soul, which now, having attained the Kingdom of Christ, rests and is illumined by the divine life.

Glory to his compassion and mercy because he shows pity on his servants, illumines and frees them from the kingdom of darkness. And he bestows on them light and his kingdom. To him be glory and power forever and ever. Amen.

HOMILY 3

That the brethren ought to conduct themselves with each other in sincerity, simplicity, love, and peace and they should struggle with and wage war against their inner thoughts.

1. The brethren should conduct themselves toward one another with the greatest love, whether in praying or reading Scripture or doing any kind of work so that they may have the foundation of charity toward others. And thus their various tasks or undertakings may find approval with those who pray and those who read and those who work, all can conduct themselves toward each other in sincerity and simplicity to their mutual profit. For why else is it written: "Thy will be done also on earth as in heaven" (Mt 6:10)? It is in order that, as the angels in heaven live together in accord with each other in the greatest unanimity, in peace and love, and there is no pride or envy there but they communicate in mutual love and sincerity, so in the same way the brethren should be among themselves. In the case where some thirty live together, they cannot continue at one thing the whole day and night. But some of them devote themselves to prayer for six hours and then they wish to read. Others readily and kindly serve the others, while still others do their own work.[11]

2. The brethren, therefore, regardless of what work they are doing, ought to conduct themselves toward each other in love and cheerfulness. And the one who works should say of him who is praying: "I also possess the treasure which my brother possesses since it is common." And let him who prays say of him who reads: "What he gains from reading redounds also to my advantage." And he who works let him thus say: "The work which I am doing is for the common good." For as the members of the body, being many, are one body (1 Cor 12:12) and help each other while each still performs its own function—as the eye sees for the whole body and the hand labors for all the members and the foot

47

walks, sustaining all the members, and another member suffers with all the others—so also the brethren should be among themselves.

Thus he who prays should not judge the one working because he is not praying. Neither should he who works condemn the one praying because he is resting while he himself is at work. Neither should he who is serving condemn another. But let each one do whatever he is doing for the glory of God. He who reads should regard the one praying with love and joy with the thought: "For me he is praying." And let him who prays consider that what the one working is doing is done for the common good.

3. And thus the highest concord and peace and oneness of souls "in the bond of peace" (Eph 4:3) will bind them together so that they can live together in sincerity, simplicity, and the blessing of God. It is evident that the most important element among these is the perseverance in prayer.[2] Above all, one thing is required: that one should have treasure in his soul and the life which is the Lord in his mind, so that, whether he works or prays or reads, he should have that possession which cannot be lost, which is the Holy Spirit.

There are always those who say that the Lord requires only visible fruits from men. The interior ones God will rectify. But this is not the way things are. For as one defends himself against the exterior man, so also he must enter into the lists and do battle against his thoughts. For the Lord demands of you that you be angry with yourself and engage in battle with your mind, neither consenting to or taking pleasure in wicked thoughts.

4. Still, to uproot sin and the evil that is so imbedded in our sinning can be done only by divine power, for it is impossible and outside man's competence to uproot sin. To struggle, yes, to continue to fight, to inflict blows, and to receive setbacks is in your power. To uproot, however, belongs to God alone. If you could have done it on your own, what would have been the need for the coming of the Lord? For just as an eye cannot see without light, nor can one speak without a tongue, nor hear without ears, nor walk without feet, nor carry on works without hands, so you cannot be saved without Jesus nor enter into the Kingdom of Heaven.

Suppose you say: "I do not outwardly corrupt myself by fornication or adultery nor do I commit the crime of avarice, therefore it follows that I am justified." You are completely off the mark in such thinking that you have perfectly fulfilled everything. There are not just three categories of sin against which one must guard oneself, but the number is legion. Arrogance, presumption, unbelief, hatred, envy, deceit, hypocrisy, where do these come from? Are you not obligated to war against these in your inner thoughts? If a robber invades your house, are you not at once greatly distressed? He does not allow you to be freed from anxious worries. You begin to fight back against him. You exchange blows. So ought also the soul to strike back, to resist, to strike blow for blow.

5. Consequently, when the will fights back in its trouble and affliction, it begins to gain the upper hand. It may fall; it rises. Then sin pounces on the soul and wages ten or twenty conflicts. It overcomes the soul and pins it down. But then the soul, after a while in a momentous struggle, overcomes sin. If the soul perseveres without letting down its guard in any area, it begins to emerge victorious as it sees through the deceits of sin and so it wins the crown of victory over sin.

If man is sincere in examining himself in this matter, he will see that sin still has a power over him until he "become the perfect man, fully mature" (Eph 4:13) and completely conquers death. For it is written, "The last enemy that shall be destroyed is death" (1 Cor 15:26) and in this way men will come out on top and gain the victory over the devil. But if, as we already said, one should say: "I do not commit fornication or adultery, I am not avaricious; that's enough for me," he has indeed in this way contended against three types of sin. But against the other twenty kinds by which sin attacks him, he has not waged war, but has been conquered. Therefore, he must contend and struggle against all types of sins. For the mind, as we said often, is an equal opponent squared off against sin so that it has equal powers to stand up against the attacks of sin and to repel its suggestions.

6. If you say that the enemy has too great a power and that evil completely dominates man, you make God unjust, who would condemn human nature for surrendering to Satan since Satan is really stronger and forces man into submission by his power. "You make him greater and more powerful than the soul. But will you ever listen to my plea?" It is like a young man wrestling a child. If the child loses, he is condemned for having been weaker. This is a great injustice. But we again insist that the mind is a good match and is equipped with equal powers of combat. A soul like this, if it seriously seeks aid and strength, will obtain it and

will be considered worthy of redemption. The contest and battle is one of equal forces. Let us glorify the Father and the Son and the Holy Spirit forever. Amen.

HOMILY 4

Christians ought to run the race in the arena of this world with alertness and exactitude so as to receive the heavenly reward from God and the angels.

1. Those who strive to live the Christian life with great zeal must above all else develop with greatest care their soul's faculty of understanding and discerning so that, having acquired an exact discernment between good and evil, always distinguishing those things with which nature has been unnaturally tainted, we may conduct ourselves properly and without offense. By using this faculty of discerning as an eye, we may avoid any depravity and binding union with evil. And thus we may receive the divine gift and become worthy of the Lord. Let us take an example from the visible world. There is indeed a similarity between the body and the soul, between the things of the body and those that pertain to the soul, between those things that are visible and those that remain hidden.[13]

2. In a similar way the body has the eye as a guide. The eye, by seeing, keeps the whole body on the right path. Imagine a certain traveler going through a wooded area, full of thorns and very swampy, with fires all around and swords stuck into the ground and precipices all about with flooding waters everywhere. The agile, attentive, unswerving traveler, guided by the eye, goes through those difficult places with great alertness, pulling up his cloak on all sides with his hands and feet to avoid tearing in the thickets and thorns or being dirtied by mud or being rent by a sword. And his eye directs the whole body, being his light, saving him from falling over the precipices or drowning in the waters or being injured by some dangerous happening. Such a person, alert and cautious in his travels, who pulls his garment tightly around himself, with maximum vigilance of mind, is guided straightway by his eye and keeps not only himself from injury but also his own cloak from burning and tearing.

But if anyone is less alert, idle, lazy, careless, sluggish, and cowardly and passes through such places, his cloak, floating about him, is torn off by the thickets and thorns, or is burnt by fire because he does not hold it tightly around himself. Or else it is tattered and torn by the swords stuck into the ground or is dirtied by the mud. The point is that in one way or another he quickly ruins his elegant and new garment because of his negligence, inattention, and slothful spirit. Moreover, if he does not attend with diligence and alertness to where his eye leads him, he will fall into a ravine or be drowned in the waters.

3. In the same way also the soul, which is clothed with the attractive garment, namely, the body, possesses the faculty of discernment which directs the whole soul along with the body as it passes through the brush and thorns of life, through the mud, fire, and precipices, that is, the lusts and sensuous pleasures and the other vanities of this world. It also should wrap around itself vigilance, courage, diligence, and attentiveness, and control itself and the vesture of the body in such a way so as not to be torn by the thickets and thorns of this world, which are the anxieties, busyness, and earthly worries. And it should not be burned by the fire of lust.

Clothed in such a way, it turns the eye from seeing evil, likewise the ears from hearing slanders, the tongue from speaking vanities, the hands and feet from unbecoming acts and pursuits. Indeed the soul has a will to turn away and prevent the members of the body from participating in unseemly spectacles, from its hearing what is evil and base, from indecent conversation and worldly, perverse preoccupations.

4. The soul also turns itself away from unbecoming mental distractions, keeping the heart from being dispersed by worldly thoughts. And thus with struggle and labor, it attentively disciplines the members of the body from evil. It preserves the attractive vesture of the body, freed from all tearing, burning, and staining. It will preserve itself, finally, through its will, which is endued by the ability to know, understand, and discern, a gift completely of the Lord. It holds itself with all its strength by turning away from all worldly lust. It is thus helped by the Lord to be truly protected from evils, those which we have enumerated above. For whenever the Lord sees anyone courageously turning away from the pleasures, distractions, the crass cares and worldly ties, from the preoccupation of vain reveries, he gives him his special help of grace and protects the soul that unwaveringly journeys courageously through the present corrupt world.

And thus the soul gains heavenly praise from its God and the angels for having kept unstained the garment of its body as well as itself. This is because it has turned away, as far as it was in its power to do so, from all worldly lust and with God's help has completed victoriously the race of this life's course.

5. But if anyone journeys through this life with sluggishness and carelessness, not attentive, but seeking his own will by refusing to turn away from all worldly lust and seeking after the Lord and only him, he is thrown into the thorns and thickets of this world. His garment, the body, is burned by the fire of concupiscence and soiled by the muck of sensuous pleasures. And the soul without such confidence is found lacking all "boldness in the day of judgment" (1 Jn 4:17), because it did not preserve its raiment unsoiled, but rather soiled it by the deceits of this world. And for this reason it is cast out from the kingdom.

What will God do with one who freely has given himself over to the world and, blinded by pleasures, has been led astray by earthly preoccupations? God indeed gives help to one who turns away from sordid pleasures and from his former habits, who centers with might and main all his thoughts always on the Lord and who denies himself and seeks ardently only the Lord. This is the one God takes care of, he who ever guards himself from the snares and enticements of the forest of this world, who "works out his own salvation with fear and trembling" (Phil 2:12), who passes with every caution through the snares, enticements, and concupiscences of this world, and who seeks the Lord's help and through the grace of his mercy hopes to be saved.

6. Take, for example, the five prudent and vigilant virgins (Mt 25:1ff.). They enthusiastically had taken in the vessels of their heart the oil of the supernatural grace of the Spirit—a thing not conformable to their nature. For this reason they were able to enter together with the Bridegroom into the heavenly bridal chamber. The other foolish ones, however, content with their own nature, did not watch nor did they betake themselves to receive "the oil of gladness" (Ps 45:7) in their vessels. But still in the flesh, they fell into a deep sleep through negligence, inattentiveness, laziness, and ignorance or even through considering themselves justified. Because of this they were excluded from the bridal chamber of the kingdom because they were unable to please the heavenly Bridegroom. Bound by ties of the world and by earthly love, they did not offer all their love and devotion to the heavenly Spouse nor did they carry with them the oil. But the souls who seek the sanctification of the Spirit, which is a thing that lies beyond natural power, are completely bound with their whole love to the Lord. There they walk; there they pray; there they focus their thoughts, ignoring all other

things. For this reason they are considered worthy to receive the oil of divine grace and without any failure they succeed in passing to life for they have been accepted by and found greatly pleasing to the spiritual Bridegroom. But other souls, who remain on the level of their own nature, crawl along the ground with their earthly thoughts. They think only in a human way. Their mind lives only on the earthly level. And still they are convinced in their own thought that they look to the Bridegroom and that they are adorned with the perfections of a carnal justification. But in reality they have not been born of the Spirit from above (Jn 3:3) and have not accepted the oil of gladness.

7. The five rational senses of the soul, if they have received grace from above and the sanctification of the Spirit, truly are the prudent virgins. They have received from above the wisdom of grace. But if they continue depending solely on their own nature, they class themselves with the foolish virgins and show themselves to be children of this world. They have not put off the spirit of the world, even though, in their false thinking by some exterior word, opinion, or form, they believe themselves to be brides of the Bridegroom.

Just as the souls who have completely given themselves totally to the Lord have their thoughts there, their prayers directed there, walk there, and are bound there by the desire of the love of God, so, on the contrary, the souls who have given themselves to the love of the world and wish to live completely on this earth walk there, have their thoughts there, and it is there where their minds live (Lk 12:34). For this reason they are unable to turn themselves over to the kind, prudential guidance of the Spirit. Something that is foreign to our basic nature, I mean, heavenly grace, necessarily demands being joined and drawn into our nature in order that we can enter into the heavenly bridal chamber of the kingdom and obtain eternal salvation.[14]

8. We have received into ourselves something that is foreign to our nature, namely, the corruption of our passions through the disobedience of the first man, which has strongly taken over in us, as though it were a certain part of our nature by custom and long habit. This must be expelled again by that which is also foreign to our nature, namely, the heavenly gift of the Spirit, and so the original purity must be restored.[15] And unless we will now receive the heavenly love of the Spirit through ardent petition and asking by faith and prayer and a turning away from the world, and unless our nature will be joined to love, which is the Lord, and we are sanctified from the corrupting power of evil by means

of that love of the Spirit, and unless we will persevere to the end un-shaken, walking with diligence according to all of his commands, we will be unable to obtain the heavenly kingdom.

9. I would wish to speak about a more subtle and profound topic to the best of my ability. Therefore, listen attentively to me. The infinite, inaccessible, and uncreated God has assumed a body, and on account of his immense and ineffable kindness, if I may so say it, he diminished himself (Phil 2:6), lessening his inaccessible glory so as to be able to be united with his visible creatures, as with the souls of the saints and angels, so they can be made participators of divine life (2 Pt 1:4). For each of these is a body, each according to his own nature, namely, an angel, a human soul, and a demon.[16] Although they are subtle in sub-stance, form, and figure according to the subtlety of their nature, so too are their bodies subtle. So too with this body of ours, although it is in substance heavy and solid. And so the soul, which is subtle, is aided by the eye by which it sees, by the ear through which it hears, likewise the tongue by which it can communicate in words, the hand, and, in a word, the whole body. The soul blends with these and through them accomplishes all of its actions or performs all of its works.

10. In the same way God, who transcends all limitations and far exceeds the grasp of our human understanding, through his goodness has diminished himself and has taken the members of our human body. He withdrew himself from the inaccessible glory. And through his compassion and love for mankind he transformed his nature (Phil 2:6), taking upon himself a body. He mingled himself totally with the body and thus he takes to himself holy souls acceptable and faithful. He becomes "one Spirit" (1 Cor 6:17) with them according to Paul's statement—a soul, if I may so put it, in a soul, substance in substance, so that the soul may live in newness of immortal life and become a participator of eternal glory, that is, I say, if it be a soul worthy and pleasing to God.

How, indeed, could God have created this visible creature out of what was not existing, with such great difference and variety? He willed and with no effort created from the nonexistent things solid and hard, as the earth, mountains, trees (you see what hardness such nature is) and also waters that course between such creatures. He commanded birds to be brought forth from them, and he created even more subtle crea-tures as fire and winds and so forth which are too subtle and escape the bodily eye.

11. How could the infinite and ineffable ability "of the manifold wisdom of God" (Eph 3:10) create out of those things that did not exist

bodies that are grosser and more subtle and more simple which subsist by his will? And how much more can he who is as he himself wishes and is what he wishes, through his ineffable compassion and incomprehensible goodness, not change and diminish and assimilate to himself holy, worthy, and faithful souls by means of an assumed body? By such a body he, the invisible, is able to be seen by such souls, He, the untouchable one, may thus be felt according to the subtlety of the soul's nature. In this way also such souls may taste his sweetness and enjoy in actual experience the goodness of the light of inexpressible pleasure.

When God wishes, he becomes fire, burning up every coarse passion that has taken root in the soul. "For our God is a consuming fire" (Dt. 4:24; Heb. 12:29). When he wishes, he becomes an inexpressible and mysterious rest so that the soul may find rest in God's rest. When he wishes, he becomes joy and peace, cherishing and protecting the soul.

12. If God also should wish to make himself similar to one of his creatures for the exultation and happiness of his intelligent creatures, as, for example, Jerusalem, the city of light, or the heavenly Mount Sion, he can do all things as he wishes, as it is said: "You come to Mount Sion and to the city of the living God, the heavenly Jerusalem" (Heb 12:22). All things are easy and possible for him who can transform himself into any form that he wishes for the benefit of those souls who are worthy of and faithful to him. Should anyone only strive to be pleasing to him and be acceptable, he certainly will see the heavenly good things in actual experience. He will have an experience of the unspeakable delights and truly immense riches of God which "eye has not seen nor ear heard nor has it entered into the mind of man to conceive" (1 Cor 2:9).

The Spirit of the Lord also becomes the rest of worthy souls and their joy and delight and eternal life. For the Lord transforms himself into bread and drink as it is written in the Gospel: "whoever eats of this bread will live forever" (Jn 6:58). In this ineffable way he recreates the soul and fills it with spiritual happiness. For he says: "I am the bread of life" (Jn 6:35). Similarly he transforms himself into the drink of a heavenly fountain as he says: "Whoever will drink of the water which I shall give him, it shall be in him a fountain of water springing up into eternal life" (Jn 4:14). And it is also said: "And we have all drunk of the same drink" (1 Cor 12:13, 10:4).

13. Thus he appeared to each of the holy fathers, exactly as he wished and as it seemed helpful to them. In one manner he appeared to Abraham, in another to Isaac, in another to Jacob, in another to Noah, Daniel, David, Solomon, Isaiah, and to each of the holy prophets. Still in

another way to Elijah and again differently to Moses. Indeed, I hold that Moses, when he was on the mountaintop, fasting for forty days, approached the spiritual table and feasted on many delights. To each of the saints, likewise, God appeared as he wished so as to refresh them, to save and lead them into a knowledge of God. For all things are easy for him, whatever he only desires to do. And when it pleases him, he diminishes himself by taking on a bodily form. He transforms himself to become present to the eyes of those who love him, showing himself in an unapproachable glory of light. He shows himself out of his immense and ineffable love for those who are worthy according to his power.

For the soul that has been considered worthy through its consuming desire, expectation, faith, and love to receive from on high that power, the heavenly love of the Spirit, and has obtained the heavenly fire of eternal life, is one that is being stripped of every worldly affection and freed from every bond of evil.

14. Just as iron or lead or gold or silver, if thrown into fire, will melt and be transformed from its natural hardness to a soft substance, and as long as it remains in the fire becomes all the more a molten liquid, losing its natural hardness because of the powerful heat of the fire, the same is true for the soul that has turned away from the world in its desire for the Lord alone. It perseveres in much searching of the mind, in struggle and labor. It awaits God, unflagging in hope and faith. It has received that heavenly fire of the Godhead and the love of the Spirit. It is then truly freed from all attachment to the world and liberated from every evil affection. It rejects everything in its life and corrects all of its natural habit and hardness of sin. It considers all other things superfluous compared to the heavenly Bridegroom alone. It rests in his fervent and ineffable love.

15. I tell you that even those brothers, loved in God, whom the soul thinks so highly of, if they are a source of leading it away from that love for God, it, I would say, would reject such. For that is its life and rest, namely, the mystical and ineffable participation of the heavenly kingdom.[17] For if an earthly, loving participation of spouses can separate the pair from their fathers, brothers, mothers, and all other things become for them rather extrinsic in their way because of their deep conjugal love for each other—for it is said: "For this reason, let a man leave his father and mother and adhere to his wife and they will be two in one flesh" (Gn 2:24)—if, therefore, I say, earthly love can detach one from all other loves, how much more in the case of those who have been made worthy to enter into a true fellowship with that Holy Spirit, the heav-

enly and loving Spirit? They shall be freed from all worldly love. All other things will seem indifferent to them since they have been conquered by a heavenly yearning and have become totally one in that surrendered state.

16. Therefore, O beloved brethren, since such good things have been offered to us and such wonderful promises have been made to us by the Lord, let us get rid of all obstacles. Let us renounce all love for the world and devote ourselves to that one good by a thorough seeking and yearning so that we may become sharers in that ineffable love of the Spirit about which St. Paul urged us to hasten after: "Seek after charity," he says (1 Cor 14:1), so that we may be considered worthy to be converted from our hardness by the right hand of the Most High and reach that spiritual sweetness and rest, having been wounded by the love of the Divine Spirit.

The Lord, indeed, is the Lover of mankind,[18] so full of tender compassion whenever we turn completely toward him and are freed from all things contrary. Even though we, in our supreme ignorance, childishness, and tendency toward evil, turn away from true life and place many impediments along our path because we really do not like to repent, nevertheless, he has great mercy on us. He patiently waits for us until we will be converted and return to him and be enlightened in our inner selves that our faces may not be ashamed in the day of judgment.

17. If that seems difficult and troublesome to us because practicing virtue is hard, but, more so, because of the insidious suggesting of the adversary, still he is very full of compassion, long-suffering and patient as he waits for our conversion. And when we do sin, he is ready to lift us up for he desires our repentance. And when we fall, he is not ashamed to take us back, as the Prophet said: "When men fall, do they not rise again? Or if one turns away, does he not return?" (Jer 8:4). We only have to have a sincere heart and live in vigilance and be converted immediately after seeking his help and he himself is most ready to save us. For he looks for our ardent will, as best we can, to turn toward him. When we show good faith and promptness glowing from our desiring, then he works in us a true conversion.

Let us then, O beloved, show, as children of God, diligence and be prompt to follow him, by casting aside all preoccupation, carelessness, and laziness. Let us not postpone day after day this work of preventing evil from controlling us. For we do not know the hour when we will have to leave this life. Great and ineffable are the promises held out to Christians, so great, indeed, that all the glory and beauty of heaven and

57

earth and all the other attractions in such variety, the riches and comeliness, the delights of visible scenes, cannot measure up to the faith and riches of a single soul.

18. How is it possible that in the face of so many exhortations and promises, we still refuse to accept totally to go to him and surrender ourselves completely to him? How can we refuse, as the Gospel says, to deny all other things, even our own soul (Lk 14:26), and to seek him alone with our love and give it to nothing else? But, look, all these things and such glory given! Look at all the loving dispositions of God manifested in the times of the fathers and the prophets! What promises! And what exhortations! What great mercy of the Lord has been shown us from the very beginning! Finally, in his own coming on this earth he has shown to us an ineffable kindness through his crucifixion in order to convert us and bring us into life. And yet, we do not will to give up our love for the world nor our evil tendencies and habits. In this way we show ourselves persons of little or absolutely no good faith. And in spite of all this, he still shows himself kind to us. He protects and cherishes us invisibly, not turning us over (according to our sinful deserts) to the deceits of evil and the world. He, in his great compassion and long-suffering, watches from above, waiting for the time we shall return to him.

19. I fear lest the saying of the Apostle should be fulfilled in us as we live prejudiced according to our own evil ideas and are carried about by our preconceived thinking: "Do you despise the riches of his kindness and forbearance and long-suffering, not knowing that the kindness of God calls you to repentance?" (Rom 2:4). But if we abuse his long-suffering and kindness and forbearance and we add still more sins, and by our carelessness and contempt we store up for ourselves still more serious judgments, that saying will be fulfilled: "But according to your hardness and unrepentant heart, you store up for yourself wrath on the day of wrath and of the revelation of the just judgment of God" (Rom 2:5). God uses great and ineffable goodness and long-suffering toward mankind, if only we would be willing to be vigilant toward ourselves and strive to be totally converted to him so that we may receive the gift of salvation.

20. But if you wish to know God's long-suffering and great goodness, let us learn it from holy Scripture. Look at the Israelite fathers to whom the promises were made, from whom Christ in the flesh came, to whom "pertained the services and the Covenant" (Rom 9:5). How much have they sinned? How many times turned away? Nevertheless, God

himself did not abandon them forever, but at certain times for their own good he subjected them to chastisements. Desiring to soften the hardness of their heart through affliction, he converted and admonished them. He sent them the prophets. How long, above all, did he show himself magnanimous toward sinners and those who offended him and nevertheless he received those with joy who turned back to him. And when they again turned themselves away, he did not give up on them but he called them back through the prophets to conversion. And when they, over and over again, turned away from him and later converted back again to him, he gently bore with them and kindly received them back, until finally they committed the great sin of laying hands on their very own Lord whom they were expecting according to the tradition of the fathers and the holy prophets, namely, the Redeemer, the Savior, King, and Prophet.

For when he came, they did not receive him, but on the contrary they treated him with great ignominy and shame. Finally they inflicted upon him the punishment of the cross. And in this so great an offense, this terrifying transgression, their sins reached the limit and fullness of crime. And thus finally they were deserted. The Holy Spirit left them when the veil of the Temple was rent in two. And so their Temple was handed over to the Gentiles, destroyed and made desolate according to the Lord's saying: "There shall not be left one stone upon another which shall not be thrown down" (Mt 24:2). And thus they finally were given over to the Gentiles and dispersed throughout the whole earth by the kings who led them into captivity, and so they were forbidden ever to return to their own homes.

21. And so, even now, God is good and kind. He shows himself long-suffering toward each one of us. He sees how much each of us offends him and yet he tranquilly waits until man is converted from sin, and then he is filled with great love and joy. For this is what it means: "There is joy over one sinner that repents" (Lk 15:15), and again: "It is no part of your heavenly Father's plan that a single one of these little ones shall ever come to grief" (Mt 18:14).

If anyone, receiving such immense goodness and gentleness of God shown him, would not accept the remission of his every offense, hidden or manifest, while God regards him without a word as he holds out to him repentance, such a person, I say, would be abusing God's kindness by remaining hardened in his sins. In fact, he would add sin to sin. He would join sloth to sloth, heaping one offense upon another. Such a one reaches the limits of his sinning by coming finally to such wickedness that he can no longer extricate himself from its burden. He is crushed, and, delivered over externally to the evil one, he perishes.

22. This is what happened to those of Sodom. They committed many sins and refused to be converted until they committed, by their wicked design upon the angels, that crime of sodomy. They fell so terribly that they could no longer repent, and they were finally rejected for good. For they filled up the limits of sins and even exceeded them. For this reason they were consumed with fire by divine judgment. And so also it was in the days of Noah when the people committed such great sins. They did not repent. They fell into such enormous sins that finally the whole earth perished. So with the Egyptians. They offended God greatly, committing sins against God's people. Still God showed them his mercy by not inflicting upon them such punishments that would have totally destroyed them. Rather, for their chastisement, conversion, and repentance, he inflicted upon them smaller plagues as a flagellation. He bore them patiently, waiting for their repentance. But, after they sinned in so many ways against God's people, they did show some repentance. But then they changed their minds and fell back into their willful evil ways. They oppressed the people of God with many hardships until, finally, when God with great miracles led his people out of Egypt through Moses, they committed the serious sin of pursuing God's people. Because of this, God's judgment completely decimated and destroyed them. They were drowned in the waters since God judged them unworthy even of remaining in life.

23. In the same way, as we said above, the people of Israel corrupted themselves by many crimes and sins. They killed God's prophets and perpetrated other crimes, infinitely worse, while God quietly waited for their repentance. He used much gentleness. But finally they committed such a sin that they were so crushed that they did not rise again. They laid their hands on the dignity of the Lord. For this reason they were completely deserted and rejected. They lost prophecy, priesthood, and the cult of God. These were given to the believing Gentiles as the Lord says: "The Kingdom shall be taken from you and will be given to a nation that will bring forth its fruits" (Mt 21:43). Up to that time God bore with them. He did not forsake but showed compassion toward them. However, when they reached the limit of their sinning by laying hands on the majesty of the Lord, then they were completely abandoned by God.[19]

24. We have dealt with these things, beloved, at some length, showing from Sacred Scripture the necessity for us to turn in conver-

sion quickly and hasten to the Lord who gently awaits us to set aside completely all wickedness and evil preoccupation. He receives us with great joy for he does not wish to see us increasing day after day our contempt toward him nor for us to increase our accumulated sins so as to incur the wrath of God upon us. Let us, therefore, strive to approach him with a truly converted heart, not despairing that we will ever attain salvation (for such a thought itself is evil and depraved). The remembrance of our past sins can easily lead us to despair, to sloth, negligence, and resignation that we may not be converted to the Lord and ever attain salvation, even though the great goodness of the Lord covers the whole human race.

25. But if it truly seems difficult and impossible to us that we can ever be converted from such a great multitude of sins because we are caught in their grasp, a temptation, as we described above, of evil and a sure obstacle to our salvation, let us recall and seriously consider how our Lord, while on this earth, restored sight to the blind, cured the paralytics, healed every sickness. He raised the dead, already decaying and disintegrating. He made the deaf to hear and drove out a legion of devils from one man and restored him to full mental health after such madness. How much more, therefore, will he not convert a soul that turns back to him, seeking from him mercy and in need of his help? Will he not bring such a soul into a freedom from passions and a permanence in all virtues with a renewed mind? Will he not lead it to health and inner insight, to thoughts of peace, freed from the blindness, deafness, and death of unbelief, ignorance, and rashness, bringing such a soul to a virtuous moderation and to purity of heart? For he, who created the body, made also the soul and when he walked this earth, he gave help and health to those who approached and begged him for such favors. He granted with generosity and kindness such healings for he was the good and only true physician. So it is with spiritual matters.

26. If, then, he was moved with such great mercy toward bodies which were to dissolve and die again and if he provided promptly and kindly for each one whatever he asked, how much more when it is a question of an immortal, imperishable, and incorruptible soul, overwhelmed by the sickness of ignorance, wickedness, unfaithfulness, rashness, and all the other passions of sin? When it comes, nevertheless, to the Lord, seeking of him help and fixing its gaze on his mercy, desiring to receive of him the grace of the Spirit for its redemption and salvation and freedom from all evil and passion, will he not give more quickly and promptly his healing liberation according to his word:

"How much more shall your heavenly Father avenge those who cry unto him day and night?" (Lk 18:7). And he adds, saying: "Yes, I say unto you, he will avenge them speedily" (Lk 18:8). And in another place he exhorts: "Ask and you will receive. For all who ask receive, and whoever seeks, finds, and whoever knocks, it will be opened unto him" (Mt 7:78). And a little farther he adds: "How much more your heavenly Father will give the Holy Spirit to those who ask him" (Lk 11:9). "Truly, I say to you, even though he will not give it to him because he is his friend, yet because of his importunity he will rise and give him as much as he needs" (Lk 11:8).

27. In all that has been said in these pages he has exhorted us to seek from him without shame, incessantly and unflaggingly, his gift of grace. It was indeed for sinners that he came in order to convert them to himself and to bring healing to all who would believe in him. We need only to get rid in our lives of all evil pursuits, as best we can, and despise evil works. Let us have nothing to do with wicked and vain talk and in all things let us with all our might cling to him.

He certainly is ready to give us his help. We have proof of this in the fact that he is merciful and comes to bring life. He heals incurable passions and gives redemption to those who call upon him, to those who turn away from all worldly attachment as best they can, freely wishing to do so by forcing their mind away from earthly cares and holding fast to him with eager desire.

To such a soul he gives his strength provided such a person values all other things as unnecessary. He clings to nothing of this world but hopefully seeks to find rest and happiness in the tranquillity of his kindness. And thus through such faith he obtains the heavenly gift. All his desires are satisfied in perfect assurance through grace. Consequently, he serves the Holy Spirit with pleasing constancy. He daily makes progress in goodness and persevering to the end in the way of righteousness; he never yields to any shape or form of evil. He never offends grace in any matter. He is deemed worthy to enter into eternal salvation with all the saints with whom he has lived in the world as a friend and companion in imitation of their lives. Amen.

HOMILY 5

The great difference between Christians and men of this world. For the latter, imbued with the spirit of the world, are in heart and mind held captive by earthly shackles. Christians, however, are possessed by a love for their heavenly Father. They keep him alone before their eyes in all their desires.

1. The world of Christians is of a special kind, their style of living, their thinking, their speech, and all their actions. That of men of this world is completely different. There is a great difference between them. The inhabitants of this world, the children of this age, are like wheat in a sieve. They are being sifted by restless thoughts of this world. They are constantly tossed to and fro by earthly cares, desire, and absorption in a variety of material concerns.[20] Satan tosses such souls as a sifter sifts wheat. He sifts the whole sinful human race by means of such earthly pursuits, ever since Adam first fell by disobeying God's command and came under the power of the prince of evil. From that time when he gained such power, Satan is constantly sifting all the sons of this world with thoughts of deceit and agitation. He dashes them relentlessly on the sieve of this earth.

2. As the wheat in the sieve is shaken by the sifter and is continually tossed up and down, so the prince of evil holds all people engrossed in earthly concerns. By these concerns he disturbs people, keeps them anxious and in a state of nervous motion. The result is that they are disturbed by vain thoughts and base passions and are in bondage to earthly attachments to this world. Satan constantly holds them as captives. He agitates and entices the whole human race, infected by the sin of Adam.

In such a manner the Lord forewarned his Apostles about the future attack of the prince of evil against them. "Satan has sought to sift you as wheat, but I have prayed to my Father so that your faith would not fail" (Lk 22:31–32). That work spoken by the Creator to Cain, which has been a sentence openly pronounced upon him, namely, "Groaning and trembling you shall be tossed upon the earth" (Gn 4:12), is a type and image of what all sinners secretly undergo. After the race of Adam had violated God's command and entered into the sinful state, it began to live in that acquired likeness interiorly. It is tossed to and fro relentlessly with continuous thoughts of fear and terror and every sort of disturbance. The prince of this world keeps each soul that is not reborn of God tossed on the waves of various passions and lusts. As wheat is shaken up constantly in the sieve, so he keeps men's thoughts jangling in all directions. He shakes and entices them all by the seductions of this world, by the carnal pleasures, fears, and agitations.

3. So the Lord, showing that those who follow the wiles and wishes of the evil prince and bear the likeness of Cain's evil, reproved them when he said, "The lusts of your father you will do. He was a murderer from the beginning and did not abide in the truth" (Jn 8:44). In such a way the whole sinful race of Adam has received that condemnation interiorly, namely, "Groaning and trembling shall you be" (Gn 4:12) and shaken in the sieve of the earth by Satan sifting you. For just as from one Adam the race of men was multiplied over the earth, so one depravity of passion infiltrated into the entire human race. The prince of evil is thus able to sift all of them by continued crass, vain, and passionate thoughts. For as one wind is capable of shaking all the plants and seeds or as one darkness of the night spreads over all the entire earth, so the prince of evil, who is similar to a spiritual darkness of sin and death, is like a hidden yet wild wind. He shakes the entire human race on the face of the earth. He tosses them about to and fro with restless thoughts. He entices the hearts of people with the pleasures of the world. He fills every soul with a dark ignorance, blindness, and forgetfulness. Only those escape him who have been reborn from above and have been transported in mind and heart to another world, as it was said: "Our citizenship is in Heaven" (Phil 3:20).

4. In this we see the difference between true Christians and the rest of human beings, and great is the difference between them, as I said above. This difference is seen in the fact that the mind and intellect of Christians are always centered on heavenly thoughts.[21] They gazed on heavenly things because they participate in the Holy Spirit. Because they have been born above from God and are children of God in truth and power, they have arrived, through many labors and sweat endured over a long time, at a state of equilibrium, tranquillity and peace, freed from further sifting. They no longer vacillate back and forth, tossed about by crippling and vain thoughts.

In this they are greater and better than those of the world, because their intellect and thinking of the soul is permeated by the peace of Christ and the love of the Spirit, as the Lord had in mind when he said: "They had passed from death to life" (Jn 5:24). It is, therefore, not in outward shape or form that the distinguishing characteristic of Christians consists. Many Christians believe that the difference does lie in some external sign. They are in mind and thought similar to those of the world. They undergo the same disturbing restlessness and instability of thoughts, lack of faith, confusion, agitation, and fear as all other persons do. They really do differ somewhat in some external form and way of

64

acting in a limited area, but in heart and mind they are shackled by earthly bonds. They do not have the divine rest and heavenly peace of the Spirit in their heart because they never begged it of God nor did they ever believe that he would deign to grant these to them.

5. It is through the renewing of the mind and the tranquillity experienced in our thoughts and the love of the Lord and the love for heavenly things that every new creation of Christians distinguishes them from the men of this world. For this reason did the Lord come in order that he might deign to give these spiritual gifts to those who truly believe in him. Christians possess a glory and beauty and an indescribable heavenly richness that come to them with hard work and sweat, acquired in times of temptations and in many trials. All of this must be ascribed to divine grace.[22]

If the sight of an earthly king is something all wish to see, and everyone who passes through the city of the king desires at least to catch a glimpse of his beauty or the elegance of his garments or the splendor of his purple, the beauty of his many pearls, the comeliness of his crown, the impressive retinue that accompanies him, spiritual persons, however, spurn all of these things because they have experienced another heavenly, incorporeal glory. They have tasted another ineffable beauty and have participated in other riches. They have received in the inner person another Spirit.

The people of this world who possess the spirit of the world have a great yearning to see an earthly king, at least to feast upon his comeliness and glory. In proportion as his share of visible accessories is greater than that of others, so even to have only seen him, the king, is something desired by all. Each man inwardly says to himself: "I would really like someone to give me something of that glory, comeliness, and splendor." He believes that king is happy, a man like him, of the earth, having the same weakness of passions, subject to death. He makes him an object of envy because of his fleeting comeliness and desired glory.

6. If, I say, carnal persons so desire the glory of an earthly king, how much more those whom the touch of the Divine Spirit of life has touched and whose heart divine love has pierced with a desire for Christ, the heavenly King, who have been captivated by his beauty and ineffable glory and by the incorruptible comeliness and incomprehensible riches of the true and eternal King, Christ! They are held captive by desire and longing for him. Their whole being is directed completely toward him. And they desire to obtain those ineffable goods which through the Spirit they contemplate.

For the sake of Christ, such Christians regard such earthly beauty, adornment, glory, honor, and the riches of kings and princes as nothing because they have tasted divine beauty and the life of heavenly immortality has dropped like dew onto their souls. Therefore, they ardently long for that love of the heavenly King and they have him alone before their eyes in every desire. For his sake they detach themselves from every worldly love and tear loose from every earthly attachment so that they may possess that one desire always in their hearts and never mix anything else with it.

However, few indeed are those who begin well the race and successfully complete it, reaching the goal without falling, who have love for God alone and who are detached from all others. Many have a conversion experience and many become participators of heavenly grace and are wounded by heavenly love, but, because of the daily battles and struggles and the work involved and the various temptations from the evil one that they have not conquered, they do not persevere. They are overwhelmed by various worldly passions, because everyone has something of this world that he loves and he does not detach himself completely from that attachment. And so such as these have stopped in the race and have immersed themselves in the abyss of the world because of their weakness, laziness, and cowardice of will or through an earthly attachment.

Those who really wish to reach the goal by good living must not willingly allow and mix any other love or affection with that heavenly love lest they be hindered in their spiritual pursuits and fall back and finally lose their very own life. Just as God has made great, ineffable, and indescribable promises, so, too, they demand on our part great faith, hope, and effort and great struggles. The goods that a person seeks in striving for the Kingdom of Heaven are not of little importance. To reign with Christ forever, if this is what you desire, will you not be ready to bear manfully struggles and labors and temptations for the brief space of this life up until death? The Lord says: "If anyone wishes to come after me, let him deny himself and take up his cross daily with joy and let him follow me" (Mt 16:24). And again he says: "If anyone does not hate father, mother, wife, children, brothers, sister, yes, even his own life also, he cannot be my disciple" (Lk 14:26). Most wish to obtain the kingdom and desire to have eternal life, but, following their own wills, they refuse to control them. They are rather more like the sower who sows vain desires. They refuse to deny themselves and still wish to receive eternal life, which is a thing impossible.

The saying of the Lord is found to be true. For those reach the goal successfully without falling who, according to the Lord's injunction, deny themselves totally. They have spurned all things of the world: concupiscences, attachments, pride, pleasures, and impediments. They keep him alone before their eyes and seek to observe his commandments so that each person of this type goes against his own will. He would reject any kingdom of this world by denying his own interests. He would mingle no other love with the love he has for his Lord. He takes no pleasure in any of the pleasures or passions of this world. He only wishes to place his total love in the Lord as far as he can willingly wish to do so.

Let me give an example that comes to me. Take someone who is led to judge another. He knows that the thing he wishes to do, to make such a judgment, is not becoming. But when he is drawn to such a judgment by a certain pleasure in the thought and does not repulse it, he falls a victim to it. For at first in his heart there is interiorly a war. There is a struggle, a conflict, a discernment between what is of the love of God and what is of the love of the world. Then he yields and makes a judgment against his brother, which may even lead to quarreling and angry blows. He weighs the matter, dialoguing with himself: "Should I say it? or, should I not say it?" He is mindful of God, but still he wants his own glory, and he will tend not to deny himself. If the love and esteem for the world in his heart dips the scale, immediately the evil word leaps to his lips. Then the mind interiorly, like an archer, aims its arrow, using the tongue to hit the neighbor. It discharges arrows of unseemly words in a spontaneous willing bent on seeking self-glory. Then this shooting of arrows against the neighbor continues with unbecoming words, augmenting the sin until it reaches the point of blows and wounds as other members of the body enter into the war, even sometimes to the point of inflicting physical death. So you see what is the origin and end result of the love of worldly glory when it once has turned the scale in the balance of the heart toward self-will. Because such a person refused to deny himself, but rather loved something of this world, all those worldly desires and evil passions of the flesh resulted.

In this way every kind of sin and every immoral practice, all theft, also avarice, sloth, desire for money, and vainglory, so likewise envy and ambition and whatever is of evil arise. Sometimes actions that may appear to be good for the glory and praise of men are done, but God reckons these on the same level as deeds of injustice, theft, and all other sins. For God says: "He has scattered the bones of those who please men" (Ps 53:5). Thus an evil person loves to give the appearance of doing things that seem to be good, yet he is still a shifting liar in his attachments to the world. For by means of a certain love for the things of the world and the flesh by which he is held in bondage to his own will, evil entices him until it becomes an enslaving bond, a heavy chain and weight that sucks him down and stifles him in a world of evil that does not allow him to rise up and return to God. The reason is that whatever anyone loves of the world oppresses his mind, holds him and does not allow him to rise up. For from this scale and discernment which tilts man toward evil, the whole of mankind hangs and is tested, including Christians living in cities or in mountains or in monasteries or in wild places or in the desert. The reason is that a person is seduced by his own desires and loves something that binds him that is not wholly centered on God.

One person, let us say, sets his heart on possessions, another on gold and silver, another on the persuasive wisdom of the world to gain the glory of men; another has ardently sought power, another, the praise and honors of men; still another lives by anger and violence. For when one yields quickly to such a passion, he shows his love and preference for that desired object. One shows this attachment to unbecoming actions, another to jealousy, another all day long shows pride and amuses himself, another deceives himself with meaningless thoughts, another loves to parade as a teacher of law to impress people, while another takes satisfaction in laziness and carelessness. Another is absorbed by dress and clothing and still someone else gives himself to earthly pursuits. Another overindulges in sleep or trivial gossip or lewd conversation. But regardless of how anyone is bound, whether by a small or a great chain to the world, he is possessed by that attachment and is unable to extricate himself from it.[23] For whatever passion a person does not manfully fight against, that is an object of his love. Such an attachment dominates and holds him down. It becomes for him an impediment and a chain that prevents him from directing his mind to God and from pleasing him. In no way can he serve God alone and obtain the kingdom and reach eternal life.

The soul that truly tends toward the Lord completely forces itself to a total love of him. It is held fast in a willed dedication, as far as is possible, to God alone. From him it obtains the help of grace. Such a person denies himself and does not obey the will of his mind, because he knows that the mind tends to deal with us in a deceitful way, seducing us to evil. He yields himself perfectly to the Word of the Lord and frees himself from every visible bond as far as he can will it. He surrenders

himself completely to the Lord and thus will be able to undergo successfully struggles, labors, and setbacks. Wherever there is a question of
affection, there is either a help or an obstacle. If a person loves something of the world, this becomes for him a burden and a bondage drag-
ging him downward and not allowing him to rise upward to God.

If, however, he loves the Lord and loves his commandments, this
becomes his help. He is strengthened by this. His observance of all the
Lord's precepts becomes easy for him and this tilts him toward the good,
or rather, it makes lighter and easier every battle and affliction. Through
divine power he cuts through the world and through the powers of evil
which lay snares for the human soul in the world and which use all sorts
of desires as nets to ensnare the soul in the depths of the world. In such a
way he is freed from such snares by means of his own faith and great
courage and through heavenly aid. He is accounted worthy of the eternal
kingdom which was the goal of his desiring. He receives from the Lord
help and he will not lose eternal life.

To be able to illustrate all of this with concrete examples, think
how many, by their own wills, perish and are drowned in the sea or are
taken into captivity. Or suppose a house is on fire. One person wishes to
save himself. As soon as he is aware of the fire, he flees naked. He
completely leaves all else behind. He wishes only to take care for his
own life and he is saved. Another person wishes to save something of the
house furniture or other objects. He enters to get those things and when
he gets them, the fire sweeps through the whole house. He is caught
within and burned. Do you not see that by attaching himself by his own
will to some temporal object, he really perishes in the fire? Similarly, at
sea people encounter raging waves and are shipwrecked. One strips
himself naked of all clothes and throws himself into the waters, hoping
to save himself. He is tossed about by the whitecap waves and swims
through the treacherous sea and saves his life. Another person wants to
save some of his clothes. He thinks he can swim and pass through the sea
with them on but those things he carried along with himself pull him
down and sink him in the depth of the sea. For a paltry gain he loses
everything, even his own life. Do you not see how by following his own
will he perishes?

Again, take the example that comes to mind of a rumor of an invad-
ing enemy. One person, as soon as he hears of it, flees at once, escaping
without any clothing but his naked self. Another person, however, does
not believe that the enemy will come or wishing to save something of his
possessions, he delays his flight in seeking to take things with him. The

enemy comes and captures him. They carry him off as a captive into a land of foreigners and there they force him to serve as a slave. Do you not see how, by following his own will, he was captured because of his lack of attention, energy, and attachment to possessions? In a similar manner, those who do not obey the commandments of the Lord and do not deny themselves, refusing to love God above all else, freely decide to be held by earthly bonds. When the eternal fire comes, they, having been caught as captives in a foreign land and drowned in a love for the world, tossed mercilessly in a bitter sea of wickedness, are held captive by a spirit of wickedness and so come to their ruin.

If you want to learn from the lives of the saints what complete dedication to the love of the Lord means and from Holy Scripture inspired by God, look at Job. How he gave up all he possessed, so to speak: children, wealth, livestock, servants, and everything else that he had, stripping himself completely to escape and save himself. He even gave up his very clothing, throwing it at Satan; yet all the time he never blasphemed in word, neither in his heart nor with his lips before the Lord. But on the contrary he blessed the Lord saying: "The Lord gave; the Lord has taken away. As it has pleased the Lord, so be it. Blessed be the name of the Lord" (Jb 1:21). Although it was true that he had many possessions, but, tested by the Lord, he showed that God alone was his possession.

Similarly, Abraham, ordered by the Lord to leave his country and family and the home of his father, at once, so to speak, stripped himself of everything—fatherland, property, relatives, parents—and obeyed the Word of the Lord. Then he underwent many trials and temptations as when his wife was taken from him or when he, living in an alien land, was subjected to injustices. Yet through all he proved that God alone was his sole love over all things. Then when, through a promise and after many years, he had his only son whom he so very much wanted, he was ordered to sacrifice him with his own hands. Abraham stripped himself and truly went against himself. He showed how by the sacrifice of his only son he loved nothing more than God. If indeed he so generously gave up his own son, how much more, if he had been ordered to surrender all other possessions, or to give them all up in one moment, he would have willingly done it.

Do you not see the complete centering upon the Lord of a perfect love freely given? And so also those who wish to follow in their footsteps must love nothing besides God so that, when they are tried, they may be found authentically prompt in preserving their love, their perfect love for the Lord. Such as these are able to endure conflict to the end who have completely and with their whole heart loved God alone and who have freed themselves from all other loves for the world. Few, however, are found who enjoy such a love, turning away from all pleasures and desires of the world and who manfully endure the assaults and temptations of the evil one.

Are there not among the many who, in crossing the rivers, are sucked under by the waters, some who pass over the turbulent streams of worldly passions, so diverse, and successfully overcome the various temptations of evil spirits? Also, just because many ships on the sea are shipwrecked by waves, are there not some ships that succeed and pass over the waves and reach safely the haven of peace? For this there is great need always of much faith and courage, struggle, patience, labors, hunger and thirst for the good, alacrity, perseverance, discretion, and reflection. Most want to possess the kingdom without labors and struggles and sweat, but this is impossible.

As in the world certain people offer themselves to a rich man to work in his fields or to do some other work so as to obtain the necessities for their livelihood, out of these some are lazy and sluggish, not working or laboring as they should. These very ones, not having toiled or labored diligently, still want equal pay as those who manfully, with full force, have labored, as though they too had fulfilled their job.

Likewise when we read in Scripture how such and such a just man pleased God, how he was made a friend and companion of God and how all the fathers were considered friends and participators of God, we forget one thing: What great afflictions they had to suffer, how much they had to endure on behalf of God, with what great courage they struggled and fought battles! We congratulate them and we wish to enjoy rewards and honors equal to theirs. We desire ardently to receive their outstanding gifts, but we fail to notice their labors, struggles, afflictions, and crucifixions. We eagerly want honors and dignities such as they received from God, but we are not ready to accept their labors and struggles.

Truly, I tell you this. Every person, even prostitutes, publicans, and the wicked, desires and wants all this, namely, to possess the kingdom easily without labors and struggles. But because of this there lie along the path temptations and many trials and afflictions and struggles and sweat in order to sift out those who have truly loved the Lord alone with might and main right up to death itself and have desired nothing else along with their love for him.

They justly, therefore, enter into the Kingdom of Heaven who have denied themselves according to the Lord's Word and have loved the Lord alone with their whole heart. Because of their great love they will be recompensed with the greatest of heavenly gifts. For in the afflictions, crucifixions, patience, and faith are hidden the promises, the glory, the possession of heavenly good things just as in the seed that is thrown into the earth the fruit lies already hidden or in the tree that is covered with thorns and grows amid vile and dirty dung. Then they will reveal that in them were the dignity and glory and manifold fruit as the Apostle says: "Through many tribulations we must enter into the Kingdom of Heaven" (Acts 14:22). And the Lord says: "In your patience you will possess your souls" (Lk 21:19), and again: "In the world you will have tribulation" (Jn 16:33).

For there is need of effort and patience, restraint and every kind of watchfulness, of alacrity and perseverance in prayer to the Lord so that one can rise above earthly desires and the snares and traps of sense pleasures, above the enticements of the world, and avoid the attacks of evil spirits. One needs to know well by what vigilance and attentive faith and love the saints possess the heavenly treasure, that is, the power of the Spirit in their souls and in Heaven, which is the balm of the kingdom. Blessed Apostle Paul, in describing this heavenly treasure, that is, the grace of the Spirit, explains also the multitude of tribulations and at the same time shows what each one ought to strive for while in this life: "We know that if our earthly house of this tabernacle be dissolved, we have a building of God, a house not made by hands, eternal in Heaven" (2 Cor 5:1).

7. Therefore, let all strive and labor with all the virtues and let them believe that they, even here, may possess that house. For even if the house of our body is dissolved, we have no other house to which the soul can turn. It is said: "If, being clothed, we shall not be found naked" (2 Cor 5:3), naked, that is, of the communion and fellowship of the Holy Spirit in which the faithful soul can alone find rest.

For this reason, Christians who are genuine Christians are optimistic and are glad to leave the body because they have that house not made by hands, which house is the power of the Holy Spirit dwelling in them. Therefore, even if the house of the body is destroyed, they do not fear, for they have the heavenly house of the Spirit and the incorruptible glory, which glory in the day of the resurrection will build up and glorify the house of the body, as the Apostle says: "He that raised Christ from the dead shall raise up also your mortal bodies through his Spirit that dwells in you" (Rom 8:11). And again he says: "That the life also of Jesus might be made manifest in our mortal flesh" (2 Cor 4:11). And he says: "That mortality which is in us may be swallowed up by life" (2 Cor 5:4).

8. Let us, therefore, strive by faith and excel in every virtue to gain after this life that clothing so that when we lay aside our body we will not be naked and that there will be nothing in that day to glorify our flesh. For insofar as anyone, through faith and zeal, has been deemed worthy to receive the Holy Spirit, to that degree his body also will be glorified in that day. What the soul now stores up within shall then be revealed as a treasure and displayed externally in the body. It is something like the trees once winter has passed. They are warmed by the invisible power of the sun and winds. The trees shoot outwardly and send out leaves and flowers and fruit like external clothing. Similarly also in spring flowers of the plants blossom forth from within the bosom of the earth and the earth is thus covered and decorated. The plants are like those lilies described by the Lord that "not even Solomon in all his glory was arrayed as one of these" (Mt 6:29). For all examples of this nature are types and images of Christians at the resurrection.

9. So to all God-loving souls, I mean, true Christians, there is the first month, Xanthicus, which is called April.[24] This is, indeed, the day of resurrection in which, by the power of the Sun of Righteousness, the glory of the Holy Spirit rises up from within, covering and warming the bodies of the saints. This is the glory they interiorly had before, hidden in their souls. For what they now have, that same then pours out externally into the body. This, I say, is the first month of the year (Ex 12:2). This brings joy to every creature. It clothes the naked trees; it opens the earth. This produces joy in all animals. It brings mirth to all. This is for Christians. Xanthicus, the first month, the time of the resurrection in which their bodies will be glorified by means of the light which even now is in them hiddenly, this is the power of the Spirit who will then be their clothing, food, drink, exultation, gladness, peace, adornment, and eternal life. For the Divine Spirit, whom they were considered worthy even now to possess, will then bring about in them every beauty of radiance and heavenly splendor.

10. How, therefore, ought each of us to believe and to strive and to be dedicated to live a full virtuous life? With much hope and endurance we should now desire the privilege of receiving that heavenly power and the glory of the Holy Spirit interiorly in the soul so that then, when our bodies will have been dissolved, we may receive what shall clothe and

vivify us. It says: "If so be that being clothed we shall not be found naked" (2 Cor 5:3), and "He shall bring to life our mortal bodies by his Spirit that dwells in us" (Rom 8:11).

For blessed Moses provided us with a certain type through the glory of the Spirit which covered his countenance upon which no one could look with steadfast gaze. This type anticipates how in the resurrection of the just the bodies of the saints will be glorified with a glory which even now the souls of the saintly and faithful people are deemed worthy to possess within, in the indwelling of the inner man. It is written: "For we all with open face [that is to say, in the inward man], reflecting as in a mirror the glory of the Lord, are changed into the same image from glory to glory" (2 Cor 3:18). Likewise: "Moses for forty days and forty nights did not eat bread or drink water" (Ex 23:28). It is not possible that a natural body can live without bread so long, unless he partook of some other spiritual bread. This bread even now the saints invisibly partake by the power of the Holy Spirit.

11. In a double way, therefore, the blessed Moses shows us what glory true Christians will receive in the resurrection: namely, the glory of light and the spiritual delights of the Spirit which even now they are deemed worthy to possess interiorly. Because of this, these gifts of the Spirit will redound also in their bodies then. The saints even now possess this glory in their souls, as said above, but it will then cover and clothe their naked bodies. It will sweep them up into Heaven and we will at last come to rest, both body and soul, with the Lord forever.

When God created Adam, he did not furnish him with material wings as birds have, but he prepared for him the wings of the Holy Spirit. The same he plans on giving him at the resurrection, to lift him and direct him wherever the Spirit wishes. These wings the saints already now are deemed worthy to possess to fly up mentally to the realm of heavenly thoughts.[25]

For Christians live in another world, eat from another table, are clothed differently, prefer different enjoyment, different dialogue, and a different mentality. Because of this they exceed all other men. This power already they are considered worthy to enjoy in their souls through the Holy Spirit. Therefore, also in the resurrection their bodies will be worthy to receive those eternal blessings of the Holy Spirit. They will be permeated with that glory which their souls in this life have already experienced.

12. Therefore, each one of us should strive and make every effort to pursue diligently all virtues. We ought to believe and seek from the

Lord that the inner man receive even now this glory and that we may participate in the holiness of the Spirit so that, purged from all sordid traces of evil, we may receive also in the resurrection what will clothe our bodies as they rise naked, what will cover over any deformity, will vivify and transform them in the heavenly kingdom forever.

Christ will descend from Heaven and raise up all generations of Adam that have fallen asleep from the beginning of time, as Holy Scripture proves. And he will divide all into two parts. Those who bear his particular sign, that is, the sign of the Spirit, he will call to himself as his very own and place them at his right hand. He says: "My sheep hear my voice and I know mine own and I am known by mine" (Jn 10:27, 14). Then shall their bodies be surrounded with the divine glory because of their good works. They themselves will be filled with the glory of the Spirit which in this life they enjoyed in their souls. And thus, illumined by the divine light and caught up into Heaven "to meet the Lord in the air (as is written), we shall be always with the Lord" (1 Thes 4:17), reigning with him forever and ever. Amen.

HOMILY 6

Those wishing to please God ought to pray in peace, tranquillity, meekness, and wisdom, so as not to give scandal to all others by their loud outcries. The homily touches also on two questions: whether the thrones and crowns are creatures and concerning the twelve thrones of Israel.

1. Those who approach the Lord ought to pray in quietness, peace, and great tranquillity. They ought to attend to the Lord, not using uncalled for or disturbing outcries, but rather with an attentive heart and controlled thoughts. Take the example of someone seriously sick who needs to undergo cautery or a surgical operation. One will bear the pain with courage and patience, self-possessed without any great tumult and disturbance. Then there are others who may be afflicted with the same sickness. While cautery is being applied or they are being cut open by the surgeons, they let out horrendous cries. All the while, both types suffer the same pain, yet one screams and the other is silent, one makes a disturbance and the other none.

There are some who, when they undergo some suffering and affliction, accept it in a tranquil spirit. There are then others who have the same affliction. They accept it with much impatience. They pour out

75

prayers with disorderly noise and agitation so that those who hear them are scandalized. There are others who, although they are not really laboring under any pain, nevertheless, for the sake of ostentation or idiosyncrasy, use unbecoming cries as though by these they can be pleasing to God.

2. It is not becoming a servant of God to live in a state of disturbance, but rather in all tranquillity and wisdom as the Prophet said, "Unto whom shall I look but unto him that is meek and quiet and that trembles at my words?" (Is 66:2). And in the times of Moses and Elijah we find that in the visions granted them, even though there was a great display of trumpets and powers before the majesty of the Lord, still, amidst all of these things, the coming of the Lord was discerned and he appeared in peace and tranquillity and quietness. For it says: "Lo, a still, silent voice and the Lord was in it" (1 Kgs 19:12). This proves that the Lord's rest is in peace and tranquillity. For whatever foundation a person lays and whatever beginning he makes, he will continue in that until the end. If he begins praying in an exaggeratedly high and screeching voice, he maintains such to the end. Because the Lord is full of love for mankind, it happens that he gives grace even to such a one. Such a type, because of grace, continues in the same procedure. Still, we see that this is the thinking of the uninstructed. As a result, they give scandal to others and are a disturbance to themselves during prayer.

3. The true foundation of prayer is this: to be very vigilant over thoughts and to pray in much tranquillity and peace in order not to be a source of offense to others.[26] For such a person, if he received God's grace, will pray to the end in tranquillity and will edify many others much more. "For God is not a God of confusion but of peace" (1 Cor 14:33). Those who pray with great noises are like coxswains who exhort the rowers to keep time. They seem unable to pray anywhere as they wish, not in churches, in villages, but only perhaps in deserted places.

But those who pray in tranquillity are a source of edification to all everywhere. A person ought to labor to concentrate on his thoughts.[27] He must cut away all underlying matter that leads to evil thoughts, urging himself toward God. He should not allow his thoughts to control his will, but he needs to collect them whenever they wander off in all directions, discerning natural thoughts from those that are evil. The soul, being tainted by sin, is similar to a large forest on a mountain or like reeds in a river or thick, thorny bushes. Whoever pass through such a place need to hold out their hands before them and with force and labor push aside whatever lies in their path. So also the thoughts that come from the adverse power beset the soul. Therefore, there is need for great diligence and mental alertness so that one may distinguish those outside thoughts that rise by the power of the adversary.

4. One person may rely totally on his own power, thinking that he can clear the mountains of the brush all by himself. Another controls his mind, keeping himself in tranquillity and self-control. Without too much trouble he is more successful than the other. So also in prayer there are some who use unseemly cries as though they were relying on their own bodily grunts and groans, not realizing how their thinking deceives them, namely, that they could ever perfectly obtain success by their own efforts. There are others who attend to their thoughts and enter into an inner battle. By their understanding and discernment these are capable of success as they shake away the attacking thoughts and walk in the Lord's will.

We find in the Apostle that he says whoever edifies others is greater than he who does not. "He that speaks in tongues edifies himself, but he that prophesies edifies the Church. Greater is he who prophesies than he who speaks in tongues" (1 Cor 14:4–5). Let everyone, therefore, seek to edify others and he will then be considered worthy of the Kingdom of Heaven.

5. *Question:* Some people claim that the thrones and crowns are creatures and not of the Spirit. How are we to understand these?

Answer: The throne of the Godhead is our mind and again the throne of our mind is the Godhead and the Spirit. Similarly, Satan and the powers and princes of darkness, after the fall of Adam, have enthroned themselves in the heart and mind and body of Adam as their own special throne. For this reason the Lord came and took a body of the Virgin. If he wished to descend in his divinity, who would have been able to endure it? So he spoke with men through the instrument of his body. In such a way he threw down the evil spirits that had enthroned themselves in the body by means of the intellect and thoughts. And the Lord cleansed the conscience and made for himself a throne of the mind, the thoughts and the body.

6. *Question:* What, therefore, is meant by the text: "You shall sit on the twelve thrones, judging the twelve tribes of Israel" (Mt 19:28)?

Answer: This we find was fulfilled on earth when the Lord was taken up into Heaven. For he sent the Spirit, the Comforter, upon the twelve Apostles, along with his holy power. He came and pitched his tent and took up his throne in their minds. When those onlookers said that they were full of new wine (Acts 2:13), Peter began to judge them, saying of Jesus: "This man, mighty in words and signs, you crucified, hanging him on a tree" (Acts 2:22). And truly he does amazing things, upturning the tombstones and raising the dead. For it is written: "In the last days I will pour out my Spirit upon all flesh and your sons and your daughters will prophesy" (Acts 2:17). Therefore, instructed by Peter, many came to repentance so that a new world, the chosen of God, came into being.

7. Do you, therefore, see how the beginning of judgment appeared? A new world appeared there. Authority to sit and judge, even in this world, was given to them, the Apostles. And it is granted them also to sit and pass judgment at the coming of the Lord in the resurrection of the dead. Nevertheless, it is also done here, by the same Holy Spirit sitting on the thrones of their minds.

The crowns which Christians will receive in the age to come are not creatures. Those who say this are speaking nonsense. The Spirit uses these in a transfigured sense. What does the Apostle Paul say of the heavenly Jerusalem? "This is the mother of us all whom we all together confess" (Gal 4:26). In regard to the garment which Christians wear it is evident that the Spirit clothes them in the name of the Father and the Son and the Holy Spirit forever. Amen.

HOMILY 7

On the gentleness of Christ toward man. The homily also contains some questions and answers.

1. Take the example of a person who enters a royal palace and sees there the portraits and all the works of art, some treasures kept in one place, others in another place. Then he sits down at table with the king. Delicious food and drink are placed before him. He sits back and enjoys thoroughly the sight and grandeur. But after that he is taken from there and thrown abruptly into some noisy places.

Or take the example of a certain maiden, fairer, more intelligent, and wealthier than all others. She takes for her husband a poor man, lowly and deformed, clothed in rags. She takes the filthy clothing from him and clothes him in regal robes and places a crown on his head and marries him. At a certain point that poor man begins to be frightened and asks: "Am I, a wretched pauper, lowly and an outcast, to be given such a wife?" So also God treats poor, wretched man. He has given him a taste for another world, of other delicious food. He has shown him splendor and regal delights, ineffable, heavenly. And so, finally, man, when he compares such spiritual gifts with the things of the world, casts everything else away. Whether it be a king or princes or the wise ones that meet his eye, he turns his look to the heavenly treasure. For since God is love, man has received the heavenly and divine fire of Christ and takes enjoyment in it and is filled with happiness and there binds himself fast.

2. *Question:* Whether Satan is with God both in the air as well as in humans?

Answer: If this sun, which is a creature, still shines upon murky places and yet is not tainted in any way, how much more the Godhead? If God is with Satan, he is not tainted or sullied by that fact. God, however, has permitted evil in order to develop man. But evil is shadowy and blind and cannot see the purity and simplicity of God. If, indeed, anyone should say that Satan has his own proper place and God also has his, he is circumscribing God, placing him outside of the place occupied by the Evil One. How, then, can we say that the good is not limited to certain places and is not comprehensible and that all things are in it and yet how is the good not infected by the evil? Is it not the same parallel that, because the heavens and the sun and the mountains are in God himself and have their whole being through him, that then they are God? All created things whatsoever have their own level of being, and the Creator, who is present to them, is God.[28]

3. *Question:* When sin is transformed into an angel of light and seemingly appears as grace, in what way can man recognize the deceits of the devil? And how can he receive and discern the ways of grace?

Answer: The signs accompanying grace are much joy, peace, love, and truth. Such truth impels man to seek truth. But the signs of sin are accompanied by turmoil, not joy and love toward God. Take the example of the plant endive. It looks like lettuce. But the latter is sweet, the former bitter. Also in the matter of grace, some things resemble truth, and then there is the very substance of truth. Similarly, there is the ray of the sun and the sun itself. Take a lamp in the house. Its light shines everywhere and yet how different is the light in the very lamp, so much brighter and clearer. So there are certain features related to grace that, when a person looks at them from a distance, as certain visions, delight him. But he is quite different when the power of God enters into him, takes over his members and his heart and captivates his mind by the love of God. When Peter was seized and they threw him into prison, even though the prison door was closed, an angel came to him, broke his bonds, and led him out. Peter, indeed, was like one in an ecstasy, thinking that he was seeing a vision.

4. *Question:* But how is it possible for those led by the grace of God ever to fall?

Answer: The pure intelligences themselves in their own nature can slip and fall. For a man begins to be puffed up. He judges and says: "You are a sinner," while he regards himself as righteous. Do you not remember what Paul says: "To me was given a thorn in the flesh, the messenger of Satan, to buffet me, lest I be exalted above measure" (2 Cor 12:7). Indeed, even a pure nature also has in itself a certain amount of pride.

5. *Question:* Can anyone through light see his own soul? Some change revelation in holding that vision comes through knowledge and the senses.

Answer: All three; sense, vision, and enlightenment, are all different. The one who is enlightened is greater than the one who only sees by the senses. For his mind is enlightened insofar as he has received a greater portion of knowledge than the one who has only sense knowledge. He really sees in himself visions which give him certitude. Nevertheless, revelation is still different in which great things, mysteries of the Godhead, are revealed to the soul.[29]

6. *Question:* Does one see the soul through revelation and divine light?

Answer: Just as our eyes see the sun, so also the enlightened see the images of the soul, but few Christians attain this.

7. *Question:* Does the soul have any form?

Answer: It has a form and image similar to that of an angel. For as angels have an image and form and as the outer man has his image so also the inner man has an image that is similar both to that of the angel and that of the exterior man.

8. *Question:* Is the mind different from the soul?

Answer: As the members of the body are many parts, yet they designate one man, so also the members of the soul are many: the mind, the conscience, the will, "thoughts accusing and excusing" (Rom 2:15), yet all these are bound together in one soul even though there are many members. The soul, however, is one, the interior man. Just as the exterior eyes look ahead and spot the brambles and precipices and ditches, so also the mind, when it is quite alert, foresees the machinations and deceits of the power, the adversary of the soul. Let us, therefore, render glory to the Father and the Son and the Holy Spirit. Amen.

HOMILY 8

Concerning those things which occur when Christians pray. On the degrees of perfection, that is, whether Christians are able to reach the highest degree of perfection.

1. One kneels down in prayer and at once his heart is filled with the power of God. And his soul exults in the Lord as a bride with the bridegroom according to that which Isaiah the Prophet said: "As the bridegroom will take delight in the bride, so the Lord will take delight in thee" (Is 62:5).[30] It happens that he is the whole day occupied by his work and can give himself to prayer for only an hour. The interior man is caught up in prayer and plunged into the infinite depths of that other world with great sweetness. His whole mind as a result is lifted up and caught up in that region where he sojourns. In that time his thoughts of earthly cares recede into oblivion because now his thoughts are filled and held captivated by divine and heavenly things, by the infinite and incomprehensible, by wonderful things that escape human expression, so that for that one hour he ardently desires and says: "Would that my soul might pass over with my prayer!"

2. *Question:* Can anyone always penetrate into such things?

Answer: Grace, indeed, is unceasingly present and is rooted in us and mingled with our nature from our earliest years. It is as something natural and real which adheres to a person as though it formed one substance. Still, it operates in a person in various ways, depending on one's cooperation as far as this is given.

At times the fire flares out and burns with more vehement flames. At other times it burns more gently and slowly. The light that it gives off flames up at times and shines more brightly. At other times it goes down and barely gives off any light. So it is also with the lamp of grace. It is always burning and giving off light, but when it is especially trimmed, it burns more brilliantly as though intoxicated by the love of God.[31] But again, by a certain dispensation of God, the light is still there but it barely shines.

3. To certain persons the sign of the cross appeared as light and plunged itself deep into the inner man. At another time a man, while praying, was thrown into a trance. He found himself standing in church before the altar. There were three loaves of bread offered to him, as though leavened by oil. And the more he ate, the more the loaves multiplied.[32] To others at times there appeared a splendid robe, such as not

found anywhere in the whole world, not made by human hands. Just as when the Lord ascended the mountain with John and Peter, he transformed his garments, making them brilliant like lightning, so too was that robe so that that man, clothed in it, was amazed and struck with awe.

Sometimes indeed the very light itself, shining in the heart, opened up interiorly and in a profound way a hidden light, so that the whole person was completely drowned with that sweet contemplation. He was no longer in control of himself, but became like a fool and a barbarian toward this world, so overwhelmed was he by the excessive love and sweetness of the hidden mysteries that were being revealed to him. The result was that the person was granted liberty and arrived at a perfect degree of purity and freedom from sin.

But later grace receded from him and the veil of the adversary's power approached. Still, grace is operating there even though the person may now be on a level of lesser perfection.

4. In a manner of speaking, there are twelve steps a person has to pass to reach perfection. At times one may have reached the stage of perfection. But again grace may recede somewhat and he descends to the next lower level, now standing on the eleventh step.[33] Let us take the example of a man rich in grace. Always night and day he is on the highest level of perfection. He is free and pure, always captivated and lifted high up. Now, if such a man were constantly experiencing those marvelous things and they were always experientially present to him, he would not be able to preach the word or take on any work. He could not bear to listen to or take any interest in any affair, even if there was a need to do so in concern for himself or for tomorrow. He would only sit in a corner lifted up and intoxicated. As a result the perfect degree of grace is not given him so that he may be concerned with the care of his brethren and in ministering the word. Nevertheless, "the middle wall has been broken through" (Eph 2:14) and death has been conquered.

5. This is the way it is. It is like a certain dark power that hangs over and forms a screen like a thick column of air, even though the lamp is always burning and giving off light in spite of the veil that threatens the light. Take the man who admits that he is not perfect nor completely free from sin. He says that the middle wall of partition has been broken and knocked down and yet in a certain area it has not completely been broken down nor permanently. There are times when grace burns more brightly, consoles and refurbishes more completely. Then at other times the grace subsides and is clouded over as grace is dispensed to man's advantage.

But who, indeed, has ever arrived at perfection and tasted and directly experienced that world? I have not yet seen any perfect Christian or one perfectly free. But, although a person may be at rest in grace and arrive at experiencing mysteries, revelations, and the immense consolation of grace, nevertheless, sin still abides in him.

There may be some who, because of the immense grace and light that they receive, consider themselves perfect and free. They are deceived because of lack of experience. Even though they possess grace, I have not yet seen any person perfectly free. Yes, even I have to some degree reached from time to time that level and I have learned that no one is perfect.

6. *Question:* Tell us, in what degree of perfection are you?

Answer: After I received the experience of the sign of the cross, grace now acts in this manner. It quiets all my parts and my heart so that the soul with the greatest joy seems to be a guileless child. No longer am I a man that condemns Greek or Jew or sinner or worldling. Truly, the interior man looks on all human beings with pure eyes and finds joy in the whole world. He really wishes to reverence and love all Greeks and Jews.

At certain times he, like the son of a king, places all his trust in the Son of God as in his father. Doors are opened to him and he enters inside into "many mansions" (Jn 14:2). And the further he enters, again new doors open in a progression. From a hundred mansions he enters into another hundred. He becomes rich and yet ever richer. Other new and amazing wonders are disclosed to him. Things are entrusted to him as a son and an heir which can never be explained by human nature or expressed in syllables by mouth or tongue. Glory to God. Amen.

HOMILY 9

How to fulfill the promises and the prophecies of God by means of various trials and temptations. We are freed from the attacks of the evil one by clinging to God alone.

1. The spiritual power of God's grace, working within the soul, does so with the greatest patience, wisdom, and mystical touching of the mind. The individual also struggles with great patience in the opportunities that come his way. But then the work of grace works perfectly in him. This is seen in the fact that his free will, after great temptation, is

clearly bent on pleasing the Holy Spirit and he himself has for a good length of time demonstrated uprightness and perseverance. Let us exemplify this principle of the spiritual life from some clear examples found in Holy Scripture.

2. What I am saying is exactly borne out in the case of Joseph. What a long time it took to fulfill the predestined will of God in his regard and to fulfill his visions. By how many labors, afflictions and distresses was he not proved first, and did he not strenuously bear all of them? Through all of these he was found to be the upright and faithful servant of God. He was then made king of Egypt and provided food for his own blood family.[34] And the prophecy of all of those things not seen was accomplished and the will of God was fulfilled after a long time and much providential direction.

3. The same is handed down about David. God anointed him king by the prophet Samuel. And after he was anointed, he constantly had to flee from Saul, who persecuted him, seeking to kill him. Where, then, was the anointing of God? Where was there any promise that was being fulfilled with any immediacy? For a short time after his anointing, David was grievously afflicted and fled into the desert. He had so little to eat that he took refuge among the pagan tribes because of Saul's plots against him. This was the one whom God anointed to be king, suffering so many afflictions. After he was tried, afflicted, tempted for some time, and, having patiently endured it all by placing all his trust only in God and fully believing "what God has done for me by the prophet's anointing and what God foretold about me, without a doubt must come about (1 Sm 16:13, ff)," after a long waiting, finally God's will was fulfilled. And David reigned after so many temptations. And then the word of God was manifested and the anointing given by the Prophet was shown to be sure and true.

4. The same story with Moses. God, since he had foreknown and predestined him to be the leader and the savior of his people, arranged that he would become the son of Pharaoh's daughter. And thus he grew up with regal wealth and pomp and luxury, having been instructed "in all the wisdom of the Egyptians" (Acts 7:22). When he reached adulthood and had become very respected, he rejected all of these things, choosing rather the affliction and reproaches of Christ, as the Apostle says, "rather than to enjoy for a time the pleasures of sin" (Heb 11:24). He became a refugee from Egypt. How long a time did he spend in the tasks of a shepherd, he who was the son of a king and brought up in the lap of so many pleasures and royal luxury? And finally, after having been tested

84

by God and found faithful with much patience because he had sustained many trials, he was made the savior and leader, the king of the people Israel, and God made him "as a god for Pharaoh" (Ex 7:1). For through him God struck Egypt and showed great and amazing things to Pharaoh through him, and finally drowned the Egyptians in the sea. See, after so long a space of time, and after so many trials and afflictions, the will and plan of God was fulfilled.

5. The same also happened to Abraham. How long before God promised to give him a son? However, he did not do this immediately. But for how many years did he not have to endure trials and temptations? But he patiently bore all that came to him. He firmly believed that he who had promised would not lie but would fulfill his word. So he was found faithful and obtained what was promised.

6. So also Noah was ordered by God in his five-hundredth year to build an ark. God announced that he would bring about a flood over the whole earth. This he brought about only in Noah's six-hundredth year. For one hundred years Noah patiently waited, yet never doubted for a moment that God would do what he had said. He was completely convinced that what God had spoken without a doubt had to happen. So, tested with a firm and integrated will, faith, patience, and great docility, he alone with his family was saved since he kept perfectly God's commandment.

7. We have offered these examples from Holy Scripture to show that the power of divine grace is in man and the gift of the Holy Spirit which is given to the faithful soul comes forth with much contention, with much endurance, patience, trials, and testings. Through such, man's free will is put to the test by all sorts of afflictions.

And, when man does not grieve the Spirit in any way but is in harmony with grace by keeping all the commandments, then he is regarded as worthy to receive freedom from all passions. He also receives the full adoption of the Spirit, which is always a mystery, along with spiritual riches and wisdom which are not of this world, of which true Christians are made participators. For this reason such persons differ in all things from other men who have the spirit of this world, for they are endowed with prudence, understanding, and wisdom.

8. Indeed, a person of this type "is able to judge all men" (1 Cor 2:15), as it is written. He knows from what viewpoint he speaks, and where he stands and what levels of perfection he has already experienced. But no one of the world can know and judge him. Only a person who has the like heavenly and Divine Spirit can know one who is like

him, as the Apostle says: "We teach spiritual things spiritually. An unspiritual person is one who does not accept anything of the Spirit of God. He sees it all as nonsense. But the spiritual man judges everything, but he himself is judged by no one" (1 Cor 2:13–15). Such a one regards all the precious things of the world, riches, luxury, and all sense pleasures, and even its knowledge and everything else of this world, as an object to be spurned and despised.

9. Just as one who suffers from a burning fever is sickened by and rejects any food or drink that you may offer him even if it were very delicious, because he is on fire with a fever and is really burning up from it, so those who are burning with a holy and venerable longing for the heavenly Spirit are wounded in their soul with love for the love of God. They burn with a divine and heavenly fire which the Lord came on this earth to enkindle. How he wishes that it be quickly accomplished! They are enflamed with a heavenly longing for Christ so that everything that is of this world, considered as outstanding and precious, is reputed base and despised on account of the fire of their love for Christ who binds them, burns them, and enflames them with a passion for God and for the heavenly good things that lead to love. From such a love nothing of the earth or underworld will separate them, as the Apostle Paul testified: "Who will separate us from the love of Christ?" (Rom 8:35), and all else that follows.

10. But one cannot possess his soul and the love of the heavenly Spirit unless he cuts himself off from all the things of this world and surrenders himself to seek the love of Christ. His mind must be freed from all crass and material concerns so that he may be totally taken up with only one aim, namely, to direct all these things according to the commandments so that his whole concern, striving, attention, and preoccupation of soul may be centered on the search for transcendent values as the soul may strive to be adorned with the Gospel virtues and the heavenly Spirit and may become a participator in the purity and sanctification of Christ.

All of this is done so that, having said goodbye to everything else, and having cut himself off from all gross and earthly impediments and having freed himself from all carnal love or affection toward parents and relatives, a person may not give attention to any other thing or be distracted by such, whether it be the passion for power or glory or honors, or carnal, worldly friendships or any other earthly concerns. He can concentrate totally on seeking the soul's intellectual being and he can labor valiantly and wait in hope for the coming of the Spirit. The Lord

86

speaks in a similar way: "In your patience possess your souls" (Lk 21:19). And again: "Seek first the Kingdom of God and all these things shall be added unto you" (Mt 6:33).

11. It is, therefore, possible that anyone, who thus really strives and perseveringly attends to himself either in prayer or in obedience or in doing any work according to God, should be able to escape from the darkness of the evil demons. For the mind that never ceases to be attentive to itself and to seek the Lord can possess its soul, which loses itself in the passions. It does this by always bringing itself with a certain violence and constancy into captivity to the Lord and by clinging only to him as it is said: "Bringing into captivity every thought to the obedience of Christ" (2 Cor 10:5).

It does this so that, by such battling, longing, and diligent seeking, the mind may be rendered worthy to be with the Lord in "one Spirit" (1 Cor 6:17) of the gift and grace of Christ, resting in the vessel of the soul which has empowered the mind to do every good work. It leads the mind away from "insulting the Spirit of the Lord" (Heb 10:29) through any self-will and any temptation to yield to the concerns of this world or honors or dignities or selfish opinions or carnal passions or association with evil men.

12. For how lovely it is when a spiritual person consecrates himself totally to the Lord and clings to him alone. He walks in his commands, never forgetting. Reverently honoring the overshadowing presence of the Spirit of Christ, he becomes one spirit with him and one being, just as the Apostle says: "He that is joined to the Lord is one Spirit" (1 Cor 6:17). But if anyone gives himself over to cares or glory or dignities, or is concerned with human honors and diligently sets his heart on these, and if he is full of worldly thoughts or is disturbed or held in bondage to anything of this world, should he want to leap over such, flee from them, and get rid of such dark passions in which he is held captive by the demonic forces, he will be unable to do so. The reason is that he loves and does the will of the dark powers. He does not totally despise the pursuits of evil.

13. Let us, therefore, prepare ourselves so that we may approach the Lord with perfect promptitude and full intent. And let us become passionately in love with Christ to do his will. And let us "think upon his commandments so as to do them" (Ps 103:18). Let us separate ourselves completely from any attachment to the world and turn our souls completely to him alone. Let us keep him alone before our eyes as our concern and striving. If because of our creatureliness we give ourselves

less diligently to divine obedience, nevertheless, let the mind not swerve from love of the Lord and from ardent seeking of him. But if we strive in such an intention, keeping always straight on the path of justice and always being attentive to ourselves, we shall obtain the promise of his Spirit. Through grace we will be freed from the destructive power of the dark passions which attack the soul so that we may be considered worthy to enter into the eternal Kingdom to enjoy Christ forever, glorifying the Father and the Son and the Holy Spirit unto ages of ages. Amen.

HOMILY 10

By humility and enthusiasm the gifts of divine grace are kept alive and increased, but by pride and sloth they are lost.

1. Persons who love truth and God, who thoroughly wish to put on Christ with great hope and faith, do not need so much encouragement or correction from others. They never give up their longing for Heaven and their love of the Lord, granted that from time to time they bear patiently a bit of a diminishment in that love. But being completely attached to the cross of Christ, they daily perceive in themselves that they are spiritually progressing toward their spiritual Bridegroom.

Having been wounded by the desire for Heaven and thirsting for the justice of virtues, they await the illumination of the Spirit with the greatest insatiable longing. And should they be considered worthy to receive through their faith knowledge of divine mysteries or to be made participators of the happiness of heavenly grace, they still do not put their trust in themselves, regarding themselves as somebody. But the more they are considered worthy to receive spiritual gifts, the more diligently do they seek them with an insatiable desire. The more they perceive themselves advancing in spiritual perfection, the more do they hunger and thirst for a greater share of and increase in grace. And the richer they become spiritually, the poorer they consider themselves, as they burn up interiorly with an insatiable spiritual yearning for the heavenly Bridegroom as Scripture says: "They that eat me shall still be hungry and they that drink me shall thirst" (Eccl 24:21).[35]

2. Such persons that pursue the Lord with such ardent and insatiable love are worthy of eternal life. For this reason they are deemed worthy also to be freed from passions and obtain fully the illumination

88

and participation with fullness of grace of the hidden and mystical communion with the Holy Spirit. However, there are other persons less dynamic and more sluggish who hardly aspire, while still on this earth, to obtain such gifts, namely the sanctification of the heart, not partially, but perfectly through perseverance and long-suffering. They never had expected to receive the fullness of the Spirit-Comforter with full consciousness and certitude. They never had hoped to receive from the Spirit liberation from evil passions. But on the contrary, after having received worthily the divine grace, they yielded to sin and gave themselves to cowardliness and indifference.

3. Such ones as these, having received the grace of the Spirit, enjoy the consolation of grace in peace and longing and spiritual sweetness. But they begin to rely on this fact and become puffed up. They live securely and forget the need for a broken heart and humility of spirit. They cease stretching out to attain the perfect measure of emptiness from passions. They fail to be filled with grace in all diligence and faith. But they felt secured and became complacent with their scanty consolation of grace. Such persons measured their progress by pride rather than a humble spirit. And so whatever gifts of grace had been given them were taken from them on account of their neglectful contempt and careless vainglory.

4. The person, however, who truly loves God and Christ, even though he may perform a thousand good works, considers himself as having done nothing because of his insatiable longing for the Lord. Even if he should tear down the body with fasts and vigils, he considers himself as though he had never even yet begun to develop virtues. Although various gifts of the Spirit or even revelations and heavenly mysteries may be given to him, he believes that he has acquired nothing because of his immense and insatiable love for the Lord.

But daily he perseveres in prayer with a hungering and a thirst in faith and love. He has an insatiable desire for the mysteries of grace and for every virtue. He is wounded with love for the heavenly Spirit, having a burning desire for the heavenly Bridegroom through grace which he always possesses within himself. This stirs him to desire perfectly to be regarded as worthy to enter into the mystical and awesome communion with him in the sanctification of the Spirit.

The face of the soul is unveiled and it gazes with fixed eyes upon the heavenly Bridegroom, face to face, in a spiritual and ineffable light. Such a person mingles with him with full certitude of faith, becoming conformed to his death. He always hopes with the greatest desire to

89

yearn to die for Christ. He certainly and completely believes that he will obtain liberation from his sins and dark passions through the Spirit, so that, purified by the Spirit in soul and body, he may become a pure vessel to receive the heavenly unction and become a worthy habitation for the heavenly and true King, Christ. And then such a person is considered worthy of heavenly life, having become a pure dwelling place for the Holy Spirit.

5. For one to reach this level is not a matter of a single act guaranteeing immediate results nor is it attained without testing. But through labors and many trials, through a long period of time and much striving, with testing and various temptations such a person receives spiritual growth and increase, reaching even to the perfect level of freedom from passions[36] so that, courageously and with great effort enduring every temptation with which it is attacked by evil forces, he attains the greatest honors and spiritual gifts and heavenly riches. And thus he becomes an heir of the heavenly kingdom in Jesus Christ our Lord, to whom be glory and power forever. Amen.

HOMILY 11

The power of the Holy Spirit in the heart of man is like fire. And things we need in order to discern the thoughts that flow out of the heart. And concerning the dead serpent that was fixed by Moses on top of the pole which was a type of Christ. The homily also contains two dialogues, one between Christ and the evil Satan; the other between sinners and Christ.

1. That heavenly fire[37] of the Godhead which Christians receive interiorly in their hearts now in this life, that same fire which now interiorly directs their hearts, bursts forth upon the dissolution of the body. It again pulls together the members of the body and brings about a resurrection of the dismembered body. For just as the fire which ministered on the altar of Jerusalem in the time of the captivity was buried in a hole, and that same fire, when peace came and the captives returned to their homeland, was, as it were, renewed and again functioned as it did before, so too the heavenly fire refashions and renews this familiar body, which after its dissolution turns to dust and raises up the decayed bodies. For that interior fire, inhabiting our hearts, emerges then and brings about the resurrection of the bodies.

2. In the time of Nabuchodonosor the fire that powerfully burned

in the furnace was not divine but was a creature. But those three youths, because of their righteousness, while they were in the visible fire, had in their hearts the divine and heavenly fire which ministered within their thoughts and worked powerfully in the youths. That same fire appeared outside them. For it stood in their midst and prevented the visible fire from burning or injuring any part of the three just ones. Similarly also in the times of the Israelites when their minds and thoughts were bent on turning away from the living God and were turned toward idolatry, Aaron was forced to tell them to bring together their golden and ornamented vessels. After a while the gold and the vessels which they cast into the fire were transformed into an idol. The fire, as it were, fashioned an image of their intention.

This is worthy of our serious attention. According to their secret intention and in their thoughts, they wanted to practice idolatry, so the fire in a similar way converted the vessels that had been cast upon it into an idol. And then they openly worshiped the idols. But just as the three young men, bent on doing righteous deeds, received within themselves the fire of God and adored the Lord in truth, so also now faithful souls receive in an interior way that divine and heavenly fire in this present life, and that fire fashions a heavenly image upon their human nature.

3. As the fire fashioned the golden vessels and they were made into an idol, so too the Lord, who fashions the intentions of faithful and good persons and even now forms an image in the soul which will be manifested exteriorly in the resurrection, glorifies their bodies interiorly and exteriorly. Indeed, just as the bodies of certain persons at that time of death decay, so also their thoughts are corrupted by Satan and are dead to any life. They are buried in earthly mud. For their soul has perished. For just as the Israelites threw the golden vessels into the fire and they became an idol, so now such a person has surrendered his pure and good thoughts to evil and they have become buried in the mud of sin and have become an idol.

But how can anyone discover them, discern and lead them out of one's own fire? Here the soul has need of a divine lamp, namely, the Holy Spirit, who puts in order and beautifies the darkened house. The soul needs the shining Sun of justice which illumines and shines upon the heart. It also has need of weapons by which it can conquer in war.

4. For in that place where the widow had lost the drachma (Lk 15:8), she first lit a lamp, then swept the house. And thus, she found the drachma, once the house was swept and the lamp lit. It was found covered with dirt and impurity and earth. Truly the soul is incapable by

itself of studying its own thoughts and discerning them. But with the divine lamp lit, the light dispels the darkness from the house. Then a person sees his own thoughts, how they have been covered by impurity and the mud of sin. The sun rises and then the soul sees its loss and begins to call out the thoughts that had been so mixed with dirt and squalor. For the soul had lost its image when it had transgressed the commandment.[38]

5. Take the example of a king who has goods and servants under him ministering to him. However, it happens that he is taken captive by enemies. When he is captured and led out of his country, his servants and ministers must want to follow after him. So also Adam was created pure by God for his service. All these creatures were given to him to serve him. He was destined to be the lord and king of all creatures. But when the evil word came to him and conversed with him, he first received it through an external hearing. Then it penetrated into his heart and took charge of his whole being. When he was thus captured, creation, which ministered and served him, was captured with him.[39] Through him death gained power over every soul and completely destroyed the image of Adam because of his disobedience so that as a result men were sidetracked and fell to worshiping demons. Yes, the fruits of the earth, created good by God, are now offered to the demons. Bread, wine, and oil are offered on their altars along with animals. But not only these things, but they sacrifice even their sons and daughters to the demons (Ps 136-37).

6. Then, at this time, he who fashioned the body and soul comes and undoes all the cunning of the wicked devil and all that he has wrought in the thoughts of men. He renews and forms a heavenly image and recreates the soul anew so that Adam again may be king over death and lord over all creatures. In the shadow of the law Moses was called the savior of Israel, for he led the Israelites out of Egypt. So also now the true Redeemer, Christ, enters into the depths of the soul and leads it out of dark Egypt with its burdensome yoke and bitter slavery. He commands us to leave the world and take on poverty and to give up all tangible possessions. We are to have no earthly care, but night and day we are to stand at the door waiting for the time when the Lord will open the closed hearts and pour into us the gift of the Holy Spirit.

7. He commanded us, therefore, to give up gold, silver, and relatives. We are to sell all our goods and distribute them to the poor (Mt 19:20). Our treasure is to be sought in Heaven: "For where your treasure is, there also is your heart" (Mt 6:21). For the Lord knew that in

this matter Satan gains the upper hand over thoughts in order to turn them toward anxieties about material, earthly concerns. For this reason God, in his concern for your soul, ordered you to renounce all things so that, even if you would be unwilling, you would still seek after heavenly riches and center your heart on God. For even if you should wish to go back to creatures, you would not find any tangible possessions around you. Whether you wish it or not, you are forced to raise your mind to Heaven where you have put your whole treasure: "For where your treasure is, there also is your heart."

8. In the law God commanded Moses to fashion a bronze serpent and to lift it up high and place it on the top of a pole (Nm 21:8). Whoever would be bitten by serpents, they would be healed. This was done as a part of God's salvific economy whereby all those who were bound to Satan by earthly cares and idolatry and passions and all sorts of ungodliness might in this way at least look up to some degree to the things above. They might breathe, freed from the things below, and attend to more transcendent things from above. They might pass from these things to what is the highest and so, advancing little by little to the more sublime and superior type, they might come to know that there is the One, Most High, supreme over all creatures.

So also God ordered you to become poor and to sell all to give to the poor so that thereafter, even if you would wish again to crawl on the earth, you could not. Searching, therefore, in your heart, begin to dialogue with your thoughts: "Since we possess nothing on earth, let us pass over to Heaven where we have our treasure and where we do all our business." Your mind begins to rise above to sublime things and to seek the higher things and in doing so you make progress.

9. But what is the meaning of that dead serpent that was fixed on top of the pole and healed those that had been bitten? The dead serpent conquered over the living serpents, as a type of the body of the Lord. The body which he took from Mary he raised it up on the cross. He hung it and fastened it to the tree. And so the dead body conquered and slew the serpent, living and creeping in the hearts of men. Here is an amazing miracle! How the dead serpent slew the living serpent! But just as Moses made a new thing when he fashioned a likeness of a living serpent, so also the Lord created a new thing from Mary and put this on. He did not, however, assume a body brought from Heaven. The heavenly Spirit touched humanity and brought it to divinity.[40] He took up human flesh and fashioned it in the womb. As, therefore, there never was a bronze serpent commanded by God to be fashioned in the world

until the time of Moses, so a new and sinless body never appeared in the world until the time of the Lord. For ever since the first Adam transgressed the commandment of God, death reigned over all of his children. Thus a dead body overcame the live serpent.

10. And this marvelous event is to the Jews, indeed, a stumbling block and to Greeks foolishness. For what does the Apostle say? "But we preach Jesus Christ crucified; to the Jews a stumbling block and to the Greeks foolishness, but, to us who are saved, Christ is the power of God and the wisdom of God" (1 Cor 1:24). In the dead body there is life. Here is redemption, here is light. Here the Lord comes to death and argues with death. He orders that death release, from hell and death, the souls and give them back to him.

Behold, death is shaken by these words and approaches his servants and gathers together into a group all his powers and princes of evil. And the prince of evil bears forth the signed documents of indentured slaves and declares: "Look, these people have obeyed my word! See how they, mortal men, have bowed down in adoration to us!" But God, who is a just judge, shows then his justice and says to him: "Adam obeyed you and you did then through him capture all hearts. Humanity obeyed you. But my body, what is it doing here? It is sinless. That body of the first Adam was in bondage to you and you legally held the writ of indenture. But all bear witness to me that I have not sinned. I owe you nothing. And that I am the Son of God all universally bear witness. "For from above out of the heavens there came upon earth a voice bearing testimony: 'This is my beloved Son; hear him' (Mt 3:17). John gives witness: 'Behold, the Lamb of God, that takes away the sin of the world' (Jn 1:29). And again Scripture says: 'He who sinned not, nor was there any guile found in him' (1 Pt 2:22). And again: 'The prince of this world comes and in me finds nothing' (Jn 14:30). And, moreover, you yourself, Satan, witness to me in saying: 'I know you, that you are the Son of God' (Mk 1:24). And again: 'What do we have to do with you, Jesus of Nazareth? Have you come here to torment us before the time?' (Mt 8:29). There are, therefore, three who bear witness to me: he that sends down from the heavens a voice; and those who are on earth; and you yourself. I, therefore, bought back the body that was sold to you by the first Adam. I tore up the contract that enslaved mankind to you. Indeed, I satisfied Adam's debts when I was crucified and I descended into hell. And I command you, O Hell, O Darkness, O Death, release the

Redemption!

94

imprisoned souls of the children of Adam." And so, at last, the wicked powers, struck with fear, restore the imprisoned children of Adam.

11. Really, when you hear that at that time the Lord freed the souls from hell and the regions of darkness and that he descended into hell and did an amazing work, do not think that this does not have any personal meaning for you. Man, indeed, can readily accept the evil one. Death has its grip on the children of Adam and their thoughts are imprisoned in darkness. And when you hear mention made of tombs, do not at once think only of visible ones. For your heart is a tomb and a sepulcher. When the prince of evil and his angels have built their nest there and have built roads and highways on which the powers of Satan walk about inside your mind and in your thoughts, then, really, are you not a hell and a sepulcher and a tomb dead to God?

For there it was that Satan stamped out counterfeit coins of silver. In such a soul he sowed bitter seeds. He leavened it with old leaven. There is where a murky, muddy fountain flows. But the Lord descends into the souls of those who seek him. He goes into the depths of the hellish heart and there he commands death, saying: "Release those captive souls that seek after me, those that you hold by force in bondage." He breaks through the heavy stones that cover the soul. He opens the tombs. He truly raises to life the dead person and leads that captive soul forth out of the dark prison.

12. Take the example of a man bound with chains, hand and foot, and someone comes to remove his shackles and to set him free so he may walk unencumbered. In a similar way the Lord removes the chains of death strangling the soul and he releases it and sets the mind free so that it may amble without disturbance, but in tranquillity before God. It is similar to a man in the middle of a raging river, covered by water. He lies lifeless, drowning in the midst of horrible, dreadful monsters. If a man who does not know how to swim wishes to save the drowning person, he likewise will perish and be drowned. Certainly, what is needed is an expert swimmer to dive into the deep water, swim out, and save him who was drowning with wild monsters all around him. The very water itself, in the case of an expert swimmer, aids such a one and holds him up on the surface of the water. In a similar way, man has been plunged into the abyss of darkness and the depths of death. He is suffocating and has lost God's life within himself, surrounded by ferocious beasts. Who is able to penetrate into those depths of hell and death except that very

Workman himself, who fashioned the human body? He himself penetrates into two parts, namely, the depths of hell and the deepest region of the human heart where the soul with all its thoughts is held captive by death. And he leads out of the dark depths the dead Adam. Even death itself through training is a help to man, like water to the swimmer.

13. But what is so difficult for God to enter into death and into the depths of the human heart and there call the dead Adam forth to life? In our present world around us there are houses and mansions where human beings dwell. There are also places where wild animals, lions, dragons, and other poisonous beasts dwell. If, then, the sun, which is a mere creature, can equally enter through windows or doors into the dens of lions as well as the pits of reptiles and yet it comes out without being harmed, how much more God, the Lord of all, can enter into holes and dwelling-places where death is found and can enter also into human souls and there snatch Adam without receiving any injury. The rain also falls from the heavens and penetrates all the parts of the earth where it moistens and renews the dried roots and gives them new life.

14. A certain person may enter into conflict and war with Satan and endure affliction. He has a contrite heart. He holds himself in serious concern, sorrow, and tears. Such a person lives in a double tension. Thus he perseveres resolutely in such pursuits and the Lord is present to him in battle and keeps him steady, because he ardently seeks him and knocks at the door until he opens it for him. If you see him as a brother, strong in battle, it is because grace sustains him. But a person who lacks such a foundation has no great fear of God. He lacks a contrite heart, has no fear, and does not discipline himself and his members against any inordinate spirit. Such a one still possesses a worldly attitude. He has not yet entered into the battle. Therefore, the first one has really entered into a war and afflictions, while the second one is still quite ignorant of what it means to fight as a soldier. Even the seeds cast into the earth have to undergo afflictions from frost, winter, and cold temperature, but finally in due season new life springs forth.

15. It sometimes happens that Satan carries on a dialogue within your heart, such as: "See what great evils you have committed; see how your soul is full of so many follies. See how you are weighed down by sins so that you can hardly expect to be saved." These things he does to lead you to despair, thinking that your repentance has not been acceptable. For since evil through transgression entered into man's heart, afterward evil argues day and night with the soul, as a man to a man. But you answer him in this way: "I have the Lord's testimonies in Scripture:

'I do not wish the death of sinners but their repentance so that the sinner himself may turn from his wicked way and live' " (Ez 33:11).

For this reason the Lord descended so that he might save sinners, raise up the dead, and bring new life to those wounded by death and to enlighten those who lay in darkness. The Lord truly came and called us to be God's adopted sons, to enter into a holy city, ever at peace, to possess a life that will endure forever, to share an incorruptible glory. Let us singly strive to come to a good end after a good beginning. Let us persevere in poverty, in our pilgrimage, living in affliction and petitions to God without any shame as we continuously knock at the door.

As near as the body is to the soul in intimate interrelationship, so much nearer is God who is present to come and open the locked doors of our heart and to fill us with heavenly riches. He is, indeed, good and he loves mankind. His promises cannot deceive, provided we only persevere to the end, zealously seeking him. Glory be to the compassionate mercies of the Father and the Son and the Holy Spirit forever. Amen.

HOMILY 12

The state of Adam before he transgressed the commandment of God and after he lost his natural and his heavenly image. The homily also treats of certain very useful questions.

1. Adam, when he transgressed the commandment, lost two things. First he lost the pure possession of his nature, so lovely, created according to the image and likeness of God. Second, he lost the very image itself in which was laid up for him, according to God's promise, the full heavenly inheritance. Take the example of a coin bearing the image of the king. If it were mixed with a false alloy and lost its gold content, the image also would lose its value. Such, indeed, happened to Adam. A very great richness and inheritance was prepared for him. It was as though there were a large estate and it possessed many sources of income. It had a fruitful vineyard; there were fertile fields, flocks, gold and silver. Such was the vessel of Adam before his disobedience like a very valuable estate. When, however, he entertained evil intentions and thoughts, he lost God.

2. We nevertheless do not say that he was totally lost and was blotted out of existence and died. He died as far as his relationship with God was concerned, but in his nature, however, he still lives.[41] For look,

97

the whole world still walks on the earth and carries on its business. But God's eyes see their very minds and thoughts and, as it were, he disregards them and has no communion with them, because nothing that they think is pleasing to God.

If there exist houses of prostitution and ill-fame in which all sorts of immoral debaucheries go on and religious people should pass by them, would they not loathe such places? Seeing them, they would in a way refuse to see them (for such places for them are dead). So also God looks upon those who have turned away from his word and commandment, and yet he passes beyond them and has no communication with them, nor does the Lord find peaceful pleasure in their thoughts.

3. *Question:* How can anyone be poor in spirit, especially when he has a new interior awareness that he has changed and made progress and has obtained a knowledge and understanding that he did not possess before?

Response: Until a person acquires such and makes progress in perfection, he is not poor in spirit, but he will always entertain certain opinions about himself and his worth. But when he arrives at such understanding and progress, grace itself teaches him that he is really righteous and God's elect, never thinking himself to be anything, but holding himself in a lowly and humble attitude as one knowing or having nothing, even though he does know and does have much.

This is, as it were, natural and imprinted in the mind. Do you not see that Abraham, our first father, when he was God's chosen one, still called himself earth and ashes (Gn 18:27)? And David, anointed to be king, had God with him (1 Sm 16:13), and yet what does he say? "I am a worm and no man, the very scorn of men and the outcast of the people" (Ps 22:6).

4. Those who wish to be co-heirs with such as these and fellow-citizens of the heavenly city and to be glorified with them ought to excel in the same humility of spirit and not regard themselves as anything in themselves, but they ought to have a contrite heart. For although grace works in individual Christians in diverse ways and has different members, yet all are of the same city, of the same mind, of one tongue, mutually recognizing one another.

Just as in the human body there are many members, even though there is one soul animating all, so there is only one Spirit working in diverse ways, yet they are all of the same city and of one way. For all the just have walked the straight and narrow path, suffering persecution, affliction, and insults and "living in goatskins, in dens and caves of the earth" (Heb 11:37). The Apostles too right to this present moment say: "And we both hunger and thirst and are naked and are reviled and live with no fixed abode" (1 Cor 4:11). Some of them were beheaded while others were crucified and still others were afflicted in various ways. Moreover, did not the Lord of the prophets and Apostles himself live on this earth as though he had forgotten his divine glory? He was made an example for us. In greatest mockery he wore a crown of thorns on his head. He bore the spittings, the buffets, and the cross.

5. If God so lived on earth, then it will become you to imitate him. And if the Apostles and prophets so lived, we also, if we only would wish to be built on the foundation of the Lord and the Apostles, ought to imitate them. For the Apostle says through the Holy Spirit: "Be imitators of me as I am of Christ" (1 Cor 11:1). But if you seek the glory of men and wish to be bowed down to, and you desire the pleasures of the flesh, you have swerved from the way. You must be crucified with the Crucified (Rom 8:17), to suffer with him that suffered, so that you may be glorified with him glorified. The bride must suffer with the Bridegroom and so become partner and co-heir with Christ. It is in no way possible except through afflictions, through the rough, narrow, and straight way to pass into the city of the saints and there to rest and reign with the King forever and ever.

6. *Question:* Since Adam lost his own image and also that heavenly image, therefore, if he shared in the heavenly image, did he have the Holy Spirit?

Answer: As long as the Word of God was with him, he possessed everything. For the Word himself was his inheritance, his covering, and a glory that was his defense (Is 4:5). He was his teaching. For he taught him how to give names to all things: "Give this the name of heaven, that the sun; this the moon; that earth; this a bird; that a beast; that a tree." As he was instructed, so he named them.

7. *Question:* Did he have an experience and fellowship of the Holy Spirit?

Answer: The Word himself was with him and was everything to him: both knowledge and experience and inheritance and teaching. For what does John say of the Word? "In the beginning was the Word" (Jn 1:1). You see that the Word was in all things. If there were given to him exteriorly a certain glory, let us not take offense because of this since it says: "They were naked" (Gn 3:25) and that they did not look at each other. But after they transgressed the command, then they saw themselves as naked and they were covered with shame.

8. *Question:* Then, before this were they covered with God's glory in place of clothing?

Answer: Just as in the case of the prophets the Spirit worked in them and instructed them and dwelled within them and appeared outwardly to them, so also in the case of Adam. The Spirit, when he wished, was with him and taught and guided him: "Give such and such a name, call it such and such." The Word was everything to him and, as long as he obeyed his commands, he was pleasing to God. And yet why should it be thought strange that, living in this state, he still transgressed the command? Those who are filled with the Holy Spirit still entertain natural thoughts and possess free will to give consent to such. So also Adam, even when he was with God in Paradise, of his own free will transgressed the command and obeyed his darker side. And yet, even after the fall, he had knowledge.

9. *Question:* What kind of knowledge?

Answer: Take the example of a robber who is apprehended and brought to court. The accusation begins with the judge saying to him: "When you committed those crimes, did you not know that you could be caught and sentenced to capital punishment?" That criminal does not dare to say: "I was ignorant." For he knew, and when he is given a sentence he recalls all and confesses his guilt. Likewise the fornicator, does he not know that he is doing wrong? And the thief, does he not know he is sinning? Thus even without Scripture, solely by their natural reason, do not men know that God exists? They cannot, therefore, in that day of judgment say: "We did not know there was a God." For God speaks out to them in the thunder of the sky and the lightning: "Do you not know that God exists who rules all creatures?"[42]

Why, then, did the demons cry out: "You are the Son of God. Why have you come to torment us before the time?" (Mk 3:11). Above all, in their agonizing torments they even say: "You burn me! You burn me!" They did not, therefore, know the tree of the knowledge of good and evil. The fall of Adam brought such knowledge.

10. Everyone begins to ask: "In what state was Adam and what did he do?" Adam himself received the knowledge of good and evil. For one thing we hear from Scripture that he possessed honor and purity, but when he fell, he was cast out of Paradise and God was angry with him. In this way he learns what is good and wholesome for him. Having learned what was to his misfortune, he now is cautious not to sin further and thus fall into death's condemnation. We know, therefore, that every creature of God is under his dominion. For he himself has made heaven

and earth, the animals, reptiles, the beasts that we see, but whose number we cannot know. Who among men knows? Only God himself knows who is in all things, even in the not yet perfectly formed embryos of animals. Does he himself not know all things under the earth and above the heavens?

11. Let us, therefore, set aside such matters and seek rather, as skilled merchants, to possess the heavenly inheritance and those things that are of profit to our soul. Let us learn to lay hold of the good possessions that will remain always with us. But if man were to begin to investigate the mind of God and say: "I have discovered something and really understand it," the human mind would be found transcending the mind of God. Truly you wander far into error in such thinking. For the more you wish through knowledge to search and penetrate God, the more deeply you descend away from him and you comprehend nothing.

Those visits of God to you that happen each day, they are so mysterious and incomprehensible. You can receive them only with gratitude and belief. Have you been able to know your own soul from the moment of your birth until now? Tell me, then, from morning to night what are the thoughts that spring up in you? Tell me your thoughts over three consecutive days. If, then, you cannot understand the thoughts of your own soul, how can you scrutinize the thoughts of God and his very mind?

12. Truly, eat as much bread as you find and let go of the rest of the whole world. Go to the shore of the river and drink as much as you need and continue on your way, not worrying about the river's source or how it flows. Take pains to have your foot healed or the disease of your eye so that you may see the light of the sun. But do not investigate curiously how much light the sun contains or how high it ascends. Take whatever is given for your use. And why do you climb the mountain to find out how many wild asses or other beasts pasture there? And the baby, when it sucks the breasts of the mother, drinks of the milk and is nourished. But it does not know how to investigate the source or the well-spring from which the milk flows. For it sucks the milk and empties the whole breast. And again in an hour the breast is full. How this is done escapes the knowledge of the baby and also the mother, even though truly the milk comes from her whole being. If, then, you seek the Lord in the depths, there you will find him, "doing wonders" (Ex 15:11). If you seek him in caves, there you will find him in the midst of two lions, guarding the just Daniel. If you seek him in fire, there you will find him, a source of help to his servants. If you seek him in the mountain, there

you will discover him with Elijah and Moses. He is, therefore, everywhere, both under the earth and above the heavens and also indwelling us. He is everywhere. So also your soul is near you, within you, and outside of you. For wherever you wish to be, in remote countries, there your mind can be also found, either eastward or westward or heavenly.

13. Let us, then, strive above all to have the brand and the seal of the Lord in us,[43] because in the day of judgment, when "the severity of God" (Rom 11:22) is shown, and all the tribes of the earth, of the entire offspring of Adam, are gathered together, when the Shepherd will summon his flock, then whoever will possess the brand will recognize their own Shepherd. And the Shepherd recognizes those who carry his own seal and he will gather them together from all the nations.

Those hear his voice who belong to him, and they follow after him (Jn 10:3). For the world is divided into two parts. One flock of sheep is darkness and this group departs into inextinguishable and eternal fire. But the other flock is full of light and this is led into the heavenly inheritance. That which we now possess in our souls, that same then will shine in splendor and will be manifested and will clothe our bodies with glory.

14. Just as in the month of Xanthicus [April] the roots that have been covered by soil now put forth their own fruits, their flowers and beauties. The good roots become manifest as well as those that have thorns. Likewise in that day of judgment, everyone shows openly what he has done in the body. Both the evil and the good deeds will be manifested. For there will indeed be a universal judgment and retribution.

There is another kind of food different from what is seen. For Moses, when he climbed the mountain, fasted for forty days. He went up as a mere man; he descended, carrying God with him. And look, we see this verified in us. After the space of a very few days, unless our bodies are sustained by nourishment, they would die. But Moses after fasting forty days descended even stronger than all of the others. For he was nourished by God and his body was sustained by another, heavenly food. Indeed, the Word of God was his food and he had a glory shining on his countenance. All this, which happened to him, was a figure of something else. For that glory now shines splendidly from within the hearts of Christians. At the resurrection their bodies, as they rise, will be covered with another vesture, one that is divine, and they will be nourished with a heavenly food.

15. *Question:* What is the meaning of the saying: "A woman praying with her head uncovered?" (1 Cor 11:5)

Answer: Because in the times of the Apostles, women wore their hair loose for a covering. For this reason the Lord and his Apostles came into the created world to teach it modesty. Truly woman is a type standing for the Church. Just as in that time in the visible world women wore their hair loosely as a covering, so the Church clothes her children and wraps them in divine and glorious garments. And in the ancient times of the Church of Israel the congregation was one and it was covered by the Spirit. And they were clothed with the Spirit as with a glory, even though they did not correspond with the Spirit. Therefore, the word "church" is said of many individuals as well as of one soul. For the soul brings together all the thoughts and is thus a church to God. For the soul is by nature suited for fellowship with the heavenly Spouse and mingles with the heavenly One. This truly can be applied, not only to man, but also to the individual. Concerning Jerusalem the Prophet says: "I found you, deserted and stripped and I clothed you" (Ez 16:6), and so forth, as if he were speaking of a single person.

16. *Question:* What is the meaning of Martha saying to the Lord about Mary: "I am busy about many things and here she sits at your feet" (Lk 10:41)?

Answer: What Mary ought to have said to Martha, the Lord, anticipating her remark, said to her—that Mary had left everything to sit at the feet of the Lord and to bless God throughout the whole day. You see, the value of her sitting came from her love. To understand more clearly God's Word, listen. If anyone loves Jesus and really gives oneself attentively to him and not in a superficial way, but also perseveres in love, God is already planning to reward that soul for that love, even though the person does not know what he is about to receive or what portion God is about to bestow on him. Indeed, when Mary loved Jesus and sat at his feet, Jesus did not merely place himself alongside her, but he endowed her with a certain hidden power from his very own being. For the words which God spoke to Mary in peace were in-breathing and of a certain power. And these words penetrated her heart and brought his soul to her soul, his Spirit to her spirit, and a divine power filled her heart. That power necessarily, wherever it is released, remains there as a possession which cannot be taken away. For this reason the Lord, who knew what he had given to Mary, said: "Mary has chosen the good part" (Lk 10:42). But not long after, the works of service, that Martha kindly performed, brought her also to that gift of grace. She also received the divine power in her soul.

17. And what indeed can be so surprising if those who came to the Lord and were intimately associated with him received his power as we see when the Apostles preached the Word of God and the Spirit fell upon those believers? Cornelius received power from the Word of God when he heard it. How much more in the case of the Lord speaking with Mary or Zacchaeus or to the sinful woman who let her hair down and wiped the feet of the Lord, or with the Samaritan woman or the good thief—did not power go out and the Holy Spirit mingle with the souls?

Now those who pursue God in love, having abandoned everything else, and who persevere in prayer, are taught secretly things they had not known before. For truth itself comes to them according to their desire and it teaches them. "I am the truth" (Jn 14:6). Even the Apostles themselves, before the crucifixion, staying close to the Lord, saw great miracles, namely, how lepers were cleansed and the dead raised to life. But they did not yet know how the divine power operates or ministers in the heart. They did not yet know that they had to be reborn spiritually and be joined with the heavenly soul and become a new creature. Because of the signs that he performed, they loved the Lord. But the Lord told them: "Why do you marvel at such signs? I give you a great inheritance which the whole world does not possess."

18. However, these words were strange to them until he arose from the dead and ascended with his body into heaven for us. And then the Spirit, the Comforter, entered and mingled with them. The Truth in person shows himself to the faithful. And the heavenly Man walks with you and forms one fellowship. Whoever, therefore, dedicate themselves to different forms of service and eagerly perform all such activities, motivated by zeal, faith, and love of God, that very service, after a while, leads them to a knowledge of truth itself. For the Lord appears to their souls and teaches them how the Holy Spirit operates. Glory and adoration to the Father and the Son and the Holy Spirit forever. Amen.

HOMILY 13

What is the fruit God expects of Christians?

All visible things God created, and gave them to men for recreation and enjoyment, and he gave them also a law of justice. But ever since

Christ's coming, God demands other fruit and another righteousness, namely, a purity of heart, a good conscience, profitable speech, holy and good thoughts, and all the works of the saints. For the Lord says: "Unless your righteousness exceeds that of the Scribes and Pharisees, you cannot enter into the Kingdom of Heaven. It is written in the Law: Do not commit adultery. But I tell you. Do not lust or be angry" (Mt 5:20 ff.). For it is necessary that he who truly desires to be a friend of God keep himself from the mire of sin, but for the eternal fire which is in us.[44] This makes us worthy of the kingdom. Glory to his mercy and to his propitious will toward us, Father and Son and Holy Spirit. Amen.

HOMILY 14

This deals with those who turn over their thoughts and mind to God. This they do in the hope of having the eyes of their heart illumined. How God esteems them worthy to receive mysteries in the greatest sanctity and purity and he makes them participators in his grace. What we ought to do if we seek to obtain heavenly good things. Finally, the apostles and prophets are compared to the rays of the sun coming through a window. This homily also teaches what is the land of Satan and what is of the angels and that both of these are intangible and invisible.

1. All the works, visibly done in this world, are done out of a certain hope of enjoying one's labors and unless anyone is fully convinced that he will profit from his labors, he would see no advantage in doing them. For the farmer sows seeds in the hope of fruit and he undergoes toils on account of what he expects to receive. St. Paul says: "In hope he who plows ought to plow. And who has taken a wife does so in the hope of having offspring" (1 Cor 9:10). A merchant also exposes himself to the perils of the sea and to most imminent death, all for the sake of profit. So also in the Kingdom of Heaven—in the hope of having the eyes of his heart illumined, a person gives himself up to seek the kingdom, putting aside all worldly pursuits, intent on prayers and supplications. He awaits the Lord's coming to manifest himself to him and cleanse him from sin that indwells him.

2. He does not rely solely on his own labors and style of life until he obtains the things he hopes for, until the Lord comes and dwells in him in the full experience and the working of the Spirit. When he has tasted the goodness of the Lord and delighted in the fruits of the Spirit

and the veil of darkness has been lifted and the light of Christ shines with splendor and brings about in him an unspeakable joy, then he will be completely satisfied in having with him the Lord in much love, as in the example of the merchant rejoicing when he makes a profit. Nonetheless, he undergoes many afflictions and he fears the thieving spirits of iniquity lest, becoming remiss, he may lose the fruit of his work before he obtain the heavenly kingdom, the Heavenly Jerusalem.

3. Let us, therefore, beg also of God that he would put on us, who have shed the old man, the heavenly Christ, even now, so that established in great joy and thus led by him, we may be granted the greatest tranquillity. For the Lord, who wishes to fill us with a taste of the kingdom, says: "Without me you can do nothing" (Jn 15:5). And still, by using the Apostles, he knew how to enlighten many others. Even though they were creatures, they fed their fellow-servants.[45] They taught them how to become a brother and a son of Christ to live in a more outstanding way than the rest of men, namely, they sanctified the very heart and mind, likewise the thoughts, so that men directed those to God. And thus God secretly bestows life and all their heartfelt needs and dedicates himself to them. For when a person surrenders to God his secret possessions, that is, his mind and thoughts, not occupying himself with any other matter or thought or distraction, but subjecting himself to a certain constraint, then the Lord makes him a sharer in his mysteries, in holiness and great purity. He also gives himself as heavenly food and spiritual drink.

4. Take the example of a man who has many possessions, servants, and children. He offers one kind of food to his servants, another kind to his children, born of his own seed, because the children are the heir of the father and they eat with him, namely, they are like to their father. So also Christ is that true Lord who has created all things and nourishes the evil and ungrateful. But he has begotten children, born of his own seed whom he has made participators of his grace. In them the Lord is formed and he nourishes them with a special refreshment, nourishment, food and drink that he does not give to other men. He also gives himself to them who relate to him as to their very own father, as the Lord says: "Whoever eats of my flesh and drinks of my blood, he remains in me and I in him and he will not see death" (Jn 6:56). Those who possess the true inheritance have been begotten as sons from the heavenly Father and they dwell in their Father's house, as the Lord says: "The servant does not abide in the house, but the son abides forever" (Jn 8:35).

5. If, therefore, we wish also to be born of the heavenly Father, we

ought to act in a more outstanding way than other people, namely, to show zeal, effort, and diligence, to love and speak well in conversation, to live in faith and in fear, as seeking to obtain only good things and to possess God by right of inheritance. "For the Lord is the portion of my inheritance and my cup" (Ps 16:5). And thus, when the Lord sees that good intention and our steadfastness, he shows forth his mercy and cleanses us by the heavenly Word. He calls to new life dead and lost minds through the good example and teaching of his own apostles. Take the example of seeds of wheat or barley that are creatures protected by clouds. The rains also and the sun call them into life when they are so commanded. Like light which enters through the window and the sun which extends throughout the whole world its rays, so the prophets were lights to their own proper house of Israel. The Apostles also were suns, sending off rays in every part of the whole world.

6. There is, therefore, one earth on which four-legged animals dwell and there is also an "earth" in the air where the birds walk and live. If the birds wish to stand or walk on the earth, there are hunters who catch them. There is also an "earth" for fish, namely, the water of the sea. Wherever one is born, whether on land or in the air, there each creature sojourns and finds its nourishment and rest.

There is also a land that is the homeland of Satan where the powers of darkness and the spirits of evil dwell and walk about and find their rest. There likewise is a land, luminous with the Godhead, where the camps and armies of angels and holy spirits walk about and find their rest. But the darksome world is invisible to human eyes nor can it be touched by the senses. Neither can the luminous world of the Godhead be touched or seen with physical eyes. But to those who are spiritual, namely, who see with the eyes of the heart, both the world of Satan and darkness and also the world of divine light lie revealed.

7. There is a secular fable that describes certain mountains which are fiery because there is a permanent fire within them. There are found animals that look like sheep. Hunters who try to capture them make iron wheels and fashion hooks that they heat in fire because those animals eat fire as their food, their pleasure, their growth, their life. Fire is everything to them. If you put them in another environment, they die. Their coats, if they become dirtied, are not washed by water but by fire and they become even purer and whiter. So also Christians have that heavenly fire as their food. It is their pleasure. It purges, washes, and sanctifies their heart. It gives them growth. It is their air and their life. If they leave that, they are killed by the evil spirits, as the animals in the fable die

if they leave the fire, or as fish that leave water or the four-legged animals suffocate if thrown into the sea. As the birds walking on the earth are captured by the hunters, so also the human being that will not stay on that earth suffocates and dies. If such a one does not have that divine fire for his food, drink, clothing, and purification of his heart and the sanctification of his soul, he is taken captive by evil spirits and dies. We, however, should zealously ask ourselves whether we have been sown in that invisible earth and planted in the heavenly vineyard. Glory be to his mercies for all eternity. Amen.

HOMILY 15

This homily teaches through many ways how a soul ought to conduct herself in holiness, chastity, and purity toward her Spouse, Christ Jesus, the Savior of the world. It touches also on certain questions, namely, whether in the resurrection all the members are raised up and other questions on evil, grace, free will, and the dignity of human nature.

1.   Take the example of a certain, very wealthy man, a noble king. He sets his eyes on a poor woman who possesses nothing other than her own being. He falls in love with her and wishes to take her as his spouse and wife. If she bestows on him all kindness and continues to show love for him, behold, that poor and indigent woman, who possessed nothing, now becomes the lady of the house of all the possessions of her husband. If, however, she should act contrary to decorum and her state of life and should act in an unbecoming manner in the house of her husband, she then is cast out with shame and insults heaped upon her as she covers her head with her two hands, just as it is said figuratively of the disobedient woman who is no longer of service to her husband. Then she suffers sorrow and the greatest grief as she considers what riches befell her and what glory she has lost as she is held in contempt because of her stupidity.

2.   So also a person whom Christ, the heavenly Spouse, has asked to be his bride in a mystical and divine fellowship. Such a one has tasted the heavenly riches and ought with great diligence to strive sincerely to please the Bridegroom, Christ. This person ought faithfully to fulfill the service entrusted by the Spirit so as to please God in all things and never to grieve the Spirit in any matter. Such a person should display properly

an outstanding modesty and love toward him and behave becomingly in the house of the heavenly King and become pleasing and acceptable to him in all things according to grace received. Behold, such a person is made like the woman of the household over all the goods of the Lord. And even the splendor of his Godhead touches her body. But if she fails and acts unbecomingly in his service and does not do the things that please the Lord nor obey his will nor cooperate with the grace of the Spirit indwelling her, then she is stripped of honor with shame and indignity and is deprived of life as being useless and hardly suited for the fellowship of the heavenly King. Then that person experiences sadness and sorrow. There is weeping among all the holy, invisible spirits. The angels, powers, Apostles, prophets, martyrs, weep over such a person.

3. Just as "there is joy in Heaven over one sinner who repents," as the Lord said (Lk 15:7), so is there great sadness in Heaven over one person that falls away from eternal life. As on earth, when a rich man dies, he is led out of life with mournful music, lamentation, and wailing from his brothers, relatives, friends, and servants, so also all the saints mourn over such a person with lamentation and plaintive music. The Scriptures allude in various places to this in oblique language saying: "The pine has fallen, mourn, you cedars" (Zec 11:2). It is like the people Israel, who seemed to please the Lord, even though it was not fully as they ought. They had a pillar of cloud to overshadow them and a pillar of fire to enlighten them. They saw the sea divide before their eyes and witnessed clear water erupt from the rock (Ex 14:19). But after their mind willfully turned away from God, then they were handed over to serpents or to their enemies and were taken captive and sent into most miserable exile and suffered bitter servitude. The same applies also to our souls. This very same thing the Spirit mystically declares through the prophet Ezekiel, as he spoke of Jerusalem: "I found you stripped in the desert and I washed you of your impurity with water and I clothed you with a garment and I put bracelets on your hands and necklaces around your neck and earrings in your ears. And you became famous among all the Gentiles. Pure flour and oil and honey you ate. And after all this ultimately you forgot my kindness. You went after your lovers and committed fornication with shame" (Ex 16:6 ff.).

4. So also the person who knows God through grace is warned by the Spirit. Such a one had been cleansed of former sins and adorned with the ornaments of the Holy Spirit and had been made a participator of divine and heavenly food, but yet does not behave in a fitting way with great thoughtfulness. She does not properly persevere in a becoming

good will and love toward the heavenly Bridegroom, Christ, and so is cast out and deprived of life of which she once was made a participator.

For Satan has power against those who have arrived at these levels to rise up and attack them. And also evil attacks those who have known God in grace and power and tries to unarm them. We must, therefore, strive and be prudently attentive "to work out our own salvation with fear," as it is written (Phil 2:12). All you who have been made participators of the Spirit of Christ, may you not behave in any matter either small or great in a contemptible way, nor hold these things in contempt nor treat the grace of the Spirit with abuse so as not to be deprived of life of which you have already been made participators.

5. Let me say this same thing using a different example. Suppose a servant enters a certain palace to take charge of the serving dishes. He uses what belongs to the king's goods, since he has come owning nothing, and he serves the king with the very dishes that belong to the king. In this matter he needs great prudence and judgment lest he serve something improperly by bringing one dish to the royal table instead of a different, proper one. He should observe the proper order, serving the courses, from the first to the last in order. If through ignorance or lack of judgment he should serve the king not according to proper order, he places himself in danger of death. So also a person who serves God in grace and the Spirit requires exact discernment and knowledge so as not to err in using the divine vessels, that is, in the spiritual service, by not keeping his own will in harmony with grace. For it is possible that even in spiritual service, performed secretly by the interior man, a person can serve the Lord with his own vessels, that is, by his own spirit. But it is impossible that anyone can serve God not using God's vessels, which means without grace, and still seek to please him in all God's will.

6. But when one receives grace, there is then need for the greatest prudence and discernment. God gives these to the person that asks him for them so that he may serve God in the Spirit whom he receives, and also that he may not be conquered by evil and be deceived, led astray through ignorance, presumption, and carelessness by acting against all that the Lord wills. Punishment, death, and grief will be such a person's portion. The holy Apostle said this: "Lest, when I have preached to others, I myself should be rejected" (1 Cor 9:27). Do you see what fear he had, even though he was an Apostle of God? Let us, therefore, implore God so that we may prove to be servants of the Spirit according to his will in an exceptional way, we who have been made participators of divine grace. May we not live with a disposition of contempt so that we

may live a life most pleasing to God and may serve him with spiritual dedication according to his will and thus we may obtain the inheritance of eternal life.

7. If anyone is burdened with a sickness, it is, nevertheless, possible that he may have certain of his members sound and healthy, for example, his vision or some other faculty, while the rest of his members are weak. So also in the spiritual life. It is possible that someone may be healthy in three areas of his spirit, but he is not perfect just because of this. You see how many stages and ways of the Spirit's acting there are. Evil is cut out little by little and diminished, not all at once. All things that exist come about by divine providence and economy, both the rising of the sun as well as all creatures, all exist for the kingdom, which the elect die to possess by right of inheritance, so that they may make up the kingdom of peace and harmony.

8. Christians, therefore, should strive in all things and ought not to pass judgment of any kind on anyone, neither on the prostitute nor on sinners nor on disorderly persons. But they should look upon all persons with a single mind and a pure eye, so that it may be for such a person almost a natural and fixed attitude never to despise or judge or abhor anyone or to divide people according to categories. If you see a man with one eye, do not make any judgment in your heart, but regard him as though he were whole. If someone has a maimed hand, see him not as maimed. See the crippled as straight, the paralytic as healthy. For this is purity of heart, that, when you see the sinners and the weak, you have compassion and show mercy toward them. For it can happen that the holy ones of the Lord sit as though they were in the theater, watching the follies of the world, but in the interior they are conversing with God. According to their exterior they seem to be looking with their eyes at the things of the world.

9. Worldly-minded persons move by another power, one of error, as they eagerly thirst for the things of the earth. But Christians are motivated by another attitude, another mind. They are of another world, another city. For the Spirit of God has fellowship with them and they crush the head of the adversary. It is written: "The last enemy to be destroyed is death" (1 Cor 15:26). For those who venerate God are masters of all things. But, on the contrary, those who are slack in faith and live in sin are completely enslaved. The fire burns them and the stone and sword kill them and finally the demons will conquer over them.

10. *Question:* In the resurrection will all members rise?

Answer: To God all things are easy and thus he has promised it, even though to human weakness and thought this seems impossible. For just as God took from dust and the earth and created the human body as a completely unique nature, not at all like the earth, and he created many other kinds of parts such as hair, skin, bones, and nerves, and just as a needle that is put into a fire is changed in color, becoming like the fire, yet retaining its own nature as iron, so also in the resurrection all members will rise. "Not a hair will perish" (Lk 21:18; Mk 9:49), as it is written. All things will become light. All are immersed in light and fire and are indeed changed, but are not, as certain people say, dissolved and transformed into fire so that nothing of their nature remains. For Peter is Peter, and Paul, Paul, and Philip is Philip. Each person in his own unique nature and personality remains, yet filled by the Spirit. But if you say that the nature is dissolved, then there is no more Peter or Paul but God is alone and everywhere. Then those in hell feel no punishment and those in the kingdom receive no reward.[46]

11. It is like a garden with various fruit-bearing trees. There is a pear tree, an apple tree, and grapevines with fruit and leaves. It can happen that the garden and all the trees and leaves can be changed and transformed into another nature. The former things now are made into light. So also humans are changed in the resurrection and their members are made holy and full of light.

12. Men of God, therefore, ought to prepare themselves for the struggle and battle. As the young athlete in the wrestling bout learns to accept the blows that come upon him and he strikes back, so Christians ought to learn to bear afflictions, both exterior and those interior wars so that, when struck, they may rise to higher victories through endurance. That is, indeed, the way of the Christian religion. Where the Holy Spirit is, there follows, as a shadow, persecution and struggle. You see how the prophets suffered persecution from all of their own compatriots, yet in all these the Spirit was working. You see how the Lord, who is the way and the truth (Jn 14:6), was not persecuted by a foreign people but by his own. He suffered persecution and was crucified by his own tribe of Israel. It was the same with the Apostles. From that time when Jesus was crucified, the Spirit, the Paraclete, passed the cross down through the ages to the Christians. Moreover, no Jew suffered persecution; the Christians alone suffered martyrdom. Because of this, Christians ought not to be surprised, for it is necessary that the truth undergo persecution.

13. *Question:* Certain people say that evil enters in from the outside and that if a person wishes, he need not accept it, but can reject it.

Answer: As the serpent spoke with Eve (Gn 3:5–6), and she obeyed, the serpent entered within, so too now, on account of man's obedience, sin (which is from outside) enters in. For sin has full power and liberty to enter into the human heart. The Apostle says: "I will that men pray without anger and evil thoughts" (1 Tm 2:8). "For thoughts proceed from out of the heart" (Mt 15:19), according to the Gospel. Go, therefore, to prayer and examine your heart and mind and desire to pour out to God your prayer as pure. And see to it that there be nothing of hindrance preventing your prayer from being pure, from your mind being totally occupied with the Lord, just as the concentration of the farmer is centered on his farming, the married man's concern with his wife, the merchant with his business. Let nothing prevent you from bending your knees in prayer and not allowing others to distract your thoughts.

14. But you say, after he came by means of the cross: "The Lord has condemned sin" (Rom 8:3), and that it no longer remains within. It is similar in this example to a soldier who puts up his chariot at the home of another. When he pleases, he has access of entering and leaving that home. So also sin has the power of conversing within the human heart. For it is written: "Satan entered into the heart of Judas" (Lk 22:3). But if you insist that through the coming of Christ sin was condemned and that after Baptism evil has no more power of suggestion within the human heart, then you ignore the fact that from the coming of the Lord up to this day the many who have been baptized, have they not, thought evil things at some time? Have not some of them turned to vain desire for glory, to fornication, or to gluttony? Moreover, are all those who live in the Church, men of the world, are they endowed with a pure and blameless heart? Or do we not find after Baptism that many commit many sins and many live in error? So, even after Baptism the thief freely enters and does what he pleases.

15. It is written: "Love the Lord your God with all your heart" (Dt 6:5, 15:19). But do you remember him constantly and have a passionate love and burning desire directed always toward the Lord? Are you night and day bound fast to him? If you have such a love, then you are pure. But if you have less a love, then ask yourself whether earthly pursuits or vile and evil thoughts absorb your attention, or whether your soul is drawn always toward love and longing for God. For the thoughts of the

world drag the mind away toward worldly and corruptible things and do not permit it to love God or to be mindful of the Lord. But very often the unlearned person goes to prayer and gets down on his knees and his mind enters into tranquillity. And as long as he digs and as deeply as he gets below the surface, the wall of evil, as an impeding obstacle, breaks down. He passes into vision and wisdom where the powerful ones or the wise or the orators cannot enter to comprehend or know the subtlety of his mind, since he is absorbed in divine mysteries. One hardly knows how to judge the value of pearls nor give a price to them simply because he lacks any experience in such a matter. Wherefore Christians have nothing to do with the things of the world considered as of great value and regard them as dung (Phil 3:8) compared to the magnificence of those spiritual gifts, a magnificence that works powerfully in them.

16. *Question:* Can a man fall who has the gift of grace?[47]

Answer: If he is careless, he certainly falls. For the enemies never take a rest nor do they withdraw from the war. How much more you ought not to cease seeking God! For a very great loss comes to you if you are careless, even though you may seem to be confirmed in the very mystery of grace.

17. *Question:* Does grace remain after man's fall?

Answer: God desires to lead man back again to life and to encourage him to weep again and be converted. But if grace truly remains, it is to encourage man again to tears and repentance in order that he may repent because of those things by which he formerly sinned.

18. *Question:* Are those perfect ones threatened by affliction or battle or do they totally live in security?

Answer: The enemy never stops waging war against humanity. Satan is without mercy and hates humans. For this reason he never is hesitant to war against everyone. But he does not attack all in the same ways. Governors and noblemen pay their taxes to the king. Such men rely on their riches, their gold and silver. They take their taxes out of their abundance and suffer no loss. Just as a man who gives alms never considers it a setback, so also Satan considers these things superfluous. He lets some persons alone; they are no loss to him, who is so wealthy in possessing so many other persons as his own. But it is different with a poor man deprived even of daily bread. He is beaten and tortured since he is unable to pay the tax. He also is worn down by trials and is tortured and yet does not die. Another person, on account of only one word said, is ordered to be put to death and perishes.

So also among Christians, there are some who are vehemently attacked and beaten by sin and yet for all that they grow stronger and wiser even in the battle, as they scorn the power of the adversaries. They have no danger from this source because they are certain and firm in their salvation since they have trained well in the battle against vice and have learned by experience. Therefore, having God with them, they are under his direction and enjoy peace.[48]

19. But others, who have never received training, if they should encounter any trial and a battle ensues, fall at once into disarray and perdition. It is like travelers to a city desirous to visit their friends and relatives. Although they encounter many people in the marketplaces, they are not detained by them, for their aim is to meet their friends. When they knock on the door outside and call, their friends open the door with joy. But if they loiter in the marketplaces and squares, they are distracted or detained by those they meet. The door is shut and no one opens to them. So those who are impelled to go forward toward the Lord, our Christ, the true Friend, ought to regard all other things as irrelevant and of little value.

Take the example of noblemen and governors who enter the palace to see the king. They greatly fear how they are to give an accounting lest they should make some mistake and incur being sentenced to trial and punishment. But simple country people, who have never seen a prince, have no worry. So it is with this world under the heavens, from kings to paupers. Since they are ignorant of Christ's glory, they are occupied with worldly matters. No one is quick to recall the divine judgment. But those who entertain thoughts that raise them to the judgment seat of Christ where his throne is and live continually in his sight are always in fear and trembling so as not in any way to fall away from his holy commandments.

20. Like the rich of this earth, they have brought much fruit to their barn. Still, every day they expend even greater labor to make their stored-up treasure even more abundant and to prevent any shortage. If they sit back and rely on the supplies stored up in the barn and neglect to bring forth more and they use up what they had stored up, they soon fall into poverty and dire want. For this reason they must strive and bring forth fruit by adding and increasing their harvest, so that they may not come under the yoke of poverty.

It is like this in Christianity for anyone who tastes the grace of God. For it says: "Taste and see how sweet the Lord is" (Ps 34:8). Such a taste is this power of the Spirit working to effect full certainty in faith which operates in the heart. For as many as are sons of light and in the service of the New Covenant through the Holy Spirit have nothing to learn from men. For they are taught by God. His very grace writes in their hearts the laws of the Spirit. They should not put all their trusting hope solely in the Scriptures written in ink. For divine grace writes on the "tables of the heart" (2 Cor 3:3) the laws of the Spirit and the heavenly mysteries. For the heart directs and governs all the other organs of the body. And when grace pastures the heart, it rules over all the members and the thoughts. For there, in the heart, the mind abides as well as all the thoughts of the soul and all its hopes.[49] This is how grace penetrates throughout all parts of the body.

21. So, on the contrary, as many as are sons of darkness, sin has control over their heart and infiltrates into all the members. "For out of the heart proceed evil thoughts" (Mt 15:19). And thus diffused throughout, sin covers humanity with darkness. Those who hold that evil is in no way born into man and does not grow are not worried about tomorrow nor are they led by any passionate desire. For a certain length of time evil stops molesting them, by suggesting a certain desire, so that such a one does not blush to affirm on oath that such a passion no longer bothers him. But after a short time he burns with lust so that he is guilty of perjury. Just as water runs through a pipe, so too sin runs through the heart and the thoughts. Those who deny these statements are refuted and ridiculed by sin itself, intent always on victory. For evil tries to hide itself and remain undetected in man's mind.

22. If, then, anyone loves God, God also shares his love with him. Once a person believes in him, God bestows on such a one a heavenly faith and so he becomes twofold. As you offer God any part of yourself, he himself shares with your soul similar aspects of his own being, so that all you do, you may do sincerely and purely, loving and praying in this same way. For great is the dignity of humanity. See how great are the heavens and the earth, the sun and the moon. But the Lord was not pleased to find his rest in them but in humanity alone. Man, therefore, is of greater value than all other creatures, and perhaps, I will not hesitate to say, not only visible creatures, but also those invisible, namely, "the ministering spirits" (Heb 1:14). For it was not of Michael or Gabriel, the archangels, that God said: "Let us make according to our image and likeness" (Gn 1:26), but he said it concerning the spiritual makeup of the human, I mean, the immortal soul. For it is written: "The ranks of angels of the Lord encamp round about those that fear him" (Ps 34:7). The visible creatures, therefore, are endowed with a certain unchangeable nature.

23. The heavens were once established, the sun, moon, and the earth, but in these creatures the Lord could not find lasting pleasure. They could not be other than what he created them to be. They had no will. You, however, for this reason are made according to the image and likeness of God. Insofar as God is his own Master and does what he wishes, if it seems right to him, with power and out of justice, he can send the just into hell and sinners into the kingdom, although he hardly wishes this, nor does it please him to do so. For God is just. So are you also your own master, and if you wish to perish, you are of a changeable nature.[50]

If you prefer to blaspheme, to concoct poisons and kill someone, no one opposes you or prevents you. If a person wishes, he may live for God and walk in the way of justice and conquer his passions. For the human mind which resists and struggles can conquer, with firm purpose, the impulses of vices and the evil passions.

24. Suppose that in a mansion in which there are many objects made of gold and silver, clothing of various kinds of gold and silver, the young men and women servants restrain their desires, even though human nature, because of indwelling sin, desires inordinately everything. Because they humanly fear their masters, they repress their driving concupiscences. How much more, where the fear of God is strong, ought a person to struggle and resist any inherent evil. For God has commanded what is possible for you to do. The nature of irrational animals is fixed and unchangeable. The nature of the serpent is to bite and to spew out poison. Therefore, all serpents are of one kind. The wolf is accustomed to be rapacious. Therefore, all wolves are of this same nature. The lamb is a gentle animal and a prey to marauders. Therefore, all lambs are of the same nature. The dove is guileless and harmless. All doves also are of the same nature. But a human being is not so. One person is a rapacious wolf and another, like a lamb, is a victim of marauders. Both come from the same human race.

25. One man is fed up with his wife and commits adultery. And another does not allow the slightest concupiscence to stir in his heart. One man steals his neighbor's goods, while another, moved by piety toward God, distributes all his goods. You can see how changeable is the nature of man, equally tending toward vice and, on the contrary, also toward good. In both cases man is capable of assenting to whatever actions he wishes. Human nature, therefore, is capable of both good and evil, either of divine grace or of the evil adversary. Man is in no way submitted to necessity.

117

Adam at the beginning lived in purity. He controlled his thoughts. But from the time that he transgressed the command of God, heavy mountains weighed upon his mind, and evil thoughts mingled with it and became completely a part of the mind, and yet this was not really man's mind by nature since such thoughts are tainted by evil.[51]

26. Therefore, you ought to seek a lamp to be lighted so as to find pure thoughts. Those are the natural thoughts which God has made.[52] They are like persons who are accustomed to the sea and have learned to swim. If storms and waves rise up, they do not panic. So it is with Christians. As the mind of a three-year-old child cannot follow or comprehend the mind of a perfect dialectician because of the difference in age, so also Christians look on this world with the eyes of children, despising its worldliness and seeing the presence of grace. They are strangers to this world. Their city and their rest are elsewhere. For Christians have the consolation of the spirit, tears, grief, and groaning. And the very tears are for them a source of delight. They have a fear along with joy and exultation. And so they are like men who carry in their hands their own blood, not trusting in themselves or thinking themselves to be anything special. But they are neglected, condemned, and rejected among all men.

27. Take the example of a king who entrusted his treasure to a certain poor person. He who receives the job of taking care of the treasure does not regard it as his own, but constantly recognizes his poverty, not daring to waste any of the other's treasure. He always keeps this in mind—not only that the treasure is another's, but above all it belongs to a king, a man of greatest power who entrusted it to him. Whenever it should please him, he can take it away from him.

So, in a similar way, ought those who have received divine grace consider themselves to be humble in thoughts and confess their own poverty. As in the case of the poor man who has received a treasure entrusted to him by the king, if he relies on someone else's treasure as though it were his own and becomes puffed up, the king will take it from him. And he who received the charge remains as he was before, a pauper. So also from those who have received grace. If they are puffed up and are filled with pride, the Lord will take his grace back and they will remain what they were before they had received grace from the Lord.

28. Truly, there are many who possess grace but do not perceive that they secretly are deprived of it by sin. Take the example of a certain young maid and young man working in a household. She is captured by

his unseemly words and consents to him. She commits fornication and loses her purity and is expelled. So that terrible serpent of sin is always present to the soul, enticing and provoking it. And if it consents, the spiritual soul communicates with the incorporeal evil of that spirit, that is, spirit enters into a fellowship with spirit, and he who commits adultery in his heart receives the suggestion of the most wicked one. This is the measure of your struggle, not to commit adultery in your thoughts, but to resist and to take up the interior war, and to battle and not to yield nor to delight in evil thoughts. And if the Lord finds in you such promptitude of mind, in the last day he will receive you into the Kingdom of Heaven.

29. For there are certain things which the Lord so directs that he cannot do without violating his own divine grace and election. And there are others that God governs by permitting in order that man may be tested and exercised and his free will may be manifested. Those oppressed by afflictions and temptations, if they bear them, will not fail to come into the Kingdom of Heaven. Therefore, Christians in hardships are not overcome by sadness or sorrow. If they are burdened by poverty or insults, they ought not to be surprised, but rather they should delight in poverty and consider it a richness. They should consider fasting a pleasure and ignominy which they accept as glory. On the other hand if they should receive in this life the better things which draw them to worldly ease, to riches, to glory, or to pleasures, they ought not to take pleasure in these but flee from them as though fleeing from fire.

30. Let us take this example. Suppose a small, insignificant nation wages war against a king. The latter is not greatly perturbed, but he sends his soldiers and officers and they carry on the war. But if it is a case of a great nation capable of overthrowing his kingdom, the king himself is forced with his servants and his army to enter into the war and with all possible forces to fight it. Look, therefore, at your dignity, namely, that God has put himself in motion with his army, the angels, I say, and his holy spirits, and has come in person to save you from death.

Stand firm, therefore, and think what providence has been working on your behalf. We take an example from human life since we still live in such a manner. Suppose a king came upon a certain poor person, very sick. He is not embarrassed to treat his wounds with healing medicines. And when he brings him to his palace, he clothes him with the royal purple and the diadem and shares his table with him. In a similar way the heavenly King, Christ, came to suffering man and healed him. He made him a companion at his royal table. And this he does, not by forcefully constraining man's will, but by attraction he establishes him in so great a dignity.

31. It is written in the Gospel: "The Master sent out his servants to call them who wish to come, inviting them: 'My banquet is ready.' But those who were called began to excuse themselves, one saying: 'I bought some span of oxen.' Another: 'I have married' " (Lk 14:16 ff.). You see, he was ready who called, but the invited refused. They themselves were alone responsible in the way they answered. Thus, so great is the dignity of Christians. Consider, the Lord has prepared for them the kingdom and has called them to enter, but they have refused. Concerning the gift which Christians will receive by way of their inheritance, one could rightly say that if anyone, from the time of Adam's creation to the end of the world, should battle against Satan and put up with afflictions, it would be nothing in comparison to the glory which he is to obtain. For he will reign forever together with Christ. Glory to him who so loved such a person that he gave himself and his grace and entrusted himself to him. Glory to his greatness!

32. According to all visible signs, all of us brethren seated here are endued universally with the one image and face of Adam. Is there also in secret and in the most interior matters one will among all of us? One heart? Will we, indeed, not all together be good and religious? Or truly, are there not certain among us who have fellowship with Christ and his angels while others have it with Satan and the demons while all the time all of us appear seated here as one? All of us bear the same countenance of Adam. Do you see how different is the intellectual life, namely, the interior man, from the exterior? For all of us appear to be as one, both those who are with Christ and his angels and those who are with Satan and his unclean spirits. There are, therefore, infinite depths to the human heart. There are found reception rooms, bedrooms, doors and antechambers, many offices and exits. There is found the office of justice and of injustice. There is death and there is life. There takes place upright business as well as the contrary.

33. Take the example of a great palace that is deserted and all kinds of stench and odors from many cadavers come out of it. So also the heart is the palace of Christ and it abounds with every kind of impurity and with great crowds of evil spirits. It is, therefore, necessary to repair and rebuild it; its storerooms and bedrooms must be cleaned up. For Christ the King with his angels and spirits is coming there so that he may find his rest, he may live and move about freely and set up his kingdom. I say

it is like a ship that is equipped with much equipment over which the captain rules and directs all the sailors, urging some on with correction, directing others. In the same way, the heart has a captain in the mind, the conscience, that tests the thoughts that accuse and defend. For it says: "Thoughts accusing or else excusing one another" (Rom 2:15).

34. You see that our conscience does not approve of thoughts of the kind that lead to sin, but immediately it sets judgment upon them. It does not lie because it witnessed to what it will say before God in the day of judgment like a constant judge. It is like a chariot. The reins, horses, and the whole apparatus are under one driver. When he wishes, he drives the chariot at a fast speed. When he wants, he stops it. Wherever he wishes to steer the chariot, there it goes. For the whole chariot is under the power of the driver. So also the heart has many natural faculties within itself, but the mind and the conscience admonish and direct the heart. And they wake up the natural faculties that spring up in the heart. For the soul, even though it is one, has many members.

35. From the time that Adam transgressed the command, the serpent entered and became master of the house and became like a second soul with the real soul.[53] For the Lord says: "Whosoever does not deny himself and hate his own soul is not my disciple" (Lk 14:26) and "He that loves his soul shall lose it" (Mt 10:39). Indeed, sin, after it entered into man's soul, became its members, adhering to the corporeal person and from this source there pour out from the heart many unclean thoughts. Wherefore, he who does the wish of his soul, does the wishes of evil, because it is so intimately connected and mixed with the soul. He who subjugates his soul and is irate with the innate passions is like one who has captured a city from his enemies. Such a person is deemed worthy to possess the good measure of the Spirit and is endowed by divine power with the pure man and transcends his very self. For such a one as this is made a participator of the divine nature (2 Pt 1:4) and made a son of God, receiving the heavenly stamp on his soul. For his chosen ones are anointed with the sanctifying oil and are raised up in great dignity to be kings.

36. For such is humanity's nature, that may be immersed in the depths of evil and be a slave to sin, yet it can still turn to good. One who is totally surrendered to the Holy Spirit and intoxicated with heavenly things is also capable of turning to evil. It is similar to a woman, clothed in tattered rags, starving and dirty. Not without much work does she reach a royal rank and put on the purple and the crown and become the spouse of the king. She may recall in memory her past filth and it may

come to her to turn back to that former state. But she, nevertheless, does not wish to return to her past, for that would be sheer stupidity. And it is similar to those who "have tasted the divine grace, have been made partakers of the Spirit" (Heb 6:4). Unless they are attentive, they can defect and even become worse than they were before when they were worldly-minded.

It is not that God is changeable or of a foolish mind or that the Holy Spirit is quenched, but the fact is that human beings themselves do not consent to grace and on account of this they go astray and fall into infinite sins. For those who have tasted that gift have both things in happy tension, namely, joy and consolation, fear and trembling, exultation and weeping. They mourn for themselves and the whole race of Adam because mankind is one. And tears are to them like bread and their compunction is like sweetness and repose.

37. If you should see a person puffed up by arrogance and pride because he is a participator of grace, and even if he should perform signs and should raise up the dead, if he, nevertheless, does not hold his soul as abject and humble and he does not consider himself poor in spirit and an object of abhorrence, he is being duped by evil and is ignorant. Granted he should perform signs, he is not to be trusted. For the sign of Christianity is this, that one be pleasing to God so as to seek to hide oneself from the eyes of men. And even if a person should possess the complete treasures of the King, he should hide them and say continually: "The treasure is not mine, but another has given it to me as a charge. For I am a beggar and when it pleases him, he can claim it from me." If anyone should say: "I am rich. I have enough. I possess goods. There is nothing more I need," such a person is not a Christian, but a vessel of deceit and of the devil. For the enjoyment of God is insatiable and the more anyone tastes and eats, the more he hungers. Persons of this kind have an ardor and love toward God that nothing can restrain. And the more they apply themselves to the art of growing in perfection, the more they reckon themselves as poor, as those in great need and possessing nothing. This is why they say: "I am not worthy that the sun shines its rays upon me." This is the sign of Christianity, namely, this very humility.

38. But if anyone should say: "I am content and full," that one is a deceiver and a liar. For as the body of the Lord was glorified when he climbed the mount and was transfigured into the divine glory and into infinite light, so also the bodies of the saints are glorified and shine like lightning. Just as the interior glory of Christ covered his body and shone completely, in the same way also in the saints the interior power of

Christ in them in that day will be poured out exteriorly upon their bodies. For even now at this time they are in their minds participators of his substance and nature. For it is written: "He that sanctifies and the one who is sanctified are of one" (Heb 2:11); and: "The glory that you have given me, I have given them" (Jn 17:22). Similarly, as many lamps are lighted from the one, same fire, so also it is necessary that the bodies of the saints, which are members of Christ, become the same which Christ himself is.

39. *Question:* In what way are Christians superior to the first Adam? Indeed, he was immortal and not only was he incorruptible in soul, but also in body. But Christians die and decompose.

Answer: The real death takes place interiorly in the heart. It lies hidden. The interior man perishes. If anyone, therefore, has passed from death into the hidden life, that one truly lives forever and does not die. For, granted that their bodies for a time are dissolved, at last, however, they are raised in glory. For they are sanctified. We say that the death of Christians is thus a sleep and a falling off into repose. But if the [Christian] man were immortal and incorruptible in his body, the whole world, seeing the strange happening, namely, that the bodies of Christians do not corrupt, would be won over to what is good by a certain necessity and not by a spontaneous desiring.

40. In order that man's free will which God gave to man from the beginning might more clearly be manifested and confirmed, a great providence is at work in this matter, and the dissolution of the bodies takes place so that it is a question of man's will choosing to embrace what is good or evil. For even the man confirmed in evil, or the one completely immersed in sin and making himself a vessel of the devil by whom he is totally bound, caught up in a certain necessity, still enjoys free will to become a chosen vessel (Acts 9:15), a vessel of life. Similarly, on the other hand, those who are intoxicated with God, even if they are full and dominated by the Holy Spirit, still are not bound by any necessity, but they possess free will to choose and do what pleases them in this life.

41. *Question:* Is evil gradually diminished and eradicated, and thus man makes progress in grace, or is evil uprooted immediately when he has had a spiritual experience?[54]

Answer: Take the example of the undeveloped infant in the womb. It does not immediately grow into a matured person but only gradually it receives the shape and is born, and even then is not perfect, but it grows gradually over many years and finally becomes a human. It is similar to barley and wheat seeds. They do not push forth roots immediately upon falling into the earth, but winters and rains pass over them and then at the convenient time the ears form. The same for the man who plants a pear tree. He does not immediately harvest fruit. So likewise also in spiritual things, where there is a question of so much wisdom and subtlety, man makes progress gradually "and reaches to a perfect man, to the full measure" (Eph 4:13), and not as some say: "To put off one garment and put on another."

42. Whoever wishes to distinguish himself in letters first starts with learning the alphabet. When he reaches the first place of that level, he moves on to Latin school and there he is the lowest of all. Again when he becomes top of that level, he enters debating school and again he is the last of all and a beginner. Then he becomes a "scholastic" and again he is the novice and the last of all the other lawyers. After he rises to be first in that area, he then becomes an official. After reaching the position of chief magistrate, he takes on an assistant assessor.

If, therefore, in worldly affairs a person makes progress in so many steps, how much more do the heavenly mysteries admit of progressions and allow increase through many stages, and then, through many testings and through many trials, one reaches perfection. For Christians, who truly have tasted of grace and have the sign of the cross in their mind and heart,[55] such, from kings to beggars, hold all things as dung and squalor. And they are able to understand that the whole earthly world—the treasures of a king and his riches and glory, the discourses of wisdom—are only an external form and have no solid foundation, but all will pass and disappear. And whatsoever lies under the heavens is easily held in contempt by them.

43. Why is this so? Because the things which are beyond the heavens are foreign and wonderful and are not found in the treasures of kings, nor in the wisdom of words, nor in worldly glory. And also because the dignities and riches that they possess who have the Lord and Creator of all things in their inner man are a possession that never will pass away, but will remain. Christians have known that the soul is by far more precious than all other creatures. Indeed, only man has been made according to the image and likeness of God. Behold the heavens, how vast! and also the earth! How precious are the creatures that inhabit them! And how great are some of their bodies! But man is, nonetheless, much more valuable than all of these bodies, since in him alone the Lord is pleased. The whales of the sea, the mountains and the beasts, in outward appearance far excel man in size. See, then, your dignity. How

precious you are that God has made you superior to the angels since he came on earth himself visibly present to help and redeem you.[56]

44. For when did the angels come to save you? Indeed, the King's Son held council with his Father and the Word was sent and took on flesh. He concealed his own divinity so that like may be saved by like. He laid down his life on the cross. So great was the love of God toward man! Immortal though he was, he chose for your sake to be nailed to the cross. Ponder, therefore, how ardently "God loved the world so as to give his only begotten Son for it" (Jn 3:16). "How shall he not with him freely give us all things?" (Rom 8:32). And again in another place it says: "Amen, I say to you that he shall set him as ruler over all his goods" (Mt 24:47).

Also in another place it shows that the angels are the ministers of the saints. For when Elijah was on the mountain and foreigners were rising up against him, his servant said: "Many are coming against us and we are all alone." Then Elijah answered: "Do you not see the armies and multitudes of angels with us surrounding us to aid us?" (2 Kgs 6:15 ff.). You see how the Master and the multitude of angels are standing by the side of their servants. How great, therefore, is the soul and with what great honors it has been gifted by God! Indeed, both God and the angels seek the human soul to share their fellowship and kingdom! But Satan and his powers seek it for their own purpose.

45. Just as in the visible world we see that kings are not served by peasants who watch sheep, but by well-groomed and well-instructed persons, so also in the heavenly palace, those who serve the heavenly King are those who are free of all fault and reproach and are pure of heart. As in the palace, the attractive maidens without blemish and reproach, namely, the most beautiful, are called to participate in the company of the king, so also in the spiritual palace, it is those who possess all manner of good virtues that enter into fellowship with the heavenly King.

In the visible order if a prince goes to stay at a certain house, if there should be anything in that household not clean, it is set aright with much housecleaning and the whole house is perfumed. How much more the house of the soul, in which the Lord finds his rest, needs ordering so that he may be able to enter and there rest, he, who is without any reproach, spot or blemish! In such a heart both God and the whole heavenly Church find rest.

46. In the visible order open to our eyes, if a certain father possesses any goods, including diamonds and precious stones, these he

hides in storerooms and sets them aside for his son as his inheritance. So God also has entrusted his possession with all his precious things to us humans.

Finally, in the temporal order in the case of a war, if a king comes with his army to do battle and his side is weaker in number and in strength, immediately he sends legates to sue for peace (Lk 14:32). But if it be a very great nation attacking an equally great nation, and king goes out against king (for example, the king of the Persians against the king of the Romans), it is absolutely necessary that these kings go out to war with their entire army and all their soldiers. Think, therefore, how great is your dignity since God has moved with his own army of angels and spirits to enter into battle with the adversary in order to redeem you from death. God, therefore, came for your sake.

47. What, for instance, if there were a king who came upon a certain pauper whose whole body was covered with leprosy. He would not be ashamed of him, but would apply medicine to his wounds and so heal his sores. And after that, he received him at his royal table, clothed him with purple and made him a king. In this way God also has shown himself to the human race. He washed their wounds and healed mankind and led them into the heavenly bedchamber. Therefore, very great is the dignity of Christians, so great, indeed, that there is nothing to compare with it. But if the Christian is aroused to defection and is done in by evil, he becomes like a city without walls which robbers invade from any part they wish, for there is absolutely no resisting force and they plunder it and set it on fire. Thus, while you are neglecting yourself and hardly taking stock of yourself, the evil spirits enter into you and destroy and lay barren your mind, dissipating your thoughts on things of this world.

48. Many people, who are experts in some field or other of knowledge and pursue science and are conscientious about proper living, think that this makes for perfection. They do not examine the heart, failing to see how evil binds up the soul. Even if the mind is interior, evil flows throughout, sending roots into all the other members. The robber, that is, the opposing power, has entered the household. It is an opposing, even hidden power. And unless one enters into war against sin, gradually the hidden, inner evil spreads by multiplying itself and leads man to commit deliberate sins. For evil is continually bubbling up like the center of a fountain. Therefore, take diligent care so as to block up the rivers of evil, lest you should fall into an infinite amount of evil and become as one in a stupor.

It is like some nobleman who throws aside all caution and lives in affluence. The officers of the prince and those who serve warrants arrest him and bring him to the prince, saying: "You are accused of a serious crime and your head is in danger." From fear at such news, he loses all his thoughts and shudders as one struck with stupor.

49. Think that it is the same way with the evil spirits. For the world evident to your gaze, from kings to the weakest, is all in tumult, confusion, and battle, and no one knows the cause of it, nor do they understand that it is an unveiling of the evil which entered in through Adam's disobedience, "the sting of death" (1 Cor 15:56). For the sin which gained entrance, being a sort of power and an intellectual creation of Satan, sowed the seeds for all evils. It works in a hidden manner in the inner man and in the mind and contends with the thoughts. However, men are unaware that they are being moved by a certain foreign power when they do these things, but they think these are done naturally and that they do them with a certain self-determination. But those who have the peace of Christ in their mind and are enlightened by him know from whence these actions come.

50. The world thrives on evil passions and is ignorant of this fact. These passions, indeed, are an unclean fire which burns up the heart and pervades all the members and incites men to lustful actions and innumerable other evils. Those who are titillated and yield to such passion commit fornication within their heart. And so gradually evil gains control and they commit the external act of impurity. The same holds also for avarice, vainglory, pride, envy, and anger. It is like a man who is invited to a banquet before whom are placed great varieties of foods. Then sin begins to suggest that he taste all of them. And so his soul is held captive by the pleasure and he overeats. For those passions are most difficult mountains to cross in whose middle there flow rivers of dragons, poisonous beasts, and reptiles. Like a whale swallowing up a man into its belly, so also sin engulfs human souls. Those passions are the burning flames of fire and the fiery darts of evil. For the Apostle says: "That you may be able to extinguish the fiery darts of evil" (Eph 6:16). For evil spreads and lays its foundation in the soul.

51. The prudent ones, however, when passions begin to rise up, do not obey them, but they turn in anger against the evil desires and become their own enemies. For Satan greatly desires to enjoy rest inside the soul and there to set up his sleeping quarters. He is disturbed and highly annoyed when the soul does not obey him. There are not lacking those who are under the control of the divine power, who, when they see a young man with a woman, granted they may entertain certain thoughts,

their mind is not defiled nor do they commit an interior sin. Still they must not be confident in such matters. There are others in whom concupiscence is completely extinguished and dried up. Truly, these are the ranks of the very great ones. Take the example of divers who swim in the bottom of the sea and risk death in the water in order to find there pearls for a royal crown and purple dye. In a similar fashion there are also those who live the eremitical life. They leave the world, stripped of everything, and descend into the depths of darkness. And from there they gather up and take back precious stones fit for the crown of Christ, for the heavenly Church, for a new world, for a lighted city and an angelic people.

52. As many kinds of fish fall into a net and the least useful ones immediately are tossed back into the sea, so also the net of grace is spread over all men and seeks tranquillity. But men do not surrender and for this reason they are thrown back again into the same depths of darkness.

Just as gold is found, washed out of a great amount of sand and it amounts to very small grains like millet, so also out of many human beings few will be approved. For those who seek the kingdom are clearly manifested, while those who merely wear its word as a beautiful ornament are the ones most conspicuous. For the same reason those are manifested who are seasoned with the heavenly salt and who speak out of the Spirit's treasures. The vessels appear in whom God is pleased and to whom he gives his grace. There are also others, who, with much patience, receive the sanctifying power in many different ways, as God wishes.

He who speaks, unless he be directed by a heavenly light and wisdom, cannot meet the needs of each person, since there are so many different levels that people are at. For some are undergoing an interior war; others, however, enjoy a much more peaceful existence.

53. Let us take the example of someone who wishes to rebuild a city that has been totally destroyed. He must first get rid of the ruins and knock down whatever is a menace, and thus he begins to build and to lay his foundations in the excavation he has made and upon this he constructs his building, even though as yet there is no house built. Likewise, for one who wishes to develop a garden in barren or swampy, dirty places, he must first begin to clean up the place and put a fence around it and prepare irrigation and so finally he can begin to plant. And the plants grow, so that after much time the garden bears fruit. In a similar manner the intentions of men, after the fall, are barren, devastated, and thorny.

For God said to man: "Thorns and thistles shall the earth bring forth for you" (Gn 3:18). Therefore, there is need of much labor and sweat so as to seek and lay down a foundation until fire comes into men's hearts which will burn up and get rid of the thorns. And in this way men begin to grow in sanctity, glorifying the Father and the Son and the Holy Spirit forever. Amen.

HOMILY 16

Spiritual persons are subject to temptations and afflictions that flow out from the first sin.

1. All intellectual creatures, namely, angels, humans, and demons, have been created by the Creator, innocent and completely simple. That some fell away from these traits and turned to evil was a result of their free will. By their own will they turned away from right reason. If we assert that such fallen ones were created as such by the Creator, we are saying that God is an unjust judge who would cast Satan into fire. There are certain heretics who say that matter was eternal and that matter is the root and the root is where the power is, equal to God's power.[57] To such you can rightly reply: "Which power finally is the victorious one?" Without doubt it has to be the power of God. Therefore, in time or in power the one who is conquered can in no way be an equal to God. Those who affirm that evil exists in itself are really most ignorant.[58] For in God no evil can exist by itself since he himself is not subject to passions and he possesses his divinity. In us, however, it works with full power, especially in our senses, suggesting all sorts of obscene desires. In us it is not like, say, wine mixed with water. It is more like wheat in the same field by itself and the tares by themselves. It is like a robber in one part of the house and the owner in another.[59]

2. Take a spring which pours forth pure water and yet has mud lying under it. When someone stirs up the mud, the whole spring is dirtied. So also the human soul, when it is stirred up, is dirtied and is mixed with evil. And Satan becomes one in consent with the soul, for both are spirits, in committing fornication or murder. For this reason, "who clings to the harlot is one body" (1 Cor 6:16). But at another time the soul exists all by itself, and, stricken by repentance for what it has committed, it weeps and prays and remembers God. For if the soul always were completely immersed in evil, how could it do such things?

Satan never wishes that men return to repentance for he is completely without compassion.

It is like a wife, who, when she contracts marriage with her husband, is one with him. But at another time they are separated since it often happens that one or the other dies, while the other party survives. In a similar way is the fellowship with the Holy Spirit; such become one spirit, "For he that is joined to the Lord is one Spirit" (1 Cor 6:17). This happens when man is absorbed by grace.

3. There are some who, even though they have begun to develop a taste for divine things, nevertheless are disturbed and hassled by the adversary, so that they are surprised (still lacking experience) that after the divine visitation, they should still harbor doubts about the mysteries of the Christian religion. Those who have grown old in them are not surprised at all. As skilled farmers from long experience, if they have had a year of bountiful harvest, they do not live without some planning, but they foresee the time of dearth and tight times. On the contrary, if famine and penury hit them, they do not become despondent, as they think positively about the future. It is the same way with things in the spiritual world. When the soul falls into various temptations (Jb 1:1), it is not surprised nor does it lose all hope, because it knows that by God's permission it is being exposed to trials and is being disciplined by evil. Nor does it forget other circumstances when things go well and there is consolation, but it expects the time of trial.

The sun, being a material, created thing, shines down also upon swampy places full of mud and slime and yet is not affected or defiled. How much more the pure and Holy Spirit that is joined to the soul which still is afflicted by evil, without himself being tainted by the evil. For: "The light shines in darkness and the darkness comprehended it not" (Jn 1:5).

4. When, therefore, a man is deep and rich in grace, there still remains inside of him a remnant of evil.[60] But he has close at hand one who can help him. Wherefore, if one is overwhelmed by temptations, caught in the raging waves of passions, he ought not to lose hope. For if he acts in this way, sin builds up and takes over from within. If, however, one constantly puts his hope in God, evil to a certain degree diminishes and dries up. Certain people are afflicted with paralysis: some with mutilated members, others with fever, while others have sickness. All of this comes from sin. For sin is the root of all evils.[61] The passions caused by the concupiscible powers of the soul and by evil thoughts also flow from sin.

130

If there is a flowing spring, the places that lie in the vicinity become wet and swampy. But when hot weather comes, both the spring and the nearby areas dry up. So also it happens to God's servants who abound in grace. For grace not only dries up the concupiscences suggested by the evil one, but also those flowing out of nature. This is because now the men of God are greater than the first Adam.

5. God is without limits and is incomprehensible. He appears everywhere, both in the mountains and the sea and below in the abyss. Yet he is not present by a movement, such as angels enjoy in their descent from Heaven to earth. God is in Heaven and he is also here. But you rightly object to my statement: "How can God be in hell or in what way is he in the darkness or in Satan or in filthy places?" I answer you that he himself cannot undergo any change and he contains all things since he is infinite. But Satan, who is his creature, is bound. What is good is not tainted nor plunged into darkness. But if you deny that he contains all things, including hell and Satan, you make him finite as far as that place where the wicked one dwells, so that as a result we should look for another, superior to him.

It is necessary that God be always superior. Because of the mystery of the Godhead and his simplicity, the darkness, though having its being in him, does not comprehend him. Nor can the evil participate in the purity that is in God. Therefore, for God no evil exists as a separated substance, since he is in no way affected by it.

6. For us, however, evil is real since it lives in our heart and there it operates by suggesting wicked and obscene thoughts and by not allowing us to pour out pure prayers. It leads our mind into captivity to this world.[62] It has entered into our souls and has touched all our bones and members. Just as Satan is in the air and God, who is also there, is not harmed by being there, so sin is in our souls and God's grace also, with the latter suffering no harm.

As a servant, who is near his master, is always under fear, being so close to him, and he does nothing without his master's order, so also we should place our thoughts under our Master, Christ, who knows our hearts. We should open them to him and we ought to place hope and trust in him, saying: "He is my glory; he is my Father; he is my riches."

You ought, therefore, consciously to have a sensitivity and fear. Even if a person does not have divine grace firmly planted and fixed in him, let him night and day conduct himself so that what guides, stimulates, and directs him each hour to those things that are good be joined to his soul as something natural so that he has this sensitivity, this fear and task fixed as though they were a natural and unswerving contrition set constantly in the heart.

7. Like a bee that secretly fashions its comb in the hive, so also grace secretly forms in hearts its own love. It changes to sweetness what is bitter, what is rough into that which is smooth. It is similar to a silversmith or engraver, working on a plate, who partly covers up those various little animals that he is sculpturing. But when he has finished his work, then he holds it up, shining in the light. So the Lord, that true Artisan, engraves our hearts and secretly renews them until they leave the body. Then the real beauty of the soul is manifested. Those, who fashion a bowl and wish to depict little animals on it first trace their design in wax and then cast them in that image, so that the work comes out in accord with that image. Likewise with sin, since it is a spirit, it has an image and takes on many shapes. In a similar way the inner man is like one of those little animals, with an image and form, for it is a likeness of the outer man. Great then and precious is that vessel, because of all creatures it alone pleased the Lord. The good thoughts, indeed, are similar to precious stones and pearls while impure thoughts are filled with the bones of dead men and all uncleanness (Mt 23:27) and evil smelling.

8. Christians are of another world, children of the heavenly Adam, a new race, children of the Holy Spirit, shining brothers of Christ, similar to their Father, the spiritual Adam.[63] They belong to his city, his race and power. They are not of this world, but of another one. For he himself says: "You are not of this world, even as I am not of this world" (Jn 17:16).

Like a merchant on a long journey, after successfully completing his business and being on his way home, he sends word to his friends to build him houses and gardens, to buy him necessary clothes. And when he returns home, he brings with him great riches, and his friends and relatives receive him with great happiness. So also is it with spiritual things. If any invest in heavenly riches, their fellow citizens, the spirits of the saints and angels, are filled with admiration and say: "Our brothers, living on earth, have acquired immense riches." Therefore such, who have the Lord with them, when they leave this life, come to those living above with great happiness. Those who belong to the Lord receive them. They have prepared for them there houses and gardens and splendid and elegant garments.

9. There is a need for sobriety in all things lest those things that we seem to possess as good things may not turn to our destruction.[64] For

those who by nature are kind, let them be on their guard, lest they be gradually drawn away by their very goodness. And those who are strong in wisdom, let not their wisdom deceive them. A person should be well balanced in all characteristics, showing warmth, moderated by a severity, wisdom with discretion, words with action. And let him place his complete confidence in the Lord and not in himself. For virtue is seasoned in various ways, like a certain food is necessarily seasoned by a special spice, not only by honey, but also even by pepper, and so it is considered useful in food.

10. There are those who claim that there is no sin in man. They are like people immersed in deep waters who still are afraid to recognize the fact, but say: "We have heard the sound of waters." So plunged into the depths of the waves of evil, they deny that there is sin in their minds or thoughts.

Some people talk a great deal, but they are not seasoned with a heavenly salt. They speak a great deal about the royal table, but they have never eaten there or enjoyed it. But different is the one who has seen the king, one to whom the treasures have been opened. He enters in and inherits them. He eats and drinks of those costly foods.

11. Take the example of a mother who has an only son, very handsome, wise, possessing great gifts of goodness and charm, in whom she puts all her hope. If it should happen that he should die, then constant sorrow comes upon her and her grief knows no comfort. So also the mind, when the soul is dead to God, ought to mourn and shed tears. It ought to be affected with constant distress, to have a broken heart, to be in fear and concern and at the same time to have a continued hunger and thirst for what is good. Such a one is covered by God's grace and has hope. He no longer is in sadness, but is overwhelmed with joy as one who finds a treasure. Again, he trembles lest for any reason he may lose it.

For thieves are attacking. Just like a person who has suffered many muggings by robbers and undergone dangers, and then escapes with great difficulty, who then later comes into great wealth and good fortune and fears no more dread of loss because of his abundance of wealth, so too spiritual persons, who before passed through many temptations and dangerous places and then were filled with grace and heaped up good things, are no longer afraid of those who seek to rob them since their wealth is so great. Still they are not without fear—fear, I say, not of those who quake before evil spirits, but fear and concern as to how they may best use the spiritual gifts entrusted to them.

12. Such a one regards himself as the greatest of all sinners.[65] He carries this thought ever with him as a part of his very makeup. And the more he progresses in knowledge of God, the more simple and unlearned he considers himself. And the more he studies and learns, the less he feels he knows. This grace acts as a guiding force, almost second nature to him. Just as an infant is carried about by a young man who carries him and does with him whatever he wishes, so also the grace that operates in the depths of the soul's powers. It feeds the mind and lifts it up to Heaven, to the perfect world, to everlasting rest. But in such a grace there are many degrees and perfections.

The general of the army who has free access to the king is different from the captain. Just as a house, full of smoke, belches it out into the outside air, so also the evil that abounds in the soul is poured outside and produces its own kind of evil. Take the example of those who are given a government job or are entrusted with the royal treasury. They never are without concern lest in any way they offend the king. So also those to whom a spiritual work has been entrusted are always filled with solicitude. And even though they may enjoy some rest, it is as if they do not really have it. For the kingdom of darkness, which has infiltrated into the city of the soul, and the barbarians who occupy its grazing lands, are being expelled from it.

13. Christ the King sends a heavenly army to recapture the city and to throw the usurpers into chains and to set up the heavenly army and the ranks of holy spirits there as in their own native land. Then the sun shines gloriously in the heart and its rays penetrate through all the members and the greatest peace reigns in power there.

The genuine struggle and battle of man, his testing and his good will toward God, then appear when grace is withheld, and he shows himself brave as he cries out to God. When you hear that there are rivers of dragons and mouths of lions and dark forces under the heavens and fire that burns and crackles in all the members (such that the earth could never contain), you will remain ignorant of such things unless you receive the pledge of the Holy Spirit (2 Cor 1:22). These forces will hold your soul and when you depart from this life will not allow you to rise to Heaven.

Likewise, when you hear about the dignity of humanity, how it has substantially been endowed with intellect, do you not understand that God had spoken these words, not of angels, but of human nature: "Let us make man according to our image and likeness" (Gn 1:26), and that *bride ?*

Heaven and earth would pass away, but you have been called to immortality, to be a son, a brother and a spouse of the King?

In the things around us, everything that belongs to the spouse belongs to the bride as well. So also everything that belongs to the Lord, no matter how much it is, he entrusts to you. He came to your aid in person to call you back to what once was yours. Yet you do not understand this nor do you perceive your dignity. Rightly does the Psalmist, full of the Spirit, deplore your fallen state when he says: "My being in honor has no understanding, but is compared with the brute beasts and is made like unto them" (Ps 49:20). Glory to the Father and to the Son and to the Holy Spirit forever. Amen.

HOMILY 17

The spiritual anointing and glory of Christians. Without Christ it is not possible to be saved or to participate in eternal life.

1. Perfect Christians,[66] who are considered worthy to reach a degree of perfection and to come close to the King, are continually dedicated to the cross of Christ. Just like the anointing in the times of the prophets was considered absolutely a most precious thing, since kings and prophets were anointed, so also now spiritual persons, who are anointed with a heavenly anointing, become Christians by grace, so that they too become kings and prophets of heavenly mysteries. Indeed, these are sons and lords and gods, bound and held captive, plunged deeply, crucified and consecrated. For the anointing with oil, a thing which came from a material plant, a visible tree, had so great a power that those who were anointed obtained a dignity beyond questioning (for it was decreed that they were thus made kings). David was anointed and immediately was exposed to persecutions and afflictions, and after the seventh year was he made king. How much more do all who have been anointed in mind and the interior man with the sanctifying and joy-giving, heavenly and spiritual "oil of gladness" (Heb 1:9), receive the sign of that kingdom of imperishable and eternal power, namely, "the pledge of the Spirit" (2 Cor 5:5), the Holy Spirit and Paraclete? Understand by Paraclete the one who consoles and pours out joy upon all who are heavily burdened.

2. These, having been anointed with the ointment from the tree of

135

life, Jesus Christ, the heavenly plant, are considered worthy to reach the degree of perfection of the Kingdom, and of the adoption. Indeed, they are participators of the secrets of the heavenly King and enjoy the confidence of the Almighty. They enter into his palace, where the angels and spirits of the saints are, even while they are in this world. Even though they have not yet entered into the full inheritance prepared for them in that age, nevertheless, they are most certain because of the pledge which they have already received, as if already crowned and reigning. Nor are they surprised, as though it were a strange and new thing, that they are about to reign with Christ, because of the abundance of grace and child-like abandonment to the Spirit. Why? Because while still in the flesh, they enjoyed that relish of sweetness and that effective working of power.

3. It is the same as one who was a friend of the king, employed in the palace, who knew the secrets of the king, being around him always. Now should he be made king and crowned, he would not be frightened by any new happenings, nor fearful since he had long been trained in the secrets of the palace. In no way does it usually happen that an uncouth or uneducated person or a stranger to the secrets can reach the task of running a kingdom, but only those who have been instructed by training and experience. So also Christians, who are going to reign in that age, are not surprised at anything new, since they have already long before known the mysteries of grace.

Because of the fact that man had violated the command, the devil has covered the soul completely with a dark veil. But then grace comes and completely removes the veil so that the soul, now restored to its former and proper purity, created pure and without blame, continually and without blemish, looks with its pure eyes on the glory of the true light and the true "sun of righteousness" (Mt 4:2), shining brilliantly in the depths of the heart.

4. As at the end of the world when the firmament will pass away and the just thereafter will live in the kingdom and the light and the glory, seeing nothing but how Christ is perpetually in glory at the right hand of the Father, so also with these who even now are caught up into that other age and are taken captive. They contemplate there the beautiful and wonderful things that take place.

We, who are still on earth, have "our citizenship in Heaven" (Phil 3:20). We pass our lives in that world, living according to our mind and the inner man. For just as the visible eye, when it is clear, always sees the sun clearly, so also the mind, completely restored by purity, always sees the glory of the light of Christ, and night and day is with the Lord, just as the body of the Lord was always joined to the Godhead with the Holy Spirit.[67] However, people do not attain those levels immediately, but only with labor, temptation, and much struggle.

There are some persons in whom grace is operative and working in peace. Within, however, evil is also present hiddenly, and the two ways of existing, namely, according to the principles of light and darkness, vie for dominance within the same heart.

5. But you will say to me: "What fellowship does light have with darkness?" (2 Cor 6:14). Where is divine light darkened and made evil? And where is that which is undefiled and pure made defiled and dirtied? For it is written: "The light shines in darkness and the darkness does not comprehend it" (Jn 1:5). These things must not be understood simply or only one way.

There are certain persons who so rest in God's grace that they become stronger the more that evil abounds. They are drawn toward God by their deep prayer life and great repose in God. However, at another time, they are disturbed by evil thoughts and are done in by sin, even though they still remain in God's grace. Simple-minded and foolish persons, when grace begins to some degree to work in them, believe that they are simply freed from sin. But those who have discretion and prudence would never dare to deny that, even when we are gifted by divine grace, we are still tested by wicked and obscene thoughts.

6. Very often we have found certain ones among the brethren who have received so much joy and grace that, for five or six years, they asserted, concupiscence had been burnt up and from that time on they thought themselves freed from passion.[68] Yet the hidden potential for evil rose up in them and they so burned with the fire of concupiscence that they were amazed and crushed, saying: "After so long a time where did the evil come from?" Therefore, no one in his sane mind should dare to say: "Because I am in grace, I am thoroughly freed of sin." But the two principles exercise their proper force upon the human mind. Inexperienced persons in this matter, when grace has begun to operate in them, think that they have already won the battle and are now perfect Christians.

I look at it in this way. It is like the sun in the sky which shines in the clear air. Clouds come and cover over it, making the air heavier. And in no way (since the sun hides inside) is the sun robbed either of its light or of its proper essence. So is it with those who are not yet completely purified. Granted they are given God's grace, still they are held deep down by sin. They experience at the same time natural movements along with strong thoughts toward God, even though they are not yet totally given to good.

7. So also, contrariwise, there are those who deep down are guided by the good principle, namely, by grace and yet they are held in bondage and subjected to bad thoughts and the evil principle. Therefore, it requires the greatest discretion for anyone to know from experience this matter. I tell you, even the Apostles, to whom was given the Paraclete, still were not completely secure. They entertained at the same time joy and gladness along with fear and trembling, and this came from the principle of grace itself and not the evil one. It was, indeed, grace itself that was guarding them so that they might not swerve, not even a bit. Like one who throws a small stone against a wall, it hardly injures the wall or moves it at all. Or like a dart hurled against one wearing a breastplate, it hardly hurts the iron nor the body of the wearer. The dart hits and is dashed down. So even if a bit of evil came close to the Apostles, it in no way harmed them, since they were clothed with the perfect power of Christ. And they, since they were perfect, were able freely to carry on the works of justification.

8. Therefore, since certain persons insist that once they have accepted grace, they need have no further solicitude. But God demands even in those perfect the soul's will to cooperate in the service of the Spirit, namely, that they freely consent. For the Apostle says: "Do not quench the Spirit" (1 Thes 5:19). Some of them do not wish to be a burden to others, while others carry on for themselves. Others receive gifts from those in the world and distribute them to the poor. This latter is better. Certain persons endowed with grace have only one concern, about their own affairs. Others seek also to help others. These latter are more outstanding than the former.

Others have the grace to expose themselves to suffer insults and afflictions for the name of God. These are superior to the others. Some in pursuing virtue seek glory and honors from others, saying that they are Christians and participate in the Holy Spirit. In contrast, others strive to hide themselves, even from encountering other human beings. These excel by far the first. Do you see how in the matter of perfection, goodwill toward God (which is developed along with our own cooperating natural will) is found superior and richer?

9. Take the example of one who is dressed in ragged clothes. In a dream he sees himself rich. He wakes up and sees that he is still poor and naked. So also those who speak on spiritual topics seem to speak with

138

ease, but if they have not experienced personally that about which they speak what they say comes across as empty words. Or take a woman, elegantly dressed in silks and pearls. She offers herself in a brothel. So also the heart of men who discourse about justice without having experienced what they speak about is like a brothel of unclean spirits.

10. Just as it is impossible for fish to live outside of water, a human being cannot walk without feet or see light without eyes or speak without a tongue or hear without ears. So also without the Lord Jesus and the working of divine power, no one can know the mysteries and the wisdom of God or be rich and be a Christian.

Those who truly are wise, the brave soldiers and philosophers of God, are those directed and guided in the interior man by divine power. The philosophers of the Greeks learn eloquence. Others are simple in their speech (2 Cor 11:6), but they rejoice and are glad in the grace of God that they are, namely, men addicted to serving God. Let us, therefore, judge who are the superior ones. It is said: "The Kingdom of God is not in a word, but in deed and in power" (1 Cor 4:20).

11. It is easy for someone to say that bread is made of wheat. But he should rather be able to describe how in detail the bread is prepared and baked. To speak truly about freedom from passions and perfection is given to few. The Gospel succinctly says: "Thou shalt not be angry, thou shalt not covet. If any man smites thee on the cheek, turn also the other cheek. If any one drags thee to court to have your tunic, give him also your cloak" (Mt 5:39ff.). The Apostle, tracing out how the work of purifying the heart must be done with patience and perseverance, teaches in many ways how first there is feeding with milk as with babies; then there is a movement or progress to growth and to full perfection. For the Gospel said that the garment is made of wool. The Apostle, however, declared in detail just how it is sewn together.

12. Those who speak about spiritual topics without tasting or experiencing are like a man who, walking in the desert, has an overwhelming, raging thirst, so he draws for himself to satisfy his thirst a picture of a fountain flowing with water, while all the while his lips and tongue burn with thirst. If one were to lecture on the sweet qualities of honey without ever having tasted honey, he would be ignorant of the power of that sweetness. In a similar way are those who talk about perfection, about joy or freedom from passions, yet lack personal experience and knowledge of them. For sure, not all things are as they tell it. When a man of this type deigns to wake up from his state and discovers that things are really different, he will judge himself: "It was not really as I judged it to

be. I was saying one thing while the Spirit was acting in a different manner."

13. The Christian religion is a food and drink. The more one eats of it, the more strongly his mind is enticed by its sweetness, so much so that he can never be restrained or satisfied, but insatiably asks for more and continually eats more. If a man has a great thirst and is given a pleasing drink, then, as he begins to taste of it, the more he wants to have it, the more eagerly he drinks of it. So is the taste of the Spirit; it can hardly be stopped or satisfied, just like the above comparison. And these are not idle words, but the working of the Holy Spirit, working in a hidden way in the mind.

Some believe that, since they have given up marriage and other material things, they are already saints. It is not true in reality. For evil still inhabits the mind, lives in the heart. He is a saint who is purified and made holy in the interior man. For where truth begins ever so gradually to show itself, there error attacks and seeks to conceal and cover over the truth.

14. When the Jews possessed the priesthood, those of that race surely suffered persecution; they were grievously afflicted because they persisted in the truth, namely, Eleazar and the Maccabees. Now, since from the time of the cross and the rending of the Temple's veil, the Spirit left them; the truth has now been revealed here and works in us. For this reason certain people of this nation suffer persecution. From the Jewish nation some were oppressed by persecution and affliction, as martyrs, to witness to the truth. For how will the truth appear unless it encounter adversaries who are liars and attack it?

Even among the brethren there are also those who suffer great passions and afflictions. They must show great caution lest they fall. One of the brethren, praying with another, was swept up by the divine power and carried away where he saw the heavenly city of Jerusalem and shining persons and a great light. And he heard a voice saying: "This is the place of rest for the just." And shortly after, he became puffed up and thought that what he had seen concerned himself. After that he fell into committing the most heinous sins, committing innumerable evils.

15. If a person leading such an interior and sublime life has fallen, how can the ordinary person say: "Because I fast, practice hospitality and distribute my wealth, I am already a saint"? Real perfection does not consist in refraining from evil, but only if, entering into your darkened mind, you put to death the serpent that lies inside your mind, deep down in your thoughts. That serpent kills you by digging itself deeply into the

secret chambers of your soul, and there sets up its nest (for the soul is an abyss)—unless, I say, you put it to death and get rid of all the uncleanness that dirties you.

All the philosophers, the Law and the Apostles, even the coming of the Savior, all were concerned with purity. Indeed, all men, whether Jews or Greeks, eagerly desire purity, even should they be unable to attain it. We must, therefore, inquire how and by what means we can obtain purity of heart. There is no other way than through him who was crucified for us. For he himself is the way, the life, the truth, the door, the pearl, the living and heavenly bread.

No one can know and serve truth without that truth. In regard to the exterior man and the visible things around us, if you have given up everything and distributed your wealth, so also in the matter of worldly wisdom. If you have knowledge of things or an ability to speak, you ought to reject all things in such areas and consider them as nothing so that you may be built on the "foolishness of preaching" (1 Cor 1:21), which preaching alone is true wisdom. This wisdom lacks fancy words but is charged with power working through the holy cross. Glory to the consubstantial Trinity forever. Amen.

HOMILY 18

The treasure of Christians, namely, Christ and the Holy Spirit, and the various ways of exercising them in order to attain perfection.

1. If any person in this world is extremely wealthy and possesses a secret treasure, through that and his riches he buys anything he may like. And whatever possessions in the world he would wish, without any difficulty, relying on his treasure, he can have. He easily obtains by means of it every possession he wishes. So it is for those who above all else seek all things from God and find and possess the heavenly treasure of the Spirit, who is the Lord himself shining in their hearts. They perform all things in the justice of virtues and do good in every relationship according to the commands of the Lord out of the treasure of Christ living in them. And by means of this treasure they acquire even greater heavenly riches.

By means of this heavenly treasure they work to acquire every virtue, relying on the fullness of the spiritual richness within them.

They easily observe all righteousness and every commandment of the Lord by means of the invisible richness of grace within them. The Apostle says: "Having this treasure in earthen vessels . . ." (2 Cor 4:7), that is, the treasure which they were deemed worthy to possess in this material life within themselves, the sanctifying power of the Spirit. And again, St. Paul says: "He who was made for us the wisdom from God and justification and sanctification and redemption" (1 Cor 1:30).

2. Therefore, one who has found and possesses within himself the heavenly treasure of the Spirit fulfills all the commands justly and practices all the virtues without blame, purely without forcing and with a certain ease.

Let us, therefore, beg God, seeking and praying him to gift us with the treasure of the Spirit in order that we may be empowered to walk in all of his commands without blame and purely, and to fulfill every justice asked of the Spirit with purity and perfection by means of the heavenly treasure which is Christ. For he who is indigent and poor and a beggar in the world cannot acquire anything. His destitution restrains him. But he who possesses the treasure, as I said, easily acquires whatever possessions he wishes without much effort. The soul that is naked and stripped of the fellowship of the Spirit and lives under the terrible poverty of sin is unable, even if it wished to do so, to produce the fruit of the Spirit of righteousness in truth, unless it becomes a participator of the Spirit.

3. However, everyone should push himself to beg the Lord to make him worthy to receive and find the heavenly treasure of the Spirit in order to be able easily and promptly to fulfill all the commandments of the Lord, without blame and with perfection, which before he could not successfully do, no matter how he tried. Being poor and stripped of the fellowship of the Spirit, how could he acquire such spiritual possessions without the spiritual treasure and wealth? But the person who has found the Lord, the true treasure, by seeking the Spirit, by faith and great patience, brings forth the fruits of the Spirit, as I said earlier. All righteousness and the commands of the Lord which the Spirit orders he does by himself, purely and perfectly and without blame.

4. Let us again use another example. Take a rich man who plans an extravagant banquet. He spends out of his wealth and treasure and does not fear that he will run out of money since he possesses great riches. And so he entertains his guests sumptuously, sparing nothing, as he serves them a variety and a great novelty of food. But a poor man who

has nothing to his name, if he wishes to give a meal for certain friends, must borrow everything, the very dishes, tablecloths, and everything else. And after his guests have dined at the poor man's table, afterward he gives back to each one from whom he borrowed, a silver dish, cloths, or whatever else was used. When he has given all the things back to their individual owners, he himself remains again poor and naked, having no wealth of his own with which he can entertain himself.

5. So also it is with those who are rich in the Holy Spirit. They truly possess the fellowship of the Spirit within themselves. And when they speak words of truth or deliver any spiritual conference and wish to edify persons, they speak out of the same wealth and treasure which indwells within them and out of this they edify persons who listen to their spiritual discourses. And they do not fear lest they run short since they possess within themselves the heavenly treasure of goodness from which they draw to feed those who hunger for spiritual food.

But the poor man, who does not possess the riches of Christ nor have within himself a spiritual wealth which can bring forth a stream of goodness in words and deeds and of divine ideas and ineffable mysteries, even if, I say, he wishes to speak a word of truth and refresh his listeners, he does not possess in himself the Word of God in power and in truth. He repeats things he memorized or borrowed from some writings or from what he has heard from spiritual persons and these he organizes and teaches. Yes, he may even seemingly entertain some, and certainly some profit from his sermons. But when he has delivered his discourse, each word returns to its source from which it came. Then he again remains naked and poor, not possessing the treasure of the Spirit as his own from which he draws to help and refresh others, but he himself first of all is not refreshed nor does he rejoice in the Spirit.

6. For this reason we must first beg of God with struggle in the heart through faith that he grant us to discover his riches, the true treasure of Christ in our hearts, in the power and energy of the Spirit. In such a way, first, by finding the Lord to be our help within us and our salvation and eternal life, we may be of help and profit to others also, insofar as it is possible and attainable, by drawing upon Christ, the treasure within, for all goodness of spiritual discourses and in teaching the heavenly mysteries. Thus the goodness of the Father was pleased to wish to dwell in every believer who asks this of him. Christ says: "He that loves me, he will be loved by my Father and I will love him and I will

manifest myself to him" (Jn 14:21). And again: "I and my Father will come and make our mansion in him" (Jn 14:23). Thus, the infinite kindness of the Father decreed. Thus, the incomprehensible love of Christ was pleased. Thus, the ineffable good of the promised Spirit. Glory to the ineffable compassion of the Holy Trinity.

7. Those who have been deemed worthy to become children of God and to be reborn by the Holy Spirit from above, who have within themselves Christ, illuminating and bringing them rest, are guided in many and various ways by the Spirit. They are invisibly acted upon in the heart, in the spiritual tranquillity, by grace. Let us take as examples figures of evident things in the world, of persons in order to suggest in what way grace works in the soul. Sometimes persons are guided by grace in the manner of those who rejoice at a royal banquet. They are filled with joy and ineffable happiness. At other times, they are like a spouse who enjoys conjugal union with her bridegroom in divine resting. At other times they are like incorporeal angels, they are so light and transcendent, even in the body. Sometimes, they are as if they have become intoxicated with a strong drink. They delight in the Spirit, being inebriated, namely, by the intoxication of the divine and spiritual mysteries.

8. Sometimes they find themselves immersed in weeping and lamenting over the human race and in pouring out prayers on behalf of the whole human race of Adam. They shed tears and are overwhelmed by grief because they are consumed by the love of the Spirit toward mankind. At another time, they are so enflamed by the Spirit with such joy and love that, if it were possible, they would gather every human being into their very hearts, without distinguishing the bad and good. Again they are so filled with humility regarding themselves below all men in the humility received from the Spirit, so they consider themselves as the least significant and worthless of all human beings. Sometimes they are lifted up in "joy unspeakable" (1 Pt 1:8). At other times they are like some powerful person, who has donned the king's whole armor and has come down to do battle against the enemies. He fights courageously against them and conquers. Similarly, the spiritual takes up the heavenly weapons of the Spirit and attacks the enemies and battles them and puts them under his feet.

9. At other times, in deepest silence and tranquillity, one reposes with no other attitude but one of spiritual pleasure and ineffable rest and

well-being. At another time, one is instructed in an understanding and unspeakable wisdom and knowledge of the unknowable Spirit through grace in matters that cannot be expressed by tongue and speech. At another time one becomes one with all human beings. So varied are the ways that grace affects such persons and leads the soul in so many different paths, refreshing it in accord with the will of God. Grace exercises the soul differently in order to restore it to the heavenly Father perfect and faultless and pure.

10. These things spoken of here concerning the workings of the Spirit belong to the level of those who are not far from perfection. Those various manifestations of grace that we spoke of, even though they are expressed differently, still they act on such persons in a progression, one operation following another. Finally, when a person reaches the perfection of the Spirit, completely purified of all passions and united to and interpenetrated by the Paraclete Spirit in an ineffable communion, and is deemed worthy to become spirit in a mutual penetration with the Spirit, then it becomes all light, all eye, all spirit, all joy, all repose, all happiness, all love, all compassion, all goodness and kindness. As in the bottom of the sea, a stone is everywhere surrounded by water, so such persons as these are totally penetrated by the Holy Spirit. They become like to Christ, putting on the virtues of the power of the Spirit with a constancy. They interiorly become faultless and spotless and pure.

11. Having been restored by the Spirit, how can they produce externally any evil fruit? But always and in all things the fruits of the Spirit shine forth in them. Let us then beg God and believe with love and much hope so that he may gift us with the heavenly grace of the gift of his Spirit in order that the Spirit himself may direct and guide us into the complete will of God and refresh us with his various reposeful touches. "Let us beseech God so that, through this guidance and exercise of grace and spiritual progress, we may be deemed worthy to attain to the perfect fullness of Christ" (Eph 3:19). And again, ". . . until we all come into the perfect man, unto the measure of the stature of the fullness of Christ" (Eph 4:13). The Lord has promised all who believe in him and ask in truth to bestow on them the mysteries of the ineffable communion of the Spirit. Let us, therefore, give ourselves completely to the Lord and hasten to receive the good things spoken of above. Consecrated in soul and body and nailed to the cross of Christ, let us become worthy of

the eternal kingdom, glorifying the Father and the Son and the Holy Spirit forever. Amen.

HOMILY 19

Christians, wishing to advance and grow, ought to push themselves toward every good so as to free themselves from every habitual sin and be filled by the Holy Spirit.

1. The person that wishes to come to the Lord and to be deemed worthy of eternal life and to become the dwelling place of Christ and to be filled with the Holy Spirit so that he may be able to bring forth the fruits of the Spirit and perform the commandments of Christ purely and blamelessly ought to begin first by believing firmly in the Lord and giving himself completely to the words of his commands and renouncing the world in all things so that his whole mind may not be taken up with anything ephemeral. And he ought to persevere constantly in prayer, always waiting in faith that expects his coming and his help, keeping the goal of his mind ever fixed upon this. Then he ought to push himself to every good work and to doing all the commandments of the Lord, because there is sin dwelling within him. Thus let him strive to show humility before every person and to consider himself the least and the worst. Let him not seek honor or praise or the glory of men as it is written in the Gospel (Jn 12:44). But let him only have always before his eyes the Lord and his commands, wishing to please him alone in the meekness of his heart, as the Lord says: "Learn of me, because I am meek and humble of heart and you will find rest for your souls" (Mt 11:29).

2. Likewise, let him accustom himself to be merciful, compassionate, and good according to his power, as the Lord says: "Be good and kind, even as your heavenly Father is merciful" (Lk 6:36). And again he says: "If you love me, keep my commandments" (Jn 14:15). And again: "Strive to enter through the narrow door" (Lk 13:24). Above all, let him take the humility and conduct of the Lord, his meekness and conversation, as his model by ever remembering him. Let him continue incessantly in prayers, always beseeching and believing that the Lord may come to dwell in him and may perfect and give him power to accomplish all his commands and that the Lord himself may become the dwelling place for his soul.

And thus, the things he now does with effort of a reluctant heart, he may perform one day willingly, accustoming himself always to the good and remembering the Lord and waiting for him always in great love. Then the Lord, seeing such an intention and his good diligence, how he strives to remember the Lord and always seeks to do good and is humble and meek and loving, how he guides his heart, whether he wishes or not, to the best of his ability with force, has mercy on him and frees him from his enemies and the indwelling sin. He fills him with the Holy Spirit. And gradually without force or struggle he keeps all the Lord's commandments in truth. Or, rather, it is the Lord who keeps in him his very own commandments and then he brings forth purely the fruits of the Spirit.

3. It is, however, necessary at first for one coming to the Lord to force himself thus to do good and, even if he should not in his heart be so inclined, he must constantly await his mercy with unshaken faith and push himself to love, even if he does not have love. He ought to push himself to meekness, even if he has none, to mercy and to have a merciful heart. He must force himself to be disregarded, and when he is looked down upon by others, let him rejoice. When he is made light of or dishonored, let him not become angry according to the saying: "Beloved, do not avenge yourselves" (Rom 12:19). Let him push himself to prayer even when he does not possess the prayer of the Spirit. And so, God, seeing him striving so and pushing himself by determination, even if the heart is unwilling, gives him the authentic prayer of the Spirit, gives him true charity, true meekness, "the bowels of mercies" (Col 3:12), true kindness, and, simply put, fills him with the fruits of the Spirit.

4. If a person pushes himself to attain prayer alone, when he has none, in order to attain its grace, without striving earnestly for meekness and humility and charity and all the other commandments of the Lord, neither taking pains nor struggling and battling to succeed in these as far as his choice and free will go, he may at times be given a grace of prayer with some degree of repose and pleasure from the Spirit according as he asks. But he has the same traits he had before. He has no meekness, because he did not seek it with effort and he did not prepare himself beforehand to become meek. He has no humility, since he did not ask for it and did not push himself to have it. He has no charity toward all men, because he was not concerned with it and did not strive for it in his asking for the gift of prayer. And in doing his work, he has no faith or trust in God, since he did not know that he was without it.

And he did not take the pains to seek from the Lord for himself to have a firm faith and an authentic trust.

5. For just as he forces himself to prayer, even when unwilling, so everyone must push himself likewise to trust, so also to humility, so to charity, so to meekness, sincerity, and simplicity, so "unto every patience and long-suffering with joy" (Col 1:11), so also to regard himself as little and to consider himself as poor and the least of all. He strives not to speak without profit, but always to be concerned to speak the things of God with mouth and heart. He is attentive not to become angry and loud-mouthed according to the saying, "Let all bitterness and anger and clamoring be put away from you, with all malice" (Eph 4:31). He strives to live according to all the ways of the Lord, in the practice of virtue and good and noble conduct, to possess all manifestations of goodness, of humility, of meekness, never being proud and high-minded and puffed up and never to speak against anyone.

6. In all of these matters a person must push himself if he desires to gain the approval of and be pleasing to Christ so that the Lord, seeing his determination and purpose in forcing himself to all goodness and simplicity and kindness and humility and charity and prayer with full determination, may give himself completely to him. The Lord himself does all of these things in truth in him without labor and force, which before he could not perform, even by his own determination, because of sin that indwelled in him. And now all the practice of virtues comes to him as though the virtues are a part of his nature. The reason is really that the Lord comes and dwells in him and he is in the Lord. The Lord himself operates in him to accomplish his own commandments, effortlessly now, filling him with the fruit of the Spirit. But if anyone forces himself only to possess the virtue of prayer, until he receives that gift from God, but does not similarly push himself to those other virtues, he cannot really perform them purely and faultlessly. He must orientate himself toward what good he is capable of doing.

Sometimes the divine grace comes to him as he is asking and imploring. For God is good and kind and he gives to those who ask him whatever they are seeking. If one does not strive to be good, does not possess the virtues already mentioned and has not even prepared himself for them, he loses the grace which he has acquired and falls because of pride, or he does not make progress nor increase in the grace that came to him because he does not give himself purposefully to the Lord's commandments. For the dwelling place and the repose of the Spirit is humility, charity, and meekness and the other commandments of the Lord.

7. Therefore, it is necessary that whoever wishes truly to please God and receive from him the heavenly grace of the Spirit and to grow and be perfected in the Holy Spirit should force himself to observe the commandments of God and to make his heart submissive, even if he is unwilling according to the saying, "Therefore, I observe all thy commandments and every false way I abhor" (Ps 119:128). As one pushes and compels himself to persevere in prayer until he succeeds, similarly, if he wishes and forces and compels himself to practice all the virtues and develops a good habit, he thus asks and begs of the Lord always. And obtaining his request and receiving a taste for God and becoming a participator of the Holy Spirit, he makes the gift given to him to increase and to thrive as he rests in humility, in charity, and in meekness.

8. The Spirit himself graces him with all of these virtues and teaches him authentic prayer, authentic charity, authentic meekness, for which he pushed himself and sought to possess them. And he had a concern and thought about them and they were given him. And thus, growing and becoming perfect in God, he is deemed worthy to become an heir of the kingdom. For the humble person never falls. Where would he fall since he is lower than all others? A proud mind is a great humiliation, while humility is a great uplifting of the mind and an honor and dignity. Let us, then, push ourselves and strive to obtain humility, even though our heart is unwilling, to obtain meekness and charity by praying and begging God in faith and hope and love unceasingly with such expectancy and purpose so that he may send his Spirit into our hearts in order that we may pray and "worship God in spirit and in truth" (Jn 4:24).

9. Let us pray that the Spirit may teach us true prayer which now we are unable to accomplish even through our earnest striving. He will teach us how to accomplish, with hearts of compassion, kindness and all the other commandments of the Lord truly without any trouble and force since the Spirit himself knows how to fill us with his fruit. And so we fulfill the commandments of God through his Spirit, who alone knows the will of the Lord. The Spirit has perfected us in himself and he is perfected in us as we are purified from all defilement and stain of sin, as he presents us as beautiful brides, pure and spotless, to Christ. We rest in God, in his kingdom, and God rests in us for all ages unending. Glory to his tender compassion and mercy and love that he has deigned

to bestow such honor and glory to the human race and to deign to make them sons of the heavenly Father and has called them his own brothers. To him be glory forever. Amen.

HOMILY 20

Only Christ, the true Physician of the interior man, can heal the soul and adorn it with the garment of his grace.

1. If anyone is naked and lacks the divine and heavenly garment which is the power of the Spirit, as it is said: "If anyone does not have the Spirit of Christ, he does not belong to him" (Rom 8:9), let him weep and beg the Lord that he may receive from Heaven the spiritual garment. Let him beg that now stripped of any divine energies, he may be clothed, since the man who is not clothed with the garment of the Spirit is covered with great shame of "evil affections" (Rom 1:26). Just as in the material world, if anyone is naked, he is overcome with great shame and disgrace. Also friends turn away from naked friends, relatives from their own family members, and children turn away from the father whom they see naked so as not to look upon his naked body (Gn 3:7). Such children turned their backs and covered him and only then turned their faces to him. In the same way also God turns away from those who are not clothed with the garment of the Spirit with certainty, from those who have not "put on the Lord Jesus Christ" (Rom 13:14) in power and in truth.

2. The very first man, seeing himself naked, was filled with shame. So great a disgrace accompanies nakedness. If, therefore, in physical matters nakedness carries with itself so great a shame, how much more shame for the person that is naked of divine power, who does not wear nor is clothed with the ineffable and imperishable and spiritual garment, namely, the Lord Jesus Christ himself? Is he not really covered with a greater shame and the disgrace of evil passions?

Everyone who is naked of that divine glory ought to be as much overcome by shame and ought to be aware of his disgrace as Adam was when he was naked. He then made for himself a covering of fig leaves. Nevertheless, he bore shame and acknowledged his poverty. Let such a person, therefore, beg of Christ, who gives and adorns with glory in ineffable light. Let him not sew for himself a garment of vain thoughts, deceiving himself with the impression of his own righteousness or thinking himself in possession of the garment of salvation.

3. If anyone stands solely on his own righteousness and redemption, he labors in vain and to no purpose. For every fancy of one's own justification will appear on the last day as a filthy rag, as the Prophet Isaiah says: "All our justification has been as a filthy rag" (Is 64:6). Let us, then, beg and implore God to clothe us with "the garment of salvation" (Is 61:10), namely, our Lord Jesus Christ, the ineffable Light, which those who have borne it will never put off for all eternity. But in the resurrection their bodies also will be glorified by the glory of the Light with which the faithful and noble persons are even now clothed, as the Apostle says: "He that raised up Christ from the dead will also raise up our mortal bodies by his Spirit that dwells in us" (Rom 8:11). Glory to his ineffable compassion and his ineffable mercy.

4. And again, just as the woman afflicted with an issue of blood believed truly and touched the hem of the garment of the Lord and immediately received a healing and the flow of the unclean fountain of blood dried up, so everyone afflicted by the incurable wound of sin, the fountain of unclean and evil thoughts, if he only approaches Christ and begs prayerfully and truly believes in him, receives a salvific healing from the incurable fountain of passions. That fountain, which has been sending up unclean thoughts, now fails and dries up through the power of Jesus alone. For nothing else can cure this wound. For the enemy, when Adam fell, used such cunning and diligence that he wounded and darkened the interior man, the mind that directs man, since it looks upon the face of God. Thereafter, man's eyes looked with favor on vices and passions, but away from the good things of Heaven.

5. Man was, therefore, so wounded that no one else could cure him except only the Lord. To him alone it is possible. He came and "took away the sin of the world" (Jn 1:29), that is, he dried up the unclean fountain of the evil thoughts of the soul. That woman with the blood hemorrhage spent all her money on those who were supposed to be able to cure her, but she was not healed by any of them until she approached the Lord with genuine faith and touched the hem of his garment. And at once she experienced a healing and the issue of blood was stopped. So also no one, whether he was of the just ones or of the fathers or of the prophets or of the patriarchs, could cure mankind wounded from the beginning with an incurable wound of evil passions.

6. Indeed, Moses came, but he was unable to bring a perfect healing. Priests, gifts, titles, sabbaths, new-moons, purifications, sacrifices,

holocausts, and all other kind of justification were performed under the law and yet the soul could not be healed and purified from its unclean issue of evil thoughts. No self-justification had power to heal man until the Savior came, the true Physician, who cures without costs. He gave himself as a ransom on behalf of the human race. He liberated him from slavery and led him out of darkness by shedding his light upon him. He dried up in him the fountain of unclean thoughts. It says: "Behold, the Lamb of God that takes away the sins of the world" (Jn 1:29).

7. For no earthly medicines, that is, mankind's own justifying actions, had any power to cure the human race of so great an interior plague. But this could be done only by the heavenly and divine nature of the so great gift of the Holy Spirit. Man could be healed only by the help of this medicine and thus could attain life by a cleansing of his heart by the Holy Spirit.

However, just as that woman, although afflicted, could not yet be cured, she still had feet by which she could hasten to the Lord, and, approaching him, she obtained a cure. Likewise, as that blind man, even though he could not approach and come to the Lord because he had no sight, yet he let out a cry, swifter than the angels, saying, "Son of David, have mercy on me" (Mk 10:47), and so believing he received his healing by the Lord's coming to him and restoring his sight, so too a person, even though he is heavily afflicted by evil passions and is blinded by the darkness of sin, nevertheless still possesses the ability to will to cry out and beg Jesus that he come and bring eternal salvation to his soul.

8. Just as that blind man, unless he had cried out, and that woman who had suffered from the issue of blood, unless she had approached the Lord, would not have received a cure, so in a like manner, unless a person comes to the Lord of his own movement and with firm desire and begs him with fullness of faith, in no way can he receive a cure. Why were they cured as soon as they believed, but we have not yet truly received our sight, nor have we been cured of our hidden passions? Indeed, the Lord has greater concern for the immortal soul than the body. For the soul, when it has been restored to sight, according to the Psalmist who says "Open my eyes" (Ps 118:18), will never for all eternity again be blinded, and, once cured, will never again be afflicted.

For if the Lord had such concern for the perishable bodies when he came into this world, how much more does he concern himself with the immortal soul, made according to his own image? It is on account of our lack of belief and our fickleness of mind, because we do not love him with our whole heart. Nor do we really believe him. These are the reasons that we have not yet obtained spiritual health and salvation. Let us, therefore, believe in him and approach him in truth, so that he may speedily bring us to full and authentic health. For he promised that he would give to those who asked him the Holy Spirit and that he would open to those that knocked and by those seeking he himself would be found (Lk 11:9–13; Mt 7:7). And "he cannot lie who promised" (Ti 1:2). To him be glory and power forever. Amen.

Homily 21

There is a double war that involves a Christian, namely, one that is interior and the other exterior. The exterior war consists of man withdrawing himself from worldly distractions. The interior war takes place in his heart against the temptations from evil spirits.

1. Whoever truly wishes to please God and truly makes himself an enemy against the adversary must wage battle on a double front. One battle takes place in the material affairs of this life by turning completely away from the earthly preoccupations and the attraction of worldly bonds and from sinful passions. The other battle takes place in the interior against the evil spirits themselves of whom the Apostle spoke: "For it is not against human enemies that we have to struggle but against the Sovereignties and the Powers, against the rulers of the darkness of this world, against the spiritual armies of evil in the heavens" (Eph 6:12).

2. Man was enchained by two binding forces when he transgressed the commandment and was exiled from Paradise. One bond came in this life in the concerns of living and in the love of the world, namely, the pleasures of the flesh and passions, of riches and glory and possessions, of wife and children, of relatives, of native country, of places, of clothes, and of all other things of the senses from which the Word of God bids him to be freed by his own free choice (since whatever binds every man to all things of the senses is from his own free will) so that, having freed himself from all these concerns, he may be able to master perfectly the commandment.

And, besides, in the interior area of his being, man is walled up and bound with the chains of darkness by the evil spirits. He is unable, as he would wish, to love the Lord and to believe as he wishes and to pray as he wishes. For everywhere in the visible as well as in the invisible there is opposition which has come down to us from the fall of the first man.

3. Whenever anyone listens to the Word of God and enters into the battle and throws off all the concerns of this life and the bonds of the world and denies himself all fleshly pleasures and breaks away from these, then, as he attends to the Lord perseveringly, he is able to find in his heart another struggle, another hidden opposition, and another war of the temptations of the evil spirits, and another battle opens up. And thus by standing firm and calling on the Lord in unshaken faith and with great patience and expecting help to come from him, he can obtain from him inward deliverance from the bonds and the barriers and the ambushes and the darkness of the evil spirits, who operate in the area of the hidden passions.

4. But this war can be brought to a conclusion through grace and the power of God. No man can deliver himself by his own power from the opposition and error of temptations and of interior passions and wiles from the evil one. But if a person is held back by the material affairs of this world, meshed by various earthly bonds and seduced by evil passions, he cannot even recognize that there is another struggle, a battle and a war going on inside.

It can happen that, if anyone struggles by going against himself and frees himself from the external worldly bonds and from the material things and the pleasures of the flesh and he begins to cling to the Lord by emptying himself from this world, then he can recognize the interior battle of passions that is being waged inside. He is aware of the inner war and the evil temptations. Unless, as I said above, he struggles to go against the world[69] and frees himself from the earthly passions with all his heart and desires to become attached completely and totally to the Lord, he will not know about the deception of the hidden, evil spirits and about the hidden evil passions. He remains a stranger to himself, as one who is unaware of his wounds. He has hidden passions and yet he is not aware of them. He is still given over to exterior things and willingly consents to being tied to the preoccupations of this world.

5. But the person who really has rejected the world and has taken effort to cast from him the weight of this earth and has thrown off the vain passions and desires of the flesh, of glory, of authority, and of human honors, and has withdrawn from them with his whole heart (since in this open struggle the Lord secretly helps him to the degree that the person denies himself of the world), and has stood manfully in the service of the Lord and has persevered wholeheartedly in body and soul,

such a person, I say, discovers the opposition, the hidden passions, the invisible bonds, the unseen warfare, the battle and interior struggle. And thus, as he beseeches the Lord, he receives the heavenly armor of the Spirit, which the blessed Apostle described as "the breastplate of justice, the helmet of salvation, the shield of faith and the sword of the Spirit" (Eph 6:14). Armed with these weapons, he is able to stand against the hidden deceits of the devil, even though he is surrounded by the pressing evil forces. Having armed himself by all prayer and perseverance and supplication and fasting and by faith, he will be able to wage war against the principalities.

HOMILY 22

On the two possible states of those who depart from this life.

1. When the soul of a man departs from the body, a certain great mystery is there enacted. If a person is under the guilt of sin, bands of demons and fallen angels approach along with the powers of darkness which capture that soul and drag it as a captive to their place. No one should be surprised by this fact. For if, while a man lived in this life, he was subject to them and was their obedient slave, how much more, when he leaves this world, is he captured and controlled by them? You can understand this, however, from what happens to those on the better side. Indeed, angels even now stand alongside God's holy servants and holy spirits surround and protect them. And when they leave their bodies, the bands of angels receive their souls and carry them to their side into the pure eternity. And so they lead them to the Lord.

HOMILY 23

As only those can wear the royal and precious pearl who are born of royal parentage, so in a similar way only those who are children of God are allowed to wear the heavenly pearl.

1. The great and most precious and royal pearl, which serves for the royal crown, is befitting only a king. Only a king can wear this pearl. No one else is allowed to wear such a pearl. Thus, unless one is born of the royal and divine Spirit and becomes a part of the heavenly and royal

family and a child of God according to what is written, "But to those who received him, he gave them the power to become children of God" (Jn 1:12), he cannot wear the heavenly and most precious pearl, the image of the inexpressible light which is the Lord, since he is not the son of the king. For those who possess and wear the pearl live and reign with Christ forever. Thus the Apostle said: "As we have worn the image of the earthly, we shall also wear the image of the heavenly" (1 Cor 15:49).

2. Take the example of a horse. Just as long as it grazes in the wilderness with wild animals, it refuses to become obedient to men. But when it is captured to be tamed, they put on a heavy bridle until it learns to walk orderly and properly. Then it is trained by an experienced rider so as to become useful in war. Then they put on it armor, I mean, the breastplate and the coat of mail; but first they hold up to it a bridle and shake it before its eyes so that they may get it used to it and not be frightened by it. Thus taught by the rider, it is capable of taking part in a war. When it is trained and used to war, all it has to do is smell the war and hear the sound of it and it immediately attacks the enemy of its own accord, so that by its mere sound that it makes it is sufficient to strike terror in the enemy. So also in the same way a person, who after the fall is wild and indomitable, wanders in the desert of the world with wild animals, which are the evil spirits. He is under sin and resists serving. But when he hears the Word of God and believes, he is bridled by the Spirit. He puts away his wild habits and carnal thoughts, being now guided by Christ, his rider. Afterward, he falls into conflict and experiences difficulties in submitting to the yoke as a part of being tested and thus gradually to be brought into docility by the Spirit. Sin in him diminishes little by little and eventually disappears. So he puts on "the breastplate of justice" and "the helmet of salvation" and "the shield of faith" and "the sword of the Spirit" (Eph 6:14), and is taught to wage war against his enemies.

And thus, armed by the Spirit of the Lord, he fights against the spirits of evil. He quenches the fiery darts of the wicked one. Without the armor of the Spirit, he does not advance to the battle line. But, having the Lord's armor, as soon as he hears and senses the heated wars, he advances with enthusiasm and a cry, as Job says, "because at the very sound of his prayer the enemies fall prostrate" (Jb 39:25). And so, having fought the war and shared in the victory with the help of the Spirit, he receives crowns of victory with great assurance. He thus finds rest with the heavenly King. To him be glory and power forever. Amen.

HOMILY 24

The condition of Christians is similar to merchandise and leaven. Just as merchants collect earthly profits, so Christians collect together their thoughts scattered throughout the world. And, as yeast ferments the whole batch of dough into leaven, so the leaven of sin infects the whole race of Adam. But Christ pours into the souls of the faithful a heavenly leaven of goodness.

1. Christians are like merchants who make great profits in trading. Just as they gather from the earth earthly profits, so also Christians collect together from the whole earth the thoughts of their heart that have been scattered throughout the world. They do this by the help of all the virtues and the power of the Holy Spirit. This is the greatest and genuine merchandise. For this world is opposed to the world above. And this age is pitted against the age to come. It is necessary, therefore, that the Christian, according to Holy Scripture, deny the world, be lifted up and pass over in mind out of this age in which the mind is now found and is exposed to enticements, ever since Adam's fall, into another age. He must live in thought in the world above of the Godhead, as it is said: "Our conversation is in Heaven" (Phil 3:20).

2. This cannot be attained unless the Christian, denying this world, believes in the Lord wholeheartedly. And the power of the divine Spirit can thus gather the heart, now dispersed throughout the whole earth, and bring it to the love of the Lord and lead the mind into the eternal world. For from the time of Adam's fall, the thoughts of the soul have been dispersed away from the love of God toward this world, because it is being mingled with crass and earthly thoughts.

Indeed, as Adam took into himself after his transgression a leaven of evil passions, so also ever since, those who were born of him and the whole race of Adam by participation shared in that leaven. And it has grown and increased so that in men the sinful passions have developed into fornications and debaucheries and idolatries and murders and other absurdities until mankind is permeated with the leaven of evil. And to such a degree has evil increased in humans that they think there is no God, but they worship inanimate stones. They cannot so much as take in an understanding of God. To such an extent has the leaven of evil passions permeated the race of the old Adam.

3. In the same way the Lord was pleased, when he came on this

157

earth, to suffer on behalf of all and to buy them back with his blood and to put the heavenly leaven of goodness into faithful souls once they were humbled by sin. And then he was pleased through growth and development to perfect in them every justification commanded them and all virtues until they [are leaven into one in the good] and they can become with the Lord, "one Spirit" according to Paul's phrase (1 Cor 6:17), so that evil and fornication may not even in thought enter into the soul, so completely leavened by the divine Spirit, as it is said, "Love thinks no evil," and so forth (1 Cor 13:5). But without the heavenly leaven which is the power of the divine Spirit it is impossible that a person be leavened with the goodness of the Lord and reach life. In this way the race of Adam would have been unable to be seduced to such evil and wickedness unless the leaven of evil, which is sin, had crept into Adam. That evil leaven was a power of Satan of a spiritual and intellectual nature.

4. Take the example of a person kneading flour without putting into it a leaven. However much be the efforts he makes, turning it over and over and thoroughly working it up, still the lump remains unleavened and unfit to eat. But if leaven is put into the dough, it draws to itself the whole mass of dough and works it all into leaven, as the Lord said in his parable about the kingdom: "The Kingdom of Heaven is like a leaven which a woman took and hid in three measures of flour until the whole was leavened" (Mt 13:33).

If there were some meat and someone were to take great pains with it, but did not salt it with the salt that kills the worms and destroys the foul odor, the meat would smell and decay and become unfit for men. In the same way picture to yourself the whole of mankind as meat and unleavened dough. Realize that the salt and the leaven belong to another world, the divine nature of the Holy Spirit.

If, therefore, the heavenly leaven of the Spirit, this good and holy salt of the Godhead from that other land, be not mixed and inserted into the lowly nature of men, a person will not be able to get rid of the foul odor of evil. Nor will such a person be leavened so as to put away the heaviness and be freed from the unleavened state of evil.

5. For whatever a person seems to do by himself and whatever diligence he exerts and successful completion he brings about relying solely on his own powers, if he thinks he can effect a perfect work by himself without the help of the Spirit, he is totally in error. Such an attitude is unbecoming one who strives for heavenly places, for the kingdom. Such a person believes that by himself and himself alone, without the Spirit, he can bring about perfect purity.

Unless a person who is swayed by passions approach God by denying the world, and believe with hope and patience that he will receive something good, yet different from his own nature (namely, what is the power of the Holy Spirit), and unless the Lord drop down from above upon him divine life, such a one will never experience true life. He will never recover from the intoxication of materialism. The illumination of the Spirit will never shine brightly upon his soul nor will it illumine him with a "holy day." He will never be aroused from the deepest sleep of ignorance in order in this way truly to know God through God's power and the efficacy of grace.

6. For unless a person is deemed worthy through faith to obtain grace, he is ineffective and unsuited for the Kingdom of God. But on the other hand, whoever has received the grace of the Spirit and does not in any way change his mind, or through negligence or wrongdoing resists grace, if he for some time strives not to grieve the Spirit, he will be able to become a participator of eternal life. Just as one is aware of the operations of evil from the very passions, I mean, by anger and concupiscence, envy and heaviness, by evil thoughts and other absurdities, so also ought one to perceive grace and the power of God by the virtues, I mean, by love, kindness, goodness, joy, simplicity, and divine gladness so as to become like to and mingled with the good and divine nature, with the kind and holy efficacy of grace.

Indeed, a person's free choice is tested by progress and growth in time and according to opportunity to see whether a person is always united with grace and found pleasing. He gradually comes to be totally one with the Spirit and thus is rendered holy and pure by the Spirit, made fit for the Kingdom. Glory and adoration to the undefiled Father and to the Holy Spirit forever. Amen.

HOMILY 25

This homily teaches that no one, unless he is empowered by Christ, is capable of overpowering the stumbling blocks of the evil one. It deals with what those who eagerly seek the divine glory need to do. It also teaches that through the disobedience of Adam we have descended into a slavery to fleshly passions from which we are delivered by the mystery contained in the cross. It teaches us, moreover, that great is the power of tears and of the divine fire.

1. Those upon whom the divine law is stamped not with ink and

letters, but implanted in hearts of flesh, illumined with the eyes of the mind and intent with a constant yearning for a hope that is not sensible or visible but interior and immaterial, have the power to conquer the stumbling blocks of the wicked one, this by the power that can never be surpassed. But those who have not been honored by the Word of God nor instructed in the divine Law are "vainly puffed up" (Col 2:18). They believe that by their own free will they can abolish the sources of sin, something which is condemned only by the mystery found in the cross. For that free deliberation lies in the power of man to resist the devil, but this power is not absolute control over the passions. "Unless the Lord builds the house" (Ps 127:1).

2. It is in vain to go against the asp and the basilisk (Ps 91:13) and tread under foot the lion and the dragon, unless one also first purges himself as far as one has strength and is strengthened by him who said to his Apostles: "Behold, I have given you power to trample upon serpents and scorpions and upon all the power of the enemy" (Lk 10:19).

If man's nature had the ability outside of the complete armor of the Holy Spirit "to stand against the deceits of the devil" (Eph 6:11), the Apostle would surely not have said: "The God of peace will bruise Satan under your feet shortly" (Rom 16:20); and again: "Whom the Lord will destroy with the Spirit of his mouth" (2 Thes 2:8). This is why we have also been commanded to beg the Lord: "Do not lead us into temptation, but deliver us from the evil one" (Mt 6:13). If we are not delivered by the more powerful assistance from the fiery darts of the evil one and not deemed worthy to be the adopted sons, then we live on this earth with no purpose. We are found far from the power of God.

3. Therefore, whoever wishes to become a partaker of the divine glory and to see, as in a mirror, the form of Christ in the ruling power of his mind,[70] must, with unquenchable love and inexhaustible desire, with all his heart and strength, by night and day, seek the help of God which powerfully comes from him, in which help it is impossible to share unless, as I said before, a person abstains from the pleasure of the world, from the desires of the opposing power, which is foreign to the light and is an activity of evil, having no likeness to good activity and is completely alien to it. Therefore, if we want to know why we, since we were created for honor and placed in Paradise, became finally "compared to the beasts that possess no understanding and were made like to them" (Ps 99:12, 20), having fallen from the pristine glory, know that we, by transgression, became slaves of carnal passions. We excluded ourselves from the blessed region of the living (Ps 116:9) and were led into captiv-

ity. We still sit along the shore of Babylon (Ps 137:1). The fact that we are still held in Egypt means that we do not yet possess the land of our inheritance, "flowing with milk and honey" (Ex 3:8). We have not yet been immersed in the leaven of sincerity (1 Cor 5:8), but we are still in the leaven of evil. Our heart has not yet been sprinkled by the blood of God, for "the snare of hell" (Prv 9:18) and the hook of evil is still lodged in it.

4. We have not yet accepted the happiness in Christ's salvation, for "the sting of death" (1 Cor 15:55) has its roots in us. "We have not yet put on the new man who has been created after God in holiness" (Eph 4:24), because we have not yet put off "the old man that is corrupt according to the sinful lusts" (Eph 4:22). We have not yet "given birth to the image of the heavenly" (1 Cor 15:49) nor have we been made "conformed to his glory" (Phil 3:21). We have not yet adored "God in spirit and in truth" (Jn 4:24), since "sin reigns in our mortal body" (Rom 6:12). We have not yet seen "the glory of the incorruptible" (Rom 1:23), because we work under "the moonless night" (Ps 11:2). We have not yet put on the armor of light (Rom 13:12) because we have not yet thrown off the armor and the spears and the works of darkness. We have not yet been "transformed by a renewal of the mind," since we are still "conformed to this world" (Rom 12:2) "in the vanity of the mind" (Eph 4:17).

We are not yet "glorified with Christ" because we have not yet "suffered with him" (Rom 8:17). We do not yet "carry the marks of him in our body" (Gal 6:17), since we do not live in the mystery of Christ's cross. For we are still "in the passions and lusts" of the flesh (Gal 5:24). We have not yet become "heirs of God and co-heirs with Christ" (Rom 8:17) because the "spirit of bondage" is still in us and not that "of adoption" (Rom 8:15). We have not yet been made "the temple of God" (1 Cor 3:16) and the dwelling place of the Holy Spirit, for we are still the temple of idols and the receptacle of evil spirits because of our attachment to the passions.

5. Indeed, we have not yet attained to the simplicity of a life-style and to the enlightenment of our mind. We have not yet been deemed worthy to receive "the guileless and spiritual milk" (1 Pt 2:2) and intellectual growth. The day has not yet dawned upon us, nor "the day star risen in our hearts" (2 Pt 1:19). We have not been mingled with "the sun of righteousness" (Mal 4:2), nor do we yet shine by his rays. We have not yet received the likeness (Gn 1:26) of the Lord nor have we become "participators of the divine nature" (2 Pt 1:4). We have not yet become

the true royal purple nor the authentic image of God. We have not yet been captivated by divine love nor wounded by the spiritual love of the Bridegroom. We have not yet known that ineffable fellowship and have not known the power and peace that are found in sanctification. In a word, we are not yet "a chosen people, a royal priesthood, a holy nation, a people set aside" (1 Pt 2:9), because we are still "serpents, a brood of vipers" (Mt 23:33).

6. How can we be found to be anything but serpents, we who do not obey God but are in the disobedience that has come by the serpent? I cannot discover how to weep befittingly over this situation. I do not know how to cry aloud and weep to him who can expel from me the error planted within me. "How shall I sing the song of the Lord in a foreign land?" (Ps 137:4). How shall I weep over Jerusalem? How am I to flee from the severe slavery of Pharoah? How am I to abandon the foul dwelling place? How shall I deny the bitter tyranny? How shall I go forth out of Egypt? How shall I pass over the Red Sea? How shall I journey through the vast wilderness? How shall I not perish, if bitten by the snakes? How shall I conquer the foreigners? How shall I destroy the pagans within me? How shall I receive the messages of the divine Law upon my tablets? How shall I see the true pillar of light and the cloud from out of the Holy Spirit? How shall I take delight in the manna of eternal delight? How shall I drink the water from the life giving rock? How shall I pass over Jordan and come into the good land of promise? How shall I see the Leader of the Lord's army whom, when Josuah, son of Nun, saw, he fell down at once and worshiped him?

7. For unless I pass through all these and kill the pagan tribes living within me, in no way will I enter and find rest "in the sanctuary of God" (Ps 73:17) nor will I become a participator in the King's glory. For this reason work diligently so as to become a child of God, having no fault and "to enter into that rest" (Heb 4:11) whither the precursor, Christ, has entered on our behalf (Heb 6:20).

Strive to be numbered in the heavenly church with "the firstborn" (Heb 12:23) so that you may be found "on the right hand of the majesty" (Heb 1:3) of the Most High. Strive to enter the holy city, the Jerusalem, full of peace, that is above where Paradise is. You have no other way to become worthy of these amazing and blessed types, except that day and night you pour out tears according to him who says: "Each night I wash my bed and water my mattress with my tears" (Ps 6:6). For you are not ignorant that "those who sow in tears will reap in joy" (Ps 126:6). For this reason the Prophet boldly declares: "Do not silence my tears" (Ps

39:13). And again: "Keep my tears before your sight as you have promised" (Ps 56:8). And, "My tears have been my bread day and night" (Ps 42:3). And in another psalm: "I have mingled my drink with weeping" (Ps 102:9).

8. For such a tear, that truly is shed out of much sorrow and anguish of heart in the knowledge of the truth and with the burning in the bowels, is food for the soul, supplied by the heavenly Bread of which Mary preeminently partook as she sat at the feet of the Lord and wept, as the Savior himself testified. For he says: "Mary has chosen the better part which will not be taken from her" (Lk 10:42, 7:38). Oh, what precious pearls, those contained in the flowing of blessed tears! Oh, that immediate and prompt hearing! Oh, what a strong and wise mind! Oh, the intensity of the love of the Lord's Spirit that moves powerfully toward the spotless Bridegroom! Oh, what a concentration of desire in the soul toward God the Word! Oh, what intimate communion of the bride with the heavenly Bridegroom!

9. Imitate her, O child, imitate her, I say, who saw nothing but him alone who said: "I have come to cast fire on the earth and how I desire but that it be already enkindled" (Lk 12:49). For there is a burning of the Spirit which puts hearts on fire. For that reason the immaterial and divine fire enlightens souls and tests them as pure gold is tested in the furnace. But it burns out any evil, as if it were thorns and stubble. For "our God is a consuming fire" (Heb 12:29), "taking revenge on those who do not know him in flaming fire and who do not obey his Gospel" (2 Thes 1:8). This fire exerted its power over the Apostles when they spoke with tongues of fire (Acts 2:35). This fire surrounded Paul in the voice that enlightened his mind while blinding his sense of sight (Acts 9:3). For it was not in the flesh that he saw the power of that light. This fire appeared to Moses in the bush (Ex 3:2). This fire, in the form of a chariot, caught up Elijah from the earth (2 Kgs 4:11). The blessed David, while seeking out the power of this fire, said: "Search me, Lord, and try me. Burn out my reins and my heart" (Ps 26:2).   *cf. note 37*

10. This fire inflamed the heart of Cleophas and his companion when the Savior spoke to them after the resurrection. From the same source also angels and the ministering spirits partake of the shining fire according to what has been said: "Who makes his angels spirits and his ministers a flaming fire" (Heb 1:7). This fire burns up the beam in the interior eye; it renders the mind pure so that recovering its natural power of seeing, it may constantly gaze on the wonderful works of God according to him who says: "Open my eyes and I will ponder the

wonders of thy law" (Ps 119:18). This fire also drives out demons, takes away sins, and has the power of resurrection. It develops immortality, the illumination of holy souls, and the strengthening of the rational powers. Let us beg that this fire come also to us so that, constantly walking in the light, we may never for even a moment "dash our feet against the stone" (Ps 91:12), "but shining as lights in the world," we may "hold forth the word of eternal life" (Phil 2:15), so that, enjoying ourselves among the saints of God with the Lord, we may find rest in life, glorifying the Father and the Son and the Holy Spirit, to whom be glory forever. Amen.

HOMILY 26

On the dignity and value and the power and works of the immortal soul. How it is tempted by Satan and how it obtains freedom from temptations. It touches on certain questions full of important teaching.

1. Do not, Beloved, consider lightly the intellectual quality of the human soul. The immortal soul is like a precious vessel. See how great are the heavens and the earth and yet God did not take pleasure in them but only in you. Consider your dignity and nobility since not on behalf of angels but for you the Lord came to your protection in order to call you back when you were lost, when you were wounded, and he restored to you the first created condition of the pure Adam. For man was lord over the heavens and the things below. He was the discerner of his passions and was totally alien to the demons. He was pure of any sin or evil, made in the likeness of God. But by the transgression he was lost and was wounded. Satan darkened his mind. In one thing this is so, yet in another way he still lives and can discern and possesses a will.

2. *Question:* Is it not true that, when the Holy Spirit comes, the natural concupiscence is uprooted along with sin?

Answer: I have said above that both sin is uprooted and man receives again the first creation of the pure Adam. By the power of the Spirit and the spiritual regeneration, man not only comes to the measure of the first Adam, but he also reaches a greater state than he possessed. For man is divinized.

3. *Question:* Is Satan let loose on us in a certain measure, or does he war against us as he wishes?

Answer: He attacks not only Christians but also idolators and the whole world. Therefore, if he were allowed to wage war as he wishes, he would have destroyed all human beings. Why is this? Simply because this is his need and desire. Just as the potter puts his vessels into the oven and heats it in a controlled way, not too much because they crack if overheated, and not too little so as not to be useless by being under-baked, and like the silversmith and goldsmith who measure out the fire exactly (for if the fire is too great, the gold and silver melt and turn to water and are sheer waste), likewise, if the human mind knows exactly how to measure the burden of the pack animal and the camel or other such animals according to what weight they can carry, how much more God, who knows what sort of vessels humans are, permits also the enemy power in various ways!

4. Take the example of the earth. Even though it is one, neverthe-less, some earth is rocky, some quite fertile. And some is good for vines while other ground is suited for raising wheat and barley. So also there are different types of human hearts and wills. Likewise also gifts from above are distributed differently. To one is given a ministry of preach-ing, to another that of discernment, to another the gifts of healings (1 Cor 12:9). For God knows how a person is able to fulfill his stewardship and so he gives his various gifts accordingly. In a similar way in regard to the interior battles, the enemy power is permitted to attack humans in the certain measure that each person is able to receive and withstand.

5. *Question:* Does a person who has received divine power and is to some degree changed by it remain in the state of nature?

Answer: In order that the will, once it has received grace, may be tested, in what direction it tends and where it gives consent, nature remains the same: strong in the strong person, and light-minded in the light-headed person. It sometimes occurs that an illiterate person may be reborn spiritually and change to a state of wisdom. Hidden mysteries are revealed to him. Still he remains by nature an uneducated person. An-other person is rough by nature. He applies his will to divine services which God accepts. However, the roughness of his nature persists and yet God is pleased with him. Another is kind in his habits, gentle and good. He offers himself to God and the Lord accepts him. But if he not persevere in good works, God is not pleased with him, since the whole nature of mankind is changeable for good or for evil. It is capable of evil, yet if it desires, it has the power not to carry it out.

6. Take the example of writing on a parchment. You write some-thing not intended and so you erase it. The parchment receives any kind of writing. So also a self-willed man gave his will over to God. He was

converted to what was good and God accepted him. In order that God may manifest his compassion, he accepts every sort of person, with varying dispositions. The Apostles came into a certain city and worked there for a certain time. They healed ones who were sick; others they did not heal. The Apostles personally would have wished to give life to all the dead and to bring to health all the sick, and yet they did not perfectly have their own way. For it was not permitted to them to do all they had wished.

Likewise, also Paul, when he was captured by the ethnarch; if the grace that was with him had desired it, he would have arranged it that the ethnarch and the wall would be toppled, since he was a man possessing the Paraclete. But the Apostle was let down by a basket (2 Cor 11:32). And where was the divine power that was with them?

These things happened providentially with the result that in some cases they performed signs and wonders and in other cases they were without power in order that the faith of the unbelievers and the believers may be distinguished and in order to test and show forth the free will, whether or not some would be scandalized at their weaker sides. For if the Apostles had accomplished everything they wished, they would have brought men and free will into God's service by a certain compulsory force and not by faith or by unbelief. Christianity is "a stone of stumbling and a rock of scandal" (Rom 9:33).

7. Moreover, what was written about Job is not lightly to be considered, just how Satan sought after him. For Satan was unable to do anything by himself without permission. What does the devil say to the Lord? "Give him into my hands, for he will surely bless thee to thy face" (Jb 1:22, 2:5). In this way even now Job is the same and also God and the devil. Therefore, insofar as a person seeks God's help and is eager and fervent in grace, Satan desires him. And he says to the Lord: "Since you help him and come to his rescue, he serves you. But let go of him and hand him over to me. Surely he will bless you to your face." In a word, because a person is comforted, grace can withdraw and he can be delivered up to temptations. The devil comes, bringing thousands of evils as temptations: despair, apostasy, evil thoughts. He afflicts the soul as to weaken and alienate it from the hope in God.

8. The prudent person, beset by evils and in affliction, does not give up hope, but he holds on to what he holds and as much as the devil brings against him, he endures in the face of innumerable temptations, saying, "Even if I shall die, I shall not let him go." And then, if a person endures faithfully to the end, the Lord begins to converse with Satan:

166

"You see how many evils and afflictions you have inflicted upon him and yet he has not obeyed you, but he serves me and fears me." Then Satan is overcome by shame and has nothing further to say. In the case of Job, if the devil had known that amidst temptations Job would remain faithful and would not be conquered, he would never certainly have desired him out of fear of being humiliated. So also now in the case of those who bear afflictions and temptations, Satan is put to shame and is sorry because he has attained nothing. The Lord begins to converse with him: "Look, I gave you permission. I allowed you to tempt him. Were you able to do anything? Did he obey you in any way?"

9. *Question:* Does Satan know all the thoughts and plans of man?

Answer: If one man is with another person and knows things concerning him, and if you, twenty years old, know things concerning your neighbor, can Satan, who has been with you from your birth, not know your thoughts? For he is already six thousand years old.[71] Still we do not say that before he tempts he knows what man will intend to do. For the tempter tempts, but he does not know whether a person will obey him or not until one gives up his will as a slave. Neither again do we maintain that the devil knows all the thoughts of a person's heart and its desires. Like a tree, it has many branches and limbs. So the soul has certain branches of thoughts and plans and Satan grasps some of them. There are other thoughts and intentions that are not grasped by Satan.

10. For in one matter the side of evil takes an upper hand in thoughts that arise. In another matter, again, the thought of man is superior as he receives help and deliverance from God and he resists the evil. In one thing he is overcome and in another he has his will. For sometimes he comes to God with fervor and Satan knows this and sees that man is repelling him and that he is incapable of restraining him. Why is this? Because a person has the desire to cry out to God. He has the natural fruits of loving God, of believing in him, of seeking him and coming to him.

In the material world of things around us, the farmer works the earth. So also in the spiritual world there are two elements to be considered. It is necessary for man to work the soil of his heart by a free deliberation and hard work. For God looks to man's hard work and toil and labor. But if the heavenly clouds from above do not appear and the showers of grace, the farmer for all his labor avails nothing.[72]

11. This is the sign of Christianity. However much man should do and how many justifying works he should perform, he should feel that he has accomplished nothing. And when he fasts, he should say, "I have

not fasted." When he prays, let him think, "I have not prayed." Persevering in prayer he should say, "I have not persevered. I have only begun to practice asceticism and to labor." And even if he is righteous before God, he must say: "I am not righteous. I am not working, but I begin each day." He ought every day to have the hope and joy and confidence in the future kingdom and in redemption and say: "If today I have not been delivered, tomorrow I will be." It is like the man who plants a vineyard. Before he ever begins work, he entertains hope and joy as he ponders in his mind the vineyards and counts up his profits, even though there is no wine yet. And in this way he puts himself to work. Hope and expectation make him toil enthusiastically and for some time even he undergoes great expenses, paid out of his pocket. It is like one who builds a house or cultivates a field. At first he undergoes expenses to himself, but in the hope of future profits. It is the same way in this matter. Unless a person keeps before his eyes joy and hope, namely, "I shall obtain salvation and life," he cannot bear patiently afflictions or the burden or accept to travel along the narrow road. For it is the presence of hope and joy that allow him to labor and bear afflictions and the burden of traveling along the narrow path.

12. Just as it is not very easy for a branding iron to escape the fire, so also neither can a person avoid the fire of death except by the greatest work. In many cases Satan, under the pretext of good thoughts such as "In this way you can please God," suggests to a person and cunningly leads him astray to subtle and half truths. Such a person does not know how to detect that he is secretly being seduced and so he "falls into the snare and perdition of the devil" (1 Tm 6:9). The most important weapons for the athlete and combatant are these: to wage war against Satan in the depths of his heart; to hold himself as an object of hatred; to deny his soul; to be angry with it and rebuke it; and to resist the passions and to struggle with thoughts and to fight the battle with himself.

13. But if you outwardly keep your body from corruption and defilement, but inwardly commit adultery and fornication in your thoughts, you are an adulterer before God. It profits you nothing, whatever physical virginity you may possess. Take the example of a young maiden and a young man. He entices her by deceit and his lascivious words and thus corrupts her. Afterward she is loathed by her husband because she had committed adultery. So also the spiritual soul, if it has anything to do with the serpent that lies hidden in the interior recesses, commits adultery with the evil spirit against God, as it is written, "Everyone that looks upon a woman to lust after her has already committed

adultery in his heart" (Mt 5:28). For there is a fornication committed through the body and another one of the soul in fellowship with Satan. The same soul is partner and sister either of demons or of God and angels. And if it commits adultery with the devil, it is useless for the heavenly Bridegroom.

14. *Question:* Does Satan ever become quieted and is man ever freed from war or, as long as he lives, is he plagued by war?

Answer: Satan is never quieted, at peace and not at war. As long as a person lives in this world and is living in the flesh, he is subject to warring. But when "the fiery darts of the wicked one are quenched" (Eph 6:16), what harm can he inflict upon man, if Satan comes with his suggestions?

If someone is a friend of the king and has a court case against an adversary, since he has the king already favorably disposed and kind toward him and the king does extend him help, he in no way can suffer injury. When someone is able to pass successfully through all the ranks and degrees and become a friend of the king, what harm can anyone inflict on him? In the world there are some cities that receive gifts and subsidies from the king. If, therefore, they render some service, they suffer no great loss since they receive so much help from the king. So also Christians, even if they are attacked in war by the enemy, still they turn to the Godhead as to their strength. They have put on from on high the power and the rest and have no concern about the war.

15. Just as the Lord put on the body, leaving behind every principality and power, in a similar way Christians put on the Holy Spirit and are at peace. Even if war starts externally and Satan attacks, they are still fortified interiorly by the Lord's power and are not anxious about Satan. As he tempted the Lord in the desert for forty days, what harm did he inflict on him by attacking him externally in his body? For interiorly he was God. So also Christians, granted they may be tempted exteriorly, nevertheless, interiorly they are filled with the Godhead and suffer no injury. If one has reached this degree, he has arrived at the perfect love of Christ and the fullness of the Godhead. But one who is not of this type still wages an interior war. For a certain hour he delights in prayer, but at another time he is bombarded by affliction and at war. This is what the Lord wishes.

Because such a person is still an infant, the Lord trains him in wars. And both things, like two personalities, spring up inside the same person: light and darkness; rest and affliction. Such persons pray in peace, but at another time they are found in distress.[73]

16. Do you not hear what Paul says? "If I have all gifts, if I hand my body over to be burnt, if I should speak with the tongues of angels and, yet, I have no charity, I am nothing" (1 Cor 13:1ss). These gifts really are to encourage us. And those who settle for these, even though they are in the light, they still are infants. For many of the brothers have reached this degree and enjoyed the gifts of healings and revelation and prophecy. But because they did not reach perfect charity which is the "bond of perfection" (Col 3:18), war came upon them and, because they were negligent, they fell.

But if anyone does reach perfect charity, he is bound and taken captive by grace.[74] If anyone approaches somewhat the level of charity, yet does not succeed in being completely bound by charity, such a one is still under fear and war and the possibility of falling. And unless he is strengthened, Satan overthrows him.

17. In such a way many who have been given grace went astray and lost grace. They thought that they had obtained perfection and said: "It is enough for us. We need nothing more." But the Lord neither has an end nor is he totally comprehended. And Christians do not dare to say, "We have comprehended" (Phil 3:13), but they are humble night and day in their search. In the changeable world, there is no end to education and no one understands this better than a person who has begun to learn. So in this case, God is incomprehensible to man and he cannot be measured except in the case of those who have begun to taste him whom they have received, and who acknowledge their own weakness. If someone journeys to a country where the people are illiterate and he knows something of learning, he is praised by them as a learned person since they are illiterate. But if the same person, not overly educated, should journey to a city where there are orators and scholars, he would not dare to appear before them or speak, lest he be judged illiterate by the scholars.

18. *Question:* If a man who is engaged in the interior war and still entertains a double principle in his soul, namely, there is sin and grace, departs from this world, where does he go, since he is tending toward the two principles?

Answer: The mind goes where it finds its goal and where it loves. Only if affliction and war beset you, you ought to resist and hate them. For the fact that war comes upon you is not your doing. To hate it, however, is up to you. And then the Lord, seeing your mind, that you are struggling and that you love him with your whole soul, drives death away from your soul in a very brief time. This is not difficult for him to do. And he receives you to his bosom and into his light. In a flashing moment he snatches you from the jaws of darkness and immediately takes you into his kingdom. For to God in a flash all things are easily accomplished, if only you show love toward him. God needs the working of man, since the human soul is meant to have fellowship with the Godhead.

19. We have already often spoken about the parable of the farmer who works and throws seed upon the earth. He must, besides, receive rain from above. Unless clouds appear and winds blow, the work of the farmer avails him nothing. The seed lies bare. Now apply this to the spiritual world. If a man relies only on his own efforts and does not receive something beyond what is due to his own nature, he cannot produce fruits worthy of the Lord. What is the working of man? To renounce, to leave the world, to remain perseveringly in prayer, to make night vigil, to love God and the brothers. It is up to him to labor perseveringly. But if he endures in his own doing and does not hope to receive something else and the winds of the Holy Spirit do not blow upon his soul and if clouds from the heavens do not appear and rain from the heavens does not fall and moisten the soul, man cannot give to the Lord fruits that are worthy of him.

20. It is written that when the farmer sees the branch bearing fruit, "he purges it, that it may bring forth more fruit" (Jn 15:2). But whatever does not bring forth fruit, he uproots and gives to be burned. Indeed, it is becoming man that if he fasts or keeps the night vigil, or prays or does anything of good, he should attribute it all to the Lord, and say, "If God had not empowered me, I could never have fasted or prayed or left the world." In this way, God sees your good intention, that you ascribe to God all the things that by your nature you accomplish and he gifts you with the things that are of him, namely, the spiritual things, the divine and the heavenly. And what are these? The fruits of the Spirit, gladness and happiness.

21. *Question:* But since there are natural fruits that similarly resemble these of love, faith, and prayer, show us: How do spiritual fruits differ from these?

Answer: The things you accomplish of yourself are good and acceptable to God, but they are not pure. An example is: You love God, but not quite perfectly. The Lord comes and gives you an unchangeable, heavenly love. You pray naturally with anxiety and distracting thoughts. God gives you a pure prayer "in Spirit and in truth" (Jn 4:23). In the visible world the soil for the most part of itself brings forth thistles. The farmer

171

digs up the soil, works it diligently, plants seed, but the thistles, which no one planted, rise up and multiply. For after the fall it was spoken to Adam: "Thistles and thorns shall the earth bring forth unto thee" (Gn 3:18). Again the farmer takes pains with the soil. He uproots the thistles and still they multiply. Apply this spiritually. After the fall, the soil of the human heart brings forth thistles and thorns. Man works at it; he takes great pains and yet the thistles of evil spirits spring up. Then the Holy Spirit himself "helps the infirmities" (Rom 8:26) of men and the Lord plants heavenly seed in the very soil of the heart and cultivates it. And, though the seed has fallen into the soil, still thistles and thorns spring up. Again, the Lord himself and man work the soil of the soul and still the evil spirits and thistles spring up and grow there, until hot weather comes and grace abounds and the thistles dry up from the heat of the sun.

22. For even though evil is found inside of nature, still it no longer has dominance over nature or the power it once exerted. For the weeds do have a power to choke the tender blades of wheat. But as soon as summer arrives, after the dying off of the fruits, the weeds have no more harming effect over the wheat. If there were thirty pecks of pure wheat and it were mixed with a quart of tares, what kind of effect would there be? The tares would be completely immersed in the wheat. So also in the matter of grace, when the gift of God and grace are more abundant in man and he is rich in the Lord; even if evil is present to some degree, still it has no power to harm a person greatly nor does it have any power or control over him. For the coming of the Lord and his providence have had this purpose—to free those who were held captive by evil and bound and in submission to it and to make them conquerors over death and sin. Therefore, the brothers should not think it so strange if they are afflicted by certain persons. It serves to vindicate them through such evil.

23. Formerly Moses and Aaron, who were given the power of the priesthood, had to suffer many things. Caiphas, when he took over their role, persecuted and condemned the Lord. However, the Lord, respecting the priesthood, permitted that to happen. Likewise the prophets were persecuted by their own nation. Also, Peter succeeded Moses, entrusted with the new Church of Christ and the authentic priesthood. For now there is a baptism of fire and the Spirit and we are given a certain circumcision of the heart. The divine and heavenly Spirit abides within the mind. Nevertheless, not even those perfect ones, as long as they are living in the flesh, are solicitous, on account of free will. But they are stricken with fear and for this reason are allowed to be tempted.

Only when a person arrives at that city of the saints, then can he live

172

his life without afflictions and temptations. For there can be no more worry or affliction or labor or old age or Satan or war, but only rest, joy, peace, and salvation. For the Lord is in their midst, who is called Savior, because he sets captives free. He is called physician because he bestows a heavenly and divine medicine and he heals the passions of the soul. For those, in some respect, hold power over man. But in a word, Jesus is King and God; Satan is a tyrant and the evil ruler.

24. To put it simply, God and his angels wish to make this man a member of his family to be with him in their kingdom. Likewise, the devil and his angels wish also to adopt man as their own. The soul is caught in between these two subsistent beings, and, to which ever side the soul's will turns, to that side he belongs and is his son. Just as if a father would send his own son into a foreign land where en route wild animals will pounce upon him. The father would give him medicines and remedies so that, if the wild beasts or dragons were to attack him, he may use the medicine to kill them. So also strive to receive the heavenly medicine, the healing and antidote of the soul, so that by means of it you may kill the poisonous wild beasts of unclean spirits. For it is not easy to maintain a pure heart unless with great effort and work a person obtains a conscience and a clean heart, in order that evil may be completely uprooted.

25. It does happen that grace befalls someone whose heart, nevertheless, is not yet purified. And this is because those who fell fell because they did not believe that, once they received grace, smoke and sin could still exert an influence on them. But all the just ones have pleased God on the narrow way full of afflictions by their persevering right to the end. Abraham, even though he was rich both in the eyes of God and the world, still considered himself as "earth and dust" (Gn 18:27). David also says: "A very scorn of men and the outcast of the people, a worm and no man" (Ps 22:6). Similarly all the Apostles and prophets were ill treated and rejected. The Lord himself, who is the Way and is God, after he came not on his own behalf but for you so that he might be an example for you of everything good, see, he came in such humility, taking "the form of a slave" (Phil 2:7), he, who is God, the Son of God, King, the Son of the King. He himself gave healing medicines and he healed all the wounded when he appeared externally as one among "the wounded" (Is 53:5).

26. Do not despise his divine dignity, as you look at him, externally humiliated as one like us. For our sakes he so appeared, not for himself. Consider at that hour when they cried out: "Crucify him, crucify him"

(Lk 23:21), and the crowd gathered together, how he was humiliated more than all men. In the world around us, if there is a criminal and he receives a sentence from the judge, then by all the people he is scorned and rejected. So also the Lord in that hour of the cross. As a man about to die, he was despised by the Pharisees. And when again they spat in his face and placed a crown of thorns on him and hit him, what more humiliation could he have yet undergone? For it is written that "I gave my back to the smiters and I hid not my face from the shame of those who spat on me and my cheeks not from buffeting" (Is 50:6).

If God condescends to such insults and sufferings and humiliation, you, who by nature are clay and are mortal, no matter how much you are humiliated, will never do anything similar to what your master did. God, for your sake, humbled himself and you will not be humbled for your own sake, but you remain proud and inflated. He came to take upon himself your afflictions and burdens and to bestow his rest on you. But you refuse to bear any difficulties and to suffer in order that in this way you may obtain the healing of your wounds. Glory be to his patience and long suffering forever. Amen.

HOMILY 27

This homily, as the preceding one, deals at greater length with the dignity and status of the Christian person. Then it teaches many profitable things about free will, intermingling certain questions full of divine wisdom.

1. Know, O man, your nobility and dignity. How precious you are, the brother of Christ, the friend of the King, the bride of the heavenly Bridegroom. For he who is capable of knowing the dignity of his soul is able to know the power and the mysteries of the Godhead and thereby is capable of being all the more humbled, since in the light of God's power does a person see his fallen state. But as he passed through the sufferings and the cross and thus was glorified and sat at the right hand of the Father, so likewise it is necessary for you to suffer with him to be co-crucified and thus to ascend and to be seated with him and to be joined to the Body of Christ and reign with him forever in that world, "if so we suffer with him in order that we may also be glorified with him" (Rom 8:17).

2. Those who are able to conquer and pass over the obstacles of evil enter into the heavenly city, which is full of peace and many good

things, where "the spirits of just men" (Heb 12:23) find their rest. Therefore, it is necessary on this point to take great pains and to struggle manfully. Indeed, it is not right that the Bridegroom came to suffer and to be crucified while the bride, for whom the Bridegroom came, should live in luxury and worldly distraction. Just as in worldly matters the prostitute gives herself promiscuously to all, so also the soul has given itself to every demon and is corrupted by those spirits. For there are some who have sin and evil by free choice, while others have it against their will. What does this mean? Those who have evil by their own choice have given away their will to evil and they take pleasure in it and make friends with it. Such as these have made peace with Satan and do not wage a war in their thoughts with the devil. But those who entertain sin against their own choice have sin "warring in their members" (Rom 7:22), according to the Apostle. And the shadowy force and darkness are against their willing. They do not consent in their thoughts and do not take pleasure in it nor do they surrender to it, but they oppose it in word and deed. They are angry with themselves. These are far more noble and honorable before God than those who give over their will freely to evil and take pleasure in it.

3. Take the example of a king who would find a certain poor maiden, dressed in rags. He would not be ashamed, but he would take away her dirty rags and would wash off her blackness. He would adorn her in elegant clothes and make her a partner of the king. He would give her a place at his table and share with her a banquet. Thus also the Lord found the wounded soul that was stricken. He gave it medicine and removed the black garments and the shame of evil and he clothed it with royal, heavenly garments, those of the Godhead, all shining and glorious. And he placed a crown upon it and made it his partner at the royal table unto joy and gladness.

And just as in the case of a beautiful garden where there are fruit-bearing trees and the air is saturated with sweet odors and there are many beautiful and refreshing places to delight in and put at rest those who go there, so also are those persons who reach the kingdom. They are all in joy and happiness and peace. They are kings and lords and gods. For it is written: "King of kings and Lord of lords" (1 Tm 6:15).

4. The Christian religion is not, therefore, an ordinary thing. "This mystery is great" (Eph 5:32). Acknowledge your nobility, that you are chosen to a kingly dignity, "a chosen race, a royal priesthood and a holy nation" (1 Pt 2:9). For the mystery of Christianity is foreign to this world. The visible glory of the king and his wealth are earthly and

175

perishable and pass away. But that kingdom and riches are divine things, heavenly and full of glory, never to pass away or be dissolved. For such Christians co-reign with the heavenly King in the heavenly Church. "And he is the firstborn from the dead" (Col 1:18) and they also are the firstborn. Still, granted that they are all this, chosen and approved by God, nevertheless, they regard themselves as the least and completely worthless. And this is natural for them, to hold themselves as lowly or as nothing.

5. *Question:* Do they not know, therefore, that they have received something added that they did not naturally possess before?

Answer: I tell you that they do not consider themselves approved. They think they have made no progress. They are oblivious as to how they obtained what they have. But even though they are such persons as described, grace itself comes and teaches them not "to count their soul as honorable" (Acts 20:24), even though they have made progress, but rather to regard themselves as naturally dishonorable. And even though before God they are honored, still they see themselves as not so. And though they progress and have knowledge of God, still they regard themselves as if they know nothing. Being rich before God, they regard themselves as poor. As Christ, having taken on "the form of a servant" (Phil 2:7), through humility conquered the devil, so at the beginning through pride and vainglory the serpent overthrew Adam. And now the same serpent, hiding in human hearts, through vainglory destroys and dissolves the race of Christians.

6. Take the example of a certain free and well-born man, according to the world, who has much wealth and continues to prosper and bring forth much fruit. He loses his balance and puts his confidence in himself. He becomes intolerable, kicking and beating everybody. So it is with certain persons lacking discretion, who, as soon as they begin to experience some bit of quiet and peace in prayer, begin to be puffed up spiritually. They lose their balance and begin to criticize others. And so they fall to the lowest parts of the earth. That very serpent who threw Adam out of the garden through pride, saying, "You shall be as gods" (Gn 3:5), now also suggests pride in human hearts, saying, "You are perfect, you are sufficient unto yourself, you are rich, you need nothing, you are blessed."

There are other persons who according to the world are wealthy and continue to amass more wealth. Yet they exercise a certain discretion. They neither boast nor are puffed up, but they are balanced. For they realize that after abundance comes the pinch. And again when they fall into financial straits, they are not dejected but keep their balance. They know that prosperity will return. And by long training in these matters, they are not taken back nor are they puffed up in times of success and prosperity nor are they dejected when misfortune hits them.

7. Christianity is similar to tasting deeply of truth, eating and drinking of truth—to eat and drink on and on unto power and energy. It is like a certain spring when someone very thirsty begins to drink from it. But then, while he is drinking, someone rushes him off before he has drunk his full. Afterward, he burns more ardently, because he has tasted the water and eagerly seeks it. So also in the spiritual life, a person tastes and partakes of the heavenly food, but while he is eating it is taken away and no one gives him to eat his full.

8. *Question:* Why do they not allow him to eat his full?

Answer: The Lord knows the weakness of man, that he is quickly puffed up and for this reason he withdraws and allows the man to be tested and afflicted. If you receive only a little and no one can stand you, because you are puffed up, how much more would you act in this way if someone allowed you to take your full without stopping you? But God, knowing your weakness, providentially arranges that you are given afflictions so that you may become humble and all the more eagerly seek him. A certain man, poor according to worldly standards, found a purse of gold. He was so elated that he began to shout out: "I found a purse; I am rich." Then the party that lost it heard about it and recovered it. Another rich man became immoderate and began to kick people about, becoming arrogant to everybody. The king learned of it and took away all his possessions. So it is in the spiritual life. When some persons taste a bit of refreshment, they lose their balance and that which they had received they even lose, for sin leads them astray and darkens their mind.

9. *Question:* How do certain persons fall after the visitation of grace? Is not Satan rendered weaker by grace? Where there is day, can there also be night?

Answer: Grace is not extinguished or diminished, but so that your free will and liberty may be put to the test to see which way it tends, grace permits the presence of sin. And then you draw near to the Lord by your free choice and beg that his grace may come upon you. For it is written: "Do not quench the Spirit" (1 Thes 5:19). The Spirit cannot be extinguished, but is always light. But it is you, if you are neglectful and do not willingly cooperate, who are done in and lose the Spirit. In a similar way it says, "Sadden not the Holy Spirit in whom you were sealed unto the day of salvation" (Eph 4:30). You see that it is up to your will and freedom of choice to honor the Holy Spirit and not to grieve him. I guarantee you that free choice remains, even in the perfect Christians who are captivated by what is good and have become inebriated with it. The result is that, even though they are tested by thousands of evils, they move toward what is good.

10. Take the example of persons who are dignified and wealthy and of noble birth. By their very own desire and choice they give up their wealth and noble birth and dignities and go away and put on poor, dirty clothes and accept dishonor instead of honors. They put up with afflictions and are held of no repute and these things they accept by their own desire. You can trust me that grace did not prevent the Apostles, who were brought to perfection by grace, from doing whatever they wished to do, even if they preferred occasionally to do something that was not in keeping with grace. For, indeed, our human nature tends toward both good and evil and the opposing force acts by enticement, not by necessity. You possess free choice to move in the direction that you wish. Do you not read that Peter "was to be blamed" (Gal 2:11), and that Paul went and corrected him? And Paul, as spiritual as he was, freely engaged in a quarrel with Barnabas and they were so sharp that they both left each other (Acts 15:39). This same Paul says: "You, who are spiritual, restore such a one, considering yourself so as not also to be tempted" (Gal 6:1). See, the spiritual persons are put to the test because their free will remains and the enemies harass them as long as they remain in this world.

11. *Question:* Were the Apostles capable of sinning if they chose, or was grace too powerful for their will?

Answer: We do not say that they were incapable of sinning because they were in light and possessed such grace. Also we do not imply that grace was weak in them. But what we say is that grace permits even the spiritually perfect persons to have their free wills and to enjoy the power to do whatever things they wish and to incline toward wherever they wish.[75] And human nature itself, being weak, enjoys the power to turn away in the presence of good. Take the case of those persons fully armed with breastplate and other arms. In a word, they are interiorly protected and enemies do not attack them. Or should the enemies attack, it is within their free will either to use those arms and to fight against and repel the enemies and to be victorious, or to take pleasure and make peace with the enemies and give up fighting, even though they possess the armor. Likewise also Christians, who have put on the perfect power and have the heavenly armor, can, if they wish, take a liking to Satan and make peace with him and no longer do battle. For nature is changeable, and, if anyone wishes, he can become a son of God or again become a son of perdition. Before such, his free will remains.

12. It is one thing to give a description of bread and the banquet table and another thing to eat and enjoy the delicious taste of bread and to be strengthened in all your bodily members. It is one thing to speak about a delicious drink in words and it is another thing to go and draw forth from the very fountain and drink to your full of the delicious draught. It is one thing to lecture on war and about the brave athletes and warriors, and it is another thing for someone to go out to the battlefront and to attack the enemies and to make a front attack and a rear withdrawal, to take and to give and to win victoriously. It is similar in spiritual matters. It is one thing to lecture with a certain intellectual knowledge and ideas, and another thing in substance and reality, in full faith and in the inner man and in the consciousness to have the treasure and the grace and the taste and the working of the Holy Spirit.

Those who speak only barren words live in illusions and are "puffed up by their mind" (Col 2:18). It says: "For our speech and our preaching was not with persuasive words of human wisdom, but in the proof of the Spirit and of power" (1 Cor 2:4). And again elsewhere it says: "The end of the commandment is love out of a pure heart and a good conscience and faith unfeigned" (1 Tm 1:5). Such a person does not fall. For to many who seek out God the door opens and they see a treasure and they enter into it. And just as they were in joy saying, "We have found the treasure," he shuts the doors. They begin to cry out and weep and earnestly seek: "We have found the treasure and have lost it." Providentially, grace withdraws so that we may seek after it more diligently. For the treasure is shown so as to make us seek it.

13. *Question:* Some say that, once grace is accepted, a person passes from death to life. Is it possible for one who is in the light to entertain impure thoughts?

Answer: It is written: "Having begun in the Spirit, do you now finish in the flesh?" (Gal 3:3). Again it says: "Put on the whole armor of the Spirit so that you may be able to stand against the attacks of the devil" (Eph 4:30). These texts speak of two different levels: one where a person was after he put on the armor and the other where he is when he wars against the principalities and powers: namely, in light or in darkness. Again it is written: "That you may be able to quench the fiery darts of the wicked one" (Eph 6:16). And again: "Sadden not the Holy Spirit of God" (Eph 4:30). And again: "It is impossible that those who once were enlightened and tasted the gift of God and were made participators of the Holy Spirit and fell away, be renewed" (Heb 6:4). See, there are those who have been enlightened and have tasted the Lord and still fall. You see that a man possesses the free will to live in harmony with the Spirit and also has the free will to grieve him. Surely he takes up arms to go into the battle and struggle against the enemies. Surely he was enlightened so as to war against the darkness.

14. *Question:* What is the Apostle's meaning in this statement: "If I possess all knowledge and all prophecy and speak with the tongues of angels, I am nothing" (1 Cor 13:1ff.)?

Answer: We must not so understand it as if the Apostle were nothing, but when compared with that charity which is perfect these other things are of little importance, and he who possesses such things in some degree may fall. But he who possesses charity cannot fall. I tell you this, that I have seen men who received all the gifts and were participators of the Spirit, but, not reaching perfect charity, they fell. One certain nobleman renounced the world, sold all that he possessed, gave freedom to his slaves. Being a prudent and understanding man, he gained a reputation for the strictness of his life. In the meantime, entertaining an exalted opinion of himself and becoming puffed up, he finally fell completely into debaucheries and a thousand evils.

15. Another in time of persecution gave over his body and became a confessor of the faith. After these things, when peace was restored, he was set free and enjoyed a great fame. His eyelids had been injured by having been burnt. Moreover, he was glorified and his prayers were sought after. But he accepted offerings and gave them to his servant, and his mind became such as though he had never heard of God's word. Another gave his body in the time of persecution and was hanged and scraped and then he was thrown into prison. There a certain nun served him out of good faith. He became familiar with her while being in prison and fell into fornication. See how the rich man, having sold all his possessions, and the one who gave his body in martyrdom, still fell.

16. There was a certain wise athlete living with me in the same dwelling who prayed with me. He was so rich in grace that, as he prayed near me, he would be overwhelmed by compunction, for grace boiled up in him. He was given also the gift of healing and he not only drove out demons, but he also cured by imposing his hands on those who were bound hand and feet, and suffered serious sicknesses. Afterward, he became careless, and, being much glorified by the world, he enjoyed the pleasure of it and became puffed up. He fell into the very depths of sin.

See how even one who had the gift of healing fell. You see how, before they arrive at the full measure of charity, they fall. For one who has reached charity is captivated and intoxicated by it. He is immersed in it and held captive in another world, as if he had no awareness of his own nature.

17. *Question:* What is the meaning of the phrase: "Those things that eye has not seen, nor ear heard, nor has it ever entered into the heart of man" (1 Cor 2:9)?

Response: In that time, the great and just ones and the kings and the prophets knew that the Savior was coming. But they did not know nor had they heard that he would suffer, had to be crucified, and would pour out his blood on the cross. Nor did it enter into their heart that there would be a baptism of fire and of the Holy Spirit and that in the Church bread and wine would be offered up, the antitype of his flesh and blood, and that those who received of the visible bread would eat spiritually of the flesh of the Lord, and that the Apostles and Christians would receive the Paraclete and would be "endowed with power from on high" (Lk 24:49) and be filled with the Godhead and that their soul would be interpenetrated by the Holy Spirit. This the prophets and kings did not know, nor did it even enter into their heart. But now Christians enjoy a richness in another way and they are seized with desire for the Godhead. But even though they enjoy this joy and consolation, they, nevertheless, are still under fear and trembling.[76]

18. *Question:* Under what fear and trembling?

Answer: That they may not take the wrong step, but cooperate with grace. Take the example of a certain man who has a treasure and he journeys to places where there are robbers. Even though he is happy about the wealth and treasure, yet he entertains fear lest the robbers attack him and strip him of them. He is as one who carries his own body in his hands.

Look, as far as external things are concerned, all of us have renounced them and are as pilgrims without possessions, deprived of any fellowship with the world. Look at the body wrapt in prayer. The brothers must be the ones to see whether the mind also is at one with the body. Take the example of skilled workers and builders in the world. They for the most part apply their body as well as their mind both night and day to their profession. Then take a look at yourself. Your body is a stranger to the world. Do you also hold your mind alienated from the world and never get tied up with matters of the world? Every man in the world, be he soldier or merchant, wherever he applies his body, there also he concentrates his mind and there is his treasure. For it is written: "Where your treasure is, there also is your heart" (Mt 6:21).

19. Now what treasure is your mind focused on? Is it totally centered on God or not? If it is not, you must tell me what is the obstacle. Surely there exist evil spirits, Satan and his demons, who hold captive the mind and entrammel the soul. For the devil is very cunning and has many tricks and loopholes and all sorts of deceits. He captures the grazing lands of the soul and the thoughts and does not allow it to pray properly and to draw near to God. For human nature itself tends to form a fellowship with the demons and the evil spirits equally as well as with the angels and the Holy Spirit. It is the temple of Satan or the temple of the Holy Spirit. Now, give a look at your mind, brothers. With whom are you in fellowship: the angels or the demons? Whose temple are you, the dwelling place of God or the devil? With what treasure is your heart filled: grace or Satan? Just as a house that has been filled with foul smells and dung, it must be completely cleaned up and put in order and filled with every fragrance and all treasures, so it is that the Holy Spirit may come instead of Satan and may find rest in the souls of Christians.

20. Indeed, it is not immediately upon hearing the word of God that a person is ranked among the good. If the mere hearing brought him into the ranks of the good, there would no longer be any struggles or times of war or any race. But without any labor, if one merely heard the word, he would come into complete rest and perfection. But things are not quite like that.

For you deprive man of his free will in saying this and you also deny the opposing power that is struggling against the mind. This is what we say, that one who hears the word comes to repentance, and after this, through God's providence withdraws for the development of the man. He enters into training and tactics of war. He enters into the struggle and conflict against Satan. And after a long race and struggle, he carries off the victory and becomes a Christian. If anyone, by merely hearing the word, without any work, would be numbered among the good, then also actors and all prostitutes would enter into the kingdom and the life. But no one will give them this without effort and struggle because the road is straight and narrow (Mt 7:14). Along this bumpy road we must travel and patiently endure afflictions and thus enter into life.

21. For if it were possible to succeed without effort, Christianity would not be "a stumbling stone and a rock of scandal" (Rom 9:33). There would be no faith or disbelief. You would in fact make man into a

bound creature of necessity, unable to turn toward good or evil. For it is only for a person capable of turning to both sides that a law is given, namely, to one possessing free will to do battle against the opposing force. No law is given for a nature that is bound by necessity. For neither the sun nor the heavens and the earth are governed by a law, because these creatures are by nature bound by necessity and for this reason they are neither subject to reward nor punishment. Reward and glory are prepared for a nature that is capable of turning toward the good. Hell and punishment are meted out for that changeable nature that is capable of turning away from the evil and throwing its lot toward the good and the right side. Look, should you say that a man is unchangeable, you make a good man unworthy of praise. For a man who is gentle and good by nature is not deserving of praise, even if he desires it. What good is not freely chosen is not praiseworthy, even if it be desirable. That person is worthy of praise who by his very own diligence with struggle and battle makes the good his own by a free will choice.

22. Take the example of the Persian camp and the camp of the Romans opposite them and there should come out from both camps two winged young men, equal in strength, and they engage in battle. Likewise also the opposing power and the human mind are equally pitted in strength against each other. Satan has equal power to exhort and entice a person toward his own will, and yet a person has equal power to resist and in no way to obey him. Powers of both evil and of good can be turned by persuasion but not by force. Divine assistance is given to such a free choice and is able, as it battles, to receive the heavenly arms and by means of them to uproot and conquer sin. To resist sin is within a man's power, even though without God he cannot conquer and uproot evil.[77] Those who say that sin is like a mighty giant and the human soul like a child speak wrongly. For if things were so dissimilar, so that sin would be as a giant and the human soul as a child, then the Lawgiver would be unjust, in giving a law to man to battle against Satan.

23. This is the foundation of the road to God, in much patience, in hope, in humility, in poverty of spirit, in gentleness to travel along the road of life. By such means one can possess justification for himself. We mean by justification the Lord himself. These commandments, which so enjoin us, are like milestones and signposts along the royal highway that leads a journeyer to the heavenly city. For it says: "Blessed are the poor in spirit; blessed are the meek; blessed are the merciful; blessed are the peacemakers" (Mt 5:3). Call this Christianity. If anyone does not pass

along this road, he has wandered off along a roadless way. He used a bad foundation. Glory to the mercies of the Father and the Son and the Holy Spirit forever. Amen.

HOMILY 28

This homily describes and deplores the tragedy of the person in whom, because of sin, the Lord does not dwell. And concerning John the Baptist that none of those born of women is greater than he.

1. Just as once God became angry with the Jews and handed Jerusalem over to the profanation by their enemies "and they who hated them lorded it over them" (Ps 106:41), and there was no feast celebrated any longer there, or any offering, so also with the human soul, God, being angry with it because of violating his command, turned it over to its enemies, to the demons as well as to the passions. And so, when these had seduced it, they completely ruined it and no longer was there any feast or incense or offering sent up by it to God. Its monuments have been forgotten in the streets,[78] while terrifying beasts and serpent spirits of evil make their dwelling place in it. And just as a house, if it has no master dwelling in it, collects darkness and shame and abuse and becomes filled with dirt and dung, so the soul, which does not have its Lord celebrating with his angels in it, becomes full of the darkness of sin and the disgrace of the passions and with all sort of ignominy.

2. Woe to the road if no one walks along it nor hears in it the voice of man, because it has become the den of wild beasts! Woe to the soul in which the Lord does not pass along its route and from which the Lord does not drive out by his voice the spiritual wild beasts of evil! Woe to the house where the master does not abide! Woe to the earth which does not have a farmer to cultivate it! Woe to the ship without a navigator, because it is carried along by the waves and by the heaving of the sea and is lost! Woe to the soul which does not have the true navigator, Christ, in it, because finding itself on the sea of frightful darkness and tossed to and fro by the heaving of the passions and beaten by the winter storm of evil spirits, it finally gains perdition! Woe to the soul when it does not have Christ, cultivating it with care so as to bring forth good fruits of the Spirit; because left sterile and filled with thorns and thistles, its fruit finally is burning in the fire. Woe to the soul when it does not have

Christ as its Master dwelling in it, because being abandoned and filled with the foul odor of passions, it finds itself a dwelling place of iniquity.

3. Just as the farmer, when he girds himself to cultivate the soil, must take the tools and clothing for cultivating, so Christ the King, the heavenly and true cultivator, when he came to humanity made barren by evil, put on the body and carried the cross as his tool and worked the barren soul and removed from it the thorns and thistles of evil spirits and pulled up the weeds of sin and burned up with fire every weed of its sins. And in this way he cultivated it with the wood of the cross and planted in it the most beautiful paradise of the Spirit, bearing every fruit that is sweet and delectable to God as its owner.

4. And just as in Egypt, during the three-day darkness, son did not see his father, neither did brother see his brother, friend his true friend, since the darkness covered them, so likewise when Adam transgressed the commandment and fell from his former glory and became subject to the spirit of the world. The veil of darkness came upon his soul. And from his time until the last Adam, the Lord, man did not see the true heavenly Father and the good and kind mother, the grace of the Spirit, and the sweet and desired Brother, the Lord, and the friends and relatives, the holy angels with whom he was rejoicing, dancing, and celebrating. And not only up to the last Adam, but even now those for whom "the Sun of righteousness" (Mal 4:2), Christ, has not arisen and in whom the eyes of the soul have not been opened and have not been enlightened by the true Light, are still under the same darkness of sin, are plagued by the same influence of the passions and are subject to the same punishment, since they lack eyes to see the Father.

5. For everyone should realize that there are eyes deeper within than these physical eyes and there is a hearing deeper within than this hearing. Just as these eyes sensibly see and recognize the face of a friend or a loved one, so also the eyes of the worthy and faithful person, being spiritually enlightened by the divine light, see and recognize the true Friend, the sweetest and greatly desired Bridegroom, the Lord, since the soul is completely illuminated by the adorable Spirit.[79] And thus, seeing with the mind the desirable and only ineffable beauty, such a person is pierced with divine passionate love and is directed in the way of all virtues of the Spirit. And so he possesses an unlimited and inexhaustible love for the Lord he longs for. What then can be more blessed than that everlasting voice of John as he points out before our eyes the Lord, saying: "Behold the Lamb of God, who takes away the sin of the world" (Jn 1:29).

6. Indeed, "among those born of women there is no greater than John the Baptist" (Mt 11:11). For he is the fulfillment of all the prophets. But all of them prophesied about the Savior and pointed him out before the eyes of all, crying aloud and saying: "Behold the Lamb of God" (Jn 1:36). What a sweet and beautiful voice of the one who directly points out him whom he was announcing! No one of those born of women is greater than John. "But he that is least in the Kingdom of Heaven is greater than he" (Mt 11:11)—those who have been born from above, of God, namely, the Apostles. They received the first fruits of the Paraclete Spirit. For they were considered worthy to be his fellow-judges, sitting on the same throne. They were made redeemers of men. You find them dividing the sea of evil powers and leading through the souls of the faithful. You find them cultivators in the vineyard of souls. You find them bridesmen, espousing souls to Christ, for it says: "I have espoused you to one husband" (2 Cor 11:2). You find them giving life to men, and, in a word, you find them "in many ways and diverse manners" (Heb 1:1) serving the Spirit. This is the little one that is greater than John the Baptist.

7. As the farmer drives a yoke of oxen and cultivates the earth, so in a similar way the Lord Jesus, the good and true Husbandman, yoking the Apostles, two by two, sent them forth to cultivate the earth of those who hear and believe in truth. But this also is worth saying: not only in the word heard, as one who possesses the gift of speech and preaches them to others, is the Kingdom of God and preaching of the Apostles, but the kingdom comes about in the power and work of the Spirit. This happened unfortunately to the children of the Israelites who constantly studied the Scriptures. They meditated on the Lord and yet, not accepting the truth for themselves, they gave it as an inheritance to others. Likewise, in the case of those who explain the words of the Spirit to others, they do not possess the word in power, yet to others they pass on the inheritance. Glory to the Father and to the Son and to the Holy Spirit forever. Amen.

HOMILY 29

According to a twofold manner God bestows his providential dispensations of grace upon the human race, intending to demand again in a just judgment the fruits of it.

1. The wisdom of God, since it is infinite and incomprehensible,

brings about in an incomprehensible and unsearchable way the dispensations of grace toward the human race in various ways for the testing of
man's free will, so that those who love him with their whole heart and
who patiently endured every kind of danger and toil for the sake of God
may appear.

To some the charisms and gifts of the Holy Spirit come in advance.
They immediately draw near in faith and petition without work, sweat,
and toil, even while they are still in the world. God so gives them grace,
not idly nor out of season nor by chance, but he gives it with ineffable
and incomprehensible wisdom to test the choice and free will of those
who so quickly received divine grace. This happens whether they were
aware of the benefit and the goodness and sweetness of God that was
shown them in proportion to the grace bestowed without any efforts on
their part for what they were considered worthy to receive. In return for
which they should have to show zeal and to run the race and to show
effort and to bear fruit of will and determination and love, and to return
for the gifts received a reckoning by giving themselves up completely to
the love of the Lord and by accomplishing his will alone and by completely withdrawing from all carnal affection.

2. To those others, even though they may have left the world and
renounced this world according to the Gospel and spend their time in
much continuous prayer and fasting and vigilance and the other virtues,
God does not give grace and rest and the joy of the Spirit, but he shows a
patient love toward them and holds back his gift.[80]

And this God does not idly or inopportunely nor in a haphazard
way, but with ineffable wisdom unto the testing of their free will to see
whether they regarded God as "faithful and true" (Heb 11:11), who
promised to give to them that ask and to open the door (Lk 11:9-13) of
life to them who knock, to see whether, after believing his word in truth,
they patiently persevere up to the end, in fullness of faith and zeal,
asking and seeking, whether they not become remiss and pull back and
give up. In a lack of faith and hope, they despise the goal by not persevering to the end because God delayed the time of his gift and because of
the testing of their will and determination.

3. For he who does not immediately receive because of God's
delay and patient longing is enkindled much more. He is more eager to
desire the heavenly good things. And daily he adds greater desire, zeal,
running, and struggle, and every attitude of virtue, and he shows a
hunger and thirst for what is good. He does not grow remiss in attacks
from the evil of the thoughts inhabiting his soul, nor does he show any

tendency to contempt, impatience, and despair. Nor, on the contrary, under pretext of patient endurance does he give himself over to laziness, using such reasoning as, "When will I ever receive God's grace?", and from this is led into carelessness by evil. Indeed, as long as the Lord, by his delaying the gift, is patiently loving him by testing his faith and the love of his will, the person himself should all the more keenly and with greater diligence, without becoming remiss, seek the gift of God, having once for all believed and assured himself that God is without deceit and is truthful, he who has promised that he would give his grace to those who faithfully ask in all patience until the end.

4. For God is regarded as faithful and true to those who remain faithful. They "have attested that he is truthful" (Jn 3:33) according to the true Word. Therefore, in accord with this insight of faith, they judge themselves whether they on their part are remiss in labor, in effort, in zeal, or in faith, or love, or any of the array of virtues. And by examining themselves with all delicate sensitivity, they push themselves and strive to the best of their ability to please the Lord, having once and for all believed that God, being truthful, will not deprive them of the gift of the Spirit if they persevere to the end with all diligence to serve him and wait on him, but they will be deemed worthy of the heavenly grace, even while they live on this earth, and they will obtain eternal life.

5. And thus they move their whole love toward the Lord, rejecting all other things and stretching out for him with great desire and hunger and thirst. And they always await the recreating and consoling power of grace. They do not willingly seek comfort or recreation in anything of this world and are attached to nothing. But always resisting gross temptations, they seek their only help and strength in God since the Lord himself is already secretly present to such persons that take upon themselves such diligence and determination and perseverance. The Lord helps and protects them and lets shine forth in them every fullness of virtue. And even though they find themselves still in struggle and affliction and they are not adorned in the certainty of truth and in a conscious experience with the grace of the Spirit and have not yet felt the recreating power of the heavenly gift nor felt it in its fullness, this is on account of the ineffable wisdom of God and his inexpressible judgments by which he tests faithful persons in various ways in a view to bring them to a love that is freely chosen. For there are limits and measures and stages of free choice and desire to love and also of a bent of mind to obey all his holy commandments as much as possible. And thus, as persons fill up the

measure of their love and obligation, they are deemed worthy of the kingdom and of eternal life.

6. For God is just and so are his judgments. He is no respecter of persons, but he will judge each person according to the different benefits which he has bestowed on mankind, those of body or spirit, or those of knowledge or understanding or discernment. And he will seek the fruits of virtue proportionately. He will give to each according to his worth according to his accomplishments (Rom 2:6). And "the mighty ones shall be powerfully tormented for mercy will soon pardon the lowest" (Wis 6:6). The Lord says: "The servant, who knew the will of his lord and did not prepare nor did he do according to his will, shall be beaten with many stripes. But he, that did not know and did things worthy of stripes, shall be beaten with few stripes. For to whom much is given, of him much shall be required and, to whom men have committed much, of him they will ask more" (Lk 12:47–48). Consider knowledge and understanding in various ways, either according to grace and the heavenly gift of the Spirit, or according to the natural grasp of the understanding or discretion and through the instruction of sacred Scripture. For each person will be responsible for the fruits of virtue in proportion to the benefits bestowed on him by God, whether natural or given by divine grace. Therefore, each person is without excuse before God in the day of judgment. For each person will be required to correspond with his choice and will, according to what he knew, to produce the fruits of faith and love and every virtue in relationship to God, whether he heard or had never heard the word of God.

7. The faithful person, who loves truth, looks to the eternal blessings reserved for the just and to the ineffable help of the future divine grace. He regards himself and his diligence and his pains and labor as unworthy compared to the ineffable promises of the Spirit. Such a one is the poor in spirit whom the Lord declared blessed. This is he who hungers and thirsts after justice (Mt 5:3, 6). This is the one who is contrite of heart. Whoever take upon themselves this determination and diligence and labor and desire for virtue and persevere to the end in them, they will be able to obtain life and truly the eternal kingdom.

Therefore, let no one of the brothers be exalted over his brothers or proceed to entertain an arrogant opinion of himself, seduced by evil to think, "I have obtained a spiritual gift." For it is not becoming for Christians to think such things. For you cannot know what tomorrow may do for him. You do not know what is his end or what will be your own. Let every one be attentive to himself, let him examine his own conscience always, checking the movement of his heart as to his diligence and with what striving his mind tends toward God. And keeping in mind the perfect goal of liberty and freedom from passions and of the Spirit's peace, let him run without stopping and without sloth, never being complacent with any charismatic gift or even justification. Glory and adoration to the Father and the Son and the Holy Spirit forever. Amen.

HOMILY 30

It is necessary that one who wishes to enter into the Kingdom of God must be born of the Holy Spirit and the manner in which this is to be done.

1. Those who hear the word should give witness to the working of the Word in their own souls. The word of God is not an idle word, but it has its own work upon the soul. For this reason it is called a "work" so that the work may be found in those who hear it. May the Lord, therefore, grant the work of truth in the hearers so that the Word may be found fruitful in us. For just as the shadow precedes the body, but reveals it, so also, while the truth is the body itself, the Word is like a shadow of the truth of Christ. Thus the Word precedes the truth. Fathers on earth beget children of their own nature from their body and soul, and when they are born fathers educate them carefully with every attention since they are their own children until they become full grown men and successors and heirs. For the aim and every striving of fathers from the beginning is to beget children and have heirs. And if they had not had any children, they would have suffered the greatest sorrow and grief, while having had children, they had joy. Also their relatives and neighbors rejoice.

2. In the same way also our Lord, Jesus Christ, was concerned with humanity's salvation. He exercised from the beginning every providential planning and diligence through the fathers, the patriarchs, through the Law and the prophets. Finally he himself came and suffered the ignominy of the cross and endured death. And all this labor and diligence of his was done so that he might beget from himself and his very own nature children from his Spirit. He was pleased that they were to be born from above, of his own Godhead. And just as those fathers, if they have no offspring, are saddened, so also the Lord who loved man-

kind as his own image wished them to be born from his seed of the Godhead. If any of them, therefore, do not wish to come to such a birth and to be born of the womb of the Spirit of the Godhead, Christ receives great sorrow, suffering on their behalf and enduring so much in order to save them.

3. For the Lord wishes all to be considered worthy of this birth. For he died on behalf of all and he has called all to life. Indeed this life is the birth from above of God. Without this one cannot live as the Lord says: "Unless one will be born from above, he cannot see the Kingdom of God" (Jn 3:3). And so, on the contrary, as many as believe the Lord and come to be deemed worthy of receiving this birth, they bring joy and great happiness in Heaven to the parents that gave them birth. And all the angels and holy powers rejoice over a person who is born of the Spirit and has become spirit. For this body is a likeness to the soul and the soul is an image of the Spirit.[81] And as the body without the soul is dead, and cannot do anything whatsoever, so without the heavenly soul, that is, without the divine Spirit, the soul is reckoned dead as far as the kingdom goes, being unable to do any of the things of God without the Spirit.

4. Just as the portrait painter is attentive to the face of the king as he paints, and, when the face of the king is directly opposite, face to face, then he paints the portrait easily and well. But when he turns his face away, then the painter cannot paint because the face of the subject is not looking at the painter. In a similar way the good portrait painter, Christ, for those who believe in him and gaze continually toward him, at once paints according to his own image a heavenly man. Out of his Spirit, out of the substance of the light itself, ineffable light, he paints a heavenly image and presents to it its noble and good Spouse.

If anyone, therefore, does not continually gaze at him, overlooking all else, the Lord will not paint his image with his own light. It is necessary that we gaze on him, believing and loving him, casting aside all else and attending to him so that he may paint his own heavenly image and send it into our souls. And thus carrying Christ, we may receive eternal life and even here, filled with confidence, we may be at rest.

5. Just as in the case of the golden coin, if it does not receive the imprint of the king's image, it does not reach the marketplace nor is it stored up in the royal treasuries, but it is discarded, so also the soul, if it does not have the image of the heavenly Spirit in the ineffable light, namely, Christ, stamped on it, it is not useful for the treasuries above and is cast out by the merchants of the kingdom, the Apostles. For also he

191

who was invited and yet did not wear the wedding garment was cast out as a stranger into the alien darkness for not wearing the heavenly image. This is the mark and sign of the Lord stamped upon souls, being the Spirit of the ineffable light. And as a cadaver is useless and completely of no good to those of a given place, and so they carry it outside the city and bury it, so also the soul which does not bear the heavenly image of the divine light, the life of the soul, is rejected and completely cast off. For a dead soul is of no profit to that city of the saints, since it does not bear the radiant and divine Spirit. For just as in the world the soul is the life of the body, so also in the eternal and heavenly world the life of the soul is the Spirit of the Godhead.

6. Therefore, he who seeks to believe and to approach to the Lord must beg while here on earth to receive the divine Spirit. For the Spirit is the life of the soul, and on this account the Lord came, in order to give his Spirit to the soul on this earth. For he says: "As long as you have the light, believe in the light. The night comes when you can no longer work" (Jn 12:36, 9:4). If anyone, therefore, while on this earth does not seek and has not received life for his soul, namely, the divine light of the Spirit, when he departs from his body, he is already separated into the places of darkness on the left side. He does not come into the Kingdom of Heaven, but has his end in hell with "the devil and his angels" (Mt 25:41).

Or take the example of gold or silver that is thrown into the fire. It becomes purer and more tested and nothing can make it to be otherwise, such as wood or hay, for it devours all things that approach it, for they become also fire. For the soul that is plunged into the fire of the Spirit and in the divine light will suffer no harm from any of the evil spirits. Even if anything should come near to it, it is consumed by the heavenly fire of the Spirit. Or as a bird, when it flies up high, has no worry and does not fear the bird-catchers or the evil beasts, for being up so high, it laughs at all below. So also the soul that has received the wings of the Spirit. It flies up into the heights of heaven and being higher than all else, it derides them all.

7. Israel, the people of God according to the flesh, passed through after Moses had divided the sea. But these, since they are the children of God, walk from above over the sea of bitterness of the evil powers. Their body and their soul have become the house of God.

In that day when Adam fell, God came walking in the garden. He wept, so to speak, seeing Adam and he said: "After such good things, what evils you have chosen! After such glory, what shame you now bear!

What darkness are you now! What ugly form you are! What corruption! From such light, what darkness has covered you!" When Adam fell and was dead in the eyes of God, the Creator wept over him. The angels, all the powers, the heavens, the earth and all creatures bewailed his death and fall. For they saw him, who had been given to them as their king, now become a servant of an opposing and evil power. Therefore, darkness became the garment of his soul, a bitter and evil darkness, for he was made a subject of the prince of darkness. This was the person who was wounded by robbers and left half dead as he "was going down from Jerusalem to Jericho" (Lk 10:30).

8. For Lazarus also, whom the Lord raised up, exuded so fetid an odor that no one could approach his tomb, as a symbol of Adam whose soul exuded such a great stench and was full of blackness and darkness. But you, when you hear about Adam and the wounded traveler and Lazarus, do not let your mind wander as it were into the mountains, but remain inside within your soul, because you also carry the same wounds, the same smell, the same darkness.

We are all his sons of that dark race and we all inherit the same stench. Therefore, the passion that he suffered, all of us, who are of Adam's seed, suffer also. For such a suffering has hit us, as Isaiah says: "It is not a wound, nor a bruise, nor an inflamed sore. It is impossible to apply a soothing salve or oil or to make bandages" (Is 1:6). Thus we were wounded with an incurable wound. Only the Lord could heal it. For this he came in his own person because no one of the ancients nor the Law itself nor the prophets were able to heal it. He alone, when he came, healed that sore, the incurable sore of the soul.

9. Let us, therefore, receive God the Lord, the true healer, who alone can come to heal our souls, after he has borne so much on our behalf. For he is always knocking at the doors of our hearts in order that we may open up to him and that he may enter in and take his rest in our souls, and that we may wash his feet and he may take up his abode with us. The Lord in that passage admonishes him who did not wash his feet (Lk 7:44). And again he says elsewhere: "Behold I stand at the door and knock. If anyone hears my voice and opens the door, I shall come in unto him" (Rv 3:20). For this purpose he endured many sufferings, giving his body over to death and buying our ransom from slavery so that he, coming to our soul, might make his abode there.

For this reason the Lord says to those on the left side in the judgment, sent by him into hell with the devil: "I was a stranger and you did not take me in. I was hungry and you gave me not to eat. I was thirsty and you gave me not to drink" (Mt 25:42–43). For his food and drink and clothing and shelter and rest are in our souls. Always, therefore, is he knocking, seeking to enter into us. Let us receive him and lead him within ourselves, because he himself is our food and life and drink and our eternal life. And every person who has not now received him within and found rest, or rather found his rest in him, does not have an inheritance in the Kingdom of Heaven nor can he enter into the heavenly city. But you, yourself, Lord Jesus Christ, lead us into it, as we glorify your name with the Father and the Holy Spirit forever. Amen.

HOMILY 31

It is necessary that the believer be transformed in his mind and focus all his thoughts upon God. For in these truly all service of God consists.

1. The believer should beg God to be transformed in his deliberation by a change of heart, to be transformed from bitterness into sweetness. He should remember how the blind man was healed and how the woman with a hemorrhage likewise was healed by the touching of his garment—the nature of lions was tamed, the nature of fire was deadened. The reason is because God is the height of goodness. Unto him you should gather up the mind and the thoughts and to think of nothing else than to look expectantly for him.

2. Let the soul be as one who gathers together straying children and castigates the thoughts scattered abroad by sin. Let the soul lead them into the home of its body, always awaiting expectantly for the Lord in fasting and love when he will come and gather it in truth. Since the future is uncertain, let the believer set his hope more on the Pilot, being full of hope. And let him remember how also Rahab, while she was living among foreigners, believed the Israelites (Jos 2:9) and was deemed worthy to share their society. But even the Israelites out of affection turned back to Egypt. As, therefore, Rahab was not harmed at all while she lived among foreigners, but her belief gave her a home, sharing the inheritance of the Israelites, so sin shall not harm those who in hope and faith wait expectantly for the Redeemer, who, when he comes, transforms the thoughts of the soul and makes them divine, heavenly, good. And he teaches the soul how to pray, truly undistractedly without wandering.

He says: "Fear not. I go before you and will level the mountains. I will break in pieces the gates of brass and cut asunder the bars of iron" (Is 45:2). And again he says: "Attend that there be no secret thought of wickedness in your heart. Say not in your heart: This nation is strong and mighty" (Dt 15:9, 7:17).

3. If we do not dissolve ourselves in sloth and turn over the pastures of our minds to the disorderly thoughts of evil, but we force our mind to obey our will, compelling our thoughts toward the Lord, without doubt the Lord will come to us with his will and take us unto himself in truth. Everything that is pleasing and is of service is found in the thoughts. Therefore, strive to please the Lord, always waiting expectantly for him from within, seeking him in your thoughts and forcing and compelling your own will and deliberation to stretch out always toward him. And see how he comes to you and makes his abode in you (Jn 14:23). For as much as you concentrate your mind to seek him, so much more does he, by his own tender compassion and goodness, come to you and give you rest. He stands, gazing on your mind, your thoughts, your desires. He observes how you seek him—whether with your whole soul, with no sloth, with no negligence.

4. And when he sees your earnestness in seeking him, then he appears and manifests himself to you. He gives you his own help and makes the victory yours, as he delivers you from your enemies. For when he first sees you seeking after him, and how you are totally waiting expectantly without ceasing for him, he then teaches and gives you true prayer, genuine love, which is himself made all things in you: paradise, tree of life, pearl, crown, builder, cultivator, sufferer, one incapable of suffering, man, God, wine, living water, lamb, bridegroom, warrior, armor, Christ, all in all.[82]

Indeed, just as an infant does not know how to take care of itself or do for itself, but only looks to its mother, as it cries, until she, moved by pity, picks it up, so faithful persons constantly hope only in the Lord, attributing all justice to him. As without the vine, the branch is dried up, so is he who desires justification without Christ (Jn 15:5–6). Just as the robber and the thief "who does not enter through the door but climbs in by some other way" (Jn 10:1), so too is he who justifies himself without the Justifier.

5. Let us, therefore, take this body and make an altar of sacrifice, and let us place on it all our desires and let us beg the Lord that he would send down from Heaven the invisible and mighty fire and consume the altar and everything on it. And may all the priests of Baal fall, which are

the opposing powers. And then we shall see the spiritual rain, like a man's footprint (1 Kgs 18:44), come into the soul, so that it becomes in us the promise of God, as it is said in the Prophet: "I will raise up and build again the tabernacle of David which has fallen and I will build again the ruins of it" (Am 9:11), so that the Lord, with his very own kindness, may shine upon the soul that dwells in night and darkness, in the drunkenness of ignorance, and, in a word, that it may awaken with vigilance and journey without stumbling, performing the works of day and of life. For the soul is nourished where it feeds, either from this world or from the Spirit of God. And God is there nourished and lives and finds rest and dwells.

6. In a word, everyone, if he wishes, is able to prove to himself from what source he is nourished and where he lives and in what condition he finds himself, so that, understanding this and gaining an accurate judgment, he may apply himself perfectly to the impulse toward what is food. Indeed, when you are in prayer, be attentive to yourself, observing your thoughts and your activities, whence they come: whether from God or from the adversary. And see who furnishes your heart with nourishment, the Lord or the world rulers of this age. And when you have the proof and you know, O soul, beg the Lord with pain and longing for the heavenly nourishment and growth and the working of Christ as in the saying: "Our conversation is in Heaven" (Phil 3:20) and do not seek after a conceived plan or a type, as some image. Behold, the mind and understanding of those who look for a concept of godliness is like to the world. See their agitation and fluctuation in determination, their unstable opinion, their cowardliness and fear, according to the saying: "Groaning and trembling shall you be on the earth" (Gn 4:12). According to their unbelief and the confusion of their fickle thoughts, they are tossed about every hour as all the rest of mankind. Such persons only differ from the world in an exterior fashion, but not in mind, and only in bodily observances of the exterior person. For in their heart and in mind they are drawn in all directions in the world, and they are attached to earthly affections and useless worries, not enjoying the peace from Heaven in their heart, as the Apostle says: "Let the peace of God reign in your hearts" (Col 3:15). This is a peace that reigns and renews the minds of the faithful in the love of God and of all the brotherhood. Glory and adoration to the Father and the Son and the Holy Spirit forever. Amen.

HOMILY 32

The glory of the Christians, even now, dwells within their souls and will at the time of the resurrection be manifested and will glorify their bodies in proportion to their piety.

1. The languages of this world are different. For each nation has its own language. But Christians learn now only one language and all are taught one wisdom of God, a wisdom not of this world nor of this passing age. And as Christians walk in this creation, they discover newer, heavenly insights and glories and mysteries, receiving them from what things hit their senses.

There are genera of domesticated animals, such as the horse and ox. Each of them has its own proper body and voice. This is the same for wild animals. The lion has its own body and voice; likewise the deer. And among the reptiles there is also a great variety, as also among the birds there are many types of bodies. The body and voice of the eagle are of one kind, that of a hawk of another.

There are the same differences in the sea. There are many bodies that are not like to each other. And in the earth there are many seeds, but each seed has its own fruit. There are many trees; but some trees are bigger, some are smaller. And the harvests of fruit show forth a great variety. For each type of tree has its own flavor. And there are herbs and great differences exist among them. Some are useful for healing, others only for their fragrance. But each tree produces from within a cover which appears visibly: leaves and flowers and fruit. Likewise also the seeds bring forth from within the covering visible to the eye. And the lilies themselves produce from within their covering and adorn the earth.

2. So also those Christians who have been deemed worthy in this life to possess the heavenly raiment carry that raiment dwelling within their souls. And when it will be preordained by God to dissolve this creation and for heaven and earth to pass away, then the heavenly raiment that clothed and glorified their soul in this present life and which they possessed in their heart, that raiment also will adorn their naked bodies which will rise from the tombs, the bodies that will awake in that day. This invisible and heavenly gift and raiment even in this life Christians receive.

Take the example of sheep or camels when they find grass. They greedily and in quick time devour the food and store up nourishment inside themselves. In time of hunger they cough it up from their bellies and chew the cud and so they have for food what they had earlier stored up. So also those who have seized the Kingdom of Heaven and have tasted the heavenly nourishment as they live in the Spirit—at the time of the resurrection will have that same food to cover and to warm all their members.

3. Therefore, we spoke of the difference in seeds, that many are sown in the same ground and bring forth a variety of fruits, all different. It is the same in regard to trees. Some of them are bigger, some smaller, but one earth holds the roots of all of them. So also the heavenly Church, being one, yet it is without number. And each number is adorned in a very unique way by the glory of the Spirit. Take the example of birds who produce out of the body the raiment of their wings, yet great is the variety among them. For some fly close to the ground, while others fly high in the air. Or take the example of the heavens. It has many stars in itself, some brighter, some bigger, some smaller, yet all are fixed in the heavens. So also the saints are rooted in the one Heaven of the Godhead in different ways and also in the invisible earth. So likewise those thoughts which come to the sons of Adam are different, yet the Spirit, coming into the heart, makes one thought and one heart. For those below and those above are directed by the one Spirit.

4. But what is the significance of the animals that "divide the hoof" (Lv 11:3)? Since they travel along the way straightway with their two hooves, this serves as a symbol of those who walk upright in the Law. But just as the shadow of the body is from the body itself, but is unable to perform any physical service, for a shadow cannot bind up wounds or give food or speak, and yet it has its existence from the body, and, proceeding before it, manifests the presence of the body, so also the ancient Law is a shadow of the New Covenant. The shadow manifests in advance the truth, but it does not possess a service of the Spirit.

Moses, having been clothed in the flesh, was unable to enter into the heart and take away the sordid garments of darkness. But only spirit from Spirit and fire from Fire dissolves the power of the evil darkness. Circumcision, in the shadow of the Law, shows the coming of the true circumcision of the heart. The baptism of the Law is a shadow of the true things to come. For that baptism washed the body, but here a baptism of Fire and the Spirit purifies and washes clean the polluted mind.

5. There the priest, "covered with infirmity" (Heb 5:2), entered

into the Holy of Holies to offer sacrifice for himself and the people. Here the true High Priest, Christ, once and for all entered into the tabernacle, not made by hands, and the altar above, ready to purify those who beseech him and the conscience that has been sullied. For he says, "I will be with you even to the consummation of the world" (Mt 28:20).

The high priest had on his chest two precious stones that had also the names of the twelve patriarchs. This was done in that time as a figure. In a similar way the Lord put on his twelve Apostles and sent them as evangelists and preachers to the whole world. You see how the shadow precedes and points out the coming approach of the truth. Yet in the way that the shadow does not have a service nor does it heal any sufferings, so also the ancient Law was unable to heal the wounds and sufferings of the soul. For it did not possess life.

6. For two substances joined together work to effect one perfect thing, such as two covenants. Man was made according to the image and likeness of God. He has two eyes, two eyebrows, two hands, two feet. And if he should happen to have only one eye or one hand or one foot, it is something regrettable. Or take the example of a bird, if it should have one wing, it is unable to fly with it. So also the nature of mankind, if it remains naked all by itself and does not receive the union and fellowship of the heavenly nature, it is not complete.[83] But it remains naked and is to be blamed in its nature for its great baseness. For the soul itself was called the temple of God and his dwelling place and the bride of the King. For it says, "I will dwell in them and walk in them" (2 Cor 6:16). So it pleased God that, coming down from the holy heavens, he took upon himself your rational nature. He took flesh from the earth and joined it with his divine Spirit, so that you also, of the earth, might receive the heavenly soul. And when your soul has fellowship with the Spirit and the heavenly soul enters into your soul, then you are a perfect man in God and an heir and son.

7. But just as neither the ages above nor the ages below can grasp the greatness of God and his incomprehensibility, so also neither the worlds above nor the worlds on earth can understand the humility of God and how he renders himself little to the humble and small. Just as his greatness is incomprehensible, so also is his littleness. And it happens that he providentially arranges for you to be in afflictions and sufferings and humiliations. And the things you regard as in opposition to you, the very things become an advantage to your soul. If you wish to be in the world and become rich, every kind of misfortune meets you. You begin to reason with yourself: "Because I have not succeeded in the world,

should I leave it, renounce it and serve God?" After you reach this point, you hear the command saying: "Sell the things you possess" (Mt 19:21); despise carnal association, serve God. Then you begin to give thanks for your misfortune in the world, because "on that account I become obedient to the command of Christ." Well, then, in regard to externals you have changed your mind and have forsaken the world and carnal associations. Therefore, you must also change your mind from carnal wisdom to heavenly wisdom. Afterward, you begin to distinguish at the very sound of what you hear and no longer have rest, but only worry and trouble so as to obtain whatever you have heard.

8. When you think that you have done all by renouncing, the Lord takes account with you: "What do you boast in? Did I not give you your body and soul? What did you do?" The soul begins to confess and to beg the Lord and to say: "All things belong to you. The house I am in is yours. My clothing is yours. I am nourished by you and from you I am provided for every need." Then the Lord begins to answer to these: "I thank you. The possessions are all yours. The good will is yours. And, because of your love toward me, because you have taken your refuge in me, come, I will now give you what up until now you have not possessed nor what men possess on earth. Receive me, your Lord, with your soul that you may always be with me in joy and happiness."

9. Take the example of a woman espoused to a man. She brings all her possessions and her whole dowry and throws it out of great love into his hands and says: "I have nothing of my own. All that I possess is yours. Both my dowry is yours and my soul as well as my body is yours." So also the wise soul is the virgin of the Lord, having a communion with his Holy Spirit. But it is necessary that just as he, when he came upon earth, suffered and was crucified, so you also suffer with him. For when you leave the world and begin to seek God and to discern, then you enter into a battle with your nature in its old habits and custom with which you grew up. And in warring against such custom, you discover thoughts that oppose you and they war against your mind. These thoughts drag you about and keep you occupied with the material world from which you have come. Then you begin to do the struggle and fight the war, putting thoughts against thoughts, mind against mind, soul against soul, spirit against spirit. In a word, the soul enters into an agony.

10. For a certain hidden and subtle power of darkness is revealed that has been entrenched in the heart. And the Lord is near to your soul and body, seeing your battle. And he puts in you secret, heavenly thoughts and he begins interiorly to give you rest. But he allows you to

be disciplined, and grace directs you in these very afflictions. And when you reach your rest, grace makes itself known to you and shows you that it was for your own advantage that it permitted you to be exercised. It is like the case of a rich man who has a child under a tutor. For a while the tutor disciplines him with straps and the chastisement and the wounds and the blows seem heavy, until the child becomes an adult. Then indeed he begins to show himself grateful to his tutor. So also grace in God's providence disciplines you until you arrive at full manhood.

11. The farmer throws seed in all directions. And he who plants a vineyard seeks that all of it bear fruit. Therefore, after he has applied the pruning knife, if he finds no fruit, he is sad. So also the Lord wishes that his word be sown in the hearts of men. But just as the farmer is saddened by the barren earth, so the Lord is grieved with the sterile heart which produces no fruit. Just as the winds blow everywhere over all creation and as the sun illumines the whole universe, so the Godhead is everywhere and is found everywhere. If you seek him in the heavens (Ps 139:8), there he is found in the thoughts of angels. If you seek him on earth, here also he is found in the hearts of men. But few out of many are the Christians, who are found to be pleasing to him. Glory and majesty to the Father and Son and Holy Spirit forever. Amen.

HOMILY 33

It is necessary to pray to God unceasingly and with attention.

1. We ought to pray,[84] not according to any bodily habit nor with a habit of loud noise nor out of a custom of silence or on bended knees. But we ought soberly to have an attentive mind, waiting expectantly on God until he comes and visits the soul by means of all of its openings and its paths and senses. And so we should be silent when we ought, and to pray with a cry, just as long as the mind is concentrated on God. For as when the body does any task, it is completely occupied with the work and all its members help one another, so also the soul should be totally concentrated on asking and on a loving movement toward the Lord, not wandering and dispersed by its thoughts but with concentration waiting expectantly for Christ.

2. And thus he will enlighten, teaching one how to ask, giving pure prayer that is spiritual and worthy of God and bestowing the gift of worship "in spirit and in truth" (Jn 4:24). Take the example of a busi-

nessman. He is not content with only one way of making a profit, but he ambitiously stretches out in all directions to increase and multiply his profits. He tries one technique after the other and then runs still to something else, cautious only that he not incur a loss. So also let us develop in our souls versatility and expertise in order to obtain the genuine and great gain, namely, God, who teaches us how truly to pray. In this way the Lord finds rest in the well-intended soul, making it a throne of glory, and he sits on it and takes his rest. In a similar way with the Prophet Ezekiel we heard about the spiritual animals tied to the chariot of the Lord (Ez 1). He presents them to us as eyes all over. In a similar way also is the soul that carries God, or rather that is carried by God—it becomes all eye.

3. And just as a house that has its master at home shows forth an abundance of orderliness, and beauty and harmony, so too is the person who has his Lord abiding with him. He is full of every beauty and uprightness. He has the Lord with his spiritual treasures inhabiting within and as his charioteer. But woe to the house whose master is absent, whose lord is not there. It is desolate, run down, full of dirt and disorder. There, as the Prophet says, "sirens and demons" dwell (Is 34:13–14). For in the deserted house cats and dogs and all sorts of dirt take over. Woe to the person that does not get up after he has seriously fallen and that has within himself those who convince him and compel him to live as an enemy to his very own Spouse. They eagerly seek to corrupt his thoughts away from Christ.

4. But when the Lord sees that to the best of his power a person recollects himself, always seeking the Lord night and day as he cries out to him, just as he commanded "to pray incessantly in everything" (1 Thes 5:17), he will "avenge" him, as he promised (Lk 18:7), cleansing him from the evil within himself. And he will "present him unto himself," a bride "without blemish and without spot" (Eph 5:27).

If, then, you believe these things to be true, as indeed they are, look to yourself to see whether your soul has found its guiding light and the genuine meat and drink which is the Lord. If you have not, seek night and day in order to receive. When you see the sun, seek the true sun. For you are blind. When you gaze on a light, look into your soul to see whether you have found the true and good light. For all the visible things of the senses are but a shadow of the true realities of the soul. For there is another man within, beyond the sensible one. And there are other eyes within, which Satan has blinded, and ears which he has rendered deaf.

And Jesus has come to make this inner man healthy. To whom be glory and power with the Father and Holy Spirit forever. Amen.

HOMILY 34

Concerning the glory of the Christians which their bodies in the resurrection will be deemed worthy to receive and how the bodies will be made radiant along with the soul.

1. Just as the bodily eyes see all things distinctly, so also to the souls of the saints the beauties of the Godhead are manifested and seen. Christians are absorbed in contemplating them and they ponder over them. But to bodily eyes that glory is hidden, while to the believing soul it is distinctly revealed. This is the dead soul the Lord raises to life out of sin, just as he also raises up dead bodies as he prepares for the soul a new heaven and a new earth (Rv 21:1; Is 65:127) and a sun of righteousness, giving the soul all things out of his Godhead.

There is a true world and a living earth and a fruit-bearing vine and a bread of life and a living water, as it is written: "I believe to see the good things of the Lord in the land of the living" (Ps 27:13). And again: "Unto them that fear the Lord the Sun of righteousness shall arise with healing in his wings" (Mt 4:2). And the Lord said: "I am the true vine" (Jn 15:1). And again: "I am the bread of life" (Jn 6:35). And again: "Whoever drinks of the water that I shall give him, there shall be in him a fountain of water springing up into life everlasting" (Jn 4:14).

2. For the coming of the Lord was completely for man, who lay dead in the tomb of darkness, sin, of the unclean spirit and of evil powers, so that in this world now he might raise up man and give him life and purify him from all blackness and enlighten him with his very own light and cover him with his own raiment, the heavenly raiment of his Godhead. But in the resurrection of those bodies whose souls were earlier raised up and glorified, the bodies also will be glorified with the soul and illumined by the soul which in this present life has been illumined and glorified. For the Lord is their home and their tabernacle and their city. They are clothed with a dwelling place from Heaven "not made with hands" (2 Cor 5:1), the glory of the divine light, as having become children of light.

They will not look upon each other with an evil eye, for evil will have been taken away. In that place there is "neither male nor female, slave nor free" (Gal 3:28), for all are being transformed into a divine nature, being made noble and gods and children of God.[85] In that place then brother will speak peace to sister without shame. For all are one in Christ and all find rest in the one light. One will attend to the other and in mutual gazing they will straight way shine forth in truth in the true contemplation of the ineffable light.

3. So in many forms and many different divine glories they gaze upon each other and each is astonished and rejoices "with unspeakable joy" (1 Pt 1:8). You see how the glories of God are unspeakable and incomprehensible, of ineffable light and eternal mysteries and of innumerable good things. For example, in the visible things around us, it is impossible for anyone to comprehend the number of plants of the earth or of seeds or of various flowers. And it is also impossible for anyone to measure all the richness of the earth. Or in the sea, it is impossible for any man to understand the living creatures in it or their number or their kinds or their variety or the measure of the sea's water or the measure of its extent. Or in the air, it is impossible to know the number of birds or their kinds or their variety. Or it is impossible to comprehend the greatness of the heaven or the positions of the stars or their course.

So likewise it is impossible to speak or describe the richness of Christians which is immeasurable, infinite, and incomprehensible. For if such creatures as these are so infinite and incomprehensible to men, how much more he that created and furnished them! Therefore, one ought rather to rejoice and be glad because such richness and inheritance has been stored up for Christians, so that no one can speak of it nor explain it adequately. With all diligence and humility, then, we must go forth to the struggle of Christians and to receive that richness. For the inheritance and share of Christians is God himself. It says: "The Lord himself is the portion of my inheritance and of my cup" (Ps 16:5). Glory to him, who gives himself and shares his own holy nature with the souls of Christians, forever. Amen.

HOMILY 35

Concerning the old and new Sabbath.

1. In the shadow of the Law given by Moses, God decreed that everyone should rest on the Sabbath and do nothing. This was a figure

and a shadow of the true Sabbath given to the soul by the Lord. For the soul that has been deemed worthy to have been set free from shameful and sordid thoughts both observes the true Sabbath and enjoys true rest, being at leisure and freed from the works of darkness. There, in the typical Sabbath, even though they rested physically, their souls were enslaved to evils and wickednesses. However, this, the true Sabbath, is genuine rest, since the soul is at leisure and is purified from the temptations of Satan and rests in the eternal rest and joy of the Lord.[86]

2. Just as then God decreed that also the irrational animals should rest on the Sabbath—that the ox should not be forced under the yoke of necessity, that they should not burden the ass (for even the animals themselves were to rest from their heavy works)—so, when the Lord came and gave the true and eternal Sabbath, he gave rest to the soul heavily burdened and loaded down with the burdens of iniquity, of unclean thoughts, and laboring under restraint in doing works of injustice as though it were under slavery to bitter masters. And he lightened the soul from its burdens, so difficult to bear, of vain and obscene thoughts. And he took away the yoke, so bitter, of the works of injustice, and gave rest to the soul that had been worn out by the temptations of impurity.

3. For the Lord calls man to his rest, saying, "Come, all you who labor and are heavily burdened and I will refresh you" (Mt 11:28). And as many persons as obey and draw near, he refreshes them from all these heavy and burdensome and unclean thoughts. And they are at leisure from every iniquity, observing the true, pleasing, holy Sabbath. And they celebrate a feast of the Spirit, of joy and ineffable exultation. They celebrate a pure service, pleasing to God from a pure heart. This is the true and holy Sabbath. Let us, therefore, entreat God that we may enter into this rest (Heb 4:11) and that we may be freed from shameful and evil and vain thoughts so that thus we may be able to serve God out of a pure heart and celebrate the feast of the Holy Spirit. Blessed is he who enters into that rest. Glory to the Father, who is so well pleased, and the Son and the Holy Spirit, forever. Amen.

HOMILY 36

The double resurrection of souls and bodies and of the differing glory bestowed upon the risen.

1. The resurrection of the souls of the dead takes place even now

in time of death. But the resurrection of bodies will take place in that day. Just as in the heavens the stars are fixed, but all are not equal, one differing from the other (1 Cor 15:41) in brightness and magnitude, so also in spiritual matters there are degrees of progress according "to the measure of faith, in the Spirit himself" (Rom 12:3; 1 Cor 12:9), one being richer than another. And Scripture says, "He that speaks in a tongue, speaks by the Spirit of God" (1 Cor 14:2). Such a person is a spiritual man, speaking to God. But he who prophesizes, "builds up the Church" (1 Cor 14:2). Such a one possesses a greater degree of grace. For the first one edifies himself alone, the other also the neighbor. This is like the grain of wheat sown in the earth. The same grain out of the same earth brings forth many and differing grains. And again from the sheaves, some are larger while some are smaller, but all are brought together to one threshing floor, to one barn. And even though they are different, one bread is made from them.

2. Or as in a city there are crowds of people and some are infants, some are adults or some adolescents, and yet all drink water from one fountain and eat from one bread, all enjoy the same air. Or in the case of lamps, one may have two wicks and one have seven. But where there is a more abundance of light, there the illumination is greater. As many as are in fire and light, such cannot be also in darkness. But there is a great difference. It is like the case of a certain father who has two sons, one a child, the other a youth. He sends the older one abroad to cities and foreign countries. But the child he always guards since he is incapable of doing anything. Glory to God. Amen.

Homily 37

Paradise and the spiritual law.

1. "The friendship of the world," as it is written, "is enmity with God" (Jas 4:4). Therefore, Scripture enjoins everyone to "guard his own heart with all diligence" (Prv 4:23), so that anyone, guarding the word within him like a paradise, may enjoy the grace not to listen to the serpent that creeps around inside, enticing him with things that lead to pleasure, whereby the anger that slays a brother is engendered, and the soul that gives birth to it, itself dies. But may he have the grace rather to listen to the Lord saying: "Be concerned with faith and hope through which love of God and of man is engendered which bestows eternal

life." Into this paradise Noah entered, keeping the commandment and working, and through love he was redeemed from God's anger. Observing this paradise, Abraham heard the voice of God. Keeping this, Moses received God's glory reflected in his countenance. Similarly David, keeping this, strove, and from there he conquered over his enemies. Even Saul, as long as he watched his heart, prospered. But when he finally transgressed, in the end he was abandoned. For the Word of God comes to each person in a proportionate measure. As long as a person possesses the Word, he is held by the Word, and as long as he keeps it, so long is he guarded.

2. For this reason the choir of holy prophets, Apostles, and martyrs guarded the Word in their hearts, concerned about nothing else. They disdained the things of the earth and abided in the commandment of the Holy Spirit. And they preferred the Spirit's love of God and the good, not merely in word or in empty knowledge, but in word and deed through all things. Instead of riches they chose poverty; instead of glory, ignominy; instead of pleasure, suffering, and also for that reason they chose love in place of God's anger.

For as they hated the pleasant things of life,[87] they loved those who took such things away from them as though they were cooperating with their own goal, even though they failed to "know good and evil" (Gn 3:5). For they neither turned away those who were good nor accused the evil ones, since they regarded all as ambassadors of the Master's providential order. Therefore, toward all they had a sympathetic attitude. When they heard the Lord saying, "Forgive and it will be forgiven you" (Lk 6:37), then they regarded those who injured them as benefactors since they received from them the occasion for their own forgiveness. When again they heard, "As you would wish that men do to you, do also unto them" (Mt 7:12), then they loved good persons consciously. Forgetting their own self-righteousness and seeking the righteousness of God, they consequently also found love naturally included in it.

3. For the Lord, in commanding many things regarding love, enjoined us to seek the "righteousness of God" (Mt 6:33). For he knows that it is the mother of love. There is no other way to be saved except through the neighbor as he has commanded: "Forgive and it will be forgiven you" (Lk 6:37). This is the spiritual law which has been written in faithful hearts, "the fulfillment of the first law" (Rom 13:10). For he says, "I did not come to destroy the Law but to fulfill it" (Mt 5:17). How is it to be fulfilled? Teach me the first Law by seizing the occasion to bless the one who sinned, who condemned his injustice. For it says: "In

whatsoever you judge another, you condemn yourself. In whatever he remits, it will be remitted him" (Rom 2:1). For the Law thus says: "In the midst of judgment, judgment, and in the midst of forgiveness, forgiveness" (Dt 17:8).

4. The fullness, therefore, of the Law consists in forgiveness. We have called it the first Law, not because God set up two laws for men, but one law, which is spiritual by its nature, but in regard to retribution it gives to each person the retribution which is just, forgiveness given to the one forgiving and contending to the one who contends. For it says: "With the chosen you are chosen and with the perverse you shall wrestle" (Ps 18:26). Therefore, those who spiritually fulfilled the Law and in proportion as they participated in grace loved with a spiritual love not only those who did good to them, but also those who reproached and persecuted them, looking forward to receive the gift of good things. Of good things, I say, not because they forgave the wrongs done to them, but because they also did good to the persons who did wrong to them. For they offered them to God as the means whereby they fulfilled the beatitude, as it says: "Blessed are you when they shall revile you and persecute you" (Mt 5:11).

5. They were taught to so think by means of a spiritual law. For while they patiently endured and maintained an attitude of meekness, the Lord, seeing the patience of the heart engaged in warfare and the love that lessened none of its ardor, broke through "the middle wall of partition" (Eph 2:14). And they got rid of so great a hatred with the result that their love was no longer forced but served as a help. In a word, the Lord took control over "the sword that turned every way" (Gn 3:24) which excited the thoughts. And they "entered into the inner sanctuary of the veil where the forerunner on our behalf had entered" (Heb 6:19), namely, the Lord. And they enjoyed the fruits of the Spirit. Having seen the things to come in the certainty of the heart, no longer as the Apostle says, "in a mirror and darkly" (1 Cor 13:12), they spoke of "what eye has not seen nor ear heard nor the things that have entered into the heart of man, what things God has prepared for them that love him" (1 Cor 2:9). But I will ask this amazing question.

6. *Question:* If these things have not entered into the heart of man, how do you know them, especially when you confess as in the Acts that you are men with the same passions as other men (Acts 14:15)?

Answer: But listen to the answer that Paul gives. He says: "But God has revealed them to us by his Spirit. For the Spirit searches all things, even the depths of God" (1 Cor 2:10). Lest any one should say that the

Spirit was given to them as Apostles, while we are by our nature incapable of it, he says elsewhere as he prays: "May God grant you to be strengthened with might according to the richness of his glory in the inner man so that Christ may dwell in your hearts" (Eph 3:16). And again: "But the Lord is Spirit, and where the Spirit of the Lord is, there is liberty" (2 Cor 3:17). And again: "But if anyone has not the Spirit of Christ, he is not of him" (Rom 8:9).

7. Let us, therefore, beg that we may partake of the Holy Spirit in the full certainty and awareness and that we may enter in where we came out, and that henceforth the serpent may be turned away from us, the destroyer of the mind, the plotter of vainglory, the spirit of worry and complaint. Let us pray that, having believed with certainty, we may keep the commandments of the Lord and we may grow up in him "unto the perfect man, unto the measure of maturity" (Eph 4:13), so that we may no longer be dominated by the deceit of this world, but we may be in the full certainty of the Spirit. May we no longer lack faith that the grace of God takes pleasure also in the sinners who repent. For what is granted through grace is not measured by comparison with former infirmity, "otherwise grace is not grace" (Rom 11:5). But believing in the all-powerful God, may we approach with a simple and not overly solicitous heart him who through faith grants the grace of participating in the Spirit and not through the merit of works done. For it says, "You have received the Spirit, not by the works of the law, but by the hearing of faith" (Gal 3:2).

8. *Question:* You said that all the things are spiritually hidden in the soul. What, therefore, is the meaning of: "I wish to speak five words in the church with my understanding" (1 Cor 14:19)?

Answer: Church is understood in two ways: the assembly of the faithful, and the soul taken together as a whole. When, therefore, it is understood spiritually of the human person, church means man taken as a whole. "Five words" refer to the whole complex of virtues that build up the total person in various ways. For just as he who speaks in the Lord through five words comprehends all wisdom, so he who obeys the Lord builds up all piety by means of the five virtues. For they are five and embrace all the others. First is prayer, then temperance, almsgiving, poverty, long-suffering. When spoken with longing and desire, these are words of the soul which are spoken by the Lord and are heard in the heart. The Lord works and then the Spirit speaks in the mind and the heart, in proportion as it desires and also performs concretely.

9. And as these virtues embrace all other virtues, so also do they

beget each other. For if the first is missing, all the others fall apart. Likewise, through the second the others follow and so on. For how shall anyone pray if he is not working under the Spirit? And Scripture bears me out when it says, "No one can say Jesus is Lord except through the Holy Spirit" (1 Cor 12:3). Moreover, how will a person persevere patiently in temperance if he does not pray and receives no help? And whoever is not self-disciplined, how shall he give alms to the hungry or the oppressed? And he who does not give alms will not willingly accept poverty. And again, anger is similar to the desire of money, whether one actually possesses it or not. But the virtuous person is thus built up into the Church, not because of what he has done, but because of what he has desired. For it is not his own work that saves a person, but he who grants to him the power. If, therefore, anyone bears "the marks of the Lord" (Gal 6:17), let him not regard himself as anything, even if he has succeeded in any undertaking, but let him rely only on having loved and striven to attempt to do. Therefore, do not think that you have preceded the Lord in virtue according to him who says: "It is he who works in you, both to will and to do for his good pleasure" (Phil 2:13).

10. *Question:* What, therefore, does Scripture command a man to do?

Answer: We earlier said that according to his nature a person has the power to desire and this God demands. Therefore, God commands that a person should first know, and when he knows, he should love and should strive with his will. But in order that the mind be activated or endure toil or complete any work, the grace of the Lord is given to the person who desires and believes. The will of man, therefore, is like a support inserted into his nature. When the will is lacking, God himself does nothing, because of man's free will, even though he could. The successful working of the Spirit depends on man's will.[88] Again, if we give our whole will, he credits us with the whole work.

Wonderful is God in all things and he is totally beyond our understanding. But we strive to explain a portion of his wonderful works, relying on Scripture or rather instructed by it. For it says, "Who has known the mind of the Lord?" (Rom 11:34). But he himself says, "How often I have wished to gather up your children and you would not" (Mt 23:37). So from this let us believe that it is he who gathers us up. He demands of us only the desire. But what manifests the will except freely willed labor?

11. Take the example of an iron tool. As it is used to saw wood, to chop, to cultivate, to plant, it becomes worn out. But there is someone

else who puts it in motion and guides it. And when it is shattered, he fires it and fashions it anew. So likewise also man, when he becomes worn out and overcome by work that is good, still it is the Lord who works secretly in him. And when he is exhausted from his labor and totally done in, the Lord consoles his heart and renews him, as the Prophet says: "Shall the axe boast of itself apart from the one who wields it or the saw exalt itself apart from the one who draws it?" (Is 10:15).

So is it also in the case of evil, when a man obeys it and is open to it. Then Satan draws him and sharpens him as a robber does his sword. We have compared the heart to iron because of its insensitivity to things and its great hardness. But we should not be ignorant of him who holds us as insensitive iron. (If we did, we would not change so quickly from the word of the vinedresser to the temptation of the evil one.) But rather, like the ox and the ass, we should know him who drives and directs us according to his disposition. For it says: "The ox knows its owner and the ass its master's crib, but Israel does not know me" (Is 1:3). Let us, then, beg for the knowledge of God and for instruction in the spiritual law in order to accomplish his holy commandments, glorifying the Father and the Son and the Holy Spirit forever. Amen.

HOMILY 38

The need for much accurateness and right understanding in discerning who are authentic Christians.

1. Many who appear to be justified are considered to be Christians. It is proper for skilled persons and those of experience to test whether such persons really have the sign and image of the King, so that they should not be counterfeits doing the works of skilled persons, and that skilled persons should wonder at them and have to reprimand them. But those who are not experts are unable to test "deceitful workers" (2 Cor 11:13), since even such as these wear the habit of monks or Christians. For the false apostles suffered for the sake of Christ and they preached the Kingdom of Heaven. For this reason the Apostle says: "In perils more abundant, in afflictions above measure, in prisons more abundant" (2 Cor 11:23), wishing to show that he suffered more than they.

2. Gold is easily discovered. But pearls and precious stones, which are fit for the king's crown, are more rarely found. For often none are found that are suitable. So also Christians are fashioned into the crown

of Christ so that they may have fellowship with the saints. Glory to him who so loved this person and suffered on his behalf and raised him from the dead. But just as a veil was placed over the face of Moses (Ex 34:33, 35; 2 Cor 3:73) so that the people could not look at his face, so also now a veil covers over your heart so that you may not look upon the glory of God.[89] When this is taken away, then he appears and manifests himself to the Christians and to those who love him and seek in truth, as he says, "I will manifest myself to him and I will make my abode with him" (Jn 14:21, 22).

3. Let us, therefore, diligently strive to approach Christ, who is without lie, so that we may receive the promise and the new covenant which the Lord has inaugurated (Heb 10:20) through his cross and death when he burst open the gates of hell and sin. And he led out the faithful ones and gave them interiorly the Comforter and brought them back into his kingdom. Let us co-reign, then, with him, even we in Jerusalem, his city, in the heavenly Church, in the choir of holy angels. Those brethren who for a long time were tested and tried are able to help the inexperienced and show compassion to them.

4. Certain persons have become very sure of themselves and have been greatly worked on by God's grace. They found their members so sanctified that they thought that concupiscence does not happen in Christianity, that they had received a balanced and chaste mind, and that in regard to other things the interior man was raised up to divine and heavenly things so that they completely thought they already had come to the measure of perfection. And as such a one was thinking that he was already nearing the calm harbor, billows of waves rose up against him, so that he again found himself in the middle of the sea and he was being carried to where the sea is the sky and death is imminent. In such a way sin entered and "wrought all manner of evil concupiscence" (Rom 7:8).

Again, there are certain persons who have been considered worthy of a certain grace, and, having so to say received from the whole depth of the sea some drops, they find this hour by hour and day by day to be such an amazing work that anyone under its influence wonders and is astounded at the strange, paradoxical working of God to think that he should be given such enlightenment. Gradually grace enlightens him, directs and brings him peace and renders him noble, since such grace in all things is divine and heavenly. The result is that in his estimation kings and potentates, the wise and nobly born, are held as the least and lowly. But after a time and seasons pass, things change, so that he himself really regards himself as a greater sinner than all other men. And again, at another time, he sees himself as the greatest, most stupendous king or a powerful friend of a king. Again, at another time he sees himself as weak and a beggar. Then the mind falls into confusion as to why things are one way and then appear otherwise. The reason is because Satan, being full of hatred for what is good, suggests evil things to those who are pursuing virtue and he struggles to overthrow them. For this is his work.

5. But do not submit yourself to him as you work at the justification which is being accomplished in the inner man wherein stands the judgment seat of Christ, together with his spotless sanctuary, so that the testimony of your conscience may glory in the cross of Christ. He has "cleansed your conscience from dead works" (Heb 9:14) that you may adore God in your spirit, that you may know what you adore according to him who says, "We adore that which we know" (Jn 4:22). Trust in God who guides you. Let your soul have fellowship with God as bride communes with bridegroom. For "this mystery is great," it says, "but I speak of Christ" (Eph 5:32) and the spotless soul. To him be glory forever. Amen.

HOMILY 39

For what purpose was divine Scripture given to us by God?

1. Take the example of a king who writes letters to those upon whom he wishes to bestow special privileges and unique gifts. He indicates to all, "Hurry at once to come to me so as to receive from me royal gifts." And if they do not come and receive them, they will profit nothing for having read the letters. Rather, they are in danger of being put to death for having refused to come and to be deemed worthy of honor at the king's hand. So also God, the King, has sent to men the divine Scriptures as letters, pointing out to them that they are to call out to God, and, believing, they are to ask and receive a heavenly gift from the Godhead's very own being. For it is written: "That we should be made participators of the divine nature" (2 Pt 1:4). But if a man does not approach and beg and receive, it will profit him nothing for having read the Scriptures. But rather he is subject to death, because he did not wish to receive from the heavenly King the gift of life, without which it is

impossible to obtain the immortal life which is Christ. To him glory forever. Amen.

HOMILY 40

All virtues and all vices are interconnected and like a chain they are dependent one upon the other.

1. Concerning external asceticism and what practice is better and primary, know this, Beloved Ones, that all the virtues are mutually bound to each other.[90] Like a spiritual chain, one is dependent upon the other: prayer to love, love to joy, joy to meekness, meekness to humility, humility to service, service to hope, hope to faith, faith to obedience, obedience to simplicity. And likewise, on the opposite side, the vices are bound one to the other: hatred to anger, anger to pride, pride to vainglory, vainglory to disbelief, disbelief to hardness of heart, hardness of heart to carelessness, carelessness to sloth, sloth to *acedia* or boredom, boredom to a lack of perseverance, a lack of perseverance to a love of pleasure. And the other parts of vice similarly are interdependent. So also on the good side the virtues are dependent upon each other and are interconnected.

2. But the head of every good endeavor and the guiding force of right actions is perseverance in prayer. By means of it we can daily obtain the rest of the virtues by asking God for them. By this means are engendered in those deemed worthy the fellowship of God's holiness and of spiritual energy and the attachment of the mind disposed toward the Lord in ineffable love. For the person who daily forces himself to persevere in prayer is enflamed with divine passion and fiery desire from a spiritual love toward God and he receives the grace of the sanctifying perfection of the Spirit.

3. *Question:* Because certain ones sell their possessions and set their slaves free and keep the commandments, although they do not seek to receive the Spirit in this life, do they, living thus, not enter into the Kingdom of Heaven?

Answer: This is a delicate topic. For some speak of one kingdom and one hell. We, however, speak of many degrees and differences and measures, both in the kingdom and in hell itself.[91] Just as the soul "ensouls" all the members and yet operates in the brain and still moves the feet below it, so also the Godhead contains all creatures, the heavenly and those under the abyss, and is everywhere being filled up in creation, even though it is most transcendent above creatures because it is infinite and beyond any comprehension. Therefore, this Godhead is concerned with men, and it providentially guides all things according to reason. And when some pray, not knowing what they seek, others fast, while others persevere in service, God, being a just judge, gives the reward to each one according to the measure of his faith. For what things they do, they do out of fear of God. But not all of these are sons or kings or heirs.

4. In the world there are murderers, others are fornicators and others robbers. On the other hand, there are those who distribute their goods to the poor. For both of these groups the Lord has a concern and to those doing good he gives rest and a reward. For there are superior and inferior degrees. And in the very light itself and the glory there is a difference. And in hell itself and punishment there appear poisoners and robbers and others who have committed lesser sins. Those who say that there is only one kingdom and one hell and that there are not degrees, speak wrongly. How many types of worldly people are now absorbed in theaters and other disorderly things! And how many there are who only pray and fear God! Thus on these and those alike God looks down with concern, and as a just judge he prepares rest for these and for those others punishment.

5. Take the example of men who harness horses and drive chariots and race them against each other. Each one strains to overcome and conquer his opponent. Likewise, there is a contest going on in the heart of those who struggle, the evil spirits wrestling with the soul, while God and the angels watch the struggle. At each hour many new strategies are thought up by the soul and likewise by the evil that is within. The soul has many hidden strategies which it concocts and gives birth to hour by hour. And also evil itself has many strategies and tricks and hourly gives birth to new ideas against the soul. For the mind is a charioteer and harnesses the chariot of the soul as it holds the reins of the thoughts. And so it competes against the chariot of Satan, which he also has harnessed against the soul.

6. *Question:* If prayer is rest, how do certain persons say that they cannot pray nor do they persevere in prayer?

Answer: Rest itself, if it abounds, produces compassion and other forms of service, such as visiting the brethren, to serve them with the Word.[92] Also nature itself wishes to go and see the brethren to speak a word. For nothing thrown into the fire can remain in its own nature, but necessarily it becomes fire. If you throw pebbles into fire, they turn into a bit of lime. And if someone wishes to plunge completely into the sea and to go out into the middle, he is completely submerged and disappears from sight. But if someone goes in gradually by degrees, he desires to come up again and to float on top and to get out of the water at the harbor and to see other persons on land. So also in the spiritual life one enters into a degree of grace and again he remembers his companions. And nature itself wants to go off to the brethren to fulfill charity, to affirm the word.

7. *Question:* How can the two things be in the heart, both grace and sin?[93]

Answer: Take the example of a fire outside a bronze vessel. When you put wood under it, see, it becomes very hot and the inside of the vessel boils up and gets hot, because the fire outside burns from beneath it. But if anyone should become careless and not throw fire under it, the fire begins to become less hot and nearly dies out. So also grace, the heavenly fire, is also within you. Hence if you pray and give your thoughts to the love of Christ, see how you have thrown under yourself the wood and your thoughts become fire and are immersed completely in the desire for God. And even if the Spirit should withdraw as though he were outside of you, still he is within you and he manifests himself outside you. But if anyone is careless and gradually gives himself up either to worldly affairs or to anxiety, once again evil comes and covers the soul and begins to afflict the person. Then the soul remembers the former rest and begins to be afflicted and to suffer continuously.

8. Again the mind is attentive to God. The former rest has begun to draw near it. It begins to seek it with greater zeal. It says, "I beg of you, Lord!" Little by little the fire is added to it and it enkindles and refreshes the soul, as the hook gradually draws out the fish from the water. If it were not so and man were not to taste the bitterness and death, how would he be able to discern the bitter from the sweet and death from life and to have given thanks to the life-giving Father and Son and Holy Spirit forever? Amen.

HOMILY 41

The depths of the soul are very deep. It evolves according to the degree, both of grace and of vice.

1. The precious vessel of the soul possesses great depth. "He seeks

out the deep and the heart" (Sir 42:18). For when man swerved from the commandment and was under the sentence of wrath, sin took him under its power. And being itself as a certain abyss of bitterness in subtleness and in depth, it entered inside and took possession over the pasturelands of the soul, even to its deepest reaches. In this way, let us liken the soul and sin when it mixed with the soul as if it were a very large tree having many branches and having its roots in the deepest parts of the earth. So also sin had entered and took possession over the pasturelands of the depths of the soul. It became something customary and self-assertive, growing up with each person from infancy and instructing man in vices.

2. If, therefore, the working of divine grace overshadows the soul according to the degree of each person's faith and he receives help from above, grace still overshadows him only in a certain degree. Let no one think that his whole soul has been enlightened. There is still a great area of evil within, and a person needs much hard work and pain, corresponding to the grace given him. For this is why divine grace began only in degrees to pour into the soul (even though grace were capable of purifying and perfecting man in an hour's time), so as to test the determination of a person, whether he preserves entirely his love for God by not complying with the evil one in any dealing, but by lending himself completely to grace. And in this manner the person proves himself in time and saving opportunity. He in no way grieves grace, nor does he abuse it. Man is helped in this gradual method, and grace itself finds grazing land in the soul and sinks roots into the deepest levels of the soul and its thoughts, as a person on many occasions proves himself and corresponds with grace, until the whole soul is permeated by the heavenly grace which then reigns in the vessel itself.

3. But if anyone is not confirmed in great humility, he is handed over to Satan and is stripped of all divine grace bestowed on him. And he is tempted by many afflictions. Then his idea of himself is manifested because he is marked and despicable. Therefore, he who is rich in the grace of God ought to be grounded in great humility and possess a contrite heart. And he ought to regard himself as poor and possessing nothing.

What is his belongs to another. Another gave it to him and takes it away whenever he wishes. He who so humbles himself before God and men is able to guard the grace given to him, as the Lord says: "He who humbles himself shall be exalted" (Lk 14:11). Although he is a chosen of God, let him consider himself as a cast-off. And being faithful, let him regard himself as unworthy. For such persons are well pleasing to God and are brought to life through Christ, to whom be glory and power forever. Amen.

HOMILY 42

Not external things, but those that are interior advance or injure a man, namely, the Spirit of grace or the spirit of evil.

1. Take the example of a great city, but one that is deserted with the walls crumbled—it has been captured by the enemies. Its greatness has no value. Therefore, care must be taken in proportion to its greatness so that it has strong walls in order that the enemies may not enter. In like manner souls, adorned with knowledge and intelligence and sharpness of mind, are like great cities. But it must be asked whether they are fortified by the power of the Spirit so that the enemies may not enter and lay them desolate. For the wise of the world, Aristotle or Plato or Socrates, who were skilled in knowledge, were like great cities, but they were laid waste by the enemies because the Spirit of God was not in them.[94]

2. But the many simple people who are participators of grace are like little cities fortified by the power of the cross. They fall away from grace for two reasons and perish: either because they do not persevere patiently in bearing afflictions brought upon them, or they have tasted the pleasures of sin and continued in them. Those who journey cannot go through without temptations.

As in giving birth, the beggar woman and the queen both have the same sufferings, so likewise also the land of the rich and the poor man equally cannot produce worthy fruit unless there be the necessary cultivation. So too in the working of the soul, neither the wise man nor the rich man reigns in grace, unless it be through patience and afflictions and many labors. For the life of Christians ought to be of this sort. As honey is sweet and shows forth nothing of bitterness or poisonous, so likewise such Christians as these show themselves good to all who approach them, whether good or bad, as the Lord says, "Be good, as your heavenly Father" (Lk 6:36; Mt 5:48). For what injures and corrupts a person is from within. "Out of the heart proceed evil thoughts" (Mt 15:19), as the Lord says, because the things that corrupt man are within.

3. Therefore, from within is the spirit of evil, creeping and progressing in the soul. It appeals to reason. It incites. It is as the veil of

218

darkness, "the old man" (2 Cor 5:17) whom those who have recourse to God must put off and must put on the heavenly and new man that is Christ (Eph 4:22; Col 3:8). Thus nothing of the things outside can harm man except the spirit of darkness that dwells in the heart, alive and active. So therefore each person in his thoughts must engage in the struggle in order that Christ may shine in his heart, to whom be glory forever. Amen.

HOMILY 43

The progress of a Christian whose whole power depends on the heart, as it is described here in various ways.

1. As many lights and burning lamps are lighted from fire, but the lamps and lights are lighted and shine from one nature, so also Christians are enkindled and shine from one nature, the divine fire, the Son of God, and they have their lamps burning in their hearts and they shine before him while living on earth, just as he did. For it says, "Therefore your God has anointed you with the oil of gladness" (Ps 45:7). For this reason he was called Christ in order that we also, being anointed with the same oil as he was anointed, may become Christs, so to say, of the same substance and one body. Again it says: "Both he that sanctifies and those that are sanctified are all of one" (Heb 2:11).

2. Therefore, Christians from one aspect are similar to lamps with oil in them, that is, all the fruits of justification. But if the lamp be not enkindled from that of the Godhead within them, they are nothing. The Lord was "the burning lamp" (Jn 5:35) by means of the Spirit of the Godhead which abided substantially in him and set on fire his heart according to his humanity. Take the example of a dirty old pouch filled with pearls. So too Christians in the exterior man ought to be humble and of lowly esteem, while interiorly in the inner man they possess the "pearl of great price" (Mt 13:46). Others are similar to "whited sepulchers," outwardly painted and decorated, but "inwardly full of dead men's bones" (Mt 23:27), and of much foul smell and unclean spirits. They are dead to God and are clothed with every kind of shame and sordidness and the darkness of the adversary.

3. The Apostle says that "the child, as long as he is little, is under tutors and governors" (Gal 3:2) of evil spirits that do not desire him to grow up, lest he should become a mature man and begin to look to the

things pertaining to the household and assert some control. The Christian always should be mindful of God. For it is written: "Thou shalt love the Lord the God with thy whole heart" (Dt 6:5). He should love the Lord, not only when he enters into the place of prayer, but in walking and talking and eating, may he remember God and love him with affection. For it says: "Where your heart is, there also is your treasure" (Mt 6:21; Lk 12:34). For to whatever thing one's heart is tied and where his desire draws him, that is his God. If the heart always desires God, he is Lord of his heart. If man renounces himself and becomes possessionless, having no city, and he fasts, yet if he is still attached to the man he is or to worldly things or to a home or to parental affection, where his heart is attached, there his mind is held captive—that is his God. And he is found to have gone from the world through the large, front door, but he has reentered and thrown himself into the world through a little side door.

As sticks are thrown into the fire and are unable to resist the power of the fire, but are burned up at once, so too demons, seeking to wage war against a man who has received the Spirit, are burned up and consumed by the divine power of the fire, provided only that the person always clings to the Lord and has trust and hope in him. And even if the demons are strong as mighty mountains, they are burned up by prayer, like wax by fire.

In the meantime, great is the soul's struggle and war against them. There are rivers of dragons there and mouths of lions. There is fire which flames up in the soul. Just as the inveterate evil, inebriated with the spirit of error, is insatiable toward evil, either in murdering or commiting adultery, so also Christians, having been baptized in the Holy Spirit, have no experience of evil. But those who possess grace and still are flirting with sin are under fear and journey through a fearful place.

4. Take the example of merchants. While on a voyage, even if they find a suitable wind and a calm sea, still as long as they have not reached the harbor, they always are in fear lest suddenly a contrary wind should blow and the sea would be stirred up by waves and the ship would be in danger. So too Christians, even if they possess within themselves a favorable wind of the Holy Spirit blowing, they still fear lest the wind of the opposing force should rise up and blow and stir up a storm and waves for their souls. Therefore, there is need of great diligence so that we may arrive at the harbor of rest, at the perfect world, at the eternal life and pleasure, at the city of the saints, at the heavenly Jerusalem, at "the

Church of the firstborn" (Heb 12:23). If a person does not pass through those degrees, he is under great fear, lest by chance at some time the evil power should bring about some fall.

5. A woman who has conceived carries her baby inside in darkness, so to say, and in a hidden place. But if then the child comes forth at the appointed time, it sees a new creation, which it never saw, of sky and earth and sun. And at once friends and relatives with cheerful faces take it into their arms. But if it should happen that there is a miscarriage in the womb, then it is necessary that the surgeons, whose duty it is, must use the knife and the child is then found passing from death to death and from darkness to darkness. Apply this also to the spiritual life. As many as have received the seed of the Godhead have it in an invisible manner. Because of sin dwelling within also, they hide it in dark and fearsome places. Therefore, if they protect themselves and preserve the seed, these in due time are born again visibly. And then, at the dissolution of the body, the angels and all the choirs above with cheerful faces receive them. But if, after having received the weapons of Christ to wage war manfully, such a one grows slothful, he immediately is turned over to the enemies and at the dissolution of the body passes over from the darkness which now covers him to another and worse darkness and to perdition.

6. Take the example of a garden having fruit-bearing trees and other sweet-scented plants, in which all is well cultivated and beautifully laid out. It also has a small wall before a ditch to protect it. Should it so happen that a fast-moving river passed that way, even though only a little of the water dashes against the wall, it tears away the foundation. It digs a course and gradually dissolves the foundation. It enters and tears away and uproots all the plants and destroys the entire cultivation and renders it fruitless. So it is also with man's heart. It has the good thoughts, but the rivers of evil are always flowing near the heart, seeking to bring it down and draw it to its own side. If the mind should be turned ever so little toward frivolity and yield to unclean thoughts, look out—the spirits of error have roamed the pastureland and have entered and have overturned there the beautiful things. They have destroyed good thoughts and devastated the soul.

7. There is the example of the eye, little in comparison to all the members of the body and the pupil itself is small, yet it is a great vessel. For it sees in one flash the sky, stars, sun, moon, cities, and other creatures. Likewise, these things are seen in one flash, they are formed and

imaged in the small pupil of the eye. So it is with the mind toward the heart. And the heart itself is but a small vessel, yet there also are dragons and there are lions; there are poisonous beasts and all the treasures of evil. And there are rough and uneven roads; there are precipices. But there is also God, also the angels, the life and the kingdom, the light and the Apostles, the treasures of grace—there are all things. Just as a fog hangs over the whole earth, so that one does not see his fellow man, so is the darkness of this world covering all creation and humanity. Humans, obscured by the darkness, are in the night and spend their life in fearful places. Like a thick smoke in a one-room house, so is sin with its filthy thoughts. It settles down and creeps over the thoughts of the heart along with an infinite number of demons.[95]

8. As in the visible things around us, when a war is being prepared wise men and nobles do not enlist, but, fearing death, remain aloof, so that the raw recruits and beggars and simple folk are put forth. And if it happens that they carry off a victory against the enemies and chase them from their frontiers, they receive from the king part of the booty and crowns and they gain promotions and dignities. Those great ones are now found much behind them in preference of the king. So too on a spiritual plane. The simple ones begin to hear the Word, and they do the Word's work with loving attitude, and they receive from God the grace of the Spirit. But the wise and those who seek superficially the Word, these flee from the war and they do not progress. They are found behind those who entered the war and won the victory.

9. Just as the winds, blowing powerfully, shake all creatures in the sky and produce a very loud sound, so the power of the enemy pummels and carries the thoughts away and stirs up the depths of the heart at will and disperses thoughts for its own benefit. Like the tax collectors who sit along the narrow streets and snatch at the passers-by and extort from them, so also the demons watch carefully and grab hold of souls. And when they pass out of the body, if they are not completely purified, they are not permitted to go up into the mansions of Heaven there to meet their Master. For they are driven down by the demons of the air. But if, while they still live in the flesh, they shall, because of their hard toil and much struggle, obtain from the Lord on high grace, they, along with those who through virtuous living are at rest, shall go to the Lord, as he promised. "Where I am, there also my servant will be" (Jn 12:26). And for endless ages they shall reign together with the Father and Son and Holy Spirit, now and always and for all eternity. Amen.

HOMILY 44

What change and renovation Christ works in a Christian whose passions of the soul and diseases he heals.

1. Whoever approaches God and truly desires to be a partner of Christ must approach with a view to this goal, namely, to be changed and transformed from his former state and attitude and become a good and new person, harboring nothing of "the old man" (2 Cor 5:17). For it says, "If any man is in Christ, he is a new creature" (2 Cor 5:17). For our Lord Jesus Christ came for this reason, to change and transform and renew human nature and to recreate this soul that had been overturned by passions through the transgression. He came to mingle human nature with his own Spirit of the Godhead. A new mind and a new soul and new eyes, new ears, a new spiritual tongue, and, in a word, new humans—this was what he came to effect in those who believe in him. Or new wineskins, anointing them with his own light of knowledge so that he might pour into them new wine which is his Spirit. For he says, "New wine must be put into new wineskins" (Mt 9:17).

2. For just as the enemy took man under his hand and made him new for himself by covering him with evil passions and anointing him with the spirit of sin, and pouring into him the wine of all iniquity and evil teaching, so also the Lord, having redeemed him from the enemy, made him new. He anointed him with his Spirit and poured into him the wine of life, the new teaching of the Spirit. For he who changed the nature of five loaves into the nature of the multitude, and gave a voice to the irrational nature of an ass, and converted a prostitute to purity, and prepared the nature of burning fire to become dew upon those in the furnace, and tamed the nature of wild lions for Daniel, is able also to change the soul that was barren and savage from sin to his own goodness and kindness and peace by the holy and good "Spirit of promise" (Eph 1:13).

3. As a shepherd is able to heal the scabby sheep and to protect it from wolves, so the real Shepherd, Christ, came and alone was able to heal and to convert the lost and scabby sheep, namely, humanity, from the scab and leprosy of sin. For earlier the priests and levites and teachers were unable to heal the soul by means of the offering of the gifts and sacrifices and by the sprinklings of blood. With such they were unable to heal themselves. For they were also clothed in infirmity. For it

says: "It is impossible that the blood of bulls and goats should take away sin" (Heb 10:4). But the Lord said, pointing out the weakness of the physicians of that time, "You will surely say unto me this parable: 'Physician, heal thyself' " (Lk 4:23). In substance he meant: "I am not as those who are unable to heal themselves; I am the true physician and the good shepherd who 'lays down my life for the sheep' (Jn 10:15), who am able to 'heal all sickness and all disease' of soul (Mt 4:23). I am the spotless sheep, that was once offered and that am able to heal all who come to me." For the true healing of the soul comes from the Lord alone. For it says, "Behold the Lamb of God, who takes away the sin of the world" (Jn 1:29), namely, of the person that has believed in him and has loved him with his whole heart.

4. Thus the Good Shepherd heals the scabby sheep. But sheep are unable to heal sheep. And unless the intellectual sheep, humanity, be healed, he does not enter into the heavenly Church of the Lord. For in a similar way it was said in the Law through shadow and image. Concerning the leper and the person with a blemish, the Spirit speaks these things figuratively and means: "A leper and one having a blemish shall not enter" into the Church of the Lord (Lv 21:17; Nm 5:2). But it commanded the leper to go off to the priest and to beg him with much entreaty to take him to the house of his tabernacle and to lay his hands on the leper, who indicated the place where the leprosy was located and to heal him. In a similar manner also Christ, the true "high priest of good things to come" (Heb 9:11), bending over the persons stricken with the leprosy of sin, enters into the tabernacle of their body and heals and cures their passions. In this way a person can enter into the heavenly Church of the saints of the true Israel. For every person infected with the leprosy of the sin of passions that has not approached the true High Priest and has not been now healed in the assembly of the saints, will not enter into the heavenly Church. For that Church, being spotless and pure, seeks persons that are spotless and pure. It says: "Blessed are the pure in heart, for they shall see God" (Mt 5:5).

5. For the person that truly believes in Christ must be transported and changed from his present state of evil to another state, one that is good, and from his present lowly nature into another, divine nature. He must be made anew by the power of the Holy Spirit. And in this way he can be fit for the heavenly kingdom. These things come to us who believe and love him in truth and live according to all his holy commandments. For if in the time of Elisha the casting of wood, that by nature is light, upon the waters dredged up the iron that by nature is heavy, how

much more will the Lord send forth his light, subtle, good, and heavenly Spirit, and through him dredge up the soul that has sunk into the waters of evil and make it light to take up wings to the heights of Heaven and transform and change it out of its own very nature!

6. In the visible world no one can by himself pass over and cross the sea unless he has a light and buoyant boat made of wood, which alone is capable of traversing over the waters. For he will go under and be drowned. In a similar way, no person of himself can cross and pass over the bitter sea of sin and the dangerous abyss of the evil powers of the darkness of the passions, unless he receive the buoyant and heavenly and winged Spirit of Christ who walks over all wickedness and journeys on. Through him a person will be able to reach by a straight and right path the heavenly harbor of rest, the city of the kingdom.

As those on the boat do not draw up water from the sea and drink it nor have their clothing from the sea nor their food, but they carry these things aboard the ship from land, so too Christians do not receive from this world, but from above, from Heaven, heavenly food and spiritual raiment. And on these they live on the ship of the good and life-giving Spirit. They pass beyond the opposing evil powers of principalities and dominions. And as all boats are built of one nature of wood, through which boats men are able to traverse the bitter sea, so from the heavenly light of one Godhead, Christians are enabled to fly over all wickedness.

7. Since the ship needs both a pilot and a well-tempered and mild wind to navigate successfully, the Lord himself is all of these in the faithful person and carries him over the violent storms and the wild waves of evil and the forces of the violent winds of sin. Powerfully and with skilled expertise as he knows how, he dissipates their tempest. Without Christ, the heavenly Pilot, it is impossible for anyone to pass over the evil sea of the powers of darkness and the gusts of the bitter temptations. For it says: "They go up to the heavens and descend down to the depths" (Ps 107:26). But Christ has a full knowledge of a pilot in regard both to wars and temptations as he journeys over the wild waves. For it says: "He himself, having been tempted, is able to aid those who are tempted" (Heb 2:18).

8. Therefore, our souls must be changed and transformed from the present state to a new one, to a divine nature, and to become new instead of old, that is, good and kind and faithful from being bitter and faithless. And thus, having become fit, we will be restored to the heavenly kingdom. For the blessed Paul likewise writes about his transformation and his being captured by Christ: "But I follow after, if I may understand

that for which also I was apprehended by Christ" (Phil 3:12). How was he apprehended by God? Just as if some tyrant were to seize and carry off a captive, and then the latter would be apprehended by the true king, so Paul, having been under the tyrannical spirit of sin, persecuted and devastated the Church. But since he was acting in ignorance out of zeal for God, thinking he was battling for truth, he was not rejected, but the Lord apprehended him and the heavenly and true King, flooding him with ineffable light and deigning to honor him with his voice, struck him like a slave and set him free. See the goodness of the Master and his power to change, how he can transform persons steeped in evil and turned back to a wild state. And in a moment he can lead them back to his own goodness and peace.

9. All things are possible with God, as it happened in the case of the good thief. In a moment through faith he was converted and was restored to Paradise. The Lord came for this in order to change us and recreate us and make us, as it is written, "participators of the divine nature" (2 Pt 1:4), and to give to our soul a heavenly soul, that is, the Spirit of the Godhead leading us to every virtue so that we might be able to live eternal life. Therefore, may we believe with our whole heart his inexpressible promises, because "He is true that promised" (Heb 10:23). We must love the Lord and always strive to live in all the virtues and to beseech assiduously and without ceasing in order to receive the promise of his Spirit totally and perfectly so that we may be brought to life even while we are still on this earth. For if in this world a person would not receive the sanctification of the Spirit through much faith and imploring, and be "made participator of the divine nature" and permeated by grace by which he can fulfill every commandment without blame and purely, he would not be made for the Kingdom of Heaven. Whatever good anyone has obtained here, that same, in that day, will be his life through the Father and the Son and the Holy Spirit forever. Amen.

HOMILY 45

No science, no wealth of this world, but only the coming of Christ is able to heal man whose greatest kinship with God this homily explains.

1. He, who has chosen the eremitical life, ought to regard all things in this world as strange and as the cross of Christ, denying all things,

"even his own life also" (Lk 14:26). He ought to have his mind focused on the love of Christ and prefer the Lord to parents, brothers, wife, children, friends, possessions. This the Lord taught, saying: "Everyone, that has not left father or mother or brothers or wife or children or lands and does not follow me, is not worthy of me" (Mt 10:37). In nothing else is there found salvation for men and rest as we have heard.

How many kings have appeared from Adam's race, possessing dominion over all the earth, thinking great things because of their kingly power! And yet none of them, for all that they had in their favor, had the power to know the evil which had infiltrated the soul because of the first man's transgression and had darkened it. They did not know the change that had come over the mind that at first was pure and contemplated the Master and was held in honor. And now on account of its fall the mind is clothed with shame and the eyes of the heart are blinded so as not to see that glory which our father Adam before his disobedience beheld.

2. There have been diverse wise men according to the world, among whom some were noted for their ability in philosophy, others have been admired for their sophistic abilities, others for their oratorical skill, still others were men of letters and poets and composed summary histories. There also were various artisans who practised the arts according to the world. Some carved in wood types of birds and fishes and images of men and in those they diligently sought to display their talent. Some fashioned by hand bronze statues similar to real humans and other things. Others built mighty and very beautiful buildings. Others dug out of the earth silver and gold that perish; others sought precious stones. Others possessed beauty of body and were pleased with their comeliness, and, all the more enticed by Satan, they fell into sin. And all of these artisans, being captured by the serpent dwelling within them and, not knowing the sin that abode in them, became slaves of the power of evil. They profited nothing from their knowledge and art.

3. Therefore, the world, filled with every variety, is likened to a rich man who possesses splendid and big houses, gold and silver and various possessions and all kind of service in abundance. But he is still seriously laden with sicknesses and afflictions and his whole family stands around, with all his riches, and is unable to relieve him of his infirmity. Thus no pursuit in this life, no brothers, no wealth, no courage, none of all the things mentioned above relieve man of sin, man who has been submerged in sin and cannot see things clearly. Only the presence of Christ can purify soul and body. Therefore, let us put aside every care of this life, and, crying out to the Lord night and day, let us

devote ourselves to him. This visible world and the rest found in it seem to comfort the body, but they aggravate all the more the passions of the soul and increase its suffering.

4. A certain prudent man desired to apply himself diligently. He strove with care to gain experience of all the things of this world, if he might be able to find some profit from them. He went to kings, potentates, rulers, and found no healing cure there to help his soul. And after spending much time with them, he found no improvement. He went again to the wise men of this world and the orators. He left them again in the same way, not having found any help. He toured the rounds of painters and those who mine gold and silver from the earth, and all the artisans, and he was unable to find any healing for his own wounds. Finally, having left them, he sought God for himself, the one who heals the sufferings and sicknesses of the soul. But as he was pondering about himself and meditated on these things, his mind was found wandering distractedly among those things from which he had visibly withdrawn out of hatred for them.

5. Take the example of a certain woman in the world who is rich with much money and a magnificent house, but she lacks any protection. And those who attack her to injure her and lay her buildings to waste are many. She, refusing the injury, goes out to seek a powerful husband, capable and educated in all aspects. And after much struggle she finds such a man. She rejoices in him and has him as a strong wall. In the same way, the soul after transgression, and for a long time having been afflicted by the adverse power and having fallen into great devastation, "a widow and desolate" (1 Tm 5:5), was deserted by her heavenly Husband because of disobedience of the commandment. She was made fun of by all the opposing powers (for they drove her out of her mind and confused her in her heavenly knowledge), so she does not see what they have done to her, but only thinks she was born like this from the beginning. Then, after she had learned through hearing of her solitude and barrenness, she deplored her desolation before God, the Lover of mankind, and found life and salvation. Why? Because she went back to her family. For there is no other family tie and helpfulness like that between the soul and God and between God and the soul.

God made various kinds of birds. Some to fashion their nests in the earth and there to have their nourishment and rest. Others he ordained to build their nests under water and there to have life. He fashioned two worlds: one above for the "ministering spirits" (Heb 1:14), and he arranged it that they have their communication there; the other world is

228

below for men under this atmosphere. He created also sky and earth, sun and moon, waters, fruit-bearing trees, all kinds of animals. But in none of these did God rest. All creation is ruled by him, and still he did not establish his throne in them nor did he enter into fellowship with them. But it was only with man that he was pleased, fellowshipping and resting in him. Do you see the relationship of God to man and of man to God? Therefore, the wise and prudent person, after passing through all creatures, took no rest in himself, but only in the Lord. And the Lord was well pleased in nothing except man alone.

6. If you raise your eyes to the sun, you find its orb in the sky, but its light and rays stretch to the earth and all the power of its light and its splendor is aimed at the earth. So also the Lord sits at the right hand of the Father "above all principality and power" (Eph 1:21), but he casts his eye on the hearts of men on earth, in order that he may raise up to where he is those who accept help from him. For this reason he says: "Where I am, there shall my servant also be" (Jn 12:20). And again Paul says: "He has raised us up together with him and made us sit together with him at his right hand in heavenly places" (Eph 2:6). Irrational animals are much more consistent than we. For they are all joined, each to its own nature, the wild animals to the wild and sheep to their own species. But you do not rise up toward your heavenly family which is the Lord, but you give yourself over and consent in your thoughts to the thoughts of evil. You make yourself a helper of sin and you wage war with it against yourself. Thus you make yourself a prey for the enemy, like a bird caught by the eagle and eaten up, or the sheep by the wolf, or an ignorant child that would be bitten by it and would be infected. For the parables act as models in the spiritual life.

7. As a wealthy maiden, espoused to a fiancé, may receive no matter how many gifts before the consummation, either ornaments or clothing or precious vessels, she is not satisfied with these until the time of the marriage arrives and she arrives at full communion, so the soul, betrothed as bride to the heavenly Bridegroom, receives as pledge from the Spirit gifts of healing or of knowledge or of revelation. But it is not satisfied with these until it reaches the perfect communion, that is, of love, which is unchangeable and unfailing. It makes those free from passion and agitation who have desired it. Or as an infant, decked out with pearls and costly clothing, when it is hungry, thinks nothing of the things it wears, but ignores them. It cares only for the breast of its nurse, how it may receive milk. So likewise consider it to be with the spiritual gifts of God to whom be glory forever. Amen.

HOMILY 46

The difference between the Word of God and the word of the world and between the children of God and the children of this world.

1. The Word of God is God. And the word of the world is world. There is a great difference and distance between the Word of God and the word of the world and between the children of God and the children of the world. For every begotten offspring resembles its proper parents. If, therefore, the offspring of the Spirit gives itself over to the word of the world and to earthly matters and to the glory of this age, it is stricken with death and perishes, whence it came into existence. For, as the Lord says, he is "choked and becomes unfruitful" (Mk 4:19) from the Word of God who is surrounded by the cares of life and who is bound by earthly bonds. Likewise, one who is possessed by fleshly desire, that is, a man of the world, if he desires to hear the Word of God, is choked and becomes like someone irrational. For being accustomed to the entice-ments of evil when such men hear about God, they are burdened by boring conversation and their minds are bored.

2. Paul also says: "The natural man receives not the things of the Spirit. For they are foolishness to him" (1 Cor 2:14). And the Prophet says: "The Word of God was to them as vomit" (Is 28:13). You see that it is not possible to live except according to the reason according to which each one was born. And you must listen to another way of putting this. If the carnal man determines to change himself, he first dies in that area and becomes unfruitful regarding that former life of evil. But take the example of someone who is overcome by a disease or a fever. Even though the body is prostrate on the bed, unable to perform any of the works of the earth, still the mind is not at rest. It is distracted and is preoccupied with the things that need doing. And it seeks the physician, dispatching his friends to fetch him. So in the same way, a person weak from the passions because of the transgression of the commandment and in a state of languor has come to the Lord and has believed and finds his help. Having renounced his former evil life, even if he should still lie in his former weakness, unable to perform truly the works of life, neverthe-less, he can be diligently concerned about this life, he can beseech the Lord and ask the true Physician.

3. It is not as certain people say who are led astray by evil teaching, that man once for all is dead and absolutely cannot perform anything good. And yet a baby, even though it is powerless to accomplish any-

thing, or with its own feet to go to its mother, still rolls and makes noises and cries, as it seeks its mother. And the mother takes pity on it and is glad that the baby seeks after her with pain and clamoring. And though the baby is unable to come to her, because of the child's eager searching, the mother comes to it herself, all out of love for the baby. And she picks it up and fondles it and feeds it with great love. This also is what God, the Lover of mankind, does to the person that comes to him and ardently desires him. But there is even more. Impelled by love, he himself, by the goodness which is inherent in him and is all his own, enters with that person "into one spirit" (1 Cor 6:17), according to the apostolic saying. When a person clings to the Lord and the Lord has pity and loves him, coming and clinging to him, and he has the intention thereafter to remain constantly in the grace of the Lord, they become one spirit and one temperament and one mind, the person and the Lord. And though his body is prostrate on the earth, his mind has its complete conversation with the heavenly Jerusalem, rising up to the third heaven and clinging to the Lord and serving him there.

4. And he, while sitting on the throne of majesty in the heights, in the heavenly city, is totally turned toward him in his bodily existence. He has indeed placed his image above in Jerusalem, the heavenly city of the saints, and he has placed his own image of the ineffable light of his Godhead in his body. He ministers to such a person in the city of his body, while he serves him in the heavenly city. He has inherited him in Heaven and he has inherited him on earth. The Lord becomes his inheritance and he becomes the inheritance of the Lord. For if the thinking and the mind of sinners in darkness can be so far from the body and are able to travel far and journey in a moment to very remote countries, and often, when the body is stretched out on the earth, the mind is in another country, present with him or her whom he loves and he sees himself as living there, if, then, the soul of the sinner is so subtle and volatile that his mind is not hindered from places far away, much more does the soul from which the veil of darkness has been removed by the power of the Holy Spirit and whose spiritual eyes have been enlightened by the heavenly light and whose soul has been perfectly set free from the passions of shame and has been made pure through grace, how much more does this soul serve the Lord completely in Heaven in the Spirit and serve him completely in the body. Such a person finds himself so expanded in consciousness as to be everywhere, where and when he wishes to serve Christ.

5. This is what the Apostle says: "That you may be able with all the

saints to comprehend what is the breadth and length and height and depth and to know the love of Christ which surpasses knowledge that you may be filled unto the utter fullness of God" (Eph 3:18–19). Ponder the ineffable mysteries of the soul from which the Lord removes the darkness that covers it. He reveals it and is revealed to it. Think how he expands and stretches the thoughts of its mind to the breadths and lengths and depths and heights of all creation, visible and invisible. Indeed, a great and divine work and wonderful is the soul. For in fashioning it, God made it such as not to put any evil in its nature, but made it according to the image of the virtues of the Spirit. He put into it the laws of virtues, discernment, knowledge, prudence, faith, love, and the rest of the virtues according to the image of the Spirit.

6. For even now, in knowledge and prudence and love and faith, the Lord is found and manifested to the soul. He has placed in it intelligence, thoughts, will, a ruling mind. He has implanted in it also a great, different subtlety. He made it to move with ease, to be volatile, inexhaustible. He gifted it to come and go in a flash, and in its thoughts to serve him where the Spirit wishes. And in one word he created it such as to be his bride and enter into union with him so that he may interpenetrate it and to be "one spirit" with it, as it says: "He that is joined unto the Lord is one spirit" (1 Cor 6:17).

HOMILY 47

An allegorical interpretation of the things done under the Law.

1. The glory of Moses which he received on his countenance was a figure of the true glory. Just as the Jews were unable "to look steadfastly upon the face of Moses" (2 Cor 3:7), so now Christians receive that glory of light in their souls, and the darkness, not bearing the splendor of the light, is blinded and is put to flight. They were manifested as the people of God from the circumcision. But here the people of God, being very special, receive the sign of circumcision inwardly in their heart. For the heavenly knife cuts away the excess portion of the mind, that is, the impure uncircumcision of sin. With them was a baptism sanctifying the flesh, but with us there is a baptism of the Holy Spirit and fire. For John preached this: "He shall baptize you in the Holy Spirit and fire" (Mt 3:11).

2. They had an inner and an outer tabernacle, and into the latter the

priests went continually, performing the services. But into the former the high priest alone went once a year with the blood, the Holy Spirit signifying that the way into the holiest was not yet made manifest (Heb 9:6ss). Here, however, those who are deemed worthy enter into "the tabernacle not made with hands, whither the forerunner has entered for us" (Heb 6:20), namely, Christ. It is written in the Law that the priest should receive two doves and should kill one, but sprinkle the living one with its blood and should let it loose to fly away freely (Lv 14:4, 22). But that which was done was a figure and shadow of the truth. For Christ was sacrificed and his blood, sprinkling us, made us grow wings. For he gave to us the wings of the Holy Spirit to fly unencumbered into the air of the Godhead.

3. To them the Law was given, written on stone tablets, but to us, the spiritual laws written "upon fleshy tables of the heart" (2 Cor 3:3). For it says: "I will put my laws in their hearts and upon their minds will I write them" (Heb 10:16). But all those things were done away with and served for a time. But now all are fulfilled truthfully in the inner man. For the covenant is within and put briefly: "Whatsoever things happened to them were done in a figure and were written for our admonition" (1 Cor 10:11). For God foretold the future to Abraham: "Your seed shall be a stranger in a land not theirs and they shall afflict the seed and make it serve four hundred years" (Gn 15:13). This fulfilled the image of the shadow. For the people became foreigners and were enslaved by the Egyptians and were afflicted "in clay and brick" (Ex 1:14). Pharaoh placed supervisors and taskmasters over them in order that they should do their works under compulsion. And when "the children of Israel groaned to God by reason of their tasks" (Ex 2:23), then he visited them through Moses (Ex 2:25). After having inflicted the Egyptians with many plagues, he led them out of Egypt in the month of flowers, when the most pleasant spring appears and the sadness of winter passes away.

4. But God spoke to Moses to take a spotless lamb and to slay it and to sprinkle its blood on the lintels and doors so "that he that destroyed the firstborn of the Egyptians might not touch them" (Heb 11:28). For the angel that was sent saw the sign of blood from afar and departed. But the angel entered into the houses not signed and slew every firstborn. Besides, God also ordered all leaven to be removed from the house and commanded that they should eat the slain lamb with unleavened bread and bitter herbs (Ex 12:13). He ordered them to eat with their loins girded and shoes on their feet and holding their staves in their hands.

And so he commands them to eat the Passover of the Lord with all haste in the evening and not to break a bone of the Lord.

5. "He brought them forth with silver and gold" (Ps 105:37), ordering each of them to borrow from his Egyptian neighbor golden and silver vessels. But they left Egypt while the Egyptians were burying their firstborn. And joy was theirs because they were throwing off their squalid slavery, but grief and wailing were the lot of the Egyptians because of the loss of their children. Wherefore Moses says: "This is the night in which God promised to redeem us" (Ex 12:42). All these things are a mystery of the soul redeemed at the coming of Christ. For Israel is interpreted as being the mind contemplating God. Therefore, it is set free from the slavery of darkness, from the spiritual Egyptians.

6. For after man in disobedience died the grievous death of the soul and received curse upon curse: "Thistles and thorns shall the ground bring forth for you" (Gn 3:18), and again: "You will cultivate the earth and it shall not yield henceforth unto you its fruits" (Gn 4:12), thorns and thistles sprouted and grew up in the earth of his heart. His enemies took away his glory through deceit and clothed him with shame. His light was taken away and he was clothed in darkness. They killed his soul and they scattered and divided his thoughts. And they dragged down from on high his mind and Israel became the man who is slave to the true Pharaoh. And he set over him his supervisors and taskmasters, to do his evil works and to complete the construction of mortar and brick. And these spirits led him away from his heavenly wisdom and led him down to the material and to earthly and muddy evil works and to words and desires and thoughts that are vain. Having fallen from his proper height, man found himself in a kingdom of hatred toward humanity and there bitter rulers forced him to construct for them the wicked cities of sins.

7. But if man groans and cries out to God, he sends him the spiritual Moses, who redeems him from the slavery of the Egyptians. But man first cries out and groans and then he receives the beginning of deliverance. And he is delivered in the month of new flowers (Ex 13:4), in the springtime when the ground of the soul is able to shoot forth the beautiful and flowering branches of justification. The bitter winter storms of the ignorance of darkness have passed, as also the great blindness that was born of sordid deeds and sins. Then he commands that all "old leaven" (1 Cor 5:7) be removed from each household, to cast away

the acts and thoughts of "the old man that waxes corrupt" (Eph 4:22), the evil thoughts and sordid desires.

8. The lamb must be slain and sacrificed and its blood sprinkled on the doors. For Christ, the true and good and spotless Lamb, was slain and his blood anointed the lintels of the heart so that the blood of Christ poured out on the cross would be unto life and deliverance for humanity and unto grief and death for the Egyptians, the demons. The blood of the spotless Lamb is indeed grief to them, but joy and gladness for the soul. Then after the anointing, he orders them to eat the lamb toward evening and the unleavened bread with the bitter herbs with their loins girded and shoes on their feet and holding their staves in their hands. For unless the soul is prepared beforehand on all sides to perform good works, as far as it can, it is not given to the soul to eat of the lamb. And even though the lamb is sweet and the unleavened bread tasty, nevertheless, the bitter herbs are bitter and coarse. For it is with great affliction and bitterness that the soul eats of the lamb and of the good unleavened bread, since sin which inhabits the soul afflicts it.

9. And it says that he ordered this to be eaten toward evening, a time that is between light and darkness. So also the soul, being brought to deliverance, is found between light and darkness, while the power of God stands by and does not allow the darkness to enter the soul and swallow it up. And just as Moses said, "This is the night of God's promise" (Ex 12:42), so also Christ, when he was given the Bible in the synagogue, as it is written, called it "the acceptable year of the Lord" and "the day of redemption" (Lk 4:19; Eph 4:30). There it was a night of retribution, here it is a day of redemption. And justly so. For all those things were a figure and shadow of the truth and in a mystical way were prefigured and they sketched out the true salvation of the soul, locked up in darkness and secretly bound "in the lowest pit" (Ps 88:6) and shut up behind "gates of bronze" (Ps 107:16) and unable to be set free except by the redemption of Christ.

10. Therefore, he leads the soul out of Egypt and the slavery in it. The firstborn of Egypt are killed in the exodus. Already a certain part of the power of the true Pharaoh is done away with. Grief overcomes the Egyptians. Grieving, they groan at the salvation of the captive. He commands them to borrow from the Egyptians vessels of gold and silver to take with them as they depart. The soul, leaving the darkness, takes back its silver and golden vessels, namely, its own good thoughts, "purified

seven times in the fire" (Ps 12:6), by which thoughts God is served and finds rest. For the demons that were its neighbors pillaged and took possession and wasted its thoughts. Blessed is the soul who is redeemed from darkness and woe to the soul who does not cry out and groan to him who is able to liberate it from those harsh and bitter taskmasters.

11. The sons of Israel, after having observed the Passover, leave. The individual person progresses, once he has received the life of the Holy Spirit and has eaten the Lamb and has been anointed by his blood and has eaten the true Bread, the living Word. A pillar of fire and a pillar of cloud went before those Israelites, protecting them. The Holy Spirit strengthens these, enkindling and guiding the soul in an awareness. When Pharaoh and the Egyptians learned of the flight of the people of God and of their loss of their slavery, he dared to pursue them, even after the killing of the firstborn. For he hastily yoked up his chariots and with all his people he followed after them to destroy them. But just at the time that he was about to pounce upon them a cloud stood between them, impeding and obfuscating the Egyptians but guiding by light and protecting the Israelites. And so as not to prolong this discourse by developing the whole story, take the parable from me in all the details according to the spiritual realities.

12. For when first the soul escapes from the Egyptians, the power of God approaches to help and leads it to the truth. But the spiritual Pharaoh, the king of darkness of sin, when it knows that the soul is in revolt and is fleeing out of his kingdom, pursues the thoughts which he so long held in his power. For these belong to him. The deceitful one plans and hopes that the soul will return back to him. Having learned that the soul is for good fleeing from his tyranny, a more impudent action than the slaughter of the firstborn and the stealing of the thoughts, he chases after it because he fears that should the soul escape completely there would be found no one who would fulfill his will and do his work. He pursues it with afflictions and trials and invisible wars. There it is put to the test; there it is tried; there appears its love toward God who led it out of Egypt. For it is handed over to be put to the test and to be tried in many ways.

13. The soul sees the power of the enemy, seeking to pounce and kill it, and yet the enemy is unable. For between it and the Egyptian spirits stands the Lord. It looks before itself at a sea of bitterness and affliction or despair. It is powerless to retreat back, seeing the enemies ready, nor can it advance forward for the terror of death and the grie-

vous and manifold afflictions surround it, making it look at death. There-fore, the soul despairs of itself, "having the sentence of death in itself" (2 Cor 1:9), because of the swarming multitude of evils around it.

When God sees the soul, overwhelmed by fear of death and the enemy, he helps and deals patiently with the soul and tests it to see whether it remains faithful, whether it has love for him. For God has planned such a road, leading to life (Mt 7:14), to be fraught with afflic-tion and narrow escapes, in much testing and extremely bitter trials so that from there the soul may afterward reach the true land of the glory of the children of God. When, therefore, the soul gives up all opinion of itself and renounces itself, because of the overwhelming affliction and the death before its eyes, in that moment, with a strong hand and an uplifted arm, God splits through the power of darkness by the illumina-tion of the Holy Spirit and the soul passes through as it avoids the fearful places and traverses the sea of darkness and of the all-consuming fire.

14. These are mysteries of the soul which truly happen in a person who diligently seeks to come to the promise of life and is redeemed from the kingdom of death and receives the pledge from God and participates in the Holy Spirit. Consequently, the soul, having been rescued from its enemies and having passed through the bitter sea by God's power and seeing its enemies to whom it formerly was enslaved killed before its eyes, "rejoices with joy unspeakable and full of glory" (1 Pt 1:8), and is consoled by God and at rest in the Lord.

Then the Spirit, whom it has received, sings a new song to God with the timbrel, which is the body, and with the spiritual strings of the cithar, which is the soul, and with the most subtle thoughts and with the key of divine grace to pluck the strings. The Spirit sends up praises to the life-giving Christ. For as it is the breath that speaks as it passes through the windpipe, so it is the Holy Spirit through holy men who are endowed with the Spirit who sings hymns and psalms and prays to God with a pure heart. Glory to him who rescued the soul from Pharaoh's slavery and established it as his very own throne and home and temple and pure spouse and led it into the kingdom of eternal life, while being still in this world!

15. In the Law, irrational animals were offered in sacrifice, and, unless they were slain, they were not acceptable as offerings. Now, unless sin is slain, the offering is not acceptable to God nor is it authen-tic. The people came to Marah (Ex 4:25) where there was a spring giving forth bitter water, unfit to drink. Therefore, God orders Moses

in despair to throw a tree into the bitter water. And when the tree was thrown into the water, the water was made sweet. And having been changed from bitterness, it became useful and drinkable for the people of God. In the same way also the soul has become bitter by drinking the poison of the serpent and becoming like to its bitter nature and becoming sinful. Wherefore God casts the tree of life into the very bitter spring of the heart and it is made sweet, having been changed from the bitterness and having been mingled with the Spirit of Christ. And so it is made very useful and goes on in the service of its Master. For it becomes spirit enfleshed. Glory to him who transforms our bitterness into sweetness and goodness of the Spirit! Woe to that one in whom the tree of life has not been cast! He cannot obtain any change for the good.

16. The rod of Moses bore two images. To the enemies it appeared as a serpent, biting and destructive. To the Israelites, however, it was as a staff on which they found support. So also the true wood of the cross, which is Christ. For the enemies, the spirits of evil, he is death. But for our souls he is a staff and a safe refuge and life upon which they rest. For the figures and shadows of earlier time were of true, present realities. For the ancient worship is a shadow and image of the present worship. And the circumcision and the tabernacle and the ark and the pot and the manna and the priesthood and the incense and the ablutions and, in a word, all such things done in Israel and in the Law of Moses and in the prophets were done in reference to this soul, made according to the image of God and fallen under the yoke of slavery and under the kingdom of the darkness of bitterness.

17. For God desired to have fellowship with the human soul and espoused it to himself as the spouse of the King and he purified it from sordidness. Washing it, he makes it bright from its blackness and its shame and gives life to it from its condition of death. And he heals it of its brokenness and brings it peace, reconciling its enmity. For, even though it is a creature, it has been espoused as bride to the Son of the King. And by his very own power God receives the soul, little by little changing it until he has increased it with his own increase. For he stretches the soul and leads it to an infinite and unmeasurable increase, until it becomes the bride, spotless and worthy of him. First he begets the soul in himself and increases it through himself, until it reaches the perfect measure of his love. For he, being a perfect Bridegroom, takes it as a perfect spouse into the holy and mystical and unblemished union of marriage. And then it reigns with him unto endless ages. Amen.

THE FIFTY SPIRITUAL HOMILIES

HOMILY 48

Perfect faith in God.

1. The Lord in the Gospel, wishing to lead his disciples to perfect faith, said: "Whoever is unfaithful in little, he is unfaithful also in much. And whoever is faithful in little, he is faithful in much" (Lk 16:10). What is the meaning of little and of much? The little are the promises of this world which he has promised to supply to those who believe in him, such as food, clothing, and the things that are for the refreshment of the body or health and so on. He enjoins us not to be anxious at all concerning these things, but with confidence in him to trust that the Lord will be the provider of those who have recourse to him in regard to all things. The much are the gifts of the eternal and incorruptible world, which he promised to supply to those who believe in him and who uninterruptedly are solicitous for those and beseech him because he so commanded. He says: "Seek first the Kingdom of God and his justice and all these things will be added unto you" (Mt 6:33), so that from these little and temporal things each one may be proved whether he believes in God because he promised to supply them while we are without worry about such things and only are concerned about future eternal things.

2. Then it is clear that he believes in the incorruptible things and really seeks the eternal, good things, if he maintains his faith strong concerning the things mentioned. For anyone of those who obey the word of truth must prove himself and examine himself or be examined and tested by spiritual persons as to how he has believed and dedicated himself to God, whether really and truly according to God's word or whether by his own idea of the justification and faith that he entertains within himself. For each one, if he is faithful in little (about temporal things I mean), is tested and proved. Listen how this is done. Do you say that you believe that you have been deemed worthy of the Kingdom of Heaven and that you have been born a son of God from above and a co-heir of Christ and for all ages will reign with him and will take delight in the ineffable light through infinite and innumerable ages like God? No doubt you will say: "Yes. For this reason I have left the world and have given myself to the Lord."

3. Therefore, examine yourself whether earthly cares have still a hold on you and much solicitude for feeding and clothing the body and other attentions and satisfaction, as though by your own power you

received them, and you were to provide for yourself instead of having been commanded not to be at all anxious about these things in regard to yourself. If you believe that you will receive the imperishable and eternal and abiding and abundant things, how much more ought you to believe that God will bestow on you these passing and earthly things which he has given also to ungodly men and beasts and birds, just as he has commanded you not to be worried at all about them, saying: "Do not be anxious about what you shall eat or drink or what you are to put on. For all these things the pagans seek after" (Mt 6:25, 32).

If you still have a concern over these things and you do not trust yourself completely to his word, know that you have not yet believed that you will receive the eternal good things which are the Kingdom of Heaven, in spite of the fact that you think you believe, while you are found unbelieving in these little, perishable things. And again as the body is more valuable than the clothing, so also is the soul more valuable than the body (Mt 6:26). Do you believe then that your soul is receiving healing from Christ for the eternal and incurable wounds among human beings, from the wounds of the passions of ignominy for which also the Lord came here in order that the souls of the faithful now may be healed of those incurable passions and may be purified of the sordidness of the leprosy of evil—he the only true Physician and Healer?

4. You will say: "Surely I believe. For in this I stand firmly and I have this as my expectation." Know, therefore, after you have examined yourself, whether bodily sicknesses do not carry you to earthly physicians, as though Christ, in whom you believe, could not heal you. See how you deceive yourself that you think you believe when you do not yet believe as you really should. For if you believed the eternal and incurable wounds of the immortal soul and the evil passions can be cured by Christ, you should also believe it possible for him to cure the temporary diseases of the body and sicknesses, and you would have had recourse to him alone while neglecting the medical tools and curing ability. For he, who created the soul, made also the body. And he who heals that immortal soul, the same can heal the body also of its temporary sufferings and sicknesses.

5. But certainly you will say such things to me: "God gave to the body for healing the herbs of the earth and drugs, and he has prepared the instruments of physicians for the sicknesses of the body, arranging that the body that comes from earth should be healed by the different species of the earth." And I agree that things are thus. But be attentive and you will know to whom God has granted these things and for whom

he has arranged them providentially according to his great and infinite love for mankind and his kindness. When man fell from the commandment which he had received and came under the sentence of wrath and was, as it were, sent into captivity and shame, or sent to labor in some mine, cast out from the delights of Paradise to this world, and when he came under the power of darkness and was reduced to disbelief through the error of the passions, he then fell under the sicknesses and diseases of the flesh, instead of being free from passion and sickness as before. It is also clear that all who have been born of the first man have fallen under the very same disorders.

6. Therefore, God has providentially arranged these things for the weak and unbelieving, not wishing completely to destroy the sinful race of humans on account of his great kindness. But he gave medicine and healing and care of the body to comfort them, namely, the men of the world and all who are living exteriorly. And he permitted them to be used by those who were not able yet to trust completely in God. But you, O monk,[96] who have come to Christ and wish to be a son of God and to be born from on high by the Spirit, you await the promises that are higher and greater than what the first man had, who enjoyed a state of passionlessness. God has been pleased to give you the good pleasure of the Lord. You, who have become a stranger to the world, must possess such a faith and understanding and style of life that is new and foreign beyond all the men of the world. Glory to the Father and to the Son and to the Holy Spirit forever. Amen.

HOMILY 49

It is not enough to put aside the pleasures of this world unless one obtains the blessedness of the other world.

1. If anyone should leave his family and renounce this world and possessions and father and mother for the sake of the Lord, and if he has crucified himself and has become a wanderer and poor and needy, but does not find in himself the divine satisfaction instead of the satisfaction of the world, nor feel in his soul, instead of the temporal pleasure, the pleasure of the Spirit and has not been clothed, instead of with perishable clothing, with the clothing of the light of the Godhead, and if he does not know with assurance the satisfaction of the communion with the heavenly Bridegroom in his soul, instead of this temporal and carnal

communion, and does not know the joy of the Spirit interiorly, instead of the sensible joy of this world, and does not receive the heavenly consolation of grace and a divine filling in the soul in the appearance to him of the glory of the Lord, as it is written (Ps 17:15), and in a word, instead of this ephemeral enjoyment, does not even now possess in his soul the imperishable enjoyment that is greatly to be desired—this person has become salt without savor. This one is pitiful beyond all. This one even here has been deprived of things and has not enjoyed the divine gifts. He does not know divine mysteries by means of the workings of the Spirit in his inner man.

2. For this is the reason why one becomes a stranger to the world so that his soul may pass in mind to the other world and to eternity, according to the Apostle. He says, "Our conversation is in Heaven" (Phil 3:20). And again, "Walking on earth, we do not war after the flesh" (2 Cor 10:3). Therefore, it is necessary that he who puts away this world must deeply believe that it is necessary to pass in mind even now through the Spirit into another age and there to have conversation and take pleasure and enjoyment in spiritual good things, and for the inner man to be born of the Spirit, as the Lord said: "He, who believes in me, has passed from death to life" (Jn 5:24). Indeed, there is another death than the physical one and another life other than the visible one. For Scripture says, "She who lives in pleasure is dead" (1 Tm 5:6), and, "Let the dead bury their dead" (Lk 9:60), because "the dead shall not praise you, Lord, but we who live" (Ps 115:17–18).

3. For as the sun when it has come up upon the earth is totally on the earth, but when it comes to the setting in the west, it brings together all of its rays, retiring to its own home, so too the soul that is not reborn from above of the Spirit is totally on the earth, scattered about in thoughts and mind over the earth, even unto its ends. When it is deemed worthy to receive the heavenly birth and communion of the Spirit, it brings together all of its thoughts, and, taking them with it, it enters unto the Lord into the heavenly dwelling, not made by hands. And all its thoughts become heavenly and pure and holy, passing into the divine air. For the soul, rescued from its prison of darkness of the wicked ruler, the spirit of the world, finds pure and divine thoughts, because it has pleased God to make man "participator of the divine nature" (2 Pt 1:4).

4. If, therefore, you are withdrawing from all the things connected with this life, and if you are persevering in prayer, you will rather

consider this labor full of rest. You will reckon the little affliction and pain to be filled with joy and refreshment exceedingly great. For if your body and soul are being wasted away hour by hour throughout the whole of life for the sake of such great good things, what is this suffering in comparison? Oh, the ineffable compassion of God that he should give himself as gift to those who believe that in a short time they would possess God and God would dwell in man's body and the Lord would have man as a beautiful dwelling place! For as God created the sky and the earth as a dwelling place for man, so he also created man's body and soul as a fit dwelling for himself to dwell in and take pleasure in the body, having for a beautiful bride the beloved soul, made according to his own image. For the Apostle says: "I have espoused you to one husband, to present you as a pure virgin to Christ" (2 Cor 11:2). And again, "Whose house we are" (Heb 3:6). For just as a husband with diligence stores up in his household all good things, so also the Lord in his house, the soul and the body, puts away and stores up treasures, the heavenly richness of the Spirit. Neither the wise ones by their wisdom nor the prudent ones with their prudence were able to understand the subtlety of the soul nor speak about it as it is, but only those to whom through the Holy Spirit comprehension is revealed and exact knowledge about the soul is known.

Give here a serious look and discern and learn how. Listen. This is God; the soul is not God. This is Lord; that is servant. This is Creator; that is creature. This is Maker; that the thing made. There is nothing common to God's nature and that of the soul. But by means of his infinite and ineffable and incomprehensible love and compassion, it pleased him to make his indwelling in this made thing, this intellectual creature, this precious and extraordinary work, as Scripture says: "For this purpose that we should be a kind of first fruits of his creatures" (Jas 1:18), to be his wisdom and communion, his very own inhabitation, his own pure bride.

5. Therefore, since such good things are offered and such promises have been given and such good pleasure of the Lord shown to us, let us not neglect, O children, nor delay progressing toward eternal life and giving ourselves up completely to the pleasing of the Lord. Let us then call out to the Lord so that, by his own power of the Godhead, he may redeem us from the prison of the darkness of the shameful passions and he may make his own image and handiwork to shine splendidly, render-

ing the soul healthy and pure. And thus we may be deemed worthy of the fellowship of the Spirit, as we glorify the Father and the Son and the Holy Spirit forever. Amen.

HOMILY 50

God is the one who works wonders through his saints.

1. Who was it who closed the doors of Heaven? Was it Elijah or God in him who commanded also the rain to fall? I believe that he who holds power over the heavens was himself seated within his mind and through his tongue the Word of God forbade the rain to fall upon the earth. And he spoke again and the gates of the heavens opened and rain poured down. Likewise also Moses laid a rod down and it became a serpent (Ex 8:10). And he spoke again and it became a rod. And he took ashes from the furnace and scattered them and there were boils. And again he struck the rod and there came forth lice and frogs (Ex 8:17). Could the nature of man do these things? He spoke to the sea and it was divided (Ex 14:16, 21), to the river and it was changed into blood. It is evident that a heavenly power was dwelling in his mind and through Moses that power did these signs.

2. How was David, without any weapon, able to go against such a giant in battle? And when he hurled the stone at the foreign enemy, through the hand of David the hand of God guided the stone. And it was the divine nature itself that killed him and brought about the victory. For David could not have done it, being weak in body. Joshua, the son of Nun, when he came to Jericho, besieged it for seven days, not able to do anything by his own nature, but when God commanded the walls came tumbling down by themselves. And when he entered the land of promise, the Lord says to him, "Go out into battle." Joshua answered, "As the Lord lives, I will not go out without you" (cf. Num 13–14). And who is it who commanded the sun to stand still for another two hours in the conflict of war (Jos 10:13)? Was it his own nature or the power that stood by him? And Moses, when he fought Amalek, if he extended his hands up to Heaven toward God, repulsed Amalek. But if he lowered his hands, Amalek was superior.

3. When you hear of such things taking place, do not let your mind wander far from you. But since those were a figure and shadow of true realities, apply them to you yourself. For when you shall raise the hands

of your mind and your thoughts toward Heaven and you shall be bent on clinging to the Lord, Satan will be worsened by your thoughts. And, as the walls of Jericho fell by God's power, so also now the walls of evil that obstruct your mind and the cities of Satan and your enemies will be totally destroyed by God's power. Thus, in the shadow the power of God was constantly at the side of the just ones, performing amazing, visible acts. And the divine grace dwelled within them. Similarly also in the prophets divine grace worked and furnished to their souls the Spirit of prophesying and to speak when there was a great need to tell about great happenings. For they were not always speaking, but when the Spirit in them desired to do so.

4. If, therefore, the Holy Spirit was poured out with such force on what was only a shadow, how much more on the New Covenant, on the cross, on the coming of Christ, where the outpouring and the intoxication of the Spirit took place? For it says, "I will pour out my Spirit upon all flesh" (Acts 2:17). This is what the Lord himself said, "I will be with you until the end of the world" (Mt 28:20). "For everyone who seeks, finds" (Mt 7:8). He says: "If you, being evil, know how to give good gifts to your children, how much more your heavenly Father will give the Holy Spirit to those that ask him" (Lk 11:13), "with power and great assurance," as the Apostle says (1 Thes 1:5)?

Therefore, such things are found by degree and pain and much work and patience and love toward him as the "senses" of the soul are exercised, as it is said (Heb 5:14), through good and evil, namely, through the machinations and deceits and manifold circumstances and ambushings of evil. They are likewise exercised by the various gifts and different helps of the working and power of the Spirit. He who knows the plotting of evil that defiles the interior man through the passions and does not realize in himself the help of the Holy Spirit of truth that strengthens his weakness and renews the soul in gladness of heart, such a one travels without yet knowing of the manifold providential care of God's grace and peace. On the other hand, he who is helped by the Lord and is found in spiritual happiness and heavenly gifts, if he should think that he no longer can be impeded by sin, he is deceived in a hidden way, since he does not discern the subtlety of evil and does not realize the growth by degrees from infancy to perfection in Christ. For through the ministering of the holy and divine Spirit, faith increases and makes progress and every citadel of evil thoughts gradually is destroyed completely in a "casting down" (2 Cor 10:4).

Therefore, each one of us must examine whether he has found the

THE FIFTY SPIRITUAL HOMILIES

"treasure in this earthen vessel" (2 Cor 4:7), whether he has put on the purple of the Spirit,[97] whether he has seen the King and has found rest by coming near to him or whether he still serves in the most exterior parts of the house. For the soul has many parts and great depth, and besides, sin has entered in and has taken charge of all of its parts and of all the pasturelands of the heart. Then when a man seeks, grace comes to him and takes charge of, let us say, two parts of the soul equally. The inexperienced person, being comforted by grace, thinks that grace has come to all the parts of the soul and has taken possession and that sin has been uprooted. But the greatest part of the soul is held under the power of sin and only one part is touched by grace. And he is deceived and does not know it.

We have much more still to clarify and call to your attention according to your disposition of sincerity, but we have briefly pointed out to you a beginning, so that, as men of understanding, you might work and examine the power of the words given and become more understanding in the Lord, and increase in the simplicity of your heart in his grace and in the power of the truth, so that you may be found with all security, safe in your salvation, and, being freed from all impediments of evil and deceit of the adversary, you may receive the privilege of being found upright and uncondemned in the day of judgment of our Lord Jesus, to whom be glory forever. Amen.

THE GREAT LETTER

INTRODUCTION TO
THE GREAT LETTER

The Great Letter of Macarius has been the source of much scholarly contention and research as to the true author for the past four decades. In 1954, when Werner Jaeger published his learned and well-documented *Two Rediscovered Works of Ancient Christian Literature: Gregory of Nyssa and Macarius* (Leiden, 1954), he gave us the first complete edition of the *Great Letter* of Pseudo-Macarius. In order to prove his thesis, that Saint Gregory of Nyssa had originally written the treatise *De Instituto Christiano*, Jaeger produced the best edition of the *Great Letter* we now possess. He used the work of H. Dörries (still unpublished) on the best manuscripts of the *Great Letter*, that is, the Greek manuscripts *Vaticanus graecus* 694 (B) and *Vaticanus graecus* 710 (A), both of the thirteenth century. He also used the Greek text of manuscript E attributed to Ephrem the Syrian, and a Greek manuscript in Jerusalem (H, codex S. Saba 157). Yet Jaeger admits that his edition is still only a provisional one, since he had practical aims other than to further Pseudo-Macarian studies.

Jaeger set out to prove not only that Gregory of Nyssa was the original author of the *De Instituto Christiano*, but also that Macarius's *Great Letter* was a paraphrase of Gregory's treatise. He summarizes thus:

> The letter has shown that even where Macarius is paraphrasing a text of Gregory of Nyssa from beginning to end, he adds much of his own. His thought can be said to take Gregory as a point of departure and then to expand and vary its model. (p. 209)

He argues that Macarius's *Letter* is a paraphrase of part 2 of Gregory's original treatise, while the Byzantine excerpt of the treatise as given in

Migne's edition (*PG* 46:287–306) belongs to the first part of the original text of the treatise. Jaeger's conclusion about the makeup of Pseudo-Macarius's *Great Letter* is that it is a compilation, with the first part, as Dörries pointed out, being literally copied from Pseudo-Macarius's Homily 40, and the second part being a paraphrase of Gregory's treatise *De Instituto Christiano.*

Conflicting Views

As I pointed out in the Introduction, recent authors (see note 5 in the Introduction) reject Jaeger's findings and accept the research of R. Staats in his *Gregor von Nyssa und die Messalianer* (Berlin, 1968). Staats quotes the opinions of other authors who consider the *Great Letter* of Pseudo-Macarius as the original work and explain the *De Instituto Christiano,* normally attributed to Gregory, as an attempt to translate the ideas of Pseudo-Macarius on the ascetical life into a language more literary and philosophical in order to lessen the Messalian expressions. It could have been done by Gregory in his late years, c. 391–395, or by some of his disciples who knew of Gregory's interest in and esteem for Pseudo-Macarius/Symeon and his school of mystics and ascetics.

When one compares the terminology, the expressions, and the biblical exegesis of the *Great Letter* with the other authentic writings of Pseudo-Macarius, one can think that Macarius is most probably the original author of the *Great Letter* and that Gregory of Nyssa's *De Instituto Christiano* is a rewriting of the *Letter.* The question, however, remains complex and invites further research into the interrelationships of the works of Gregory and Macarius.

Present Translation

For this translation I have relied basically on the text of the *Great Letter* as edited by H. J. Floss in 1860 from a thirteenth-century manuscript in Berlin, lost since World War II. Alternate readings have been adopted in places from the more comprehensive edition by Werner Jaeger (*Two Rediscovered Works,* pp. 233–301). H. Berthold in his recent edition of *Collection I* begins his text with *Logos 2* and sends the reader to Jaeger's edition for the *Logos 1,* that is, the *Great Letter.* I have preferred to use the Floss edition over Jaeger's because this version represents the text of the Pseudo-Macarian homilies and *Great Letter* that was most influential in Western spirituality since the sixteenth century. This was the text that had such an immense influence on the ascetical writers of both the Greek and Latin worlds. In comparing Floss's edition with Jaeger's reconstruction from several manuscripts, we should note that the Greek text of Floss-Migne is almost exactly the same as that found in Jaeger's edition from p. 254, line 18, to p. 281, line 14. Much that is found prior to this in Jaeger's edition of the *Great Letter* (*Two Rediscovered Works*, pp. 233–54) is available in the Macarian Homilies translated in this volume. We also find that an examination of the Migne texts *On Perfection* and *On Prayer* (*PG* 34:841A–852D and 853A–865B) proves them to be excerpts from the *Great Letter*. Thus I thought that by staying with the Migne text of both the fifty homilies and the *Great Letter* I would be able to present the most representative teachings of Pseudo-Macarius without excessive repetition and within the limits of a single volume, despite the text-critical problems.

Content of Letter

When we analyze the text of the *Great Letter*, we discover two distinct parts. The first (409C–420B) deals with the passions (*pathē*) and *apatheia*, the purging of the passions to bring the Christian into a state of tranquillity and integration (see notes 6, 26, 36 to the Homilies). Macarius takes pains to establish that God could not have created anything evil. His use of "passions" refers to the evil tendencies in a human being's heart to be self-centered and abuse the good desires created by God to serve our sanctification. He describes how a Christian cannot be sanctified and become an abode of God while still living "passionately," that is, according to carnal-mindedness. The second part (420C–441) presents a wholly different characteristic. Macarius turns toward the monastic community and gives general instructions concerning the mutual relationships between superiors and subjects, along with a picture of a very loose monastic organization with the prime accent on the development of interior humility and purity of heart to attain incessant prayer.

These themes are also found in many of the homilies translated in this volume. There can be little doubt, on the basis of the ideas, the language used, the biblical citations (often consisting merely in making a statement and backing it up by a series of biblical texts from the Old and New Testaments, without any attempt at exegesis), and the abundance of "homey," simple examples and anecdotes, that the *Letter* is a product of the author whose name is Macarius in tradition, but surely not St. Macarius of Egypt. This author, Pseudo-Macarius, like all the other monks of the "desert" spirituality, was interested in "saving" words, instructions that came out of a common, traditional, scripture-inspired way of understanding the dynamic, interpersonal relationship of God and human beings. To Macarius and the other desert authors the traditions of early Christian asceticism and mysticism belonged, not to any one individual, but to the entire Church and to all humanity. It all came from God as the source of truth.

THE GREAT LETTER OF PSEUDO-MACARIUS

I wish to know your thinking as to whether you feel it is necessary that the perfect man, who is sanctified, not only should be in God, but also God should be in him, as the Lord says, "who abides in me and I in him" (Jn 15:5). For it is necessary that a man of God should also live in the divine tabernacle and should place his abode on the holy mountain of the most pure divinity in order that God not only completely surrounds him, but that he be surrounded by God's glory, which never allows him to be brought under the power of the darkness of passions.[1] For the Savior inhabits the worthy ones by the grace of sanctification and their state of *apatheia,* so that, as the Lord is passionless, so also those who have received him he would free from passions so as to be no longer agitated and tossed about on all sides by every wind.[2]

False Teaching on Passions

There are certain persons who not only dwell far from the mysteries of Christ, but who also furnish their neighbors occasions to drink of their sordid corruption, as they bind God's truth to injustice. Of them it is said that "what is known by God has been manifested" (Rom 1:19). For they are puffed up in their thoughts and dwell in darkness in their ignorant heart and speak about natural things and declare that the passions of shamefulness are created by God. But I say that the pleasure of corruption and an unjust spirit, an unbecoming anger, and other such things can never be brought about by God.[3]

Let us, therefore, treating them and their voices as coming from those who have fallen into error, ponder the gift of free will with which our Creator has endowed us by which we can ardently seek the better

253

things and avoid the worse. For the just Judge would not punish us by endowing us with passions, if he himself were their Maker.

God Creates only Good

Please put aside such thinking. Do not even let it enter your mind. For such erroneous and foolish teaching must be found abhorrent to every pious soul. For God is the Creator of only clean and very good natures, as the Holy Spirit announces in the creation of the world: "For behold," he says, "all things are very good" (Gn 1:31). However, Jeremiah laments and questions the indignity of the passions: "Lord," he says, "did you not say, 'Who is this who said let it be done, if it were not the Lord himself commanding it? Out of the mouth of the Most High do not flow evil things, but good' " (Lam 3:36–38). And again, there is the question asked of the Lord in the Gospel by intellectual beings: "Lord," they say, "did you not sow good seed in your field? From whence came these weeds?" (Mt 13:27). In another place the Savior himself says about these things: "Every plant, which the Heavenly Father has not planted, will be uprooted" (Mt 15:13). For Paul witnesses that everything planted by God is good in quoting the words of Christ, "Because all creation is good" (1 Tm 4:4). Know, therefore, that the passions hidden deeply in us are not from our nature, but come from an outside source.[4] For it is said, "Cleanse me from my secret faults and spare your servant from foreigners" (Ps 18:13–14). And, "Foreigners have risen up against me and the strong have sought my soul" (Ps 53:5). And, "Judge, O Lord, those who do wrong to me. War against those who wage war against me" (Ps 34:1). Therefore, the hidden forces or those who do evil things and foreigners waging war, are they not spirits of evil, who oppose the virtues of Christ?

Purity of Heart

Be diligently attentive to how the law rightly cries out about the purity of the inner man. It says: "Do not usurp the name of the Lord, your God, in vain, for the Lord will not leave unpunished the person who utters his name to misuse it" (Dt 5:11). Therefore, the Apostle clearly gives the admonition: "Let us cleanse ourselves from every iniquity not only of the flesh but also of the spirit" (2 Cor 7:1). In another text it is said, "Wash your heart from any trace of a bad conscience" (Heb 10:22); and again, "May you be kept blameless and whole, body, soul, and spirit" (1 Thes 5:23). And, "That you may be perfect children of God" (Phil 2:15). As many, therefore, who wish to enjoy the dignity of being adopted children, let them preserve, not only their body in purity, but also their spirit according to the Psalmist who says, "Let my heart be pure in keeping your statutes so I shall never be put to shame" (Ps 119:5–6).

For there are certain persons who observe God's laws according to the law of the flesh. They observe only an exterior purity, while those under grace ardently seek to observe them interiorly, something which brings about a holy peace. They follow him who said, "Unless your observance of the law goes deeper than that of the Pharisees and the Scribes, you will not enter into the kingdom of heaven" (Mt 5:20). For the Pharisees, blinded in their understanding, wash only the exterior part of the vessel. So also now there are some new Pharisees, who like them justify themselves by dressing up the exterior man with a certain natural wisdom. But the Holy Spirit does not bear witness with their spirit that they are children of God according to the Apostle who says, "For God's Spirit bears witness with our spirit that we are children of God" (Rom 8:16).

Works of the Flesh

Such as those do not care to grow in sanctity in the interior man, but only abound in works of the flesh. They are ignorant of the meaning of "All the glory of the king's daughter is from without" (Ps 45:14). For whoever among us is, as it were, an intellectual fig-tree, whose inner fruit the Lord desires, and not merely the form expressed by outer leaves, such a person is he who maintains that the cause of evil passions is nature and not something that has come to human nature. He has changed God's truth into his own lie. For as I said above, the Pure and Immaculate One made his image like to himself, but death has come into the world through the envy of the devil.[5] After the human race was conceived in iniquities and was alienated by the sins of the first parents from the womb and led into error, with sin reigning from Adam to the coming of Christ, the Lamb of God came as propitiation to take away the sin of the world through his own power. After he conquered the strong one, he snatched away the captives from the evil one's domain as it has been said, "He captured the captives," and again, "He has done away with the captivity" (Ps 68:18; Eph 4:8). We ought to take care so that we may be called out of captivity to conduct ourselves according to the heavenly image, just as we once did so according to the image of the world. And let us conduct ourselves by serving justice and sanctification, just as we once showed ourselves servants to sin (Rom 6:19).

To See God Everywhere

Let us believe that walking in light we ought to see without any difficulty the wonders of God, according to the Psalmist who says, "Open wide my eyes and I will concentrate on the wonders of your law" (Ps 119:18). For just as in what pertains to the senses, whoever walks in the light does not stumble and fall, so too in what pertains to the spirit, whoever strives for spiritual perfection does not long for evil things nor think sordid thoughts. For light cannot have anything in common with darkness (2 Cor 6:14), nor can the temple of God have any common ground with idols (2 Cor 6:16). So consider yourself the temple of God. Flee from any image of spiritual idols in your heart. For every affection operating in the soul is an idol. Thus it is well said: "If anyone lets himself be dominated by anything, then he is a slave to it" (2 Pt 2:19). If we have become slaves to the pleasures of the flesh, it becomes clear we no longer are servants to the holy and passionless Spirit.[6] For no one can serve two masters. "You cannot serve God and mammon" (Mt 6:24). For the temple of God is holy, "not having any stain or wrinkle or anything like that" (Eph 5:27).

The Holy Spirit flees from any deceit and avoids any foolish thoughts. And there is no discipline to be found in an evil soul. Believing that our every law is written on our heart by the finger of God, not by ink, but by the divine Spirit, let us accept the truth of the Lawgiver who said, "I am the truth" (Jn 14:6), the truth of him, who effects a circumcision of the heart and inscribes the Law upon the minds of those worthy of his goodness, as he says in prophecy: "I will imprint my laws deep upon their hearts and upon their minds I will write them" (Jer 31:33). Thus, to whomever it has been given to be called to be "a chosen race, a royal priesthood, a holy consecrated nation, a people acceptable" (1 Pt 2:9; Ti 2:14), it is easy for them to receive the working of the life-giving Spirit in them.

So be encouraged to pray that we may be considered worthy to be brought to a knowledge of the simple way of converting totally to Christ. For a soul of this sort that has put aside any personal confusion and no longer is ruled by bad thoughts nor made an adulterer by evil, such a one, that is, who lives in the fellowship of only the divine Spouse, is totally simple in his single-mindedness.[7]

Mystical Union

For such a soul, wounded by love for Christ, dies to any other desire in order, I speak boldly, to possess that most beautiful intellectual and mystical communion with Christ according to the immortal quality of divinizing fellowship. Truly, such a soul is blessed and happy, when conquered by spiritual passion,[8] it has worthily become espoused to God the Word. Let her say, "My soul will exalt in the Lord, who has clothed me in the garments of salvation and has wrapt me in the cloak of integrity like a bridegroom wearing his crown, like a bride adorned in her jewels" (Is 61:10). For the King of Glory, ardently desiring her beauty, has deigned to regard her, not only as the temple of God, but also as the daughter of the king and also the queen. Indeed, she is the temple of God, since she is inhabited by the Holy Spirit. She is also the daughter of the king since she has been adopted by the Father of lights. She is also queen as endowed with the divinity of the glory of the Only-Begotten Son.

Titles of Christ

In what manner has the Lord, who is one in substance, received analogically many titles due to the economy of salvation for mankind? How is he called a rock and a door? How is he an axe and the way? And again a vine and bread? A rock certainly because of his unshakable and impenetrable strength. Truly a door because he is the entrance to eternal life. Also an axe because he cuts out the roots of evil. And a way because he leads the worthy to a knowledge of truth. And a vine from which wine is produced that exhilarates the human heart; and bread that strengthens the heart of the rational animal. In the same way the pure soul, inhabited by the Word of God, will be worthy to be made whole through many stages of acquiring spiritual virtues and gifts.

I speak these things so that the concept of the bride be understood, not only in three different ways,[9] but in many others. Know that this is according to our human way of understanding until we go "to the altar of God, to God who gives joy to our youth" (Ps 42:4). For the Savior wishes, as well as we who are in the flesh do, that we may be made worthy by his integrity and be filled with sanctity so that we would confidently confess: "We walk in the flesh, but we fight not with weapons of flesh. For the weapons by which we fight are not of the flesh, but in the sight of God they are strong enough to destroy fortresses. We demolish sophistries and the puffed up arrogance that pits itself against God's knowledge" (2 Cor 10:3–5).

Crucify the Passions

Therefore, we must now tie our passions of sin to the cross according to the prayer of the Prophet, "Afflict my whole being with your fear" (Ps 119–120). For flesh and blood, as the Apostle says, cannot enter the Kingdom of God. It is not this that is meant by the body which has been fashioned by God, but the "wisdom of the flesh" (Rom 8:6), which is moved by spirits of evil, "that are at work in the children of rebellion" (Eph 2:2). For "it is not against flesh and blood" that the perfect in Christ have "to struggle but against the powers that direct the darkness in this world, against the spiritual army of evil" (Eph 6:12). If, therefore, we admit that such operation is not natural, but of the powers of enemies, we will be empowered by the weapons we have received from Christ to resist their wiles (Eph 6:11–13), since we have been given by the Savior power to "tread underfoot serpents and scorpions and the whole strength of the enemy" (Lk 10:19). Thus we should dare to say, even while we are in the flesh, "Had I been guilty in my heart, the Lord would never have heard me" (Ps 66:18). Also, "I have run without iniquity and have not wavered" (Ps 59:5), that is, I walk easily the way of integrity without any carnal attachment, "stretching out toward the goal to which God calls us upwards" (Phil 3:14). For alienated from every passion, we will dare to say: Not only "I have kept the faith," but also, "I have completed the race" (2 Tm 4:7).

Suffer with Christ

For not only must we believe in Christ, but we must also suffer with him according to what has been said: "For it has been given to you, not only to believe in Christ, but also to suffer for him" (Phil 1:29). For only to believe in God is possible also for those who delight in the pleasure of the world, worse yet, even the impure spirits who say, "We know who you are, son of God" (Lk 4:34). For both groups are enemies of the cross of Christ. "They are destined to be lost whose God is their belly and they are proudest of what should be shameful to them, who delight in earthly pleasures" (Phil 3:19). Do you not see that not only heretical powers are enemies to the cross, but also those who delight in the things of this earth? However, for those who suffer with Christ, it is also given to be glorified with him, since they have crucified themselves to the things of this world. They "carry the marks of the Lord on their own bodies" (cf. Gal 6:17).

For those who know how to philosophize rightly and who have redeemed their souls from any evil iniquities, they know accurately the end of philosophy as knowledge of and a laboring to attain the goal of the race. They throw away all pride and vanity in good works, and, by denying their soul, they lead a life according to the precepts of Scripture (Mt 16:24 ff.; Lk 9:24). They keep focused on the one treasure which God has held out as a reward to those who diligently love Christ. God calls to Christ all who willingly undergo the contest of accepting the cross. For this contest they only need Christ's cross as viaticum which they, with joy and good hope, necessarily carry in order to follow God their Savior, as they make his Law and way of life the plan of salvation. So spoke the Apostle himself, "Be imitators of me as I am of Christ" (1 Cor 4:16). And again: "We are running steadily in the race we have started. Let us not lose sight of Jesus who leads us in our faith and brings it to perfection. For the sake of the joy which was still in the future, he endured the cross, disregarding the ignominy of it and he sits now on the right of God's throne" (Heb 12:1–2).

Danger of Pride

We must fear lest we who have received gifts of the Spirit and rightly would begin acting virtuously were to use that as an occasion of growing in pride and vanity before we have reached the goal of the things we hoped for. We fall away from our zeal and through pride we render everything useless that we have undertaken so laboriously. And we appear unworthy of the perfection to which the grace of the Spirit draws us. It is, therefore, to slacken off in undertaking hard work[10] when we run away from the struggles of the race. Nor should we look back on what has been accomplished, but we should confine all that to oblivion, as the Apostle writes, "Let us strain ahead for what is to come" (Phil 3:13). Let us turn our heart's attention to the concerns of asceticism, having an insatiable desire for righteousness which we ought solely to hunger and thirst after as befits those who strive for perfection. We must show ourselves to be humble and most diffident since we are far away from attaining the promises and still a great way from the perfect love of Christ.

Need for Struggle

For he who ardently desires this and looks toward the heavenly promise, yet neither fasts nor keeps the vigil nor sets about to exercise any other of the virtues, is directed toward good works which demand such asceticism. He is full of divine desire and looks eagerly to the one who is calling him, and he counts as little every battle he fights to attain him. He struggles right up to the end of this life, by heaping up difficult tasks upon difficult tasks and external virtues upon other virtues, to present himself to God as precious on account of his works. He renders himself worthy of God, not trusting in his own conscience. For this is the greatest work of philosophy:[11] to be greatly humbled in heart in works done and to despise life by rejecting through fear of God one's self-opinion, so that one may share in the promise by desiring it through belief, not as though earning it by effort. For even though the gifts are great, works are not to be considered worthy.[12]

Detachment

However, there is need of great faith and hope, for the reward comes from these and not by works. The substance of faith is poverty of spirit and an infinite love toward God. I think that enough has been said about what pertains to the hope of the goal for those who have chosen to live in a philosophical manner. Some things ought to be added about how such people ought to live in the company of others, what kinds of ascetic works they should love, and how they ought to journey together until they reach the city above. He who completely despises the splendor of this life, and gives up relatives and even all earthly glory and looks to heavenly honor, spiritually joined with his brothers in God, must deny his soul together with his life. However, to deny the soul is to deny one's will, even to suppress it. It is always to embrace the Word of God and also to lead the congregation of brothers, like a good steersman in a boat, in harmony to the port of God's will. However, you must possess nothing, not claiming anything as your own beyond what is common to all, except what garment covers your body.[13] For if one has none of these things, but gives up even the care of his own life, the community will take care of all necessities as he performs with pleasure and hope whatever it is he is commanded to do as the honest and simple servant of Christ, redeemed to serve the common need of the brethren.

Humble Service

For the Lord wishes and admonishes this when he said: "He who wishes to be first and great among you, let him be the last and the minister and servant of all" (Mk 9:34; 10:43ff.; Mt 20:26ff., 23:11). Therefore, it is necessary that service before others be without a reward, nor should it bestow on the server any honor or glory, so as not to contradict Scripture by appearing "pleasing to men" or "serving to the eyes" (Eph 6:6–7; Col 3:22). Not serving men, but the Lord alone, let him keep to the narrow path (Mt 7:14). Let him submit promptly to the single yoke of the Lord and carry it patiently in order to be brought with pleasure to his end with positive love.

Therefore, he ought to be subject to all, and as a debtor, to whom all has been given, he ministers to the brethren, putting aside all concerns for himself, he returns due love. Moreover, the superiors,[14] to whom charge has been given for the spiritual welfare of the group, must regard the great importance of the charge given them and be attentive to the wiles of evil attacking the faith in order to fight manfully by the skills learned. Let them not take such responsibility out of a desire for power. For there is danger in such a position. There are those who regard themselves as superior to others, and feel they are leading them to eternal life, yet it is hidden to them that they are destroying themselves by their pride.

The Role of the Superior

Therefore, those in charge of others ought to labor more than others, even regarding themselves as more humble than their subjects, and show their life to be a type of service to the brethren. They must consider those entrusted to them as a bequest from God. For if they so conduct themselves, exercising their holy office by their ministry and teaching correctly according to the demands of the given situation, observing the approved order, they must hiddenly exercise humility of mind as honest ministers serving faithfully. Thus they accrue to themselves by such a life a great reward. Therefore, they ought to care for those under them as good teachers toward very young children who have been entrusted to them by their fathers. For such teachers regard

the inclination of the children, giving one whippings, another correc-
tions, another praise, another some other approach used by teachers. But
they do not act as a favor or out of hatred in what they do to them; they
do what is befitting the situation and the nature of the children so that
they may be useful adults in this life. So we also must put aside all hatred
toward a brother and all arrogance and accommodate our words to his
strength and his understanding.

Rebuke this one, correct that one, exhort another, according to
each one's need, just as a good doctor prescribes medicine. For the
doctor who examines sufferings prescribes a medication, for one something mild, for another something more powerful. He does not become
angry with any of them who are in need of a cure, but he accommodates
his medical training to the wounds and the bodies. You then should
follow what the case necessarily calls for, so that listening well to the
disciple who comes to you, you may guide his pure virtue to the Father
who bestows on him the worthy inheritance of his gift. If you conduct
yourselves in such a manner toward each other, those who are the elders
and those who need teachers, with the latter obeying orders with joy, the
former with pleasure leading the brethren to perfection, and all of you
bestowing upon each other honors, you will live the angelic life here
on earth.[15]

Simplicity and Concord

Therefore, let no pride be known among you, but rather simplicity
and concord. And let a spirit that totally lacks in deceitfulness be the
binding force in the community. Let each one consider himself to be
inferior, not only to his brother with whom he lives, but also to every
human person. For he who knows this truly will be Christ's disciple. For
"Whoever exalts himself, will be humbled and whoever humbles himself will be exalted" (Lk 14:11). And again, "Whoever of you wishes to
be first, will be last of all and servant of all" (Mt 9:34). So too, "The Son
of man has not come to be served, but to serve and to give his life as a
ransom for many" (Mt 20:28). And the Apostle writes: "We do not
preach ourselves, but Jesus Christ, our Lord; ourselves, however, as
your servants for Jesus' sake" (2 Cor 4:5). Knowing, therefore, the fruit
of humility and the weeds of pride, imitate the Lord. Love one another
and do not fear death or any other punishment over good toward each
other. But as the Savior walked a path among us, so you walk that path

toward him and progress both in body and soul according to your heavenly calling, loving God and each other.

For love and fear of the Lord are the first fulfillment of the Law. It is necessary that each of you build in your soul as a certain and firm foundation fear and love and that you water these with good works and sufficient prayer. For love of God is not born simply nor automatically in us, but by many labors and great inner attentiveness and with the cooperation of Christ as the Book of Proverbs says: "For if you seek after it as if you were seeking gold and you dig for it as if for a buried treasure, then you will understand what the fear of the Lord is and you will discover the knowledge of God" (Prv 2:4–5).

Loving God and Neighbor

Discovering the knowledge of God and understanding the fear of him, you will properly succeed at what follows, namely, to love your neighbor. For the first command is attained by great labor, while the second, since it is less, is fulfilled easier than the first. But where the second command is sought, it does not mean that the first will follow purely. For how can the one who does not seek to love God with all his soul and all his heart bestow a concern of love upon the brethren in a wholesome and sincere manner? For the master of evil, finding the intellect void of the remembrance of God, and of love and longing for him, will find such a person defenseless and will easily conquer him with bad thoughts, making the divine commandments appear harsh and laborious, kindling in his soul grumbling, resentment, and complaints about having to serve the brethren. Or else it will deceive him with the presumption of self-righteousness, filling him with arrogance and making him think that he is of great importance and worthy of esteem, and that he has entirely fulfilled the commandments. Such evil is not a small one. For the upright and solicitous servant ought to submit himself to the judgment of the Lord and not set himself up before the Lord as judge and flatterer of his virtuous life. For if he makes himself the judge, while casting away the true Judge, then he will not receive any reward since according to his own judgment he has puffed himself up with praises and vain opinion about himself.

We must be judged by the statement of Paul, "The Spirit of God bears witness to our spirit" (Rom 8:16), and not judge ourselves by ourselves. For he says: "It is not the man who commends himself that will be approved, but whom God commends" (2 Cor 10:18). He who does not await God's judgment on himself falls into seeking human glory. He will seek praise for his works from those whom he serves. He does the works of an unbeliever who follows after earthly rather than heavenly rewards. As the Lord himself says in one place, "How can you have faith when you receive honor from one another and do not seek the honor that comes from God alone?" (Jn 5:44).

It seems to me such persons are really similar to those "who clean the outside of the cup and the dish and leave the inside full of all sorts of evil" (Mt 23:25). See, therefore, that you do not allow such a thing to happen, but, lifting your souls upward and having only one concern, always seek to please God and never fall away from the remembrance of heavenly things nor be enticed by honors of this life. So run that you hide your struggles undertaken for virtue, lest someone who would want to suggest something of earthly honors, seek to snatch your soul and lead you from the truth to seek vain things full of error. For the devil, not finding any opportunity nor any way to enter in order to snatch away those who have their souls lifted up to God, perishes and lies dead, for when evil is lifeless the devil is dead.

Divine Love Begets Fraternal Love

If the love of God dwells within you, it is necessary that such love bring forth other fruit, such as fraternal love, meekness, sincerity, perseverance in prayer, and zeal and all virtues. But since the treasure is precious, so also great are the labors necessary to obtain it. Such persons do not strut in show before others, but do all in order to please the Lord, who knows all hidden things, whom we must always be directed toward, and who scrutinizes the interior of the spirit. We must strengthen ourselves with thoughts of piety lest the adversary find an entrance or a place for deceits. Much struggle is needed, therefore, and much inward and unseen travail, much scrutiny of our thoughts and training of our soul's enfeebled organs of perception, before we can discriminate between good and evil. The mind that follows God knows how to exercise the soul, binding it to itself out of love for God and by hidden virtuous thoughts and good works healing what is weak and joining it to what is strong. Since inner custody and care of the soul go together, namely, to remember God with striving and always to entertain good thoughts, let us not slack in such zeal, whether eating or drinking or resting or doing anything else or in talking, so that all we do may be to God's glory and not to our own, lest anything sordid or unclean ensnare our life by the enticements of the devil.

Besides, the fulfillment of the commandments becomes easy and delightful to those who love God, since his love makes the struggle for us easy and lovable. Therefore, the devil strives by every means to drive out of our hearts the fear of the Lord. He does this by seeking to distract our love for God by turning away our soul by means of earthly forms and seductions from what is truly good toward what only appears to be good. He makes war, and when he finds a soul stripped of spiritual arms and defenseless, he destroys our efforts. He replaces heavenly glory with earthly, and he obscures true beautiful things with what only seems beautiful to deceived imagination. For the devil is terrifying if he should find any who neglect to be inwardly on guard. He seizes the opportunity and steals away the virtuous labors and sows thistles with the wheat, namely, evil and pride and empty vainglory and desire for honor and quarreling and other crimes.

Offering the First Fruits

Therefore, it is necessary to be vigilant on all sides, guarding against the enemy so that, even if the devil should brazenly present any trap, before he can ever capture our soul, we can repel him. I always remember that it was Abel who offered a sacrifice to God of the fat and firstlings of his flock, while Cain offered gifts of the fruits of the earth, but not of the firstfruits. It is said: "And God looked with favor on Abel's sacrifices, but did not regard the gifts of Cain" (Gn 4:4). This teaches us that everything that is done in fear and in faith is pleasing to God, not that which is done for display and without love.

Abraham, when he was receiving Melchisedech, the priest of God, made him an offering from the firstfruits of the earth and so obtained his blessing (Gn 14:19–20). This incident points to the first and highest elements of our constitution, the mind and the soul, and that they must initially be offered to God as a holy sacrifice. We must not offer to God anything common, the firstfruits and the highest of our true thoughts must be continually devoted to remembrance of him, engrossed in his love and in unutterable and boundless longing for him. In this way we can grow and move forward day by day, assisted by divine grace and the power which is in Christ. Then the burden of fulfilling the commandments will appear light to us, and we will carry them out faultlessly and irreproachably, helped by the Lord himself as he completes the works of justice in us.

Virtues Interlinked

But now, concerning the various virtues it cannot be said which is the most important and to be sought before all others, and which is second after it, and so on.[16] The virtues are all equal and interconnected, leading the practitioner to the summit. Simplicity leads to obedience, obedience to faith, faith to hope, hope to service, and service to humility. Meekness takes over from humility and leads to joy, joy to charity, charity to prayer. So bound together, they lead the soul who possesses them to the summit of his desire. Just as on the contrary, vices are linked to each other, but their evil leads one to extreme evil. You, however, must direct your work more to prayer. This is the superior in the chorus of the virtues. By it we seek other virtues from God so that communion and fellowship thrive through the mystical holiness and certain spiritual way of acting with an ineffable disposition of the person intent on prayer.

For the Spirit infuses the superior and fellow-combatant with a burning love of the Lord and he burns with desire, never finding weariness in prayer, but always being enflamed with a love of God, he is refreshed with alacrity, as it is said: "Whoever eat me, still will hunger and who drink of me will still thirst" (Sir 24:29). And in another place, "You have given joy to my heart" (Ps 4:7). The Lord said, "The Kingdom of Heaven is with you" (Lk 17:21). What kingdom is said to be within us unless that joy that comes through the Spirit from above and is infused into our souls? This is by way of an example and a pledge of eternal joy which the souls of the saints enjoy in the life to come.

Work of the Holy Spirit

Therefore, the Lord consoles us through the working of the Spirit in our every tribulation to save us and communicate to us all his spiritual and charismatic gifts. For it is said: "He who comforts us in all our sorrows, so that we can offer others in their sorrows the consolation we have received" (2 Cor 1:4). And, "My heart and my flesh exult in the living God" (Ps 84:2). And, "My soul feasts most richly" (Ps 63:5). All these expressions indicate through enigmas something of the joy and consolation given by the Spirit. Therefore, it has been shown what is the end of piety which all who choose to live a life pleasing to God ought to propose to themselves. This is the purification of the soul and the indwelling of the Spirit through exhortation to perform good works. Let each of you prepare your spirit to obtain this end. By rendering to God the greatest love, let each dedicate himself to prayer and fasting according to his will. Let all of you be mindful of what the Lord exhorts us to pray for without ceasing and to be vigilant in prayer, so as to receive his promises as he says: "God will see justice done to his chosen who cry to him day and night" (Lk 18:7). He says, "Then he told them a parable about the need to pray continually and never lose heart" (Lk 18:1).

Unceasing Prayer

That we need a great zeal for prayer, and that the Spirit who dwells in our spirits brings it about, is clearly shown by the words of the Apostle, who exhorts us: "Pray all the time, asking for what you need, praying in the Spirit on every possible occasion" (Eph 6:18). Whoever of the brothers dedicates himself to this, namely, unceasing prayer, possesses a beautiful treasure, which becomes the greatest possession of one who loves God with a firm and right conscience.[17] He never willingly strays away into distractions, nor does he have an unwonted debt that needs paying; but rather he fulfills the love and desires of his spirit, displaying to all the brothers the good fruits that come from perseverance. It is necessary, however, that the others in the community also make time for such unceasing prayer and rejoice in persevering in prayer so that they become sharers of such a life. The Lord himself will surely give to those who ask how they must pray, according to what is said: "He gives to him what he has asked for" (Ps 106:15).

Therefore, we ought to ask and to know that the better one makes an effort in the work of prayer, the more he must sustain the battle with great care and all virtue. For great battles demand great labors because evil insidiously rises up from all sides. Such obstacles the devil places in his path to impede his diligence, such as sleep, listlessness, physical torpor, distraction of thought, confusion of intellect, debility, and other evil passions and workings to kill the soul that is partly torn away and given over to its enemy. Therefore, it is necessary, as a wise ship captain does, that one in prayer controls the spirit and never gives the mind over to the turbulent suggestions of the evil spirit, nor allows it to be tossed about by waves. He must keep his eyes directed on the heavenly port and offer himself to God, who has believed in him and wants that from him.

THE GREAT LETTER

Nor should they in prayer be satisfied with merely standing or kneeling, seemingly to be agreeing with Scripture and well-pleasing to God, while all the while their mind wanders far from him. They must guard against every neglect of thoughts and unseemly attitude and turn the whole soul with the body back to prayer. And the superiors also ought to assist such a person, and with every solicitude and correction to nurture the one who is learning how to pray with fervor according to what is outlined for him. They should also diligently purify his soul. For those who so conduct themselves, let them share the fruit of their virtues even with the weak, not only to him who already is growing in perfection, but also with children and those uneducated in doctrine, consoling them and arousing them to imitate what they see in such advanced teachers.

Fruit of True Prayer

The fruits of sincere prayer are simplicity, love, humility, fortitude, innocence, and other things similar to these. Such fruits which precede the heavenly fruit are developed in this life by a man eager for prayer through hard labor. Prayer is adorned with such fruit. Who lacks such fruit undertakes in vain laborious tasks. This applies not only to prayer, but also to every path of philosophy, which is born out of such a growth process. It is truly a way of justice and leads to the proper goal. One who is lacking in these is left only with vanity and is similar to the foolish virgins, who did not have at the necessary time the spiritual oil to enter into the wedding feast (Mt 25:1–13). For such did not have a light in their hearts, the fruit of virtue, nor the light of the Spirit in their souls. This is why Scripture rightly called them foolish, because they lacked virtue before the coming of the Bridegroom and were abjectly excluded from the heavenly bridal chamber. They did not enjoy any reward for their efforts of virginity because the power of the Spirit was not with them. When we cultivate a vineyard, the whole of our attention and labor is given in the expectation of the harvest. If there is no vintage, all our work is to no purpose. Similarly, if through the activity of the Spirit we do not perceive within ourselves the fruits of love, peace, and the other qualities mentioned by St. Paul (Gal 5:22), then our labor for the sake of virginity, prayer, psalmody, fasting, and vigil is useless.

THE GREAT LETTER

Spiritual Harvest

For, as we said, our labors through which the Spirit is attracted should be undertaken in expectation of the spiritual harvest above. One shares in grace from this, and bears fruit with spiritual enjoyment made active by the Spirit in faithful and humble hearts. Thus, the labors and hardships of prayer and fasting and other works must be undertaken with joy and hope, believing that the flowers and fruits of labors are the works of the Spirit. If anyone should attribute this to himself and all his own efforts, he would be bearing pride and toasting rather than rich fruit. Such passions, like a certain oozing infection inserted into the depths of the soul, negate and corrupt the works. What, therefore, must one do who lives for God and his hope? The struggles to develop virtue must be undertaken with joy. He must place hope in God to be purged of passions, to reach the highest degree of perfection in the virtues, and to trust in God's kindness. Thus he is prepared and enjoys that which he has believed in, namely, grace. By grace he runs without any effort and despises the evil of the adversary, even though he is still a pilgrim. He is freed from passions by Christ's grace.[18]

Those who introduce evil passions into their nature through neglect of good works turn to such with pleasure and easily consider such as natural and a proper pleasure befitting human nature. They bring forth fruit of avarice and envy and evil and other types of the adversary's depravity. But those who are devoted to Christ and truth through faith and the practices of virtue bring forth their supernatural good fruit with ineffable joy. They perform these without effort by means of their unshakable faith, immutable peace, true goodness, and all the other gifts of the Spirit by which the soul itself becomes better and stronger against the evil of the adversary.

Indwelling Spirit

Such a person shows himself to be a pure dwelling place for the adorable and Holy Spirit from whom he receives the immortal peace of Christ, through whom he is joined and united with the Lord. Such a person, accepting the Spirit's grace and joined to the Lord, becomes one Spirit with him (1 Cor 6:17). He performs easily, not only works of virtue, never ceasing to battle against the enemy in order to become

269

stronger than the devil in his wiles, but also more importantly, he takes upon himself the sufferings of the Savior. He delights more in these than the devotees of this life delight in human honors and glory and kingdoms. For Christians, through their continued conversion and the gift of the Holy Spirit to maturity—by the grace that is given to them— prefer above the glory, pleasures, and all that is delightful, the greater desire to be held in contempt for the sake of Christ, to bear all insults and ignominy through faith in God.

Suffering Persecutions

Since this person places all his hope in the resurrection and in future blessings, every insult and beating and persecution and other suffering, even to the cross, is a delight and rest and the reward of heavenly treasures. For Jesus says: "Blessed are you when they will have spoken ill of you and all men will have persecuted you and will have spoken every evil against you by lying for my sake, be glad and rejoice because your reward will be great in heaven" (Mt 5:11). And the Apostle says, "But that is not all we can boast about; we can boast about our sufferings" (Rom 5:3). And in another place: "Therefore, I shall be very happy to make my weakness my special boast so that the power of Christ may dwell in me. And that is why I am quite content with my infirmities and with insults, in hardships, in imprisonments, for it is when I am weak that I am strong" (2 Cor 12:9–10). And again: "We prove we are servants of God in times of suffering" (2 Cor 6:4).[19] For this grace of the Spirit permeates the entire soul and floods the dwelling place with joy and virtue. The Spirit makes sweet the sufferings of the Lord by extinguishing the feeling of present sorrow by the hope of future blessings.

As you desire to obtain the highest virtue and honor by the Spirit's cooperation, may you so live that, undergoing all labor and struggles with joy, you may be reckoned worthy of the indwelling Spirit in us and never lose your inheritance with Christ, nor be cut off from him by worldly-mindedness so that you never fall into sin nor be the source of sin to others. If there are those who because of their spiritual immaturity cannot yet commit themselves entirely to the work of prayer, they should fulfill obedience in other matters, serving as they are able. They should work gladly, serving diligently with joy, not out of reward of honor, nor for human glory nor thanks from men. Let them shun negligence or sluggishness.

THE GREAT LETTER

God Wills to Save All

Let them not be servants of the bodies and souls of others, but as servants of Christ and of us, let their work appear pure and sincere before God. Let no one believe that by zeal for good works he cannot do the things which will bring salvation to his soul. For God does not enjoin the impossible upon his servants, but he shows abundant and great love and divine goodness, so that of his own good will he rewards each one by giving him some good work to do. Therefore, no one who seriously seeks salvation will lack power to do good. The Lord says: "Whoever will give even a cup of cold water to someone simply in the name of a disciple, amen, I say to you, that he will not go unrewarded" (Mt 10:42).

What can be more powerful than this commandment? Heavenly reward follows upon a cup of cold water. And look at the immense love for mankind! He says: "As long as you did it to one of these, you did it to me" (Mt 25:40). Indeed it is a small commandment, but when obeyed it brings forth from God a great and abundant gain.

A Will Toward God

Indeed, he demands nothing beyond our powers. But whether you do something small or great, your reward depends on your will. If in the name and in reverence for God you do anything, a splendid and unbelievable gift is bestowed upon you. But if you do good out of the motive of ostentation and for the praise of men, listen to the Lord himself categorically stating: "Truly I say to you, they have received their reward" (Mt 6:2). In order that we may not act in this way, he commands his disciples and through them us: "Be on your guard. Do not display your deeds of mercy or prayer or fasting before men. Otherwise you will not have a reward before your Father in Heaven" (Mt 6:1). So the Lord orders us to run away from the perishable praises of perishable men, to flee the withering glory, but truly to seek only that glory whose beauty neither can be described nor has any end. By it we ourselves will be able to become participators of those ineffable mysteries in Christ Jesus, our Lord, to whose glory be forever and ever. Amen.

271

NOTES

THE FIFTY HOMILIES

1. Though some details are obscure, the substantial meaning of the vision is clear, namely, Yahweh's transcendence of place. He is not tied to the Temple of Jerusalem, but he can follow his people into exile if he wishes. Macarius gives us here an example of his free allegorical interpretation of Holy Scripture to give his teaching of the dignity of the human person, called to be the temple-residence of the Godhead.

2. Macarius again emphasizes what he so frequently insists on, namely, that evil is not intrinsic to human nature both before and after the fall, but it comes from outside forces that are now found within the hidden layers of the psyche. Cf. H.16:11; H.26:10, 128.

3. For the Eastern fathers' common teaching on the dignity of human beings made according to the image and likeness of God, see G. A. Maloney, *Man—The Divine Icon* (Pecos, N. M., 1973).

4. The Greek word *aphtharsia* is a common patristic term, usually translated as incorruptibility, but one that comes out of a biblical anthropology with a long history going back to St. Paul. The Bible maintains a close relationship between sin and death, as Paul writes in Romans 5:12–21. But the Good News is that "just as sin has resulted in the reign of death, so also grace, which confers holiness leading to eternal life, holds sway through Jesus Christ our Lord." But such immortality, i.e., God's eternal life already living in fervent Christians, given through the Church, comes about through the working of the life-giving Spirit. See *DS* 7,2:1605; and St. Ignatius of Antioch, *To the Ephesians*, 20,2. Also, I. Hermann, *Kyrios und Pneuma. Studien zur Christologie der paulinischen Hauptbriefe* (Munich, 1961).

5. Macarius often uses the doctrine of the spiritual senses that the Holy Spirit develops in the process of divinization. No doubt he had read the mystical writings of Origen and St. Gregory of Nyssa on this subject. See J. LeMaitre in *DS* 2,1:1843–45; and K. Rahner, "The 'Spir-

itual Senses' according to Origen," *Theological Investigations,* vol. xvi (New York, 1979), pp. 81–103.

6. Macarius usually uses the Greek word *anapauosis* to express a very Semitic-Christian concept that among the Hellenic Christians under Evagrius's neo-Platonic and Stoic influence is expressed by *apatheia.* Sometimes he uses the word *hesychia,* which in general means tranquillity and shows his influence on the succeeding generations of hesychastic fathers who would build a spirituality around Christian divinization toward integration through inner attentiveness by centering on and synchronizing their breathing with the Jesus Prayer. See J. K. Mozley, *The Impassibility of God* (Cambridge, 1926); and P. Adnès, *"Impeccabilité," DS* 7,2:1614–20.

7. Macarius is one of the leading fourth century patristic writers who have stressed the consciousness of grace, as we have seen in the Introduction. Cf. A. Leonard, "Expérience Spirituelle," *DS* 4,2:c.2004–26; J. A. Cuttat: "Expérience chrétienne et spiritualité orientale," in *La Mystique et les mystiques,* ed. A. Ravier (Paris, 1965), pp. 825–1020; and D. P. Miquel: "Les caractères de l'expérience spirituelle selon le Pseudo-Macaire," *Irenikon* 39 (1966):497–513.

8. This image of Satan clothing man and woman after sin with a robe of darkness is often used by Macarius. Cf. H.8:3,42; H.26:25; H.43:7.

9. The image of the Holy Spirit as a dove (Ps 55:7) is often seen in the Old Testament (e.g., Gn 1:2) and in the New Testament, as when the Spirit overshadows Jesus in his Baptism (Mt 3:16; Mk 1:10; Lk 3:22; Jn 1:32). Plato uses the symbol of the human soul as having wings to fly into the realm of the true and eternal ideas. Macarius uses this symbol of wings of the soul often. Cf. H.1:9; H.44:5.

10. Again, Macarius stresses his teaching on the spiritual senses. See above, note 5.

11. Here we see a typical example of Macarius's openness to a loose structure in the monastery, allowing greater time for prayer and spiritual pursuits for the more spiritually advanced, and more time for work given to neophytes, who would be in need of developing the virtues of obedience and humility to serve others in charity. But all are to do their work in love and joyfulness for the common good.

12. Macarius sees incessant prayer as the goal of the monastic life. Thus, everything else in the monastery revolves around giving each member the maximum freedom to develop contemplative prayer, which for Macarius is the sign of a truly divinized and integrated Christian.

NOTES

13. This is an example of how Macarius uses concrete allegories and analogies to convey to simple people some ascetical or mystical truth. Here is his development of the sense of inner seeing through the soul's power of discernment (*diakrisis*). See above, note 5. Also his use of allegory in H.11:13; H.5:6.

14. This highlights Macarius's optimistic view of human nature and God's continued outpouring of grace so that human beings can always, by God's grace, respond and return to the true human nature that God always meant to be in loving union with himself. See Maloney, *Man— The Divine Icon*, pp. 187–99.

15. On the dignity of the human soul, See *Collection III*, H.24.

16. Macarius uses the word *body* in the Semitic sense to apply to the whole person, including good angels, demons, and saints in glory. See C. A. Van Peursen, *Body, Soul, Spirit: A Survey of the Body-Mind Problem* (London, 1966), pp. 35 ff.; and G. A. Maloney, *Inscape—God at the Heart of the Matter* (Denville, N.J., 1978), pp. 16–25.

17. Macarius is the first writer in Christian history to speak of "mystical participation" or "communion" (*koinōnia*), as here and in H.10:2 and 4,15:2 and 47:17. In *The Great Letter* he even uses the term "mystical union" (*mystikē synousia*) (see p. 257).

18. The title "Lover of Mankind" is frequently used in Eastern Christian writers for Jesus Christ. *Ho Philanthropos* is found also in liturgical prayers, as in the Byzantine Liturgy of St. John Chrysostom.

19. Here Macarius stays close to the scriptural texts that present God as cutting himself off completely from the Jewish people. Macarius is straining to preach to his readers the need of a conversion and to show what happens when one refuses God's grace. Yet in his very positive attitude toward the basic goodness of human nature, he highlights (also from Scripture) the infinite mercy of God toward all who have refused his light and grace. See below in this homily 4:24.

20. Macarius deals in a similar way in H.17 with the giving up of earthly care (*amerimnia*). Such care was one of the greatest causes for enslaving human beings into self-centeredness and away from God as the sole center. See John Climacus, *The Ladder of Perfection*, 17 (*PG* 88:1096ff); and St. Basil, *Small Rules* 206 (*PG* 31:1220a).

21. Here we find Macarius teaching an anthropology, not only of the *heart*, but also of the *nous* or intellect. This no doubt can be traced to the influence on him of the Cappadocians, especially St. Gregory of Nyssa. The *nous* or mind is to be brought into the heart. For Macarius the true contemplative, freed by the Spirit from selfishness, can freely use the

riches of creation, the mysteries in Scripture, and the inspirations of grace without having to draw into oneself, into the heart, to recollect himself. Cf. H.46 and 49, which complement this H.5.

22. Two accents among the early Eastern Fathers that in two words summarize the *ascesis* or ascetical life are weeping for tears (*penthos*) and hard work (*ponos*). Yet Macarius correctly ascribes to divine grace the power to continue in the *praxis* or the performance of ascetical acts. Even though the Christian must will to engage in ascetical practices, Macarius insists that the Christian cannot take pride in such exploits as though it depends solely on human effort. God's grace is always at work, even in bringing the individual Christian to will, and all the more, to persevere in the disciplines necessary to eradicate vices and to put on the virtues of Christ.

23. St. John of the Cross in the sixteenth century makes the identical statement with the example of the bird tied to earth by a thin thread on a chain. See *The Ascent of Mount Carmel*, Book I,4, in *The Collected Works of St. John of the Cross*, trans. Kieran Kavanaugh, OCD, and Otilio Rodriguez, OCD (Washington, D.C., 1973), p. 97.

24. This is an example that would offer proof that Macarius was a Persian, since he gives the Persian or East Syrian manner of numbering the months of the year.

25. Cf. H.2:3.

26. Again, we find Macarius using the traditional word *apatheia* for tranquillity or complete integration. The monk's first concern is to destroy the source of bad thoughts by battling always against the passions. When he reaches this stage through purifying the heart of all imaginings, he acquires *apatheia*. When the monk is "dispassioned," then he can occupy his mind and heart with the continual presence of God. See Macarius, *The Book of the Mind's Elevation* (*PG* 34:905). See notes 36 and 86.

27. This is the traditional teaching on *nepsis* of the desert fathers. This word in Greek comes from the verb *nēpho*, meaning "not to be intoxicated." It refers to a state of being always sober and vigilant. It has its scriptural foundation in the text of 1 Peter 5:8; "Be sober, watchful, your adversary, the devil, like the a roaring lion, prowls about looking for someone to devour." The hesychastic fathers of the desert are known in the collection of the *Philokalia* as "the holy *neptikoi*," those who are sober, vigilant, and attentive within to their thoughts. See *The Philokalia*, trans. G. Palmer, P. Sherrard, et al. (London, 1984), Vol. 3, p. 15.

28. Macarius is very cautious in dealing with the immanent presence of God within his creatures, especially in his indwelling presence in human beings. He avoids a simplistic fusion of God and the human soul with his accent on grace, freely given by God, who always remains totally transcendent to his creatures (and yet is made a participator in God's very own nature (2P 1:4) by grace. Cf. H.45:5.)

29. Macarius's teaching is in harmony with the more highly developed doctrine of St. John of the Cross on the three types of visions. Cf. *The Ascent to Mount Carmel*, Bk. II. (*Works*, pp. 163–212).

30. On Christ as the Bridegroom of the soul, see, e.g., H.10:2, 12:15, 15:2 and 4, 27:1, 28:5, 33:3, 38:5, 45:7, and 47:17. The theme also appears in *The Great Letter*, p. 257.

31. Macarius often speaks of a spiritual intoxication that spiritual experiences bring about, as here in H.8. Only once does he use the phrase "a sober intoxication." Cf. *Collection I*, H.63:4 and 6.

32. These experiences most certainly are autobiographical, as he shares how he received the transforming experience of the cross of light in H.8:6.

33. Macarius stresses frequently that grace may seem to recede in appearance, but it is a part of God's pedagogy of grace in order that faith and patience may be tested and grow stronger. Cf. H.8:5, 16:13, 26:7, 27:7, 8, 12, and 20.

34. Joseph was not made king of the Egyptians, but won the favor of the Pharaoh, who entrusted great responsibilities to him. He called him his chancellor and governor of all Egypt (Gn 41:40–43).

35. The continual pursuit of the divine Lover (*epektasis*, see Phil 3:13) and, in this life, of the virtues that lead to him was a major theme of Gregory of Nyssa, e.g., *Life of Moses* 2:219–55; and *Homilies on the Song of Songs*, 5, 6, 8 and 12. Macarius refers to this theme several times, e.g., H.15:37, 17:13, etc.

36. Macarius uses the word *apatheia*. The state that many of the Eastern fathers sought as the goal of all *praxis* or their ascetical practices is a state of self-control, called *apatheia*. Although it has its roots and received much influence from the Stoic concept, the Christian writers never considered human passions as evil. One could not take the first step in sanctity if he or she did not have the desire to love God and a certain basic fear of sin. After grace filters down into one's heart and true love conquers the heart, *apatheia* results in the state of integration and the goal of divinization for which God created human beings in his image and likeness.

37. Fire is a symbol of God in his many relationships to his created children. See H.1:2. It is in H.25:9 that Macarius comes closest to bringing together this symbol, especially as a manifestation of the Holy Spirit, in his cleansing and inpouring of graces to "enkindle" the human heart. For the many expressions of God as fire, see G. A. Maloney, *Why Not Become Totally Fire?* (Mahwah, N.J., 1990).

38. The theological anthropology of the early Eastern Fathers, built around the image-likeness doctrine, is very flexible, and seems on the surface to bring about confusion and contradiction, even in the writings of an individual theologian. Yet the fluidity allows the writer to emphasize either the aspect of a continual growth in a process of divinization brought about by the Holy Spirit and the individual Christian's cooperation in this, or the distinction between an image of nature and a likeness by grace. St. Athanasius, in order to highlight the absolute necessity of grace after the fall, often stressed losing the image through sin, as Macarius does in this text. Other theologians, like St. Irenaeus and those who followed a more dynamic process theology, distinguished between an imageness in the historical creation of each individual human being (*imago in plasmate*), which never could be lost, even through sin, and a likeness through grace and man's cooperation with the Holy Spirit.

39. Here Macarius, who never depreciates the nobility of the human soul and optimistically maintains the basic goodness in each human soul, seems to be stressing the power of the evil spirits when sin has taken over. Such a contagion comes from outside and is not intrinsic to the basic goodness of the human person, made according to God's image. Yet the damaging effects, which Macarius is stressing to his monastic audience, permeate throughout all parts of a human being's body, soul, and spirit levels. This would be similar to the realism of St. Paul as he describes his helplessness before the unspiritual elements in his wretched being as "sin in my members" (Rom 7:24).

40. This is similar to the teaching of Irenaeus in the second century who taught that God comes to sinful man to divinize him through the two hands of the Holy Spirit and the Word made flesh, Jesus Christ. Therefore, what he pithily described as the end of the incarnation, namely, "God became man, in order that man might become God" (*Adversus Haereses*, Bk. III, ch. 19, 1), both Irenaeus and Macarius would attribute also to the Holy Spirit: "the vivifying Spirit which causes man to become spiritual" (*Adversus Haereses*, Bk. V, ch. 12, 2).

41. Here is a clearer distinction made by Macarius as to the evil effects of sin on human beings. We could rephrase it to say that by sin

man lost his relationship with God, the likeness, but still retained his ontological nature that remains basically good, but he is unable by his own human power to enter again into God's living grace (redemption) without the power of the risen Lord Jesus and his Spirit.

42. Macarius evidently is referring to St. Paul's statement in Romans 1:20–21, where all human beings have no excuse for not knowing God, since he has given so much evidence in nature and in the power of the human intellect to recognize the power and deity of the source of goodness in creation.

43. Macarius is referring to the teaching of St. Paul concerning the "signing" or the "sealing" with the seal (*sphragis*) of the Holy Spirit: "and you too have been stamped with the seal of the Holy Spirit of the Promise" (Eph 1:13).

44. This refers to the presence of the Holy Spirit as fire within the human soul that accepts divine grace and lives in a way that becomes a living temple of the Holy Spirit. Cf. H.25:9.

45. In some of the manuscripts the remainder of section 3 through the middle of section 5 appears as the conclusion of H.13.

46. This is Macarius's argumentation against a pantheism that no doubt was a problem in some areas of the Christian East, especially through sects that went even farther than Messalianism did. See *Introduction*, on Messalianism.

47. This was a belief among certain groups that accepted Messalianism. In the seventeenth century in France it reoccurred in the form of Quietism.

48. Here again we find his favorite phrase describing the state of integration and wholeness for the Christian who comes into peace and harmony. The Greek word *anapausis*, "resting," conveys the idea of a continued growth in such harmony, thus avoiding any tinge of Messalianism, of reaching a state of perfection, of no need of further cooperation with grace.

49. Another example of Macarius integrating an anthropology of the heart with that of the *nous* or the intellect. Cf. above, note 21.

50. As we have seen so often, Macarius stresses the dignity of the human being through his or her free will to grow continuously in perfection, or turn away from God and refuse to cooperate with grace.

51. Here is another example of Macarius's optimistic view of human nature. Evil originally could not come either from the "heart" or from the "mind" of a human person, but had to come from outside nature. Most fathers of the East, including Macarius, would use the Greek

phrase *para physin* to show that evil is not within human nature as God intended it to be according to his own image and likeness, but enters and attacks human nature with its own evil thoughts and temptations. It goes against (*para*) human nature.

52. From the Gospel, Macarius learned that evil thoughts come from out of the heart. In Baptism, the light of Christ shines again within human nature. The proof of returning to one's true self in Christ is that, although evil thoughts may bombard one's heart and mind, yet the Christian has found his or her shelter in living according to the "natural" thoughts that God puts into the mind-heart.

53. Macarius is careful to describe the unspiritual self in our hearts as *though* Satan is within the soul as now a second soul. Sin becomes a part, adhering to the corporeal part of a person, and from there this almost second "soul" moves about to claim the whole person. He is always cautious to avoid anything that would convey the impression to his readers that Satan infests the Christian soul. He stretches to accentuate the immanence of evil moving freely within every member of the human personality, taking possession of the mind and heart and claiming the inhabitant, the human soul, for its own.

54. This question of how a Christian overcomes evil within himself or herself perplexed, evidently, those monks of East Syria in the region of Mesopotamia. Macarius shows by his answer a balanced judgment that one is never totally confirmed in grace by any one "peak experience," but slowly, through a long-drawn-out process that demands constant inner attentiveness. We can see in his answer how he must have been considered a wise and prudent teacher amidst much faulty Messalian teaching and practices.

55. The "peak experience" that occurred to Macarius when he received within himself the sign of the cross (see H.8:6) did not confirm him in grace so that from then on he had no struggle or suffered no temptations. As he wrote in H.8:6: "After I received the experience of the sign of the cross, grace now acts in this manner. It quiets all my parts and my heart so that the soul with the greatest joy seems to be a guileless child . . . and the further he enters, again new doors open in progression." He received a breakthrough that hurled him on to a new level of consciousness. He would know other temptations, yet he was aware of grace operating from within him in a new way, from an internal "vision."

56. St. Gregory Palamas of the fourteenth century, the defender of the hesychastic fathers of Mount Athos, who claimed that they were

seeing the Taboric light of Christ within themselves, was no doubt influenced by Macarius, as he often comes back to this very example of the great dignity given to human beings that would make them superior to angels, since God himself in Christ has taken on our humanity, while God never did that much by taking on an angelic nature for angels. See G. I. Mantzarides, *The Deification of Man: St. Gregory Palamas and the Orthodox Tradition* (New York, 1984).

57. This was the common teaching of much ancient pagan philosophy.

58. Macarius doubtless has the Manichaeans in mind—a real force in fourth-century Mesopotamia and Syria.

59. In this concrete example, Macarius more clearly shows that the evil that inhabits the human soul is there as a stranger, a robber, as someone who does not belong there, while the human person is the owner of the house.

60. Another statement stressing Macarius's principle of the cohabitation of evil and grace within the same individual Christian. See above, note 2.

61. This statement cries out for a basic distinction between moral and physical evil and God's permissive and deliberative will and yet we do not find any qualification here. Surely, what he must mean is that in all physical and psychic or moral evils sin is present, intensifying the urge through sin to become self-centered and not God-centered.

62. Here we see in most general terms the outline of the pattern of the Eastern fathers' teaching on the psychology of thought, or how a thought evolves within the human soul, leading finally to "captivity." Usually John Climacus in the seventh century is given credit for formalizing the five steps as: (1) the arising in our mind of a representation, a subject, an image; (2) the coupling or conversation or dialogue with the image; (3) consent given to the thought; (4) slavery or captivity; and (5) passion. Cf. *The Ladder of Perfection*, Step 15 (*PG* 88:896d).

63. Here Macarius calls Christ both our brother and our father, the spiritual Adam, who births us through his Holy Spirit into eternal life. Cf. H.8:6; H.16:6; H.14:4; H.30:2. Origen also calls Christ the Father of Christians—see *Homily on Exodus*, 6:2.

64. The word for sobriety is *nepsis*. It is used by Macarius often in his homilies and reflects his oneness with the traditional "neptic" fathers of the desert. The inner attentiveness over all thoughts, especially the eight capital thoughts, roots of all sins, is necessary to attain the state of integration or tranquillity, the main condition for persevering in prayer.

Nepsis is rather described than defined. The one who wrote the most about it and was greatly influenced by the writings of Macarius was Hesychius of Sinai. Cf. *Century I* (*PG* 93:1480d ff.).

65. Most Westerners, reading this, would probably not accept it, since it would imply too much negative accent on one's sinfulness and not enough on the saving power of Christ. However, this reflects a general attitude in the speech and writings of Macarius and the desert fathers. This very phrase is used by St. John Chrysostom's Byzantine Liturgy in the prayer the congregation with the priests and deacons recite together before Communion. St. Francis of Assisi also referred to himself as the greatest of sinners. Perhaps we ought not to judge such spiritual athletes of the desert who have opened their unconscious to areas most of us do not even know exist. Surely such a conviction brought them into a habitual humble mentality that filled them with the grace and joy of the risen Lord, reflected in weeping and rejoicing at the same time.

66. Macarius is not using the word *perfect* Christian, to mean that such have become confirmed in grace and no longer need to be attentive to the sinful roots within them. It means that such have advanced through long years of asceticism and inner attentiveness to the evil within and live more habitually in the contemplative union with the indwelling Trinity, a state that is always in process of greater growth, that encourages a hunger all the more to enter into the spiritual combat and never yield to sloth.

67. Here Macarius seeks to describe the inner spiritual eyes that have become purified by the Holy Spirit so that the Christian now habitually sees by intensified faith, hope, and love the glory of the indwelling risen Lord Jesus Christ.

68. No doubt among those Christians living in East Syria in Mesopotamia, where Messalianism was strong, there were many uninterested Christians who yielded to the temptation that, because of their intense spiritual experience, they no longer were capable of sinning. Here we see the balanced teaching of Macarius that no matter how intense the spiritual experiences of any Christian might be, he or she must always be humble enough to realize that one could still fall grievously into sin through pride.

69. Here Macarius uses the word *world* not in the sense of the physical world of God's creation that he would see, as Scripture teaches, as very good (Gn 1:31), but in the ascetical sense of the spirit of worldliness within the individual heart that tends toward *philautia* or self-love.

70. This "ruling power" (*hēgmonikon*) is a common term among many Greek patristic authors.

71. Macarius wrote no doubt in the vicinity of Mesopotamia and was influenced through the Old Testament chronology of creation. According to one standard dating worked out by Hippolytus in the third century, Christ came in the year 5500 from creation.

72. Macarius gives us a refreshingly simple teaching throughout his homilies about the interrelationship between God's grace and man's continued cooperation in the area of *praxis*. Most Eastern writers were never tempted to enter into the Western fixation on the Augustinian problem that involved so many theological schools in the sixteenth and seventeenth centuries in Europe, especially as led by Jesuits and Dominicans, to determine the parameters of free will and God's knowledge and the distribution of graces so as to preserve divine foreknowledge and gratuitousness of grace and yet protect human free will over any predestination. Here Macarius shows the primacy of God's gratuitous grace and yet the absolute need of man's labor to remove the obstacles preventing one from receiving the gifts of graces that are already there. It is easily understood by Macarius that anything a person does can never merit God's grace. Yet human work is necessary as dispositive to receive God's gifts.

73. This statement of Macarius is in keeping with the scheme proposed by his friend Gregory of Nyssa. One progresses continually through a triad of light to shadow to darkness. Each stage is important in God's pedagogy of grace in order that one may grow in perfection, but the dialectic continues always on different levels of intensity.

74. St. Paul often uses this language in describing the replacement of masters by no longer being a slave to sin but now a slave to Jesus Christ (Eph 6:6).

75. Macarius's concept of true freedom is common teaching among the early fathers of the Christian East. It consists in the ability to take one's life in hand and give it up to God in perfect self-surrender to do only his will and what will redound unto God's glory. For a full explanation of this subject, see E. Pousset et al., "Liberté, libération," *DS* 9:780–838.

76. Again Macarius comes back to his balanced synthesis between grace that brings joy and consolation and the cohabitation with sin or the roots of possible sin that should instill fear and trembling.

77. Macarius is not thinking here that a human person can "naturally" do anything to resist sin by his or her own power. For Macarius

and the traditional fathers of the desert of the fourth century, God's grace is always operating in the creation of even the good will to resist sin. They were convinced of Christ's teaching: "Without me you can do nothing" (Jn 15:5).

78. Reading *lēsthentōn*, "being forgotten," for the *plēsthentōn*, "being filled," found in most manuscripts.

79. This is another example of Macarius's use of the spiritual sense of inner sight, illumined by the Holy Spirit and thus able to see and believe in the union such a Christian enjoys with Christ, the true Friend and Bridegroom. "We know Jesus Christ dwells within us through the Spirit" (1 Jn 3:24).

80. The granting of grace by God to the individual Christian is a mystery for Macarius and should be for all of us. But Macarius insists here that God gives his graces differently, as Jesus has taught in the Gospel parables, but always out of his infinite wisdom. God is the wise teacher and knows how to give the graces needed to challenge the individual person to cooperate.

81. It was St. Athanasius, whose writings on the image and likeness of God in humanity may have influenced Macarius, who insisted that the *Logos* is the image of the Godhead or the Father. The Spirit is the image of the Son. And we are made according to the image and likeness that is Jesus Christ through the Holy Spirit. "The Son is the Image of the invisible God and the Spirit is the Image of the Son" (*Ad Serapionem* I, 20 (*PG* 26:577b).

82. In the Homilies, Macarius gives several lists of titles to Christ, as here. When he calls Christ the "one incapable of suffering," Macarius refers to the divinity of Christ and not to his humanity.

83. Macarius sees human nature both before the fall, as God originally planned the creation of human beings according to his own image and likeness, and after, when sin stripped man of the divine life, much in the line of St. Irenaeus. Irenaeus writes: "There are three things out of which, as I have shown, the complete man is composed—flesh, soul and spirit" (*Adversus Haereses*, Bk. IV, ch. 4,38). For both Irenaeus and Macarius all three elements, as assumed by the humanity of Christ, are essential to man as God made him and intended him to be eventually completed. The body and soul form the *plasma* or the frame of man. This is being made according to the image, which contains the potential to be realized according to the likeness of Christ, which is the life of God's grace dwelling in the total person, body and soul and spirit.

84. Macarius, in the tradition of the Eastern fathers, sees praying

incessantly not as an action, but as a state of contemplating God in every moment as the Center of all reality, and, therefore, the goal for which God created human beings. The Messalians (from the Syriac *messalleyane*, meaning, "the ones who pray always") insisted also on incessant prayer, but often to the neglect of action. In his writings Macarius insists along with Origen that good works and the observance of the commandments do not interrupt true prayer. Prayer for Origen and Macarius is a raising of the mind toward God. A person's "prayerfulness" is determined by the degree to which his actions and prayerful attitude arise from the love of God. For a compete summary of what these fathers meant by incessant prayer, see M. J. Marx, OSB, *Incessant Prayer in Ancient Monastic Literature* (Città del Vaticano, 1947).

85. By this statement—"for all are being transformed into a divine nature, being made noble and gods and children of God"—Macarius means that in eternal life the total human being will discover his or her uniqueness and fullness as a human being by becoming a participator of God's divine nature (2P. 1:4) through the divinizing grace of the Holy Spirit. A divine nature in human beings, for Macarius, would mean that they will have come into the most intimate, mystical union with the Trinity, and yet in this oneness there will always be the total humanity of each unique human person, different from the three indwelling Persons.

86. Such a Sabbath rest is described by Macarius and the traditional writers of the desert spirituality as *apatheia* or the state of complete integration of all human powers as created and intended to be developed by God with man's cooperation. G. Bardy, the famous patrologist, describes *apatheia:* "It is not a matter of insensibility toward God whom one must love above all else, nor of insensibility toward men, but of perfect liberty of spirit, perfect abandonment as the fruit of renunciation, perfect detachment from all things, humility, continual mortification and contempt for the body" (G. Bardy, "*Apatheia*," in *DS* 1:730).

87. Macarius means not that they despised any material creatures of God, but that they despised the inordinateness within their human nature under sin that made them tend toward attachment to them, bringing them a pleasure that, when it is inordinate, creates a deceitful sense of self-importance and power.

88. What this means is understood in the logic of love. The successful working of the Spirit depends on man's will since love is not merely

given by God and received by man, but man, in order to be all God intended him to be, must return that love in being transformed through his own cooperation into a holy person through the Spirit.

89. Macarius frequently uses the image of a covering veil to describe human failure to contemplate God, who is radiantly shining everywhere; see, e.g., H.8:3, 42; H.26:25; H.43:7.

90. One characteristic in Eastern Christian spirituality in the area of asceticism is this basic principle of the interrelationships of all virtues and vices. Gregory of Nyssa bases this principle on St. Paul's statement: "Does one member suffer? All members suffer with him" (1 Cor 12:26). See Gregory of Nyssa, *De Virginitate* (*PG* 46:317–416). For Stoic influence on this principle, see, J. Stelzenberger, *Die Beziehunge der frühchristlichen Sittenlehre zur Ethik der Stoa* (Münich, 1933), pp. 317ff.

91. Since Macarius views Heaven as interpersonal relationships between God and angels and human beings, we are not surprised that he insists on various degrees of perfection in Heaven and also of evil in hell. St. Gregory of Nyssa also posits that in Heaven there will be continuous growth: "For it may be that human perfection consists precisely in this constant growth in the good" (*Life of Moses, PG* 44:301c).

92. Macarius seems to employ a *double entendre* in using the term *word* (*logos*). He implies doing all things in the Word Incarnate, Jesus Christ, as the indwelling power without whom we can do nothing; but he also intends the individual's use of speech to witness to the Good News and bring a loving service to others not knowing Christ.

93. Here again is Macarius's oft-repeated principle of the cohabitation of both grace and sin within the individual human being.

94. In his narrow view that only Christians enjoy the workings of the Holy Spirit, Macarius differs from the liberal views of the Alexandrian writers, such as Clement and Origen, who could find the workings of the Holy Spirit in some pagan philosophers. Clement writes: "One true God is the sole author of all beauty, whether it is Hellenic or whether it is ours" (*Stromata* I,28).

95. This is similar to H.2:1. In using the term *demons*, Macarius does not infer that these are actual fallen angels or devils. He uses the mythology of the Canaanites and Mesopotamian religions, much of which formed the demonology of Judaism.

96. Here Macarius uses the term *monk* (*monazōn*) rather than his more usual *Christian* (*christianos*).

97. Purple is the color of regality or divinity. When the soldiers mocked Jesus as a king, they clothed him in purple and crowned him with thorns (Mk. 15:17).

THE GREAT LETTER

1. Here we see the seminal idea of God's uncreated energies as a sharing in the divine nature through the Taboric light that surrounds and transforms the Christian from within into a reflection of God's glory. See G. A. Maloney, *Uncreated Energy* (Warwick, N.Y., 1987).

2. *Apatheia* means, both for Macarius and Evagrius, the state of becoming "dispassioned," i.e., by destroying the attachments of inordinate desires called "passions." These refer not to the God-given emotions, such as the "irascible" and the "concupiscible" passions, but rather to sinful, inner attachment to selfishness, rooted by sin in the natural passions. The sign of having attained this state of integration on the body, soul, and spirit levels is when the Christian can occupy his or her mind and heart with the continual presence of God. True agapic love conquers the human heart. The two commands to love God at all times totally and to love others as oneself are being perfectly fulfilled in a process of unending growth.

3. This is a theme that Macarius continually returns to in this letter, namely, the basic goodness of all elements created by God in our human nature in contrast to the elements of evil that have infiltrated into us from the outside, beginning with the insidious suggestions of the devil. Such deception and carnal-mindedness belonging to human selfishness could never be willed nor created by God. See note 51 to H.15:25.

4. This teaching is basic to the early fathers, especially of the Christian East. Clement of Alexandria in the third century clearly distinguished between two kinds of passions and desires: one is irrational and tends toward disintegration and intemperance; the other is good as created by God. These latter are natural necessities for human beings to live fully according to their dignity as having been created by God according to his own image and likeness (Gn 1:26). This kind of passionate desire is to live dynamically in submission in all things to the moderating influence of God's Logos made flesh, Jesus Christ. See Clement, *Stromata* II,39,6.

5. With St. Paul, Macarius primarily refers to death that comes to

human nature as death to God's divine life, due to surrender to the devil's suggestion of living and acting independently of God.

6. Here "passionless" as applied to the Spirit refers, as we have seen above, to a lack of anything that would bring about self-centered love, rather than true divine passion of agapic self-giving.

7. "Single-mindedness," or being *monotropos,* is one of many ways by which Macarius and those writers who were influenced by him described the state of mystical union with the Bridegroom, Jesus Christ. It is a result of continued *askesis* to move away from disintegration and fragmentation, to move from our false ego and to enter into our true selves in ever growing oneness with Jesus Christ. St. Paul described this state of union when he wrote, "I have been crucified with Christ, and I live now not with my own life but with the life of Christ who lives in me" (Gal 2:19–20).

8. Here is one of the rare times Macarius uses the word *erōs* in a positive sense to refer to the superabundant and fiery divine love of God that abounds in our hearts through the Holy Spirit (Rom 5:5).

9. Macarius is referring to the three different ways, common to Eastern Christian writers who follow Origen's teaching, of the senses of scriptural meaning—the corporal or literal sense, the psychic or moral, and the spiritual or mystical. Origen's spiritual exegesis of the Old Testament is the manifestation of Christ as the key to the Old Testament.

10. Throughout this ascetical *Great Letter,* Macarius uses the term *ponos* for hard work, referring to any ascetical practices that involve great physical efforts in an attempt to bring the corporal powers under submission to the intellect and will, informed by grace. A more general word for asceticism that he also uses is *ergon,* which means "work." Macarius also uses the term *kopos,* which stresses the pain, suffering, and weariness that come from the physical *ponos.* St. Basil, whom Macarius follows greatly in writing on the ascetical life, explains how all spiritual goods come "through hard works (*ponois*) and sweat" (*Hom. in principium Proverbiorum,* 16; *PG* 31:421A).

11. "Philosophy" here means ascetic life, i.e., monasticism.

12. Macarius blends a happy balance between *praxis,* the ascetical practices the Christian must do by way of therapy to heal the negativity of sinful attachments and positively to acquire the mind of Christ by living virtuously, and *theoria,* or the contemplative life. *Praxis* or ascetical works cannot "buy" union with the Trinity. They are, however, necessary to dispose the Christian to discover God's sheer gift of himself through divinization.

NOTES

13. Macarius believes in a strict interpretation of poverty, not only of the spirit, but actual poverty, down to the monk's possessing only the clothes he wears. He shows how the community provides for all other needs, thus relieving the monk from any temptation to become attached to the possession of material things. See J. DeGuibert, "Abnégation," *DS* 1:67–73.

14. Macarius often addresses exhortations in this letter to superiors and spiritual guides, who have been entrusted with the responsibility to direct those who are not as well developed spiritually as the elders should be in the ways of perfection. This would indicate that Macarius enjoyed a great reputation among the leaders of monasteries in Mesopotamia and other outlying regions, as we see in his homilies.

15. The living of the "angelic life" (*bios tōn anggelōn*) here on earth was a common description of the goal of early monasticism.

16. On *praxis* of the virtues, see above, note 12.

17. On this topic of incessant prayer, cf. Homily 33, note 84.

18. Again we see Macarius using the word *passions* to refer to the inordinate tendencies to exploit the God-given natural passions in a sinful and evil manner. It is by Christ's grace that a Christian can be healed of such "unnatural" passions in order to enter into true freedom to develop God's created and good passions.

19. St. Ignatius of Antioch, so rooted in the teachings of St. Paul and St. John, was the inspiration, not only in his writings on his desire for suffering martyrdom, but in his actual undergoing martyrdom in Rome, for writers like Macarius and other desert ascetics to live the monastic life as a form of "white martyrdom."

BIBLIOGRAPHY

I. Macarius
A. Spiritual Homilies:

Texts:

Die 50 Geistlichen Homilien des Makarios. Edited by Hermann Dörries, Erich Klostermann, and Matthias Kroeger. Patristische Texte und Studien 6. Berlin: De Gruyter, 1964.

Makarios/Symeon: Reden und Briefe. Die Sammlung I des Vaticanus Graecus 694 (B). 2 vols. Edited by H. Berthold, GCS. Berlin: Akademie-Verlag, 1973.

Neue Homilien des Makarios/Symeon aus Typus III. Edited by Erich Klostermann and Heinz Berthold, TU 72. Berlin: Akademie-Verlag, 1961.

Pseudo-Macaire. Homélies propres à la collection III. Edited by Vincent Desprez, SC 275. Paris: Éditions du Cerf, 1980.

Homiliae Spirituales. PG 34:449–822.

Translations:

Fifty Spiritual Homilies of St. Macarius the Egyptian. Translated by A. J. Mason. London: SPCK, and New York: Macmillan, 1921. Reprinted with introduction by Ivan M. Kontzevitch, Eastern Orthodox Books, Willits, 1974.

Intoxicated with God. Translated by George A. Maloney. Denville, N.J.: Dimension Books, 1978.

B. Letters:

Epistola sancti Macarii Aegyptii. PG 34:409–442.

"Great Letter." In Werner Jaeger, *Two Rediscovered Works of Ancient*

Christian Literature: Gregory of Nyssa and Macarius, 233–301. Leiden: E. J. Brill, 1954.

"Great Letter" In R. Staats (ed.), *Epistola Magna. Eine messalianische Mönchsregel und ihre Umschrift in Gregors von Nyssa 'De instituto christiano.'* Abhandlungen der Akademie der Wissenschaften in Göttingen. Philol.-hist. Klasse, 3rd series, 134: Göttingen, 1984.

II. Other Primary Works:

Athanasius. *Ad Serapionem. PG* 26:529–676.

Basil. *Homilia in principium Proverbiorum (Homilia XII). PG* 31:385–424.

———. *Regulae brevius tractatae. PG* 31:1079–1306.

Clement of Alexandria. *Stromata. SC* 30–38. Paris: Éditions du Cerf, 1951–.

Diadoque de Photice, Oeuvres Spirituelles. Edited by Édouard des Places, *SC* 5 bis. Paris: Éditions du Cerf, 1955.

Epiphanius. *Panarion* 80. *PG* 42:755–74.

Gennadius of Marseilles. *De viris illustribus. PL* 58:1059–1120.

Gregory of Nyssa. *De Virginitate. PG* 46:317–416. See also *Gregorii Nysseni Opera,* Vol. 8,I:215–343. Edited by Werner Jaeger. Leiden: Brill, 1952.

———. *Commentarius in Cantica Canticorum. PG* 44:755–1120. See also *Gregorii Nysseni Opera,* Vol. 6. Edited by Werner Jaeger. Leiden: Brill, 1966.

———. *De Vita Moysis. PG* 44:297–430. See also *Gregorii Nysseni Opera,* Vol. 7,I. Edited by Werner Jaeger. Leiden: Brill, 1964.

Gregory of Sinai, Saint. *Writings from the Philokalia on Prayer of the Heart.* Translated by E. Kadloubovsky and G. E. H. Palmer. London: Faber and Faber, 1951.

Hesychius of Sinai. *De temperantia et virtute. Centuria I. PG* 93:1479–512.

John Climacus. *Scala Paradisi. PG* 88:631–1164.

John Damascene. *De Haeresibus. PG* 94:677–780.

Liber Graduum, edited by Michael Kmosko. In *Patrologia Syriaca,* edited by René Graffin, 3:CLXX–CCXCIII. Paris: Firmin-Didot et Socii, 1926.

Origen. *Homiliae in Exodum. PG* 12:297–396.

Philokalia, The. Translated by G. Palmer, P. Sherrard, et al. 3 vols. London and Boston: Faber and Faber, 1984.

BIBLIOGRAPHY

Syméon le Nouveau Théologien. Oeuvres. Edited by B. Krivocheine et al. *SC* 51 bis, 96, 104, 113, 122, 129, 156, 174, 196. Paris: Éditions du Cerf, 1957–1974.

Symeon the New Theologian. *Hymns of Divine Love.* Translated by George A. Maloney. Denville, N.J.: Dimension Books, 1975.

Symeon the New Theologian: The Discourses. Edited by C. J. deCatanzaro. Ramsey: Paulist Press, 1980.

Vie d'Hypatios. Edited by Gerhardus Johannes Marinus Bartelink, SC 177. Paris: Éditions du Cerf, 1971.

Secondary Works and Interpretations:

Adnès, Pierre. "Impeccabilité." *DS* 7:1614–20.

Bardy, G. "Apatheia." *DS* 1:727–46.

Bareille, G. "Euchites." *Dictionnaire de théologie catholique* 5:1454–1465.

Benz, Ernst. *Die Protestantische Thebais. Zur Nachwirkung des Makarios des Egypters im Protestantismus des 17 und 18 Jahrhunderts in Europa und Amerika.* Wiesbaden, 1963.

Bobrinskoy, B. "Nicholas Cabasilas and Hesychast Spirituality." *Sobornost* 5:7(1968): 483–505.

Bouyer, Louis, et al. *A History of Christian Spirituality.* 3 vols. New York: Desclée Co., 1963.

Canévet, M. "Le 'De Instituto Christiano' est-il de Grégoire de Nysse?" *Revue des Études Grecques* 82 (1969): 404–23.

Cuttat, Jacques Albert. *Expérience chrétienne et spiritualité orientale.* Paris, Desclée, De Brouwer, 1967. Also in *La Mystique et les mystiques,* edited by A. Ravier, Paris:825–1020. Desclée, De Brouwer, 1965.

Davids, E.A. *Das Bild vom neuen Menschen. Ein Beitrag zum Verständnis des Corpus Macarianum.* Salzburg and Munich: Salzburger Patristische Studien 2, 1968).

deGuibert, J. "Abnégation-I." *DS* 1:67–73.

Deseille, Placide. "Epectase." *DS* 4:785–88.

Desprez, Vincent. "Macaire (Pseudo), Macaire, Macaire-Syméon." *DS* 10:20–43.

Dörries, Hermann. *Symeon von Mesopotamien. Die Überlieferung der messalianischen "Makarios"-Schriften.* TU 55:1 Leipzig: J.C. Hinrichs, 1941.

Dörries, Hermann. *Die Theologie des Makarios-Symeon.* Abhandlungen der Akademie der Wissenschaften in Göttingen, Philol.-hist. Klasse, 3rd series, 103: Göttingen, 1978.

Guillaumont, Antoine. "Messaliens." *DS* 10:1074–1083.

Hausherr, Irénée. "L'Origine de la théorie orientale des huit péchés capitaux." *Orientalia Christiana* 30:164–75.

———. *Penthos: la doctrine de la componction dans l'Orient chrétien. Orientalia Christiana Analecta,* 132. See *Penthos: the doctrine of compunction in the Christian East.* Translated by Anselm Hufstader. Cistercian Studies Series 53. Kalamazoo, MI: Cistercian Publications, 1982.

Jaeger, Werner. *Early Christianity and Greek Paideia.* London: Oxford University Press, 1961.

Jaeger, Werner. *Two Rediscovered Works of Ancient Christian Literature: Gregory of Nyssa and Macarius.* Leiden: E. J. Brill, 1954.

Kemmer, Alfons. *Charisma Maximum. Untersuchung zu Cassians Vollkommenheitslehre und seiner Stellung zum Messalianismus.* Lowen: Dr. F. Ceuterick, 1938.

LeMaitre, J. "Contemplation chez les orientaux chrétiens. III. A.e.a. Les sens spirituels." *DS* 2:1843–845.

Leonard, Augustin. "Expérience spirituelle." *DS* 4:2004–026.

Lossky, Vladimir. *The Mystical Theology of the Eastern Church.* London: J. Clarke, 1957.

Maloney, George A. *Inscape—God at the Heart of the Matter.* Denville, N.J.: Dimension Books, 1978.

———. *Man—The Divine Icon.* Pecos, N.M. ex.: Dove Publications, 1973.

———. *Russian Hesychasm—The Spirituality of Nil Sorskij.* The Hague: Mouton, 1973.

———. *The Mystic of Fire and Light.* Denville, N.J.: Dimension Books, 1975.

———. *The Prayer of the Heart.* Notre Dame, Ind.: Ave Maria Press, 1981.

———. *Uncreated Energy.* Warwick, N.Y.: Amity House, 1987.

———. *Why Not Become Totally Fire?* Mahwah, N.J. Paulist Press, 1990.

Marx, M. J. *Incessant Prayer in Ancient Monastic Literature.* Città del Vaticano, 1947.

Meyendorff, Jean. "Messalianism or Anti-Messalianism? A Fresh Look at the Macarian Problem." In *Kyriakon. Festschrift in honor of Johannes Quasten,* 2:285–590. Münster: Aschendorff, 1970.

BIBLIOGRAPHY

————. *St. Grégoire Palamas et la mystique orthodoxe.* Paris: Éditions du Seuil, 1959.

Miquel, D. P. "Les caractères de l'expérience spirituelle selon le Pseudo-Macaire." *Irenikon* 39 (1966): 497–513.

Pousset, E., Guillet, J., et al. "Liberté, libération." *DS* 9:780–838.

Quasten, Johannes. *Patrology.* 4 vols. Volume 1, Utrecht, Brussels: Spectrum Publishers, 1950; Volume 2, Utrecht, Antwerp: Spectrum Publishers, 1953; Volume 3, Westminster, Md.: Newman Press, 1960; Volume 4, Westminster, Md.: Christian Classics, Inc., 1986.

Rahner, Karl. "The 'Spiritual Senses' according to Origen." *Theological Investigations.* Vol. XVI. New York: Seabury, 1979: 81–104.

Solignac, Aimé. "Immortalité." *DS* 7:1601–614.

Spidlik, T. "L'eternità e il tempo, la *zoe* e el *bios,* problema dei Padri Cappodoci." *Augustinianum* 16 (1976): 107–16.

Staats, R. "Die Asketen aus Mesopotamien in der Rede des Gregor von Nyssa 'In suam ordinationem.'" *Vigiliae Christianae* 21 (1967): 167–79.

————. *Gregor von Nyssa und die Messalianer.* Patristische Texte und Studien 8. Berlin: De Gruyter, 1968.

Stewart, Columba. *"Working the Earth of the Heart": The Messalian Controversy in History, Texts, and Language to AD 431.* Oxford: Clarendon Press, 1991.

Strothmann, W. *Die syrische Überlieferung der Schriften des Makarios.* 2 vols. Wiesbaden: Göttinger Oreintforschungen, 1975.

Villecourt, Dom P. L. "La date et l'origine des 'Homélies Spirituelles' attribuées à Macaire." *Comptes rendus de l'Academie des Inscriptions et Belles-Lettres,* 250–258. Paris: Auguste Picard, 1920.

Wilmart A. "Origine voeritable des homélies pneumatiques." *Revue d'Ascetique et de la Mystique* 1 (1920): 361–77.

INDEX

Aaron, 172
Abel, 265
Abraham, 55, 70, 85, 265
Adam, xiv, 41, 74, 97–98, 99, 100–01, 120, 192–93
Adelphios, 8
Affliction, 59, 71–72, 85, 96–97, 112, 119, 129–30, 166–67, 177, 200–01, 260. *See also:* Temptation
Alexandrian school of spirituality, 3
Amalek, 244
Amphilochius, 8
Angelo of Clareno, 23
Angels, 125
Antioch, 8
Antiochene school of spirituality, 2
Apatheia, 251, 253
Aphraates, 3, 7, 19
Apocriticus (Macarius), 6
Apophthegmata, xii
Apostles, 39, 104, 178–79, 207
Aristotle, 218
Armenia, 8
Arndt, John, 23–24
Arnold, Gottfried, 24
Asceticism, 9, 12, 16–17, 27, 168, 252, 259, 260
Ascetikon, 9
Athos, Mount, 13, 21

Baptism, xvii, 19, 172, 232–33
Basil the Great, St., xii, xvii, 3, 9, 10
Benedict, St., 23

Berthold, H., 5–6, 250
Blake, William, xiv
Buddhism, 1

Cabasilas, Nicholas, 22
Cain, 63, 265
Caiphas, 172
Callinicus, 21
Callistus, Patriarch, 22
Canévet, M., 10
Cappadocia, 8
Cappadocian Fathers, 9
Carthage, 8
Cassian, St. John, 23, 25
Catecheses (Symeon), 21
Charismatic movement, xii, 25
Charity, 12
Christianity: dignity of, 118, 126; emphases in, 1–4; fear and trembling in, 180–84, 212–13; fruits of, 103–04; glory of, 197–98; and judgment, 111; perfection in, 135–42, 146–48; resurrection and, 203–04; true, 26–27, 64–65, 72–73, 132, 211–12; the war in, 153–55, 170–71, 200
Christian Library (Wesley), 24
Christ Jesus: centering on, 70–71; centrality of, 19–20; and death, 94–97; gentleness of, 78–79; Heavenly Pilot, 225; High Priest, 198–99; Husbandman, 186; King, 134; Lamb of God, 235–36; love

294

INDEX

for, 226–29; Physician, 150–52, 193, 230, 240–41; and redemption, 44–47, 58–59, 119–20; resurrection in, 73–75, 111–12; and salvation, 190–91; sanctification of, 86; and Satan, 173–76; the Savior, 14–15; the Shepherd, 223–24; soul and, 40–43, 54–55, 223–24; Spouse, 108–09; suffering of, 258–59; Sun of Righteousness, 73–74, 136; Taboric light of, 11; titles of, 257–58; treasure of, 143–44; union with, 20–21, 232, 257; Word of God, 230–31, 236

Circumcision, 198
Clement of Alexandria, 2, 3
Cleophas, 163
Cloud of Unknowing, The, xvii
Combat, spiritual, 15
Commentary on the Divine Liturgy (Cabasilas), 22
Concord, 262–63
Conferences (Cassian), 23
Cornelius, 104
Council of Ephesus, xii, 9
Council of Side, 10

Dadoes, 8
Daniel, 55, 101
David, 55, 84, 163, 207, 244
Death, 94–97, 123
De Instituto Christiano (Gregory), 10, 249–50
De Segur, Msgr. L., 25
Detachment, 66–70, 87, 110, 260–61
De Vero Christiano (Arndt), 24
Devil, the: is bound, 131; enticements of, 14; God and, 79–80; and the human race, 63, 96–97, 113–14, 136, 164–67; power of, 110–11; is never quieted, 169–70
Diadochus, 20

Diatessaron, 7
Die Theologie des Makarios/Symeon (Dörries), xii
Directions to Hesychasts (Gregory), 22
Discernment, 16–17, 50–51
Dörries, H., xii, 5, 7, 249–50

Egypt, 8, 234–37
Eleazar, 140
Elijah, 56, 76, 102, 125, 163, 244
Elisha, 224
Ephrem, St., 3, 7, 19, 249
Eremitical life, 9–10
Eucharist, xvii
Euphraetes River, 7
Evagrius of Pontus, xvii, 2
Ezekiel, 37–38, 202

Faith, 239–40
First fruits, 265–66
Flesh, the, 255–56
Floss, H.J., 5, 250–51
Francis, St., 23
Free will, 14–15, 123, 182–83

Gennadius of Marseilles, 6
Gerhard, John, 24
God: all things are possible with, 226; children of, 155–56; communion with, 18; creates only good, 254; demands of, 210–11; is everywhere, 256–57; is faithful, 188, 231; faith in, 239–40; the fire of, 55, 90–91, 107–08, 163–64; goodness of, 59–60, 194–95; grace of, 14, 62, 110–11, 115–16, 133–34, 137, 209–10, 245; heals mankind, 126; help from, 159–61, 171, 243–44; humility of, 199–200; incomprehensibility of, 11; love for, 113–14; love of, 116, 125, 196, 231, 263–65; mercy of, 57, 59–61, 237; omnipotence of,

INDEX

19; otherness of, 11; seeking, 194–96; soul and, 40–44, 54–55, 80, 237–38; surrender to, 106–07; transcendence of, 4; visits us, 100–01; wills to save, 271; wisdom of, 186–88; is without limits, 131; Word of, 230–31; works through saints, 244–45

Godhead, 77, 90

Goths, 7

Grace, 14, 17, 62, 79–80, 110–11, 115–16, 133–34, 137, 177–78, 209–10, 245

Great Letter, The (Pseudo-Macarius), 5, 10

Gregor von Nyssa und die Messalianer (Staats), 250

Gregory of Nyssa, St., xvii, 3, 5, 9, 10–11, 13, 17, 249–50

Gregory of Sinai, St., 21

Gregory Palamas, St., 4, 21

Haywood, Thomas, 24

Hazzaya, Joseph, 21

Heart, the, xiii–xviii, 219–23

Hermas, 8

Hesychasm, xvi

Hinduism, 1

Hoburg, Christian, 24

Holy Spirit: action of, 12; and affliction, 85–88; armor of, 156–57, 179–80; Baptism of, 19, 172, 232–33; experience of, 11; fellowship with, 56–57, 99, 142–44, 147–48; fruits of, 104–05, 145–46, 208; gifts of, 16–17, 187; illumination of, 88; indwelling of, 19, 269–70; love of, 53–54; power of, 157–58, 224; receiving, 73, 134, 192–93; soul and, xi, 37–38, 91–93; work of, 266–67

Humanity, dignity of, 134

Human nature, 13, 117–18

Humility, 15–16, 88–89, 122, 146, 189–90, 217, 251, 259–62

Hymns of Divine Love (Symeon), 21

Hypatius, 21

Ignatius of Xanthopoulos, 22

Institutes (Cassian), 23

Irenaeus, St., 2

Isaac, 55

Isaac of Ninevah, 21

Isaiah, 55

Islam, 1

Jacob, 55

Jaeger, Werner, 3, 10, 249–51

Jericho, 244–45

Jesus Prayer, 21, 22

Job, 70, 156, 166

John the Baptist, St., 185–86

Joseph, 84

Joshua, 244

Judaism, 1

Jung, C.G., xiv

Kavsokalivites, Neophytos, 6

Kierkegaard, Søren, 24

Klostermann, E., 5–6

Koinonia, 18

Kopken, Arnold, 24

Kroeger, M., 5

Lausiac History (Palladius), 6

Law, the, 206–08, 232–33, 237–38

Lazarus, 193

Leaven, 157–58

Letter to his Children (Macarius), 6

Life, 2

Life in Christ (Cabasilas), 22

Light, 2

Love, 47–48, 53–54, 113–14, 116, 125, 196, 226–29, 231, 263–65

Lycaonium, 8

INDEX

Macarius of Corinth, St., 22
Macarius of Egypt, xi, 6, 9
Macarius Magnes, 6
Macarius the Alexandrian, 6
Maccabees, the, 140
Maloney, George, xi–xvi
Marah, 237
Mark the Hermit, St., 20
Martha, 103
Mary, 103, 104
Mason, A.J., 27
Melchisedech, 265
Messalianism, xii
Messalians, the, 8
Metaphrastes, Symeon, 21
Migne, J.-P., 5, 249–51
Modesty, 103, 109
Monasticism, 16
Moses, xiv, 56, 74, 76, 84, 93, 102,
    151, 163, 172, 192, 198, 207,
    232–35, 237–38, 244

Nabuchodonosor, 90
Nepsis, 22–23
Nicephorus the Hesychast, 21
Nicodemus of the Holy Mountain, St.,
    22
Noah, 55, 60, 85, 207

Origen, 2, 3, 11

Palladius, 6
Pamphylia, 8
Paradiesgartlein (Arndt), 24
Paradise, 206–07
Pascal, Blaise, 27
Passions, 53–54, 67–68, 127–28, 137,
    251–54, 258
Patrologia Graeca (Migne), 5
Paul, St., 163, 166, 254
Penthos, 19, 22
Perfection, 20, 135–42, 146–48
Persecution, 270

Persians, 7
Peter, St., 172
Pharaoh, 233–34
Philo, xvii
Philokalia, 22
Picot, Jean, 5, 23
Pieté et La Vie Interieure, La (De
    Segur), 25
Pietists, 23–24
Plato, 218
Platonism, 2, 3
Pleasures, 52. *See also*: Passions
Poiret, Pierre, 24
Poverty of spirit, 22, 98, 118
Prayer: foundation of, 76; incessant, 4,
    17–18, 89, 201–03, 267–68;
    interior, 12; and perfection, 81–
    83, 214–15; perseverance in, 214–
    16, 242–43; and tranquillity, 75–
    78; true, 149, 268–69
Pride, 16, 80, 118, 259–60
*Primitive Morality, or The Spiritual
    Homilies of St. Macarius The
    Egyptian* (Haywood), 24
Protestants, 23–24, 27
Pseudo-Macarius, 2
Purity of heart, 254–55

Qatraya, Dadiso, 21
Quasten, Johannes, 25

Rehab, 194
Repentance, 114
Resurrection, 73–75, 111–12, 203–04,
    205–06
Romans, the, 7

Sabbas, 8
Sabbath, 204–05
Salt of the earth, 39–40
Samuel, 84
Satan. *See* Devil, the
Saul, 84

297

INDEX

Sayings of the Desert Fathers, The, xii
Scholasticism, 23–24
Scripture, 213–14
Self-renunciation, 12
Seraphim of Serov, St., 22
"Shorter Rules," the, xii
Simplicity, 262–63
Sin, xiii, 13–14, 44–47, 48–49, 116, 121–22
Sisinnios, 8–9
Slavic spirituality, 22–23
Sobriety, 16, 132
Socrates, 218
Sodom, 60
Solomon, 55
Sorsky, Nil, St., 22
Soul, the: Christ and, 40–43; depths of, 216–17; and discernment, 50; and life in God, 40–44, 80, 237–38; the lost, 184–85; senses of, 53–54, 245; sin and, 48–49, 56; the Spirit and, 37–38, 90–93, 192; struggle of, 220–21
Staats, R., 10, 250
Stewart, Columba, xii
Stoicism, 2
Symeon, 8
Symeon Metaphrastes, 22
Symeon of Mesopotamia, 7, 8, 9, 10

Symeon the New Theologian, St., 4, 21
Synod of Side, 8

Tabor, Mount, 4
Taboric light, 11, 13, 22
Tears, 162–63
Temptations, 83–84, 87, 129–32
Tranquillity, 75–78, 128
Treatise on Virginity (Gregory), 10
Trinity, the, 1, 3, 14
Two Rediscovered Works of Ancient Christian Literature: Gregory of Nyssa and Macarius (Jaeger), 249

Velichkovsky, Paissy, 22
Villecourt, Dom L., 8
Virginity, 9–10
Virtues, 209, 266

Way of the Pilgrim, The, 22
Wesley, John, xi, 24
Wesley, Samuel, 24
Will, the, 165–66
Word of God, the, 230–31, 236
"Working of the Heart." The Messalian Controversy in History, Texts, and Language to AD 431 (Stewart), xii

Zacchaeus, 104
Zen Buddhism, xv

Other Volumes in this Series

Julian of Norwich • SHOWINGS

Jacob Boehme • THE WAY TO CHRIST

Nahman of Bratslav • THE TALES

Gregory of Nyssa • THE LIFE OF MOSES

Bonaventure • THE SOUL'S JOURNEY INTO GOD, THE TREE OF LIFE, AND THE LIFE OF ST. FRANCIS

William Law • A SERIOUS CALL TO DEVOUT AND HOLY LIFE, AND THE SPIRIT OF LOVE

Abraham Isaac Kook • THE LIGHTS OF PENITENCE, LIGHTS OF HOLINESS, THE MORAL PRINCIPLES, ESSAYS, and POEMS

Ibn 'Ata' Illah • THE BOOK OF WISDOM and Kwaja Abdullah

Ansari • INTIMATE CONVERSATIONS

Johann Arndt • TRUE CHRISTIANITY

Richard of St. Victor • THE TWELVE PATRIARCHS, THE MYSTICAL ARK, and BOOK THREE OF THE TRINITY

Origen • AN EXHORTATION TO MARTYRDOM, PRAYER, AND SELECTED WORKS

Catherine of Genoa • PURGATION AND PURGATORY, THE SPIRITUAL DIALOGUE

Native North American Spirituality of the Eastern Woodlands • SACRED MYTHS, DREAMS, VISIONS, SPEECHES, HEALING FORMULAS, RITUALS AND CEREMONIALS

Teresa of Avila • THE INTERIOR CASTLE

Apocalyptic Spirituality • TREATISES AND LETTERS OF LACTANTIUS, ADSO OF MONTIER-EN-DER, JOACHIM OF FIORE, THE FRANCISCAN SPIRITUALS, SAVONAROLA

Athanasius • THE LIFE OF ANTONY, A LETTER TO MARCELLINUS

Catherine of Siena • THE DIALOGUE

Sharafuddin Maneri • THE HUNDRED LETTERS

Martin Luther • THEOLOGIA GERMANICA

Native Mesoamerican Spirituality • ANCIENT MYTHS, DISCOURSES, STORIES, DOCTRINES, HYMNS, POEMS FROM THE AZTEC, YUCATEC, QUICHE-MAYA AND OTHER SACRED TRADITIONS

Symeon the New Theologian • THE DISCOURSES

Ibn Al'-Aribī • THE BEZELS OF WISDOM

Hadewijch • THE COMPLETE WORKS

Philo of Alexandria • THE CONTEMPLATIVE LIFE, THE GIANTS, AND SELECTIONS

George Herbert • THE COUNTRY PARSON, THE TEMPLE

Unknown • THE CLOUD OF UNKNOWING

John and Charles Wesley • SELECTED WRITINGS AND HYMNS

Meister Eckhart • THE ESSENTIAL SERMONS, COMMENTARIES, TREATISES AND DEFENSE

Francisco de Osuna • THE THIRD SPIRITUAL ALPHABET

Jacopone da Todi • THE LAUDS

Fakhruddin 'Iraqi • DIVINE FLASHES

Menahem Nahum of Chernobyl • THE LIGHT OF THE EYES

Early Dominicans • SELECTED WRITINGS

John Climacus • THE LADDER OF DIVINE ASCENT
Francis and Clare • THE COMPLETE WORKS
Gregory Palamas • THE TRIADS
Pietists • SELECTED WRITINGS
The Shakers • TWO CENTURIES OF SPIRITUAL REFLECTION
Zohar • THE BOOK OF ENLIGHTENMENT
Luis de León • THE NAMES OF CHRIST
Quaker Spirituality • SELECTED WRITINGS
Emanuel Swedenborg • THE UNIVERSAL HUMAN AND SOUL-BODY
    INTERACTION
Augustine of Hippo • SELECTED WRITINGS
Safed Spirituality • RULES OF MYSTICAL PIETY, THE BEGINNING OF WISDOM
Maximus Confessor • SELECTED WRITINGS
John Cassian • CONFERENCES
Johannes Tauler • SERMONS
John Ruusbroec • THE SPIRITUAL ESPOUSALS AND OTHER WORKS
Ibn 'Abbād of Ronda • LETTERS ON THE SŪFĪ PATH
Angelus Silesius • THE CHERUBINIC WANDERER
The Early Kabbalah •
Meister Eckhart • TEACHER AND PREACHER
John of the Cross • SELECTED WRITINGS
Pseudo-Dionysius • THE COMPLETE WORKS
Bernard of Clairvaux • SELECTED WORKS
Devotio Moderna • BASIC WRITINGS
The Pursuit of Wisdom • AND OTHER WORKS BY THE AUTHOR OF THE
    CLOUD OF UNKNOWING
Richard Rolle • THE ENGLISH WRITINGS
Francis de Sales, Jane de Chantal • LETTERS OF SPIRITUAL DIRECTION
Albert and Thomas • SELECTED WRITINGS
Robert Bellarmine • SPIRITUAL WRITINGS
Nicodemos of the Holy Mountain • A HANDBOOK OF SPIRITUAL COUNSEL
Henry Suso • THE EXEMPLAR, WITH TWO GERMAN SERMONS
Bérulle and the French School • SELECTED WRITINGS
The Talmud • SELECTED WRITINGS
Ephrem the Syrian • HYMNS
Hildegard of Bingen • SCIVIAS
Birgitta of Sweden • LIFE AND SELECTED REVELATIONS
John Donne • SELECTIONS FROM DIVINE POEMS, SERMONS, DEVOTIONS AND
    PRAYERS
Jeremy Taylor • SELECTED WORKS
Walter Hilton • SCALE OF PERFECTION
Ignatius of Loyola • SPIRITUAL EXERCISES AND SELECTED WORKS
Anchoritic Spirituality • ANCRENE WISSE AND ASSOCIATED WORKS
Nizam ad-din Awliya • MORALS FOR THE HEART